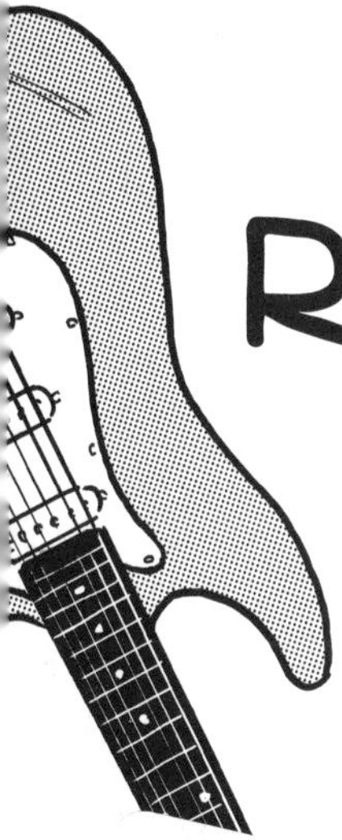

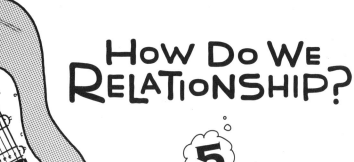

HOW DO WE RELATIONSHIP?

5

STORY AND ART BY

Tamifull

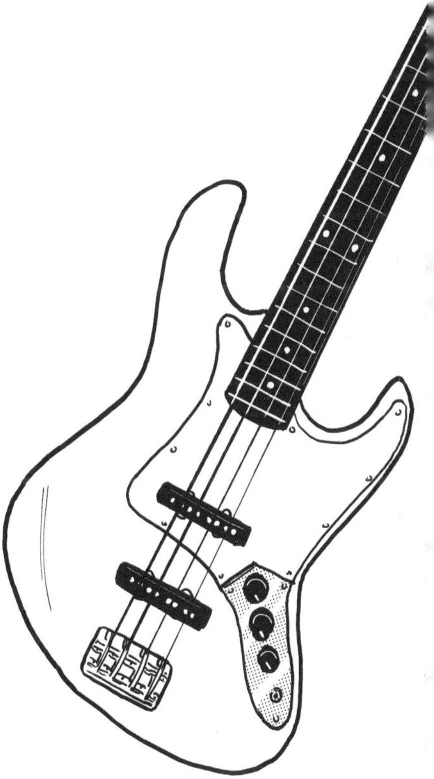

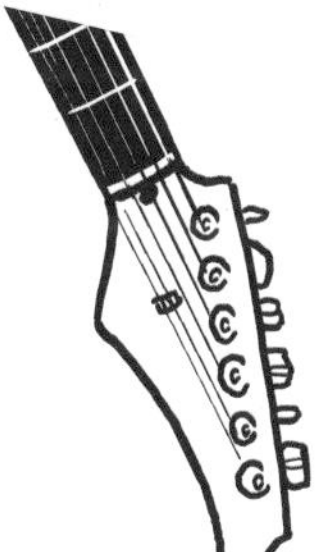

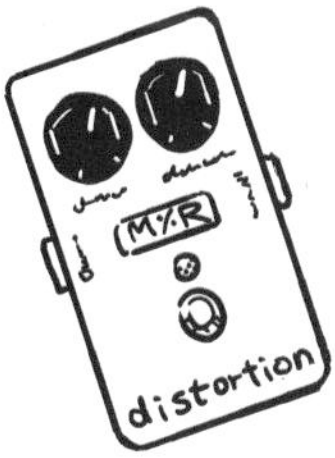
M-R
distortion

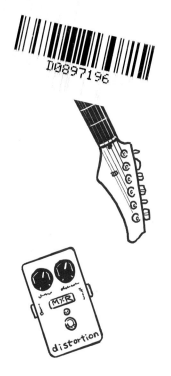

CHARACTERS

How Do We RELATiONSHIP?

SUMMARY

Miwa and Saeko started dating as soon as they entered college, but their feelings for each other were uneven, so their relationship had issues and they broke up. Now they're both single again and starting a new story.

CHARACTERS

Band Club
1ST-YEARS

Miwa Inuzuka (Bass)

She's really popular, but she's never fallen in love with someone who likes her back. Saeko was her first girlfriend.

Saeko Sawatari (Guitar)

She has an assertive presence in the club and a bad habit of getting jealous over Miwa.

They dated.

CHARACTERS

Saeko's Coworkers

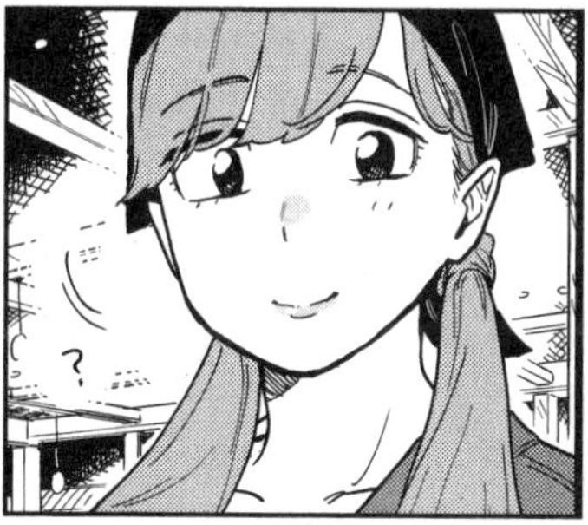

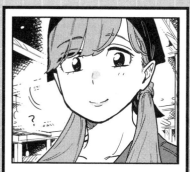

Yuria Washio

She's a student at a technical school who hopes to become a beautician. She may have recently gotten a girlfriend.

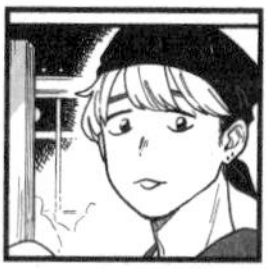

Kamedo

CHARACTERS

Miwa's First Love

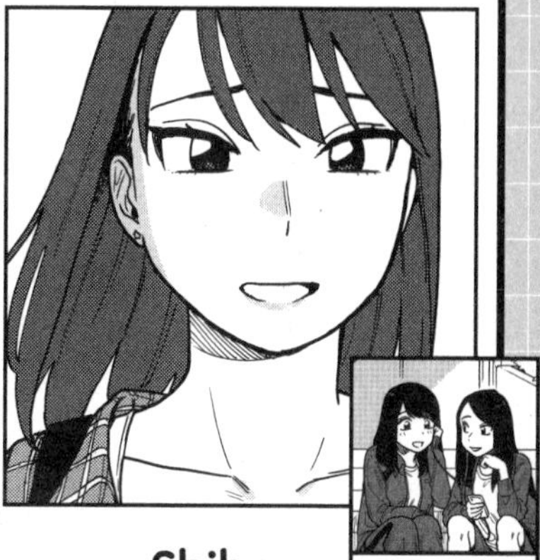

High School

Shiho Kumagai

She and Miwa went to the same high school and were both in the tennis club. Currently lives in Okinawa.

CHARACTERS

Cheerful Club Buddies

Vocals

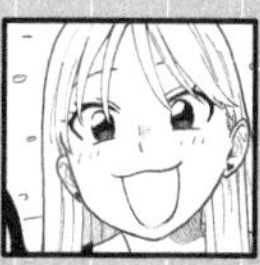

Rika

Guitar

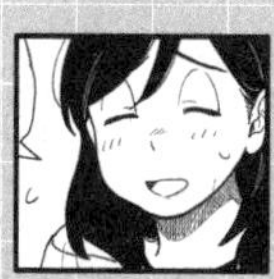

Usshi

Vocals

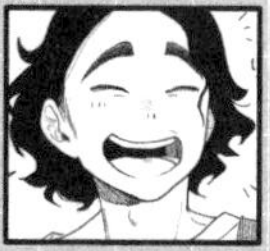

Mikkun

Guitar

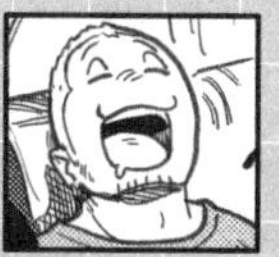

Lucha

Drums

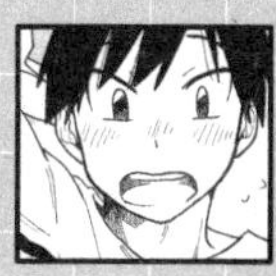

Tsuruta

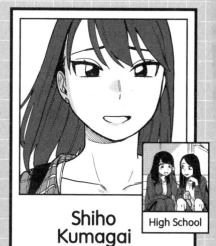

Contents.

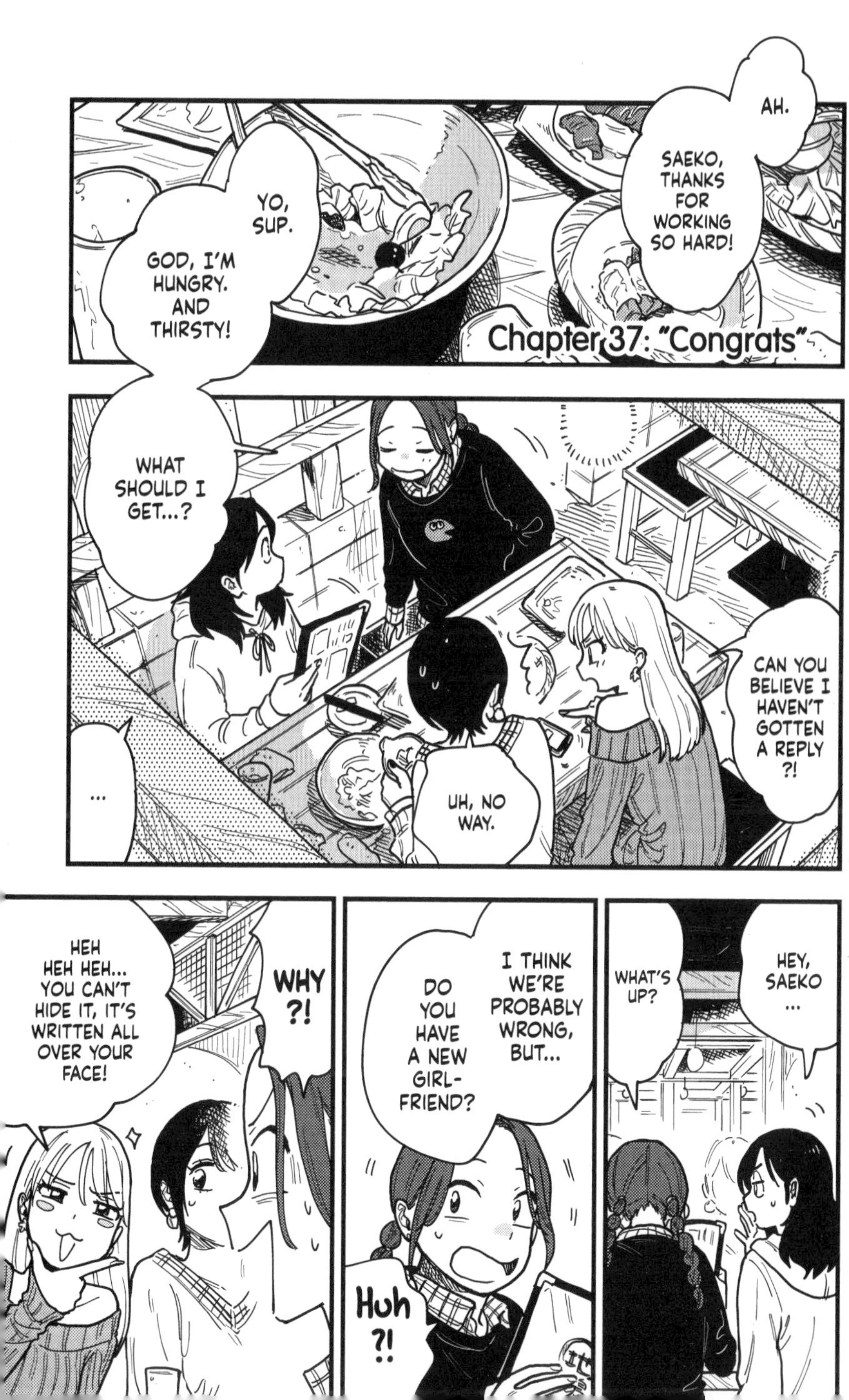
AH.
SAEKO, THANKS FOR WORKING SO HARD!
YO, SUP.
GOD, I'M HUNGRY. AND THIRSTY!
WHAT SHOULD I GET...?
Chapter 37: "Congrats"
CAN YOU BELIEVE I HAVEN'T GOTTEN A REPLY?!
UH, NO WAY.
...
HEY, SAEKO...
WHAT'S UP?
I THINK WE'RE PROBABLY WRONG, BUT...
DO YOU HAVE A NEW GIRL-FRIEND?
Huh?!
WHY?!
HEH HEH HEH... YOU CAN'T HIDE IT, IT'S WRITTEN ALL OVER YOUR FACE!

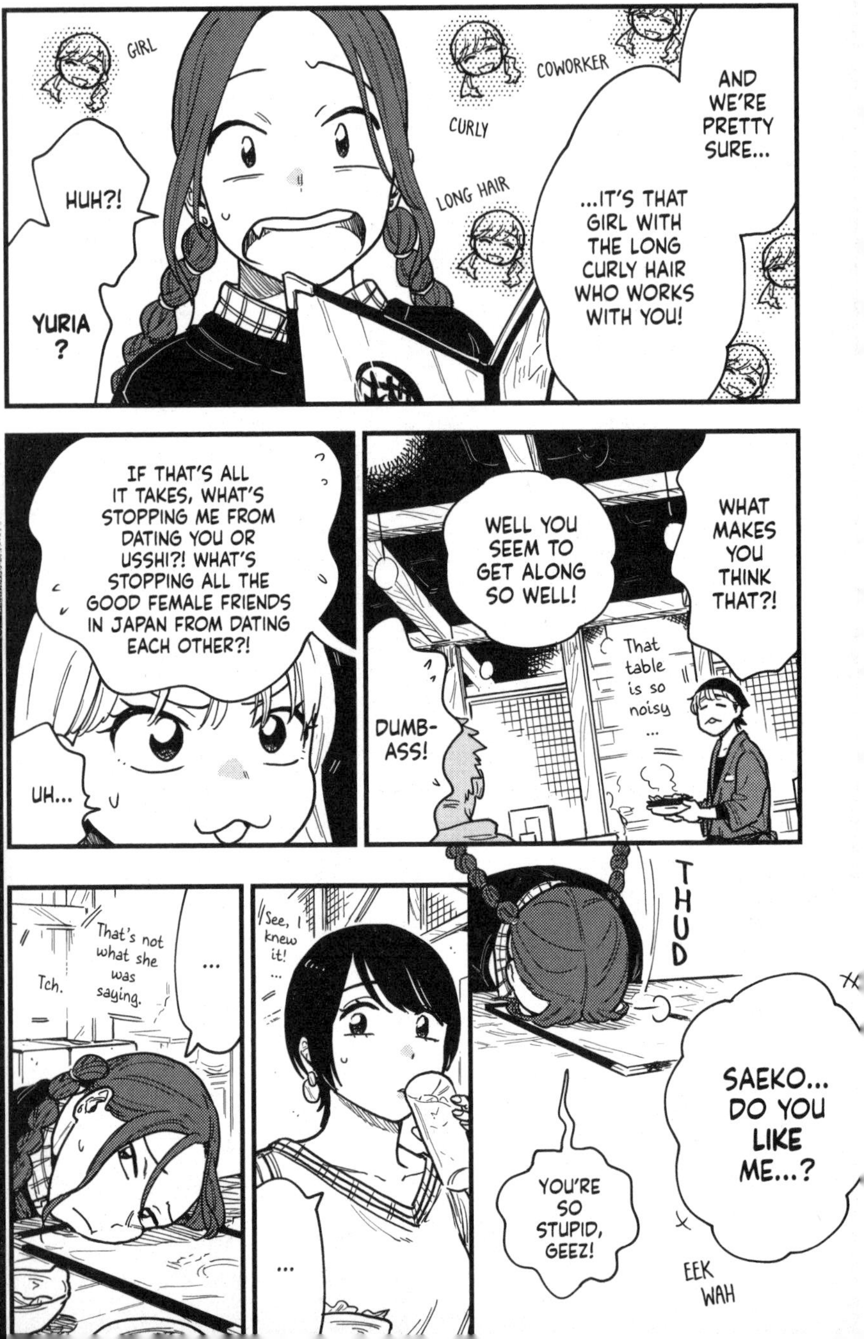
AND WE'RE PRETTY SURE...
...IT'S THAT GIRL WITH THE LONG CURLY HAIR WHO WORKS WITH YOU!
COWORKER
CURLY
LONG HAIR
GIRL
HUH?!
YURIA ?
WHAT MAKES YOU THINK THAT?!
WELL YOU SEEM TO GET ALONG SO WELL!
That table is so noisy ...
DUMB-ASS!
IF THAT'S ALL IT TAKES, WHAT'S STOPPING ME FROM DATING YOU OR USSHI?! WHAT'S STOPPING ALL THE GOOD FEMALE FRIENDS IN JAPAN FROM DATING EACH OTHER?!
UH...
THUD
SAEKO... DO YOU LIKE ME...?
YOU'RE SO STUPID, GEEZ!
EEK
WAH
See, I knew it! ...
...
...
That's not what she was saying.
Tch.

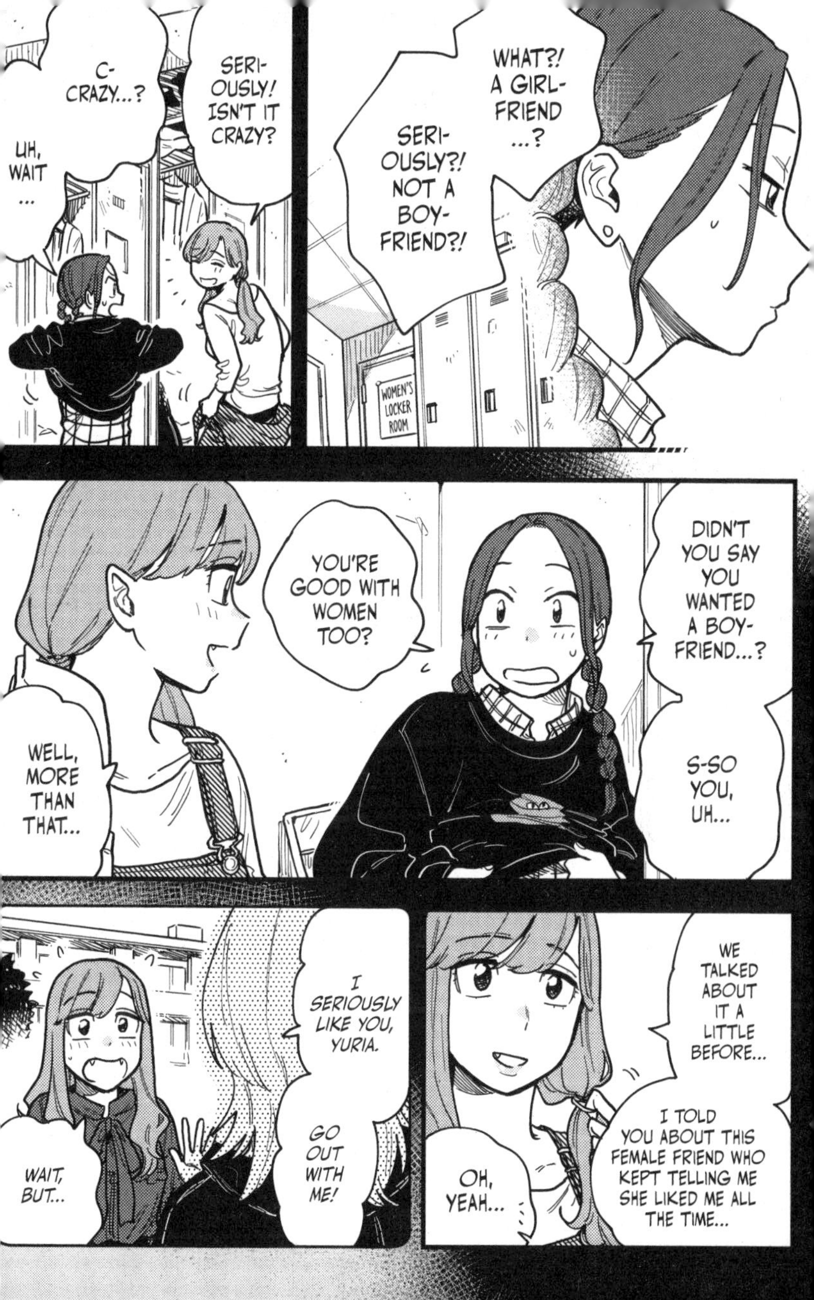
WHAT?! A GIRL-FRIEND...?
SERI-OUSLY?! NOT A BOY-FRIEND?!
SERI-OUSLY! ISN'T IT CRAZY?
C-CRAZY...?
UH, WAIT...
WOMEN'S LOCKER ROOM
DIDN'T YOU SAY YOU WANTED A BOY-FRIEND...?
S-SO YOU, UH...
YOU'RE GOOD WITH WOMEN TOO?
WELL, MORE THAN THAT...
WE TALKED ABOUT IT A LITTLE BEFORE...
I TOLD YOU ABOUT THIS FEMALE FRIEND WHO KEPT TELLING ME SHE LIKED ME ALL THE TIME...
OH, YEAH...
I SERIOUSLY LIKE YOU, YURIA.
GO OUT WITH ME!
WAIT, BUT...

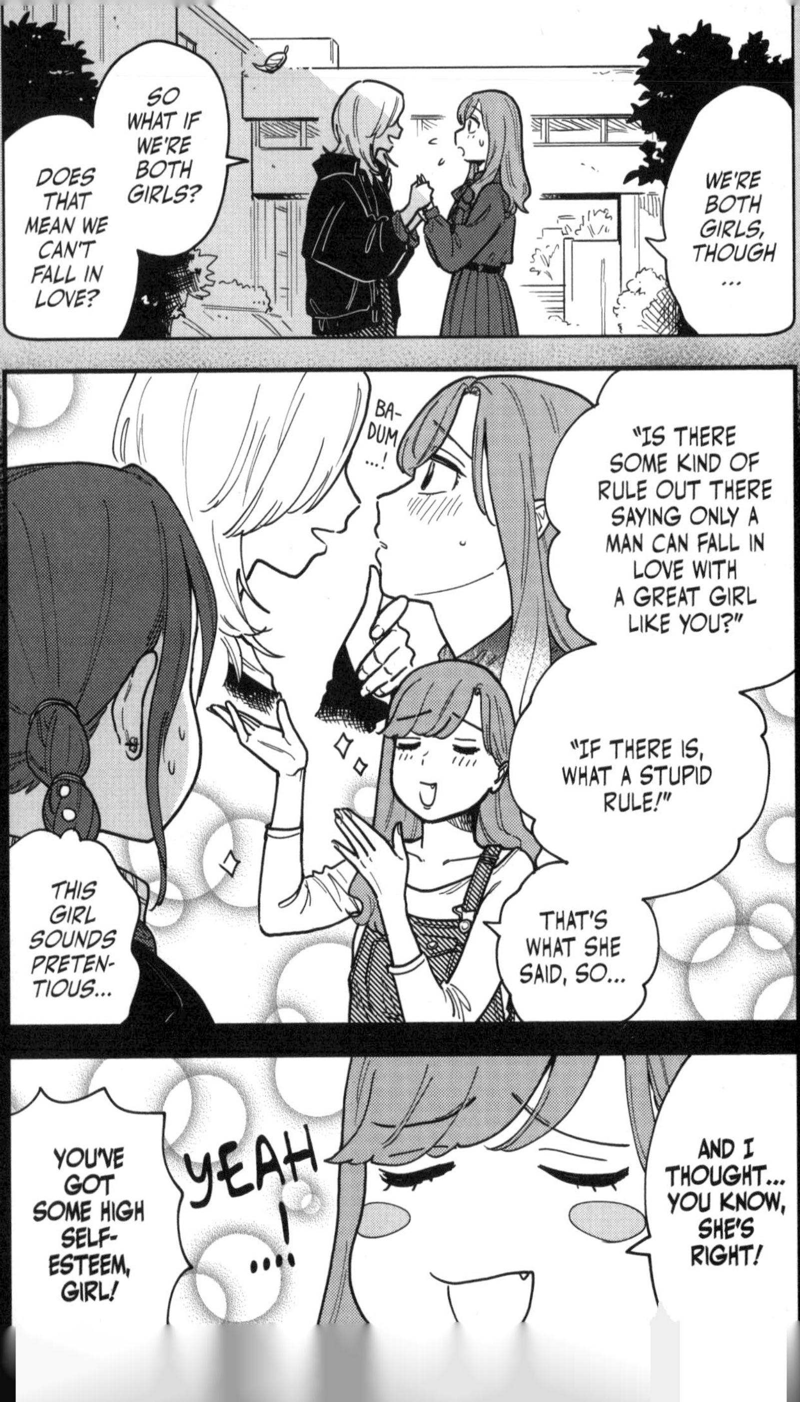
WE'RE BOTH GIRLS, THOUGH...
SO WHAT IF WE'RE BOTH GIRLS?
DOES THAT MEAN WE CAN'T FALL IN LOVE?
BA-DUM...!
"IS THERE SOME KIND OF RULE OUT THERE SAYING ONLY A MAN CAN FALL IN LOVE WITH A GREAT GIRL LIKE YOU?"
"IF THERE IS, WHAT A STUPID RULE!"
THAT'S WHAT SHE SAID, SO...
THIS GIRL SOUNDS PRETEN-TIOUS...
AND I THOUGHT... YOU KNOW, SHE'S RIGHT!
YEAH...!
YOU'VE GOT SOME HIGH SELF-ESTEEM, GIRL!

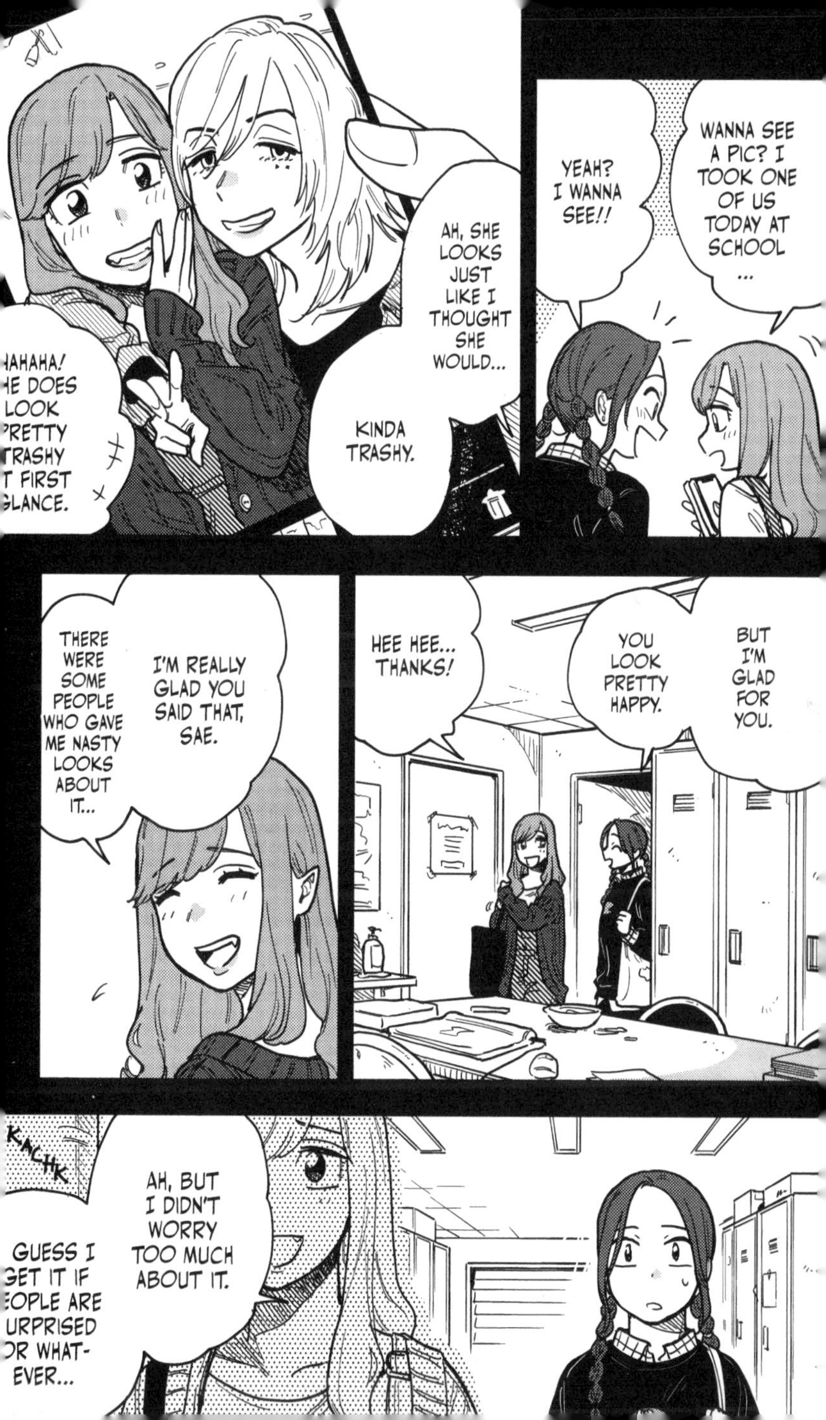

WANNA SEE A PIC? I TOOK ONE OF US TODAY AT SCHOOL ...
YEAH? I WANNA SEE!!
AH, SHE LOOKS JUST LIKE I THOUGHT SHE WOULD...
KINDA TRASHY.
AHAHA! HE DOES LOOK RETTY TRASHY T FIRST LANCE.
BUT I'M GLAD FOR YOU.
YOU LOOK PRETTY HAPPY.
HEE HEE... THANKS!
I'M REALLY GLAD YOU SAID THAT, SAE.
THERE WERE SOME PEOPLE WHO GAVE ME NASTY LOOKS ABOUT IT...
KACHIK
AH, BUT I DIDN'T WORRY TOO MUCH ABOUT IT.
GUESS I GET IT IF EOPLE ARE URPRISED OR WHAT-EVER...

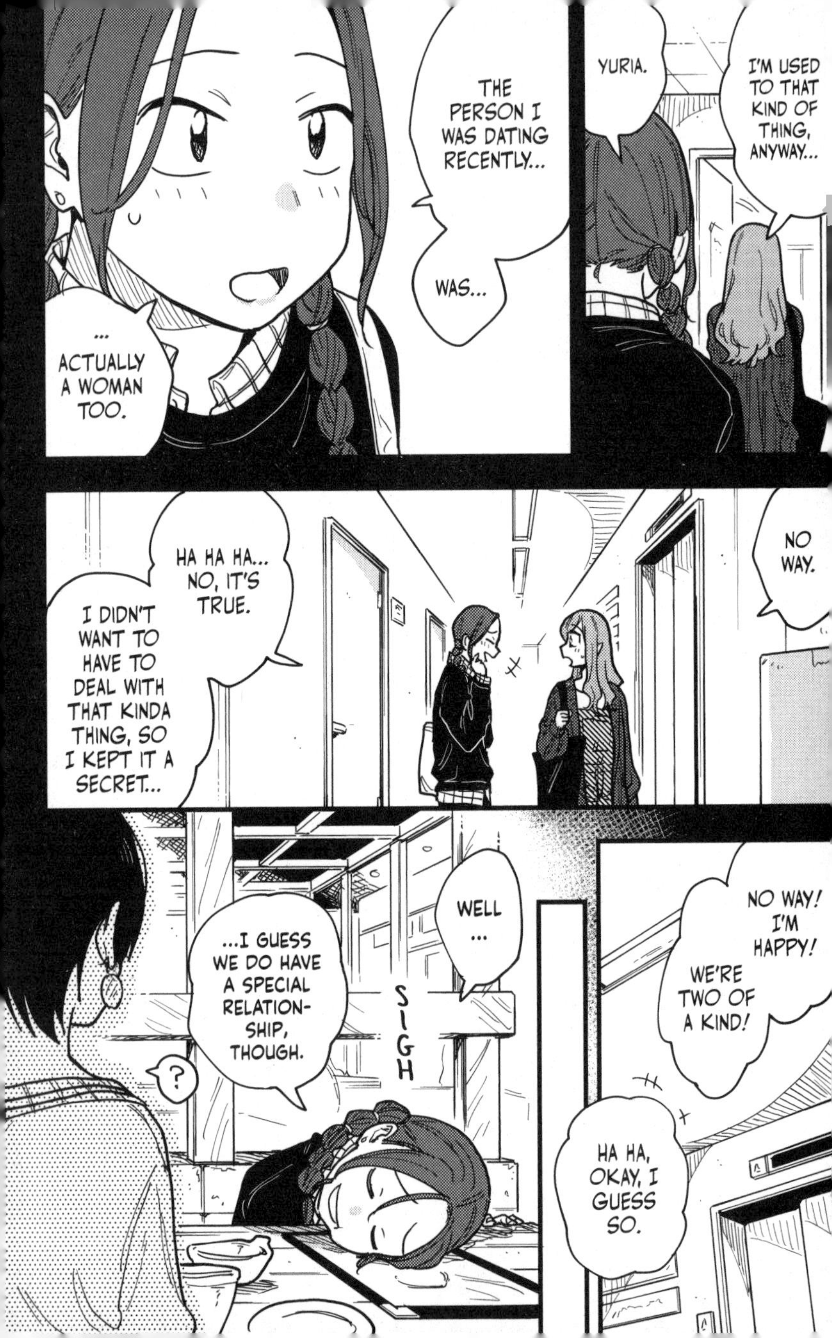
I'M USED TO THAT KIND OF THING, ANYWAY...
YURIA.
THE PERSON I WAS DATING RECENTLY...
WAS...
... ACTUALLY A WOMAN TOO.
NO WAY.
HA HA HA... NO, IT'S TRUE.
I DIDN'T WANT TO HAVE TO DEAL WITH THAT KINDA THING, SO I KEPT IT A SECRET...
NO WAY! I'M HAPPY!
WE'RE TWO OF A KIND!
HA HA, OKAY, I GUESS SO.
WELL...
...I GUESS WE DO HAVE A SPECIAL RELATION-SHIP, THOUGH.
SIGH
?

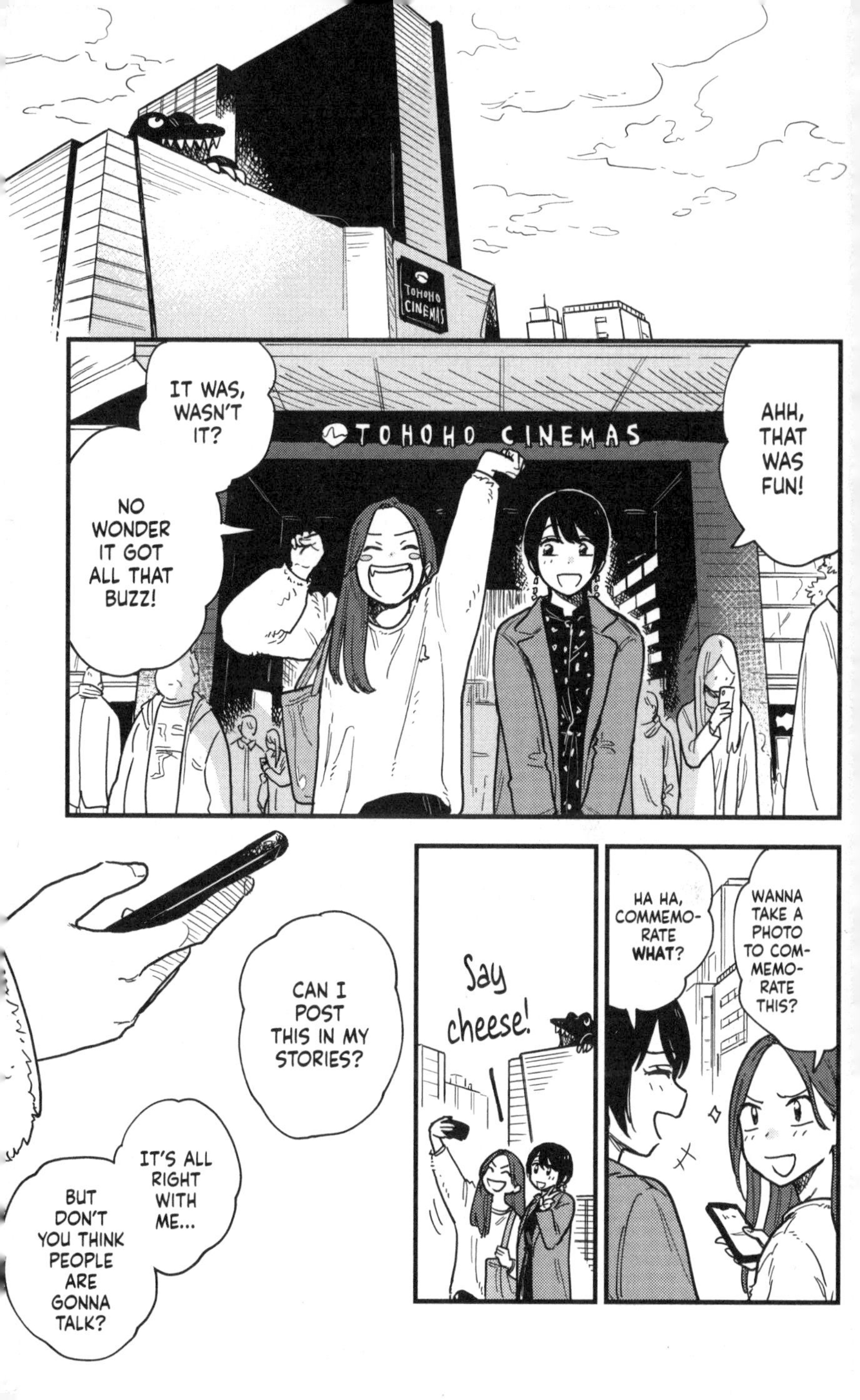
TOHOHO CINEMAS
AHH, THAT WAS FUN!
IT WAS, WASN'T IT?
NO WONDER IT GOT ALL THAT BUZZ!
TOHOHO CINEMAS
WANNA TAKE A PHOTO TO COM-MEMO-RATE THIS?
HA HA, COMMEMO-RATE **WHAT**?
Say cheese!
CAN I POST THIS IN MY STORIES?
IT'S ALL RIGHT WITH ME...
BUT DON'T YOU THINK PEOPLE ARE GONNA TALK?

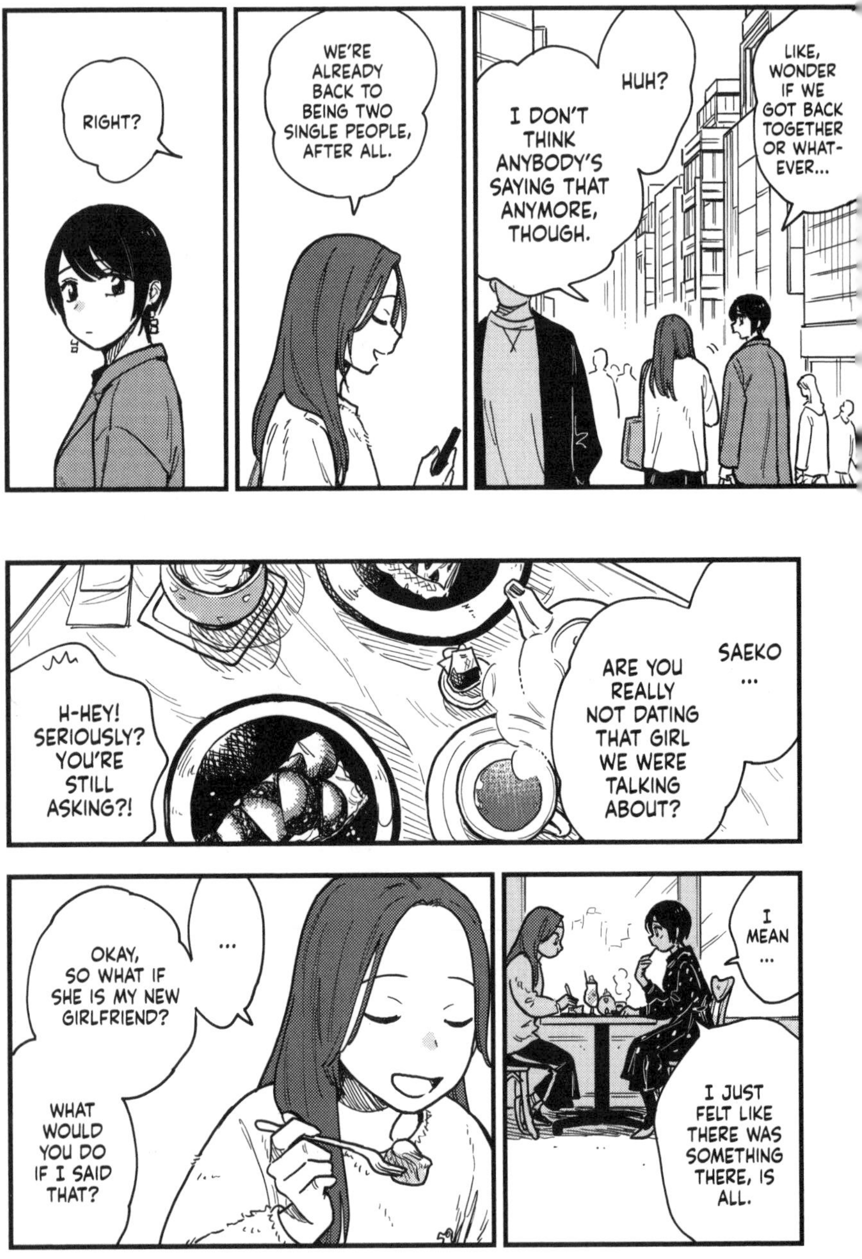
LIKE, WONDER IF WE GOT BACK TOGETHER OR WHAT-EVER...
HUH?
I DON'T THINK ANYBODY'S SAYING THAT ANYMORE, THOUGH.
WE'RE ALREADY BACK TO BEING TWO SINGLE PEOPLE, AFTER ALL.
RIGHT?
SAEKO ...
ARE YOU REALLY NOT DATING THAT GIRL WE WERE TALKING ABOUT?
H-HEY! SERIOUSLY? YOU'RE STILL ASKING?!
I MEAN ...
I JUST FELT LIKE THERE WAS SOMETHING THERE, IS ALL.
...
OKAY, SO WHAT IF SHE IS MY NEW GIRLFRIEND?
WHAT WOULD YOU DO IF I SAID THAT?

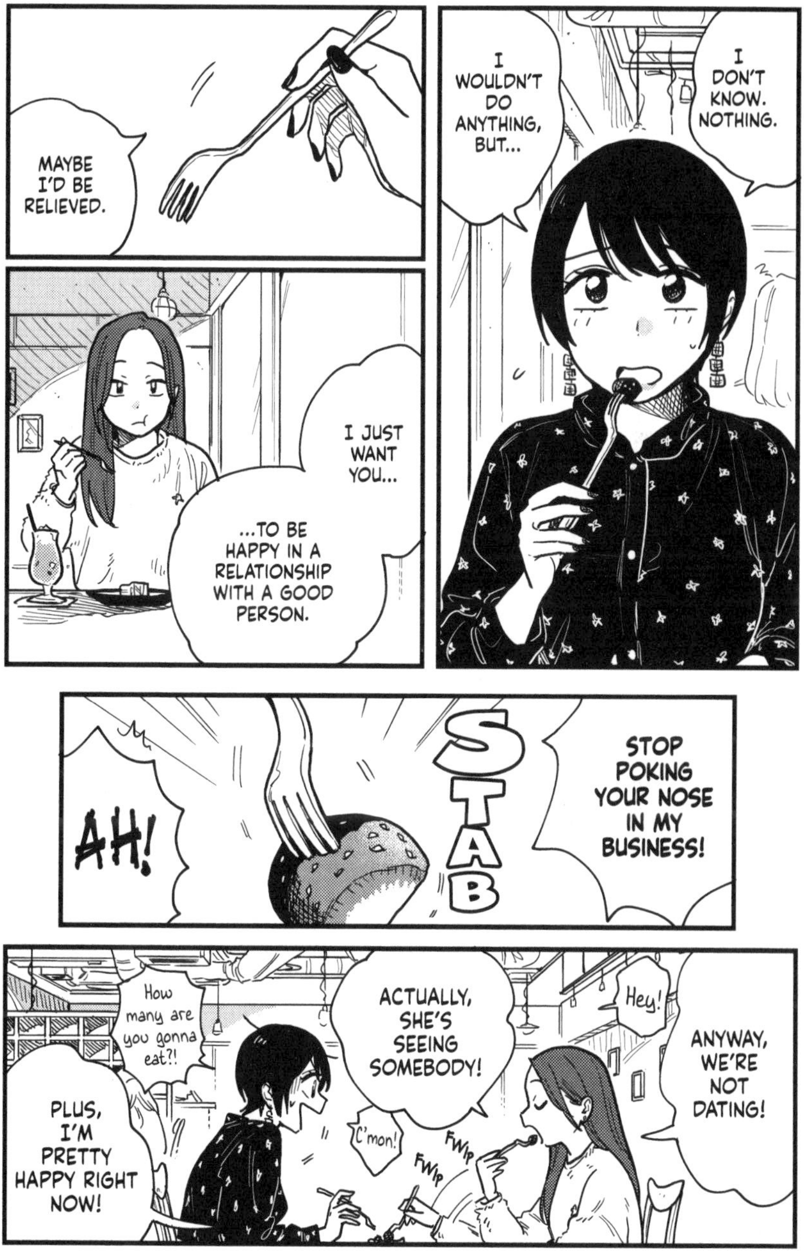
I DON'T KNOW. NOTHING.
I WOULDN'T DO ANYTHING, BUT...
MAYBE I'D BE RELIEVED.
I JUST WANT YOU...
...TO BE HAPPY IN A RELATIONSHIP WITH A GOOD PERSON.
STOP POKING YOUR NOSE IN MY BUSINESS!
STAB
AH!
Hey!
ANYWAY, WE'RE NOT DATING!
ACTUALLY, SHE'S SEEING SOMEBODY!
FWIP
FWIP
C'mon!
How many are you gonna eat?!
PLUS, I'M PRETTY HAPPY RIGHT NOW!

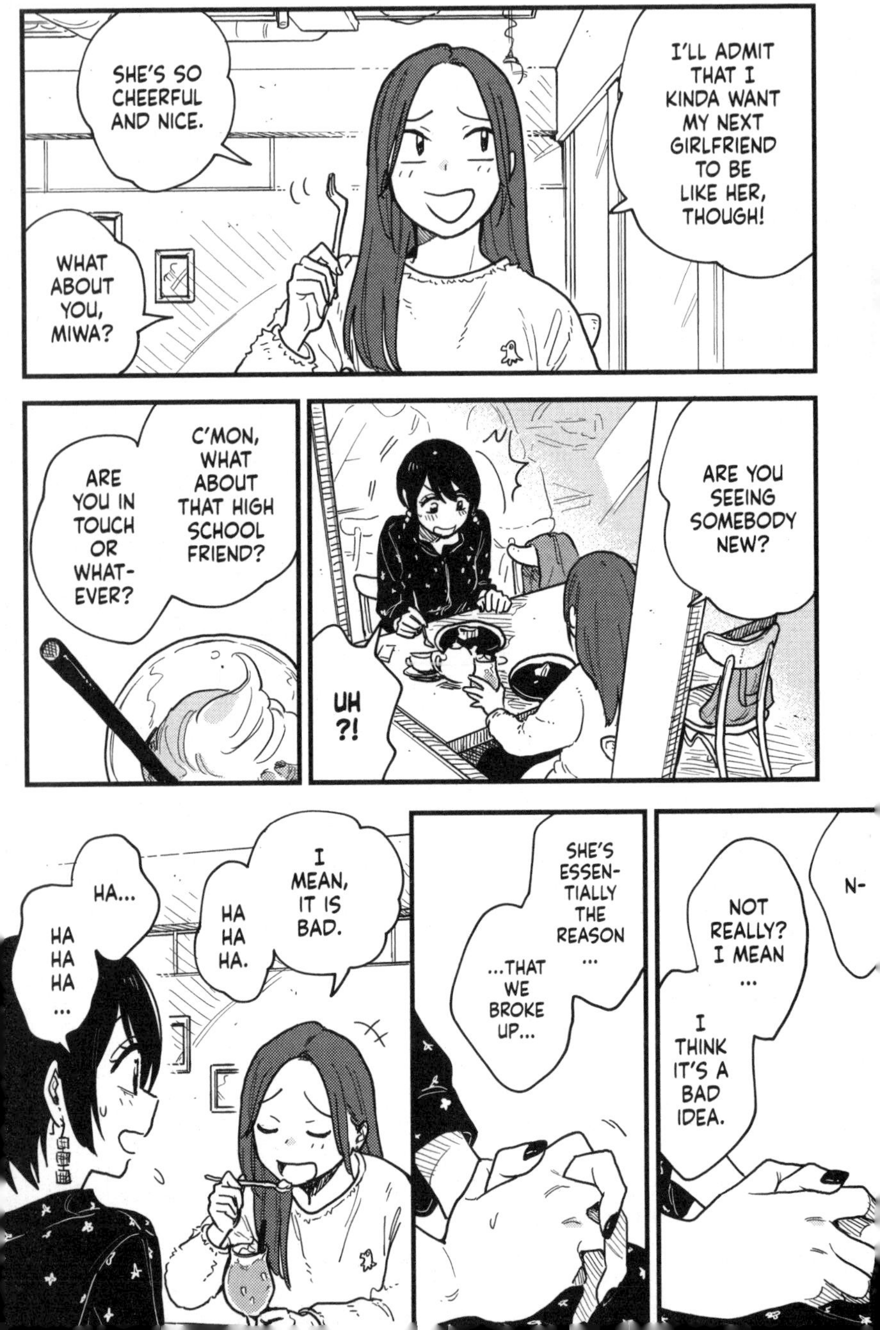
I'LL ADMIT THAT I KINDA WANT MY NEXT GIRLFRIEND TO BE LIKE HER, THOUGH!
SHE'S SO CHEERFUL AND NICE.
WHAT ABOUT YOU, MIWA?
ARE YOU SEEING SOMEBODY NEW?
UH ?!
C'MON, WHAT ABOUT THAT HIGH SCHOOL FRIEND?
ARE YOU IN TOUCH OR WHAT-EVER?
N-
NOT REALLY? I MEAN ...
I THINK IT'S A BAD IDEA.
SHE'S ESSEN-TIALLY THE REASON ...
...THAT WE BROKE UP...
I MEAN, IT IS BAD.
HA HA HA.
HA...
HA HA HA ...

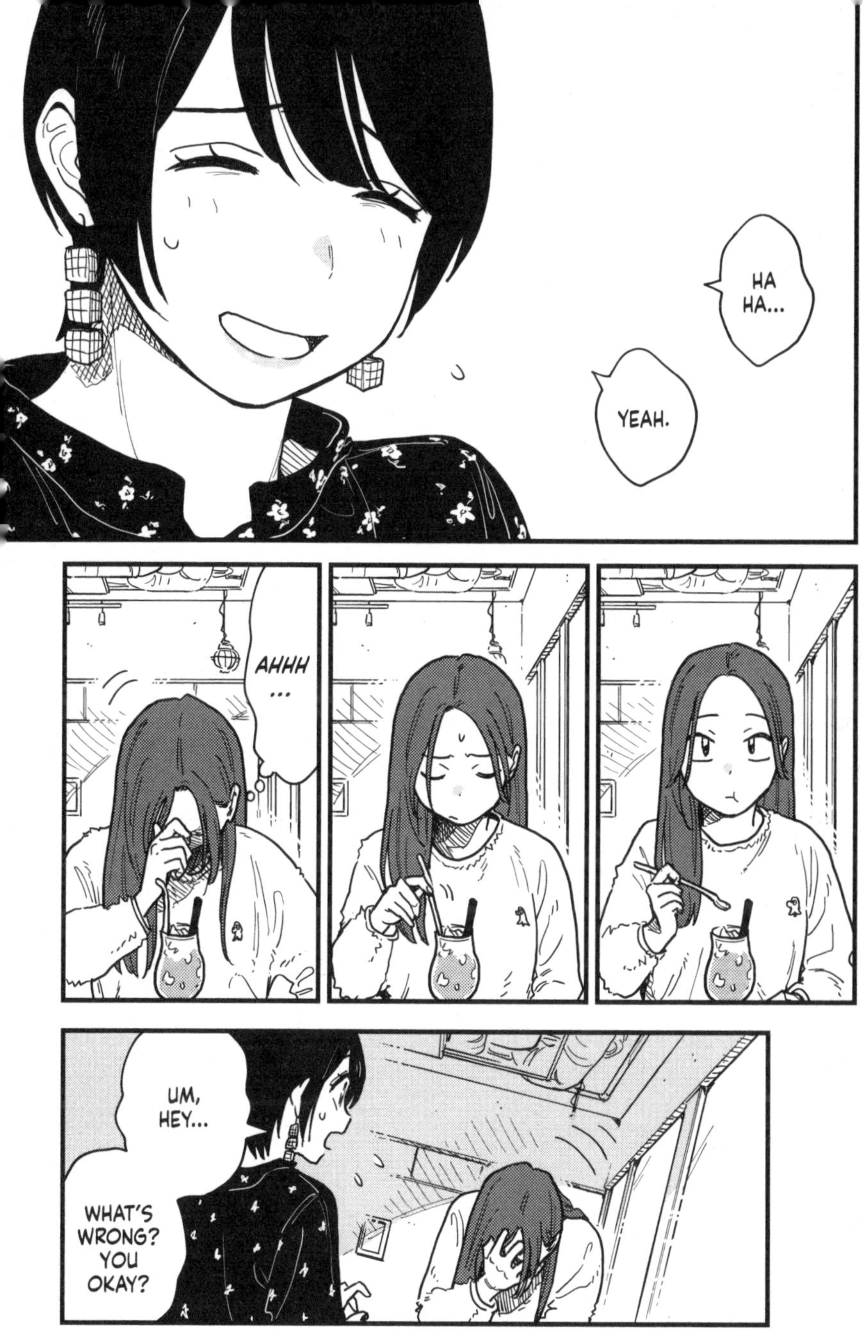
HA HA...
YEAH.
AHHH ...
UM, HEY...
WHAT'S WRONG? YOU OKAY?

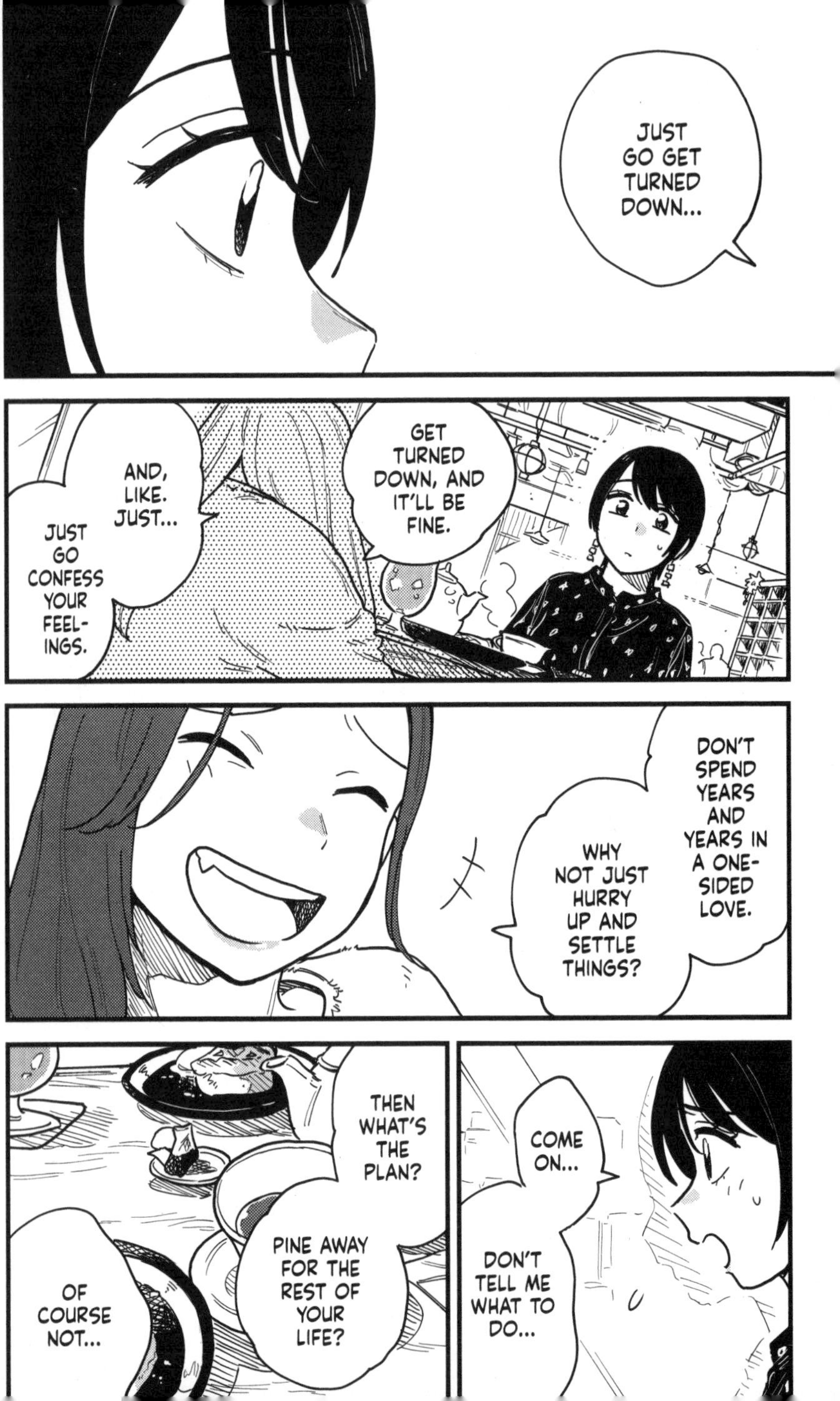
JUST GO GET TURNED DOWN...
GET TURNED DOWN, AND IT'LL BE FINE.
AND, LIKE. JUST...
JUST GO CONFESS YOUR FEEL-INGS.
DON'T SPEND YEARS AND YEARS IN A ONE-SIDED LOVE.
WHY NOT JUST HURRY UP AND SETTLE THINGS?
COME ON...
DON'T TELL ME WHAT TO DO...
THEN WHAT'S THE PLAN?
PINE AWAY FOR THE REST OF YOUR LIFE?
OF COURSE NOT...

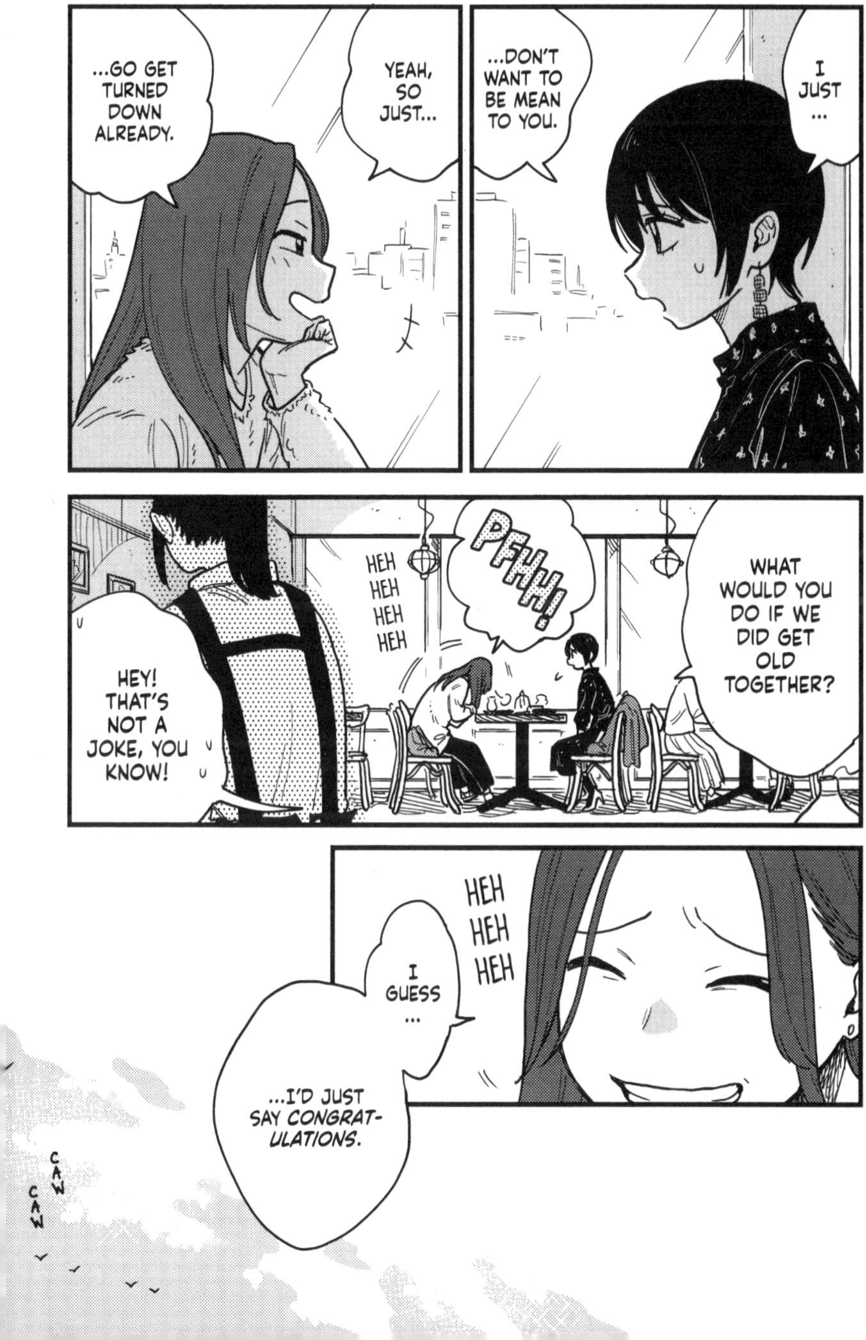
I JUST ...
...DON'T WANT TO BE MEAN TO YOU.
YEAH, SO JUST...
...GO GET TURNED DOWN ALREADY.
WHAT WOULD YOU DO IF WE DID GET OLD TOGETHER?
PFHH!
HEH HEH HEH HEH
HEY! THAT'S NOT A JOKE, YOU KNOW!
HEH HEH HEH
I GUESS ...
...I'D JUST SAY CONGRAT-ULATIONS.
CAW
CAW

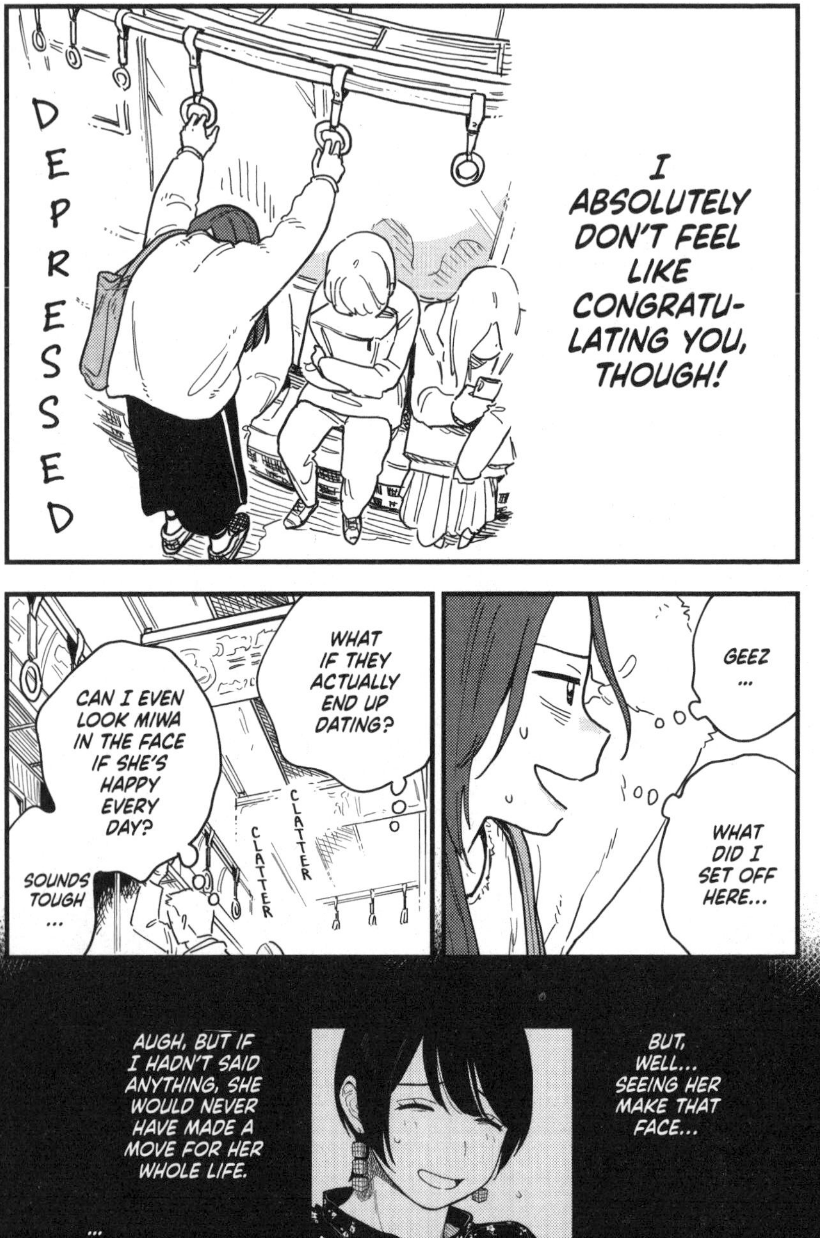
I ABSOLUTELY DON'T FEEL LIKE CONGRATULATING YOU, THOUGH!
DEPRESSED
GEEZ...
WHAT DID I SET OFF HERE...
WHAT IF THEY ACTUALLY END UP DATING?
CAN I EVEN LOOK MIWA IN THE FACE IF SHE'S HAPPY EVERY DAY?
CLATTER
CLATTER
SOUNDS TOUGH...
BUT, WELL... SEEING HER MAKE THAT FACE...
AUGH, BUT IF I HADN'T SAID ANYTHING, SHE WOULD NEVER HAVE MADE A MOVE FOR HER WHOLE LIFE.
...

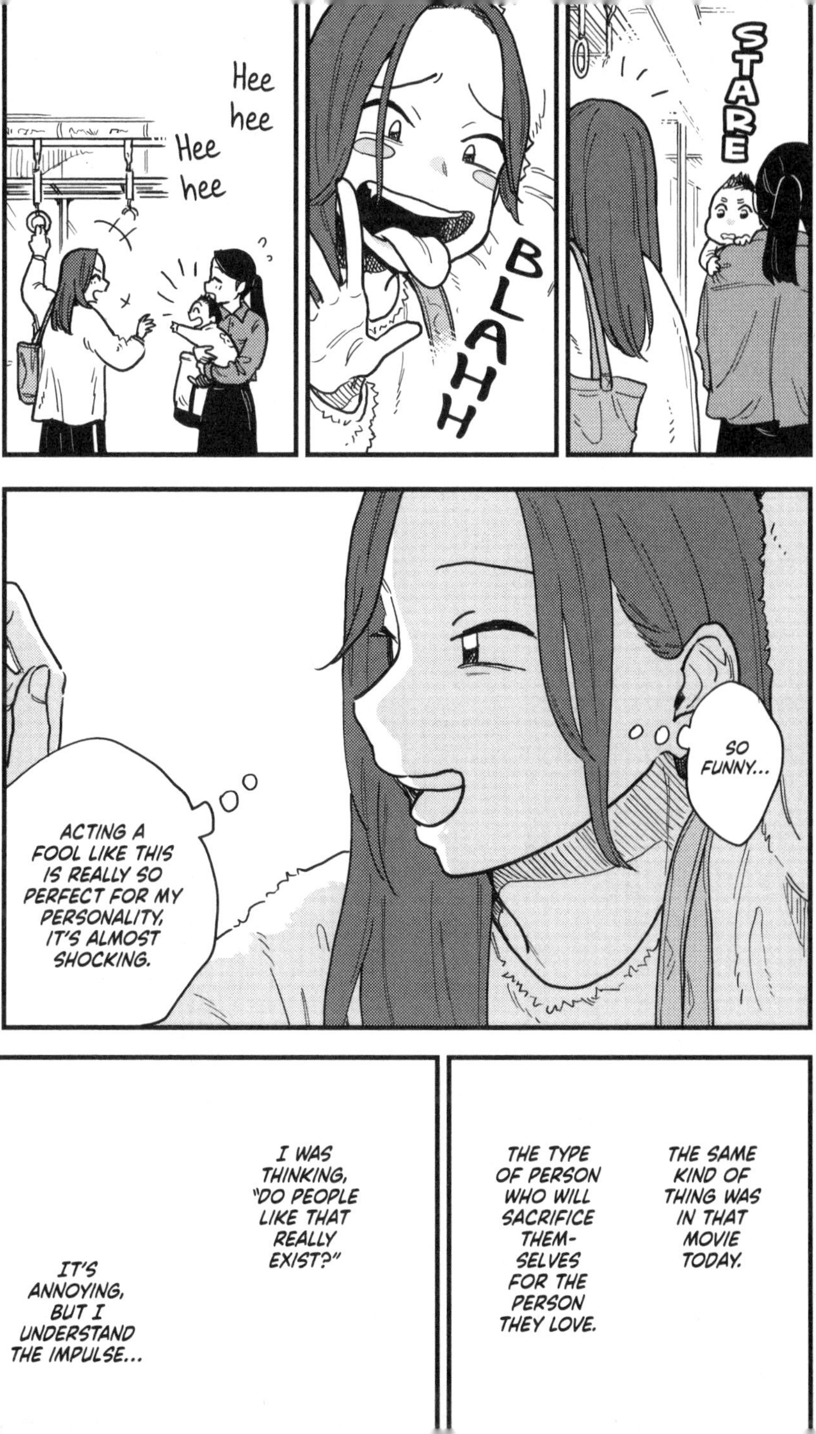
STARE
BLAHH
Hee hee
Hee hee
SO FUNNY...
ACTING A FOOL LIKE THIS IS REALLY SO PERFECT FOR MY PERSONALITY, IT'S ALMOST SHOCKING.
THE SAME KIND OF THING WAS IN THAT MOVIE TODAY.
THE TYPE OF PERSON WHO WILL SACRIFICE THEM-SELVES FOR THE PERSON THEY LOVE.
I WAS THINKING, "DO PEOPLE LIKE THAT REALLY EXIST?"
IT'S ANNOYING, BUT I UNDERSTAND THE IMPULSE...

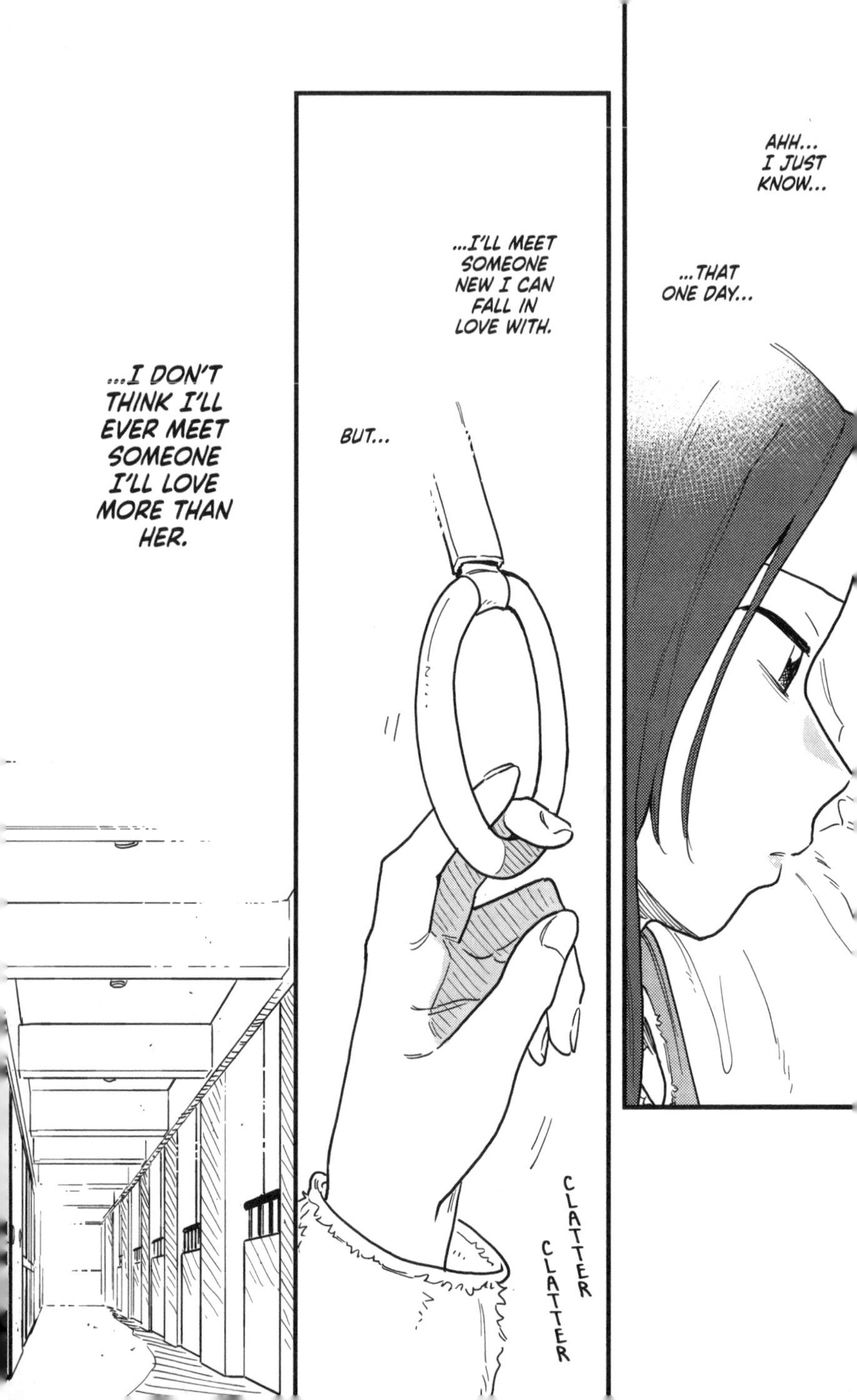
AHH... I JUST KNOW...
...THAT ONE DAY...
...I'LL MEET SOMEONE NEW I CAN FALL IN LOVE WITH.
BUT...
CLATTER
CLATTER
...I DON'T THINK I'LL EVER MEET SOMEONE I'LL LOVE MORE THAN HER.

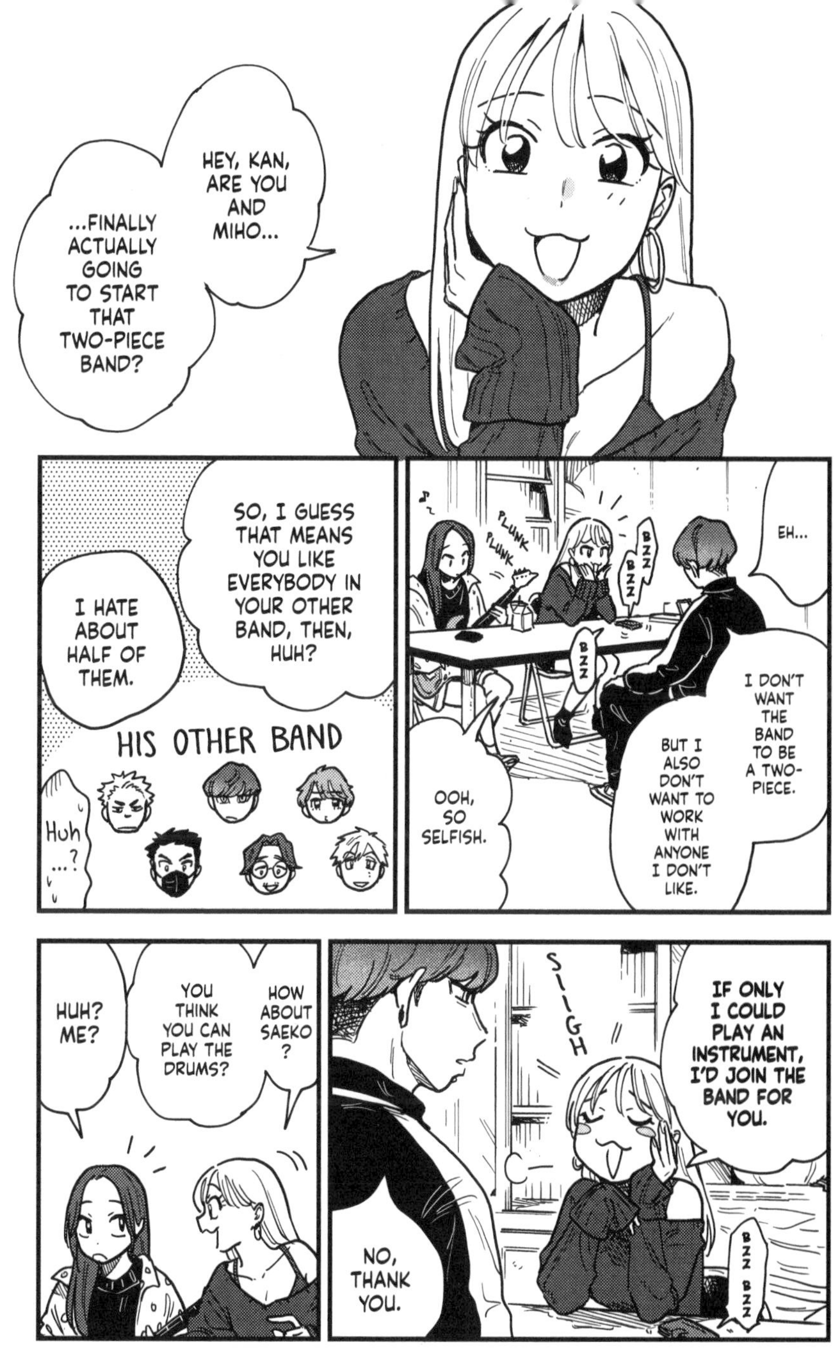
HEY, KAN, ARE YOU AND MIHO...
...FINALLY ACTUALLY GOING TO START THAT TWO-PIECE BAND?
EH...
PLUNK PLUNK
BZZ BZZ
BZZ
I DON'T WANT THE BAND TO BE A TWO-PIECE.
BUT I ALSO DON'T WANT TO WORK WITH ANYONE I DON'T LIKE.
OOH, SO SELFISH.
SO, I GUESS THAT MEANS YOU LIKE EVERYBODY IN YOUR OTHER BAND, THEN, HUH?
I HATE ABOUT HALF OF THEM.
HIS OTHER BAND
Huh ...?
SIIGH
IF ONLY I COULD PLAY AN INSTRUMENT, I'D JOIN THE BAND FOR YOU.
NO, THANK YOU.
BZZ BZZ
HOW ABOUT SAEKO?
YOU THINK YOU CAN PLAY THE DRUMS?
HUH? ME?

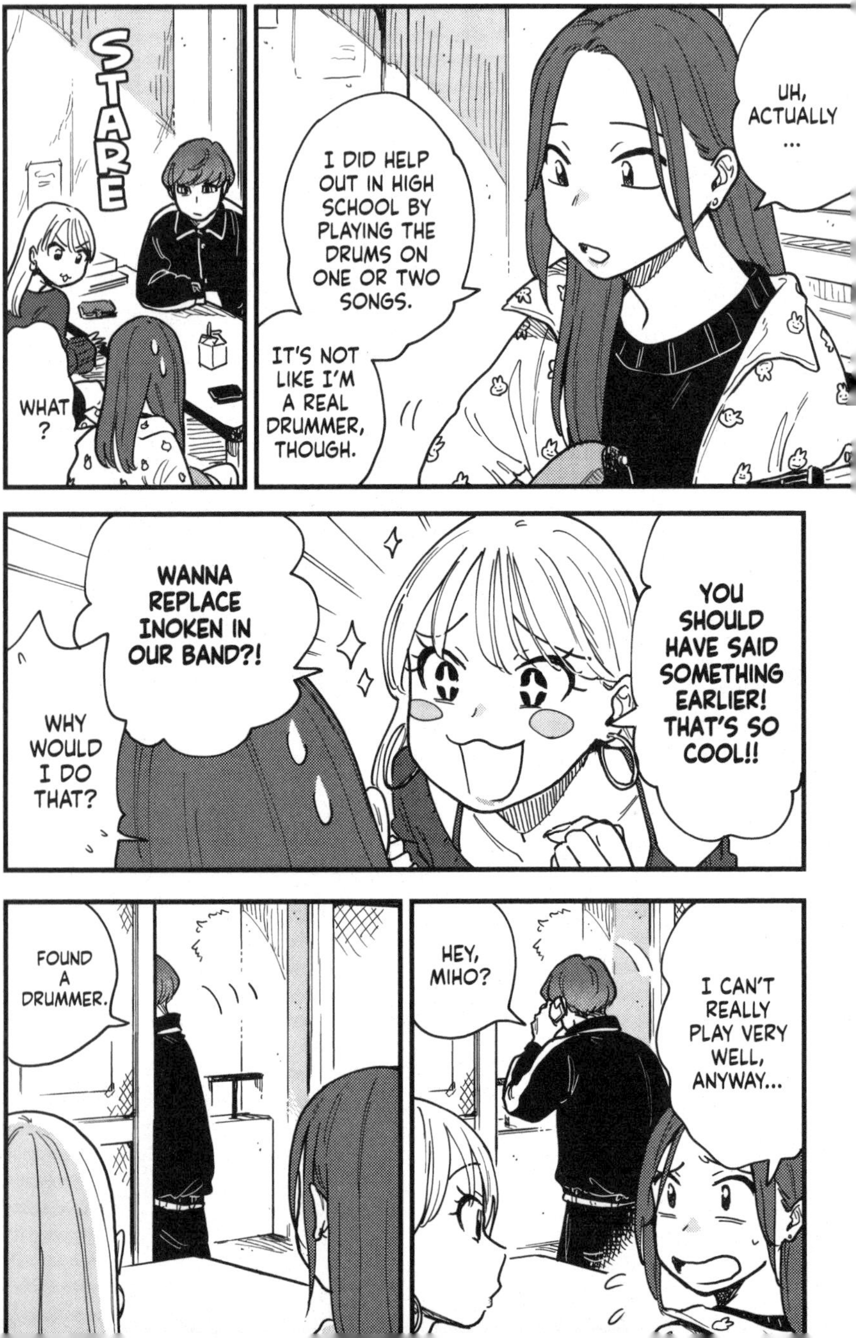
UH, ACTUALLY ...
I DID HELP OUT IN HIGH SCHOOL BY PLAYING THE DRUMS ON ONE OR TWO SONGS.
IT'S NOT LIKE I'M A REAL DRUMMER, THOUGH.
STARE
WHAT ?
YOU SHOULD HAVE SAID SOMETHING EARLIER! THAT'S SO COOL!!
WANNA REPLACE INOKEN IN OUR BAND?!
WHY WOULD I DO THAT?
I CAN'T REALLY PLAY VERY WELL, ANYWAY...
HEY, MIHO?
FOUND A DRUMMER.

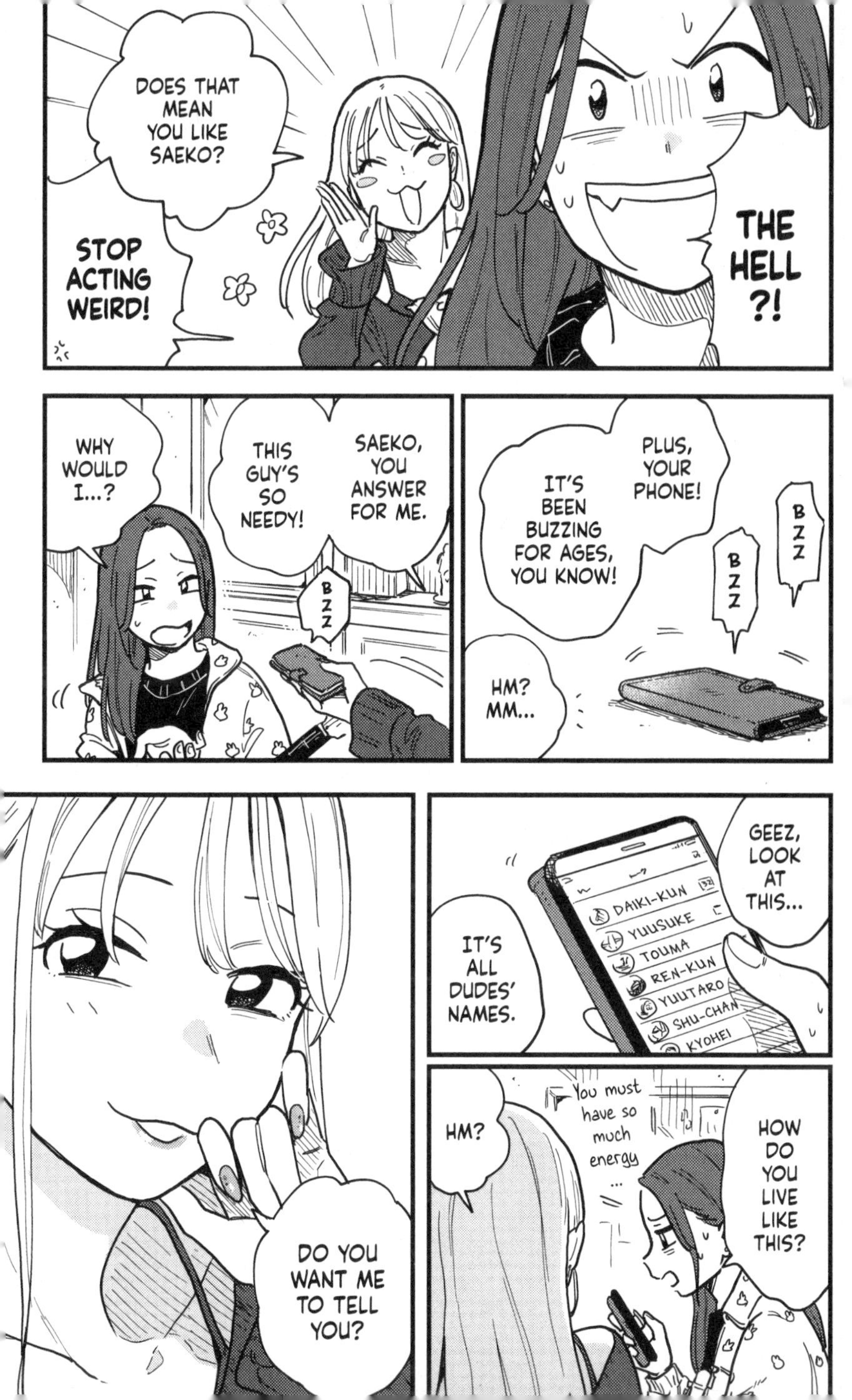
THE HELL?!
DOES THAT MEAN YOU LIKE SAEKO?
STOP ACTING WEIRD!
PLUS, YOUR PHONE!
IT'S BEEN BUZZING FOR AGES, YOU KNOW!
BZZ
BZZ
HM? MM...
SAEKO, YOU ANSWER FOR ME.
THIS GUY'S SO NEEDY!
WHY WOULD I...?
BZZ
GEEZ, LOOK AT THIS...
DAIKI-KUN
YUUSUKE
TOUMA
REN-KUN
YUUTARO
SHU-CHAN
KYOHEI
IT'S ALL DUDES' NAMES.
HOW DO YOU LIVE LIKE THIS?
You must have so much energy ...
HM?
DO YOU WANT ME TO TELL YOU?

HOW DO WE RELATIONSHIP?

Chapter 38: Little Devil's Recommendation

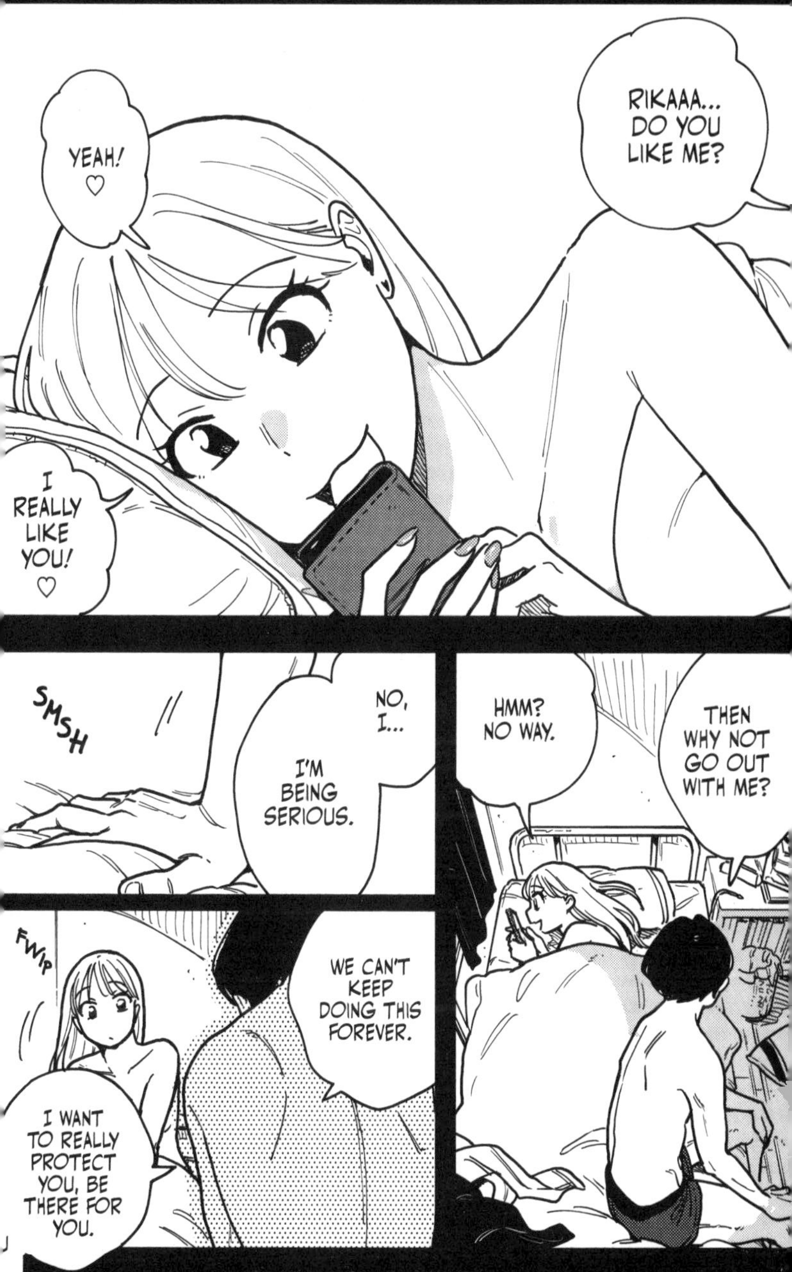
RIKAAA... DO YOU LIKE ME?
YEAH! ♡
I REALLY LIKE YOU! ♡
THEN WHY NOT GO OUT WITH ME?
HMM? NO WAY.
NO, I...
I'M BEING SERIOUS.
SMSH
WE CAN'T KEEP DOING THIS FOREVER.
I WANT TO REALLY PROTECT YOU, BE THERE FOR YOU.
FWIP

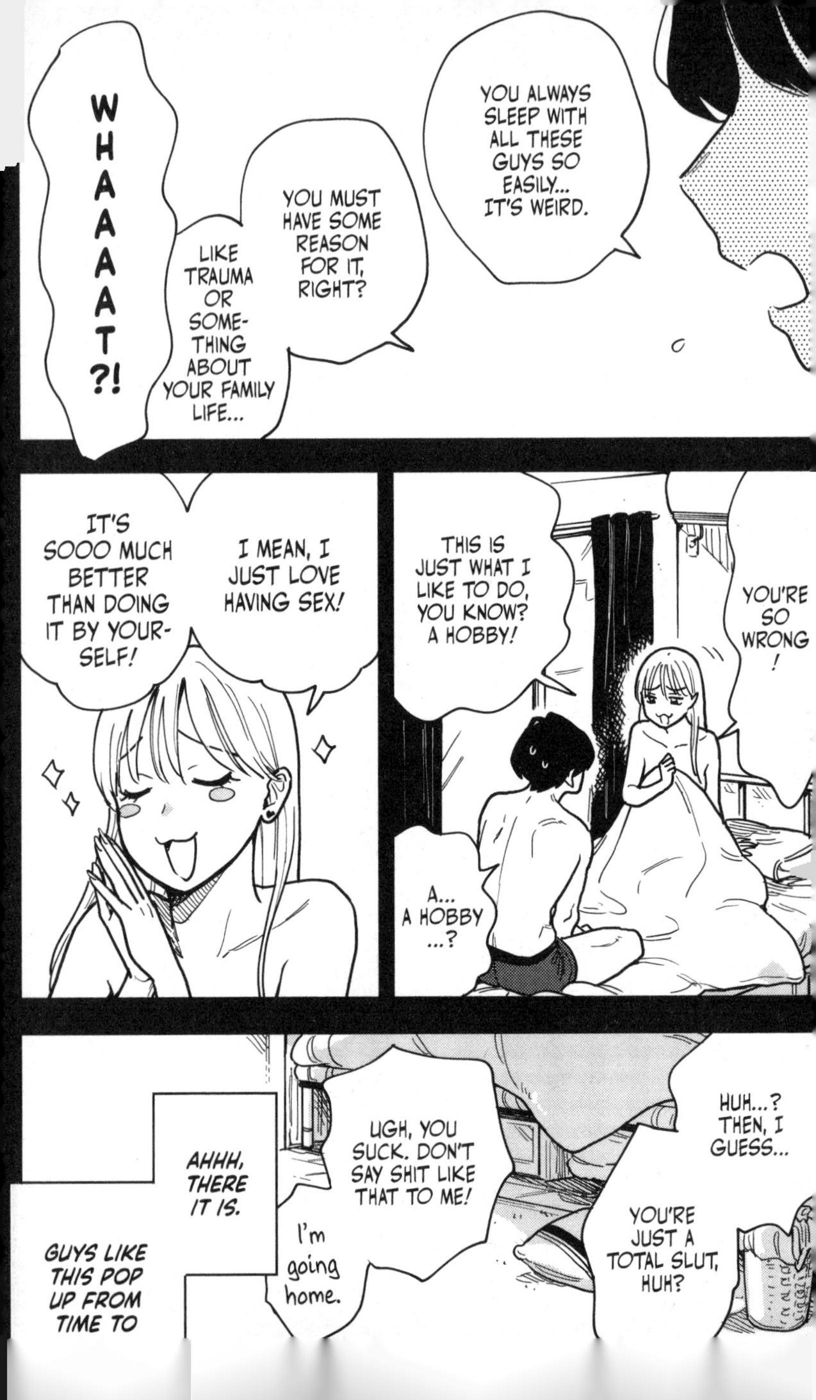
YOU ALWAYS SLEEP WITH ALL THESE GUYS SO EASILY... IT'S WEIRD.
YOU MUST HAVE SOME REASON FOR IT, RIGHT?
LIKE TRAUMA OR SOMETHING ABOUT YOUR FAMILY LIFE...
WHAAAAAT?!
YOU'RE SO WRONG!
THIS IS JUST WHAT I LIKE TO DO, YOU KNOW? A HOBBY!
A... A HOBBY ...?
I MEAN, I JUST LOVE HAVING SEX!
IT'S SOOO MUCH BETTER THAN DOING IT BY YOURSELF!
HUH...? THEN, I GUESS...
YOU'RE JUST A TOTAL SLUT, HUH?
UGH, YOU SUCK. DON'T SAY SHIT LIKE THAT TO ME!
I'm going home.
AHHH, THERE IT IS.
GUYS LIKE THIS POP UP FROM TIME TO

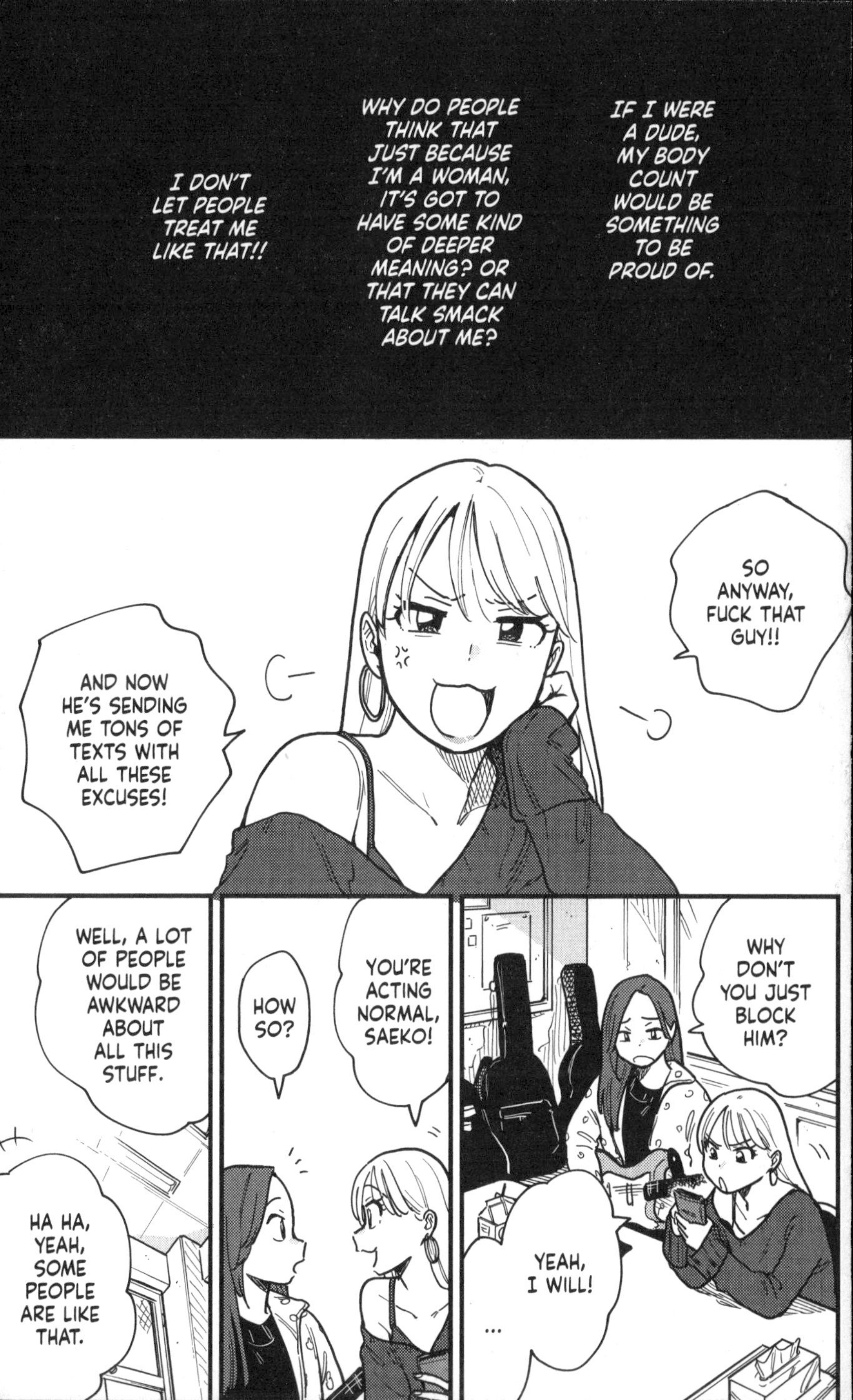
IF I WERE A DUDE, MY BODY COUNT WOULD BE SOMETHING TO BE PROUD OF.
WHY DO PEOPLE THINK THAT JUST BECAUSE I'M A WOMAN, IT'S GOT TO HAVE SOME KIND OF DEEPER MEANING? OR THAT THEY CAN TALK SMACK ABOUT ME?
I DON'T LET PEOPLE TREAT ME LIKE THAT!!
SO ANYWAY, FUCK THAT GUY!!
AND NOW HE'S SENDING ME TONS OF TEXTS WITH ALL THESE EXCUSES!
WHY DON'T YOU JUST BLOCK HIM?
YEAH, I WILL!
...
YOU'RE ACTING NORMAL, SAEKO!
HOW SO?
WELL, A LOT OF PEOPLE WOULD BE AWKWARD ABOUT ALL THIS STUFF.
HA HA, YEAH, SOME PEOPLE ARE LIKE THAT.

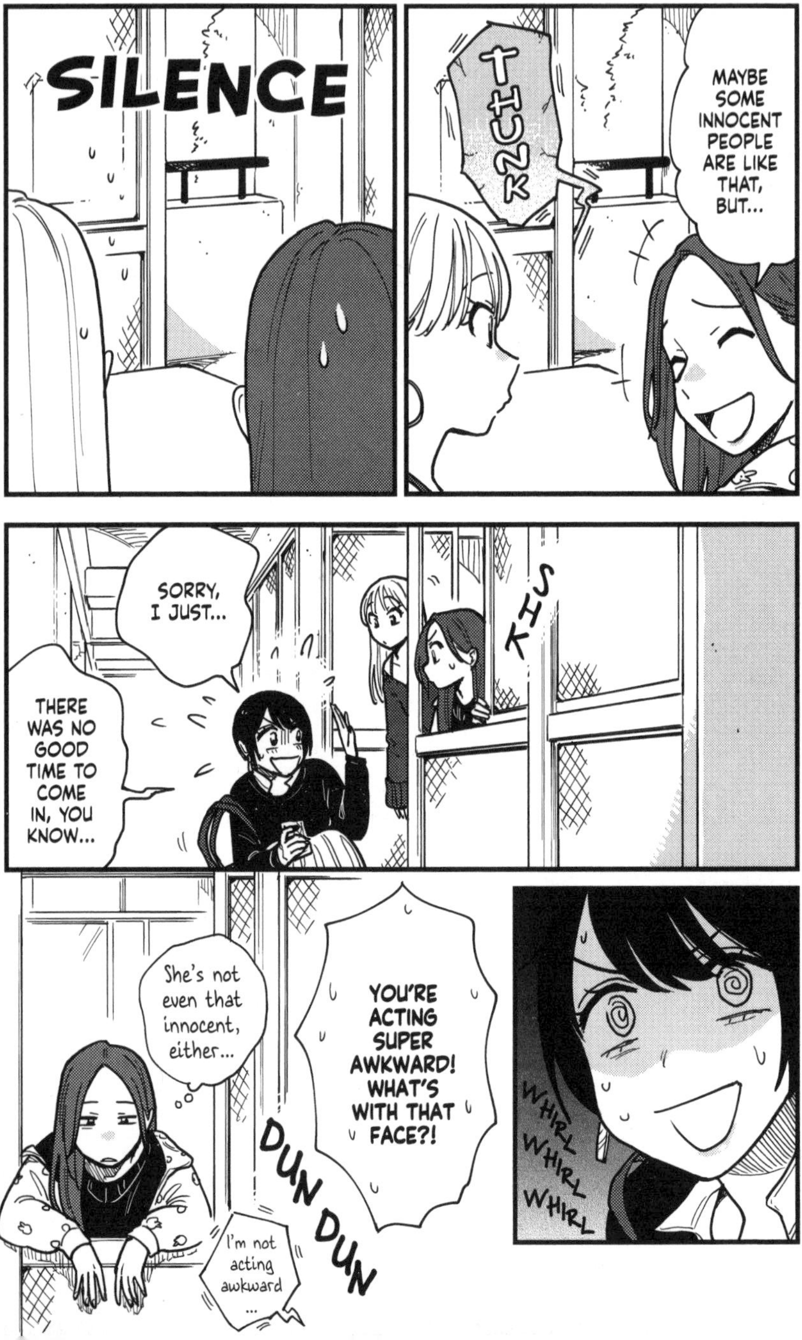
MAYBE SOME INNOCENT PEOPLE ARE LIKE THAT, BUT...
THUNK
SILENCE
SHH
SORRY, I JUST...
THERE WAS NO GOOD TIME TO COME IN, YOU KNOW...
WHIRL WHIRL WHIRL
YOU'RE ACTING SUPER AWKWARD! WHAT'S WITH THAT FACE?!
DUN DUN
She's not even that innocent, either...
I'm not acting awkward ...

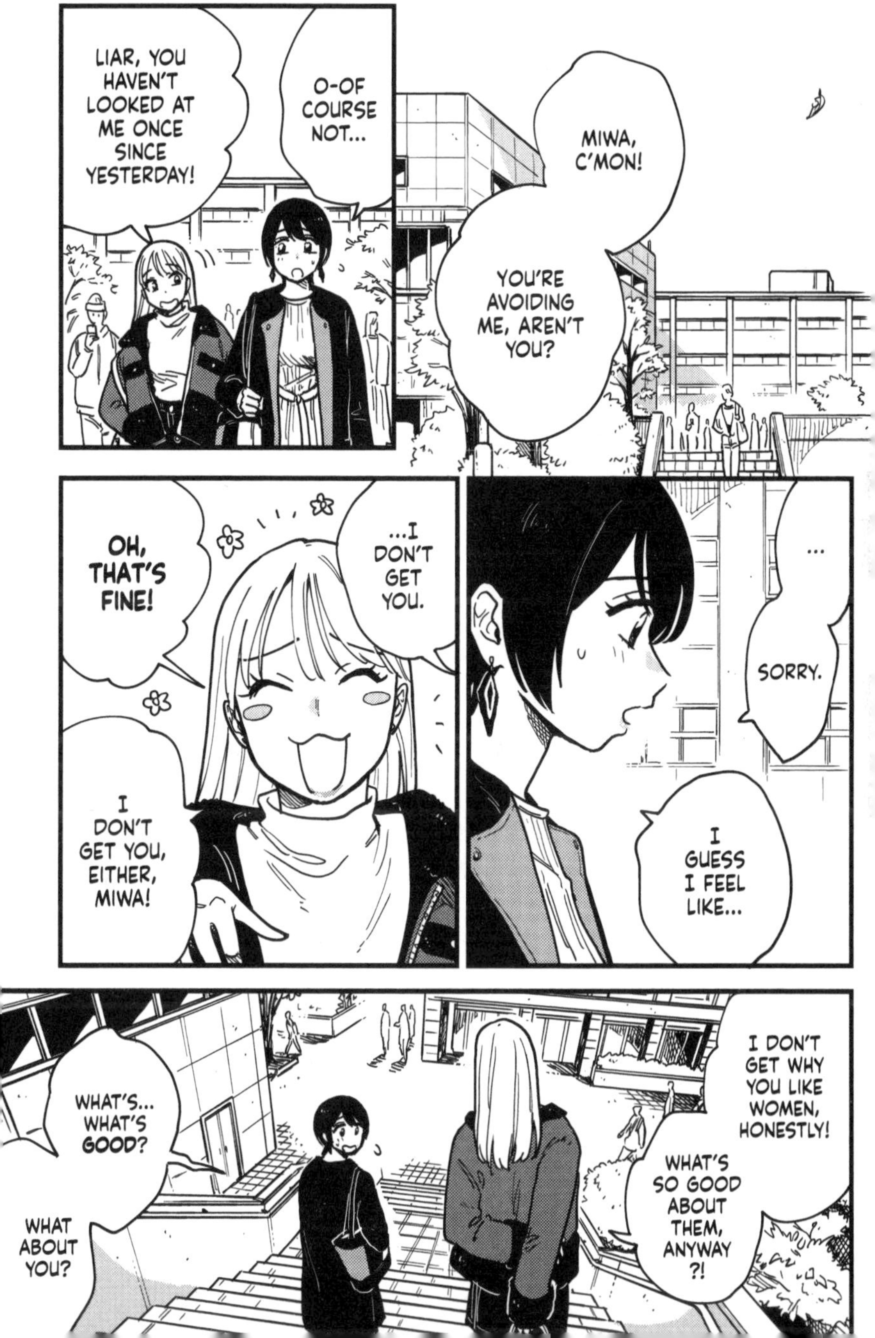
MIWA, C'MON!
YOU'RE AVOIDING ME, AREN'T YOU?
O-OF COURSE NOT...
LIAR, YOU HAVEN'T LOOKED AT ME ONCE SINCE YESTERDAY!
...
SORRY.
I GUESS I FEEL LIKE...
...I DON'T GET YOU.
OH, THAT'S FINE!
I DON'T GET YOU, EITHER, MIWA!
I DON'T GET WHY YOU LIKE WOMEN, HONESTLY!
WHAT'S SO GOOD ABOUT THEM, ANYWAY?!
WHAT'S... WHAT'S GOOD?
WHAT ABOUT YOU?

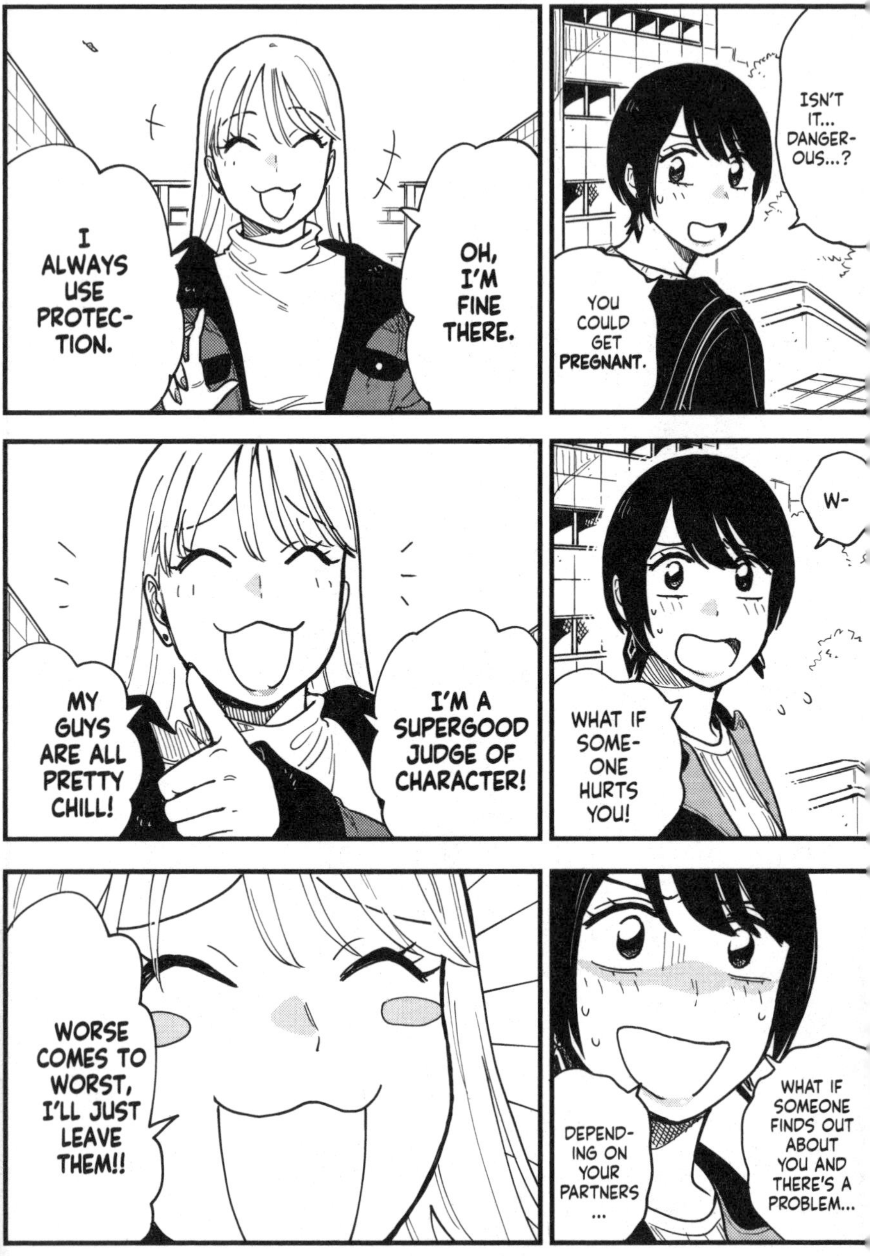
ISN'T IT... DANGEROUS...?
YOU COULD GET PREGNANT.
OH, I'M FINE THERE.
I ALWAYS USE PROTECTION.
W-
WHAT IF SOMEONE HURTS YOU!
I'M A SUPERGOOD JUDGE OF CHARACTER!
MY GUYS ARE ALL PRETTY CHILL!
WHAT IF SOMEONE FINDS OUT ABOUT YOU AND THERE'S A PROBLEM...
DEPENDING ON YOUR PARTNERS...
WORSE COMES TO WORST, I'LL JUST LEAVE THEM!!

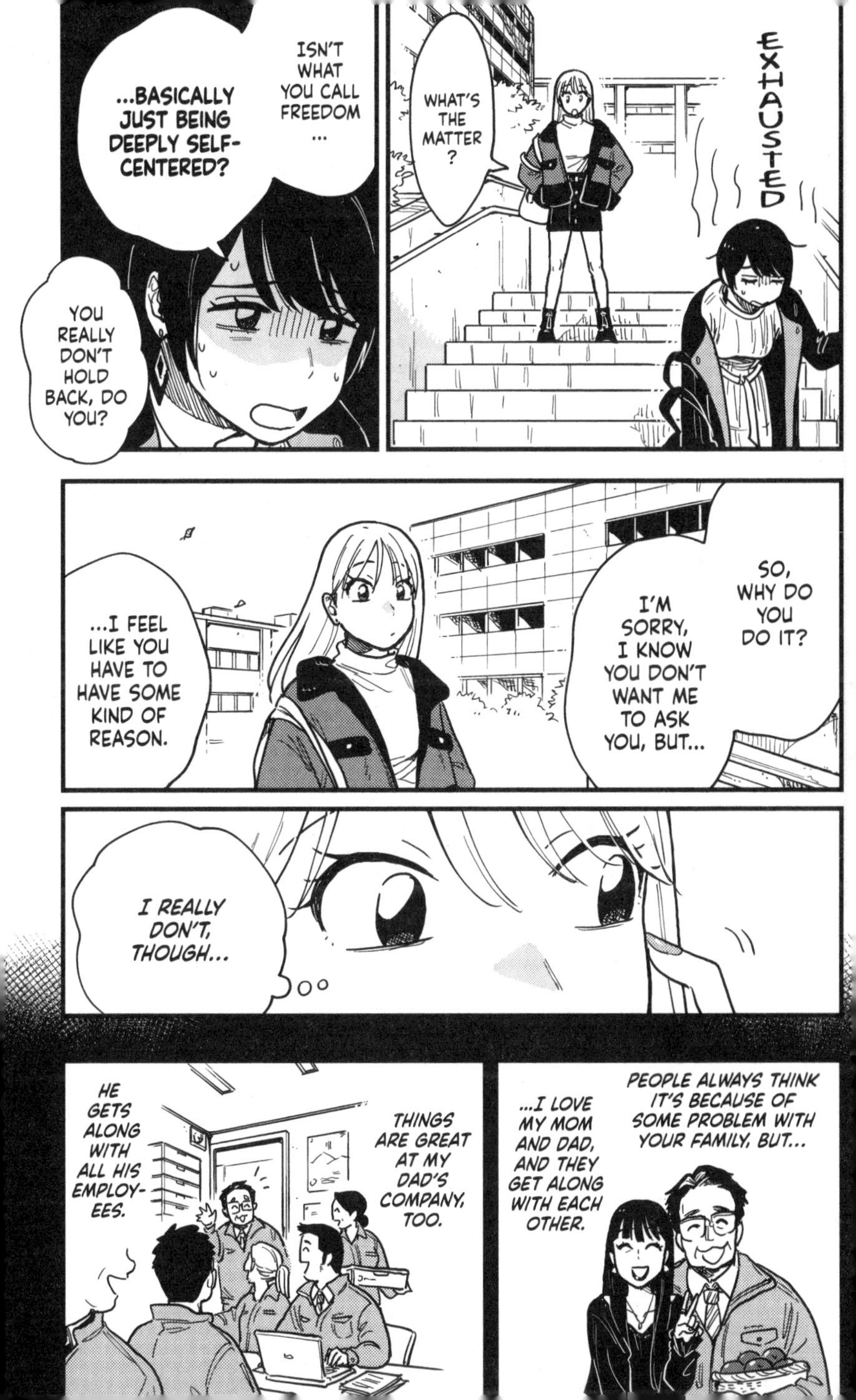
EXHAUSTED
WHAT'S THE MATTER?
ISN'T WHAT YOU CALL FREEDOM...
...BASICALLY JUST BEING DEEPLY SELF-CENTERED?
YOU REALLY DON'T HOLD BACK, DO YOU?
SO, WHY DO YOU DO IT?
I'M SORRY, I KNOW YOU DON'T WANT ME TO ASK YOU, BUT...
...I FEEL LIKE YOU HAVE TO HAVE SOME KIND OF REASON.
I REALLY DON'T, THOUGH...
PEOPLE ALWAYS THINK IT'S BECAUSE OF SOME PROBLEM WITH YOUR FAMILY, BUT...
...I LOVE MY MOM AND DAD, AND THEY GET ALONG WITH EACH OTHER.
THINGS ARE GREAT AT MY DAD'S COMPANY, TOO.
HE GETS ALONG WITH ALL HIS EMPLOYEES.

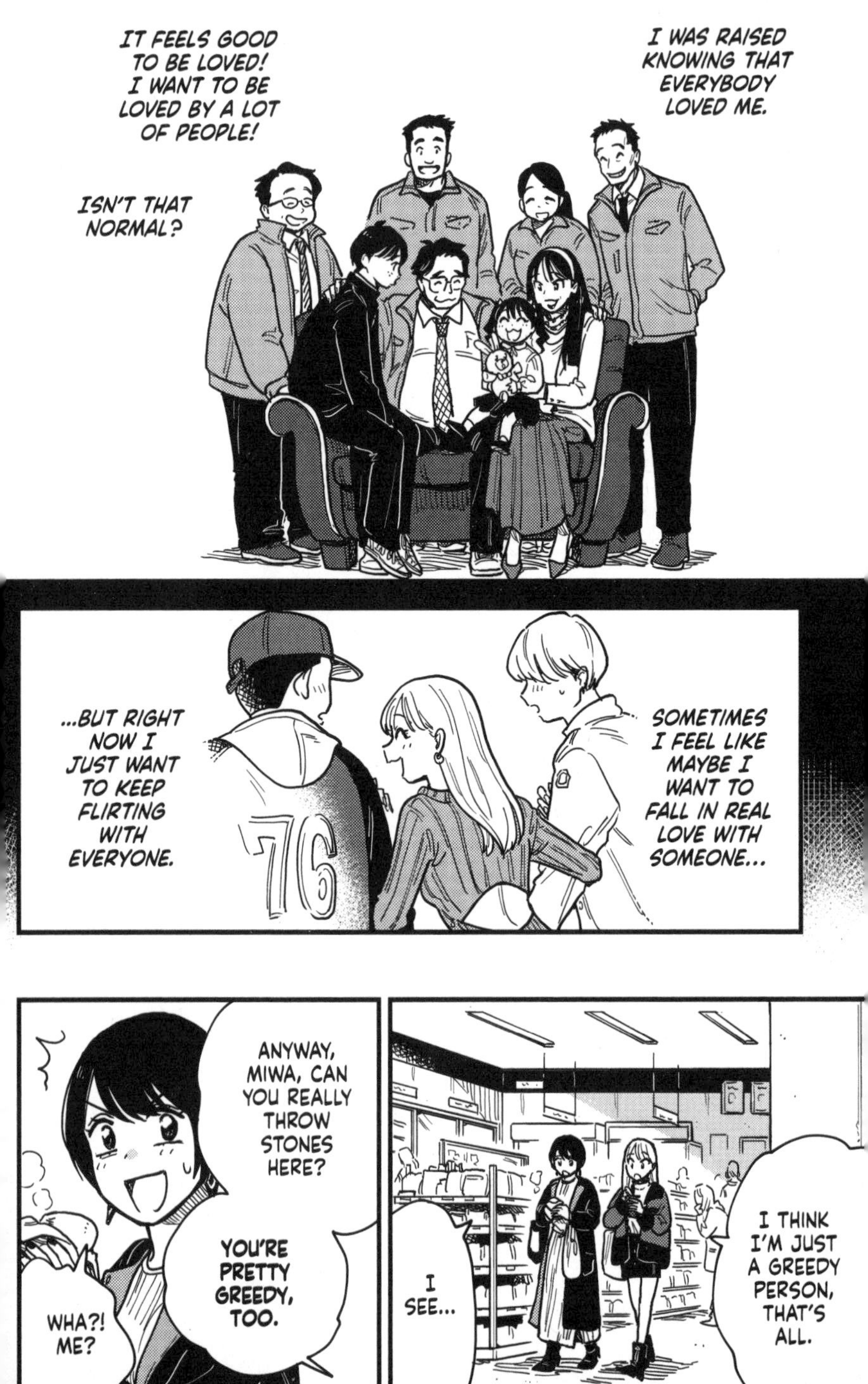
I WAS RAISED KNOWING THAT EVERYBODY LOVED ME.
IT FEELS GOOD TO BE LOVED! I WANT TO BE LOVED BY A LOT OF PEOPLE!
ISN'T THAT NORMAL?
SOMETIMES I FEEL LIKE MAYBE I WANT TO FALL IN REAL LOVE WITH SOMEONE...
...BUT RIGHT NOW I JUST WANT TO KEEP FLIRTING WITH EVERYONE.
I THINK I'M JUST A GREEDY PERSON, THAT'S ALL.
I SEE...
ANYWAY, MIWA, CAN YOU REALLY THROW STONES HERE?
YOU'RE PRETTY GREEDY, TOO.
WHA?! ME?

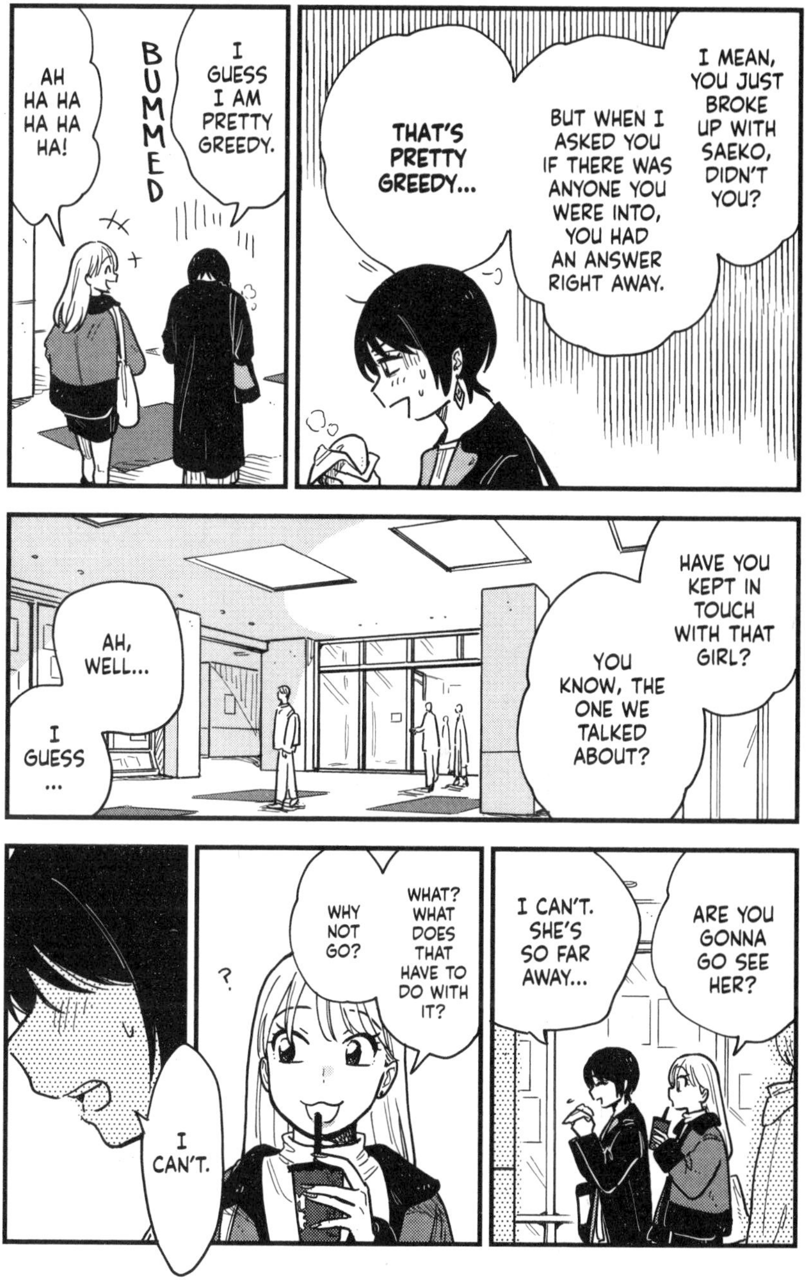
I MEAN, YOU JUST BROKE UP WITH SAEKO, DIDN'T YOU?
BUT WHEN I ASKED YOU IF THERE WAS ANYONE YOU WERE INTO, YOU HAD AN ANSWER RIGHT AWAY.
THAT'S PRETTY GREEDY...
I GUESS I AM PRETTY GREEDY.
BUMMED
AH HA HA HA HA HA!
HAVE YOU KEPT IN TOUCH WITH THAT GIRL?
YOU KNOW, THE ONE WE TALKED ABOUT?
AH, WELL...
I GUESS ...
ARE YOU GONNA GO SEE HER?
I CAN'T. SHE'S SO FAR AWAY...
WHAT? WHAT DOES THAT HAVE TO DO WITH IT?
WHY NOT GO?
?
I CAN'T.

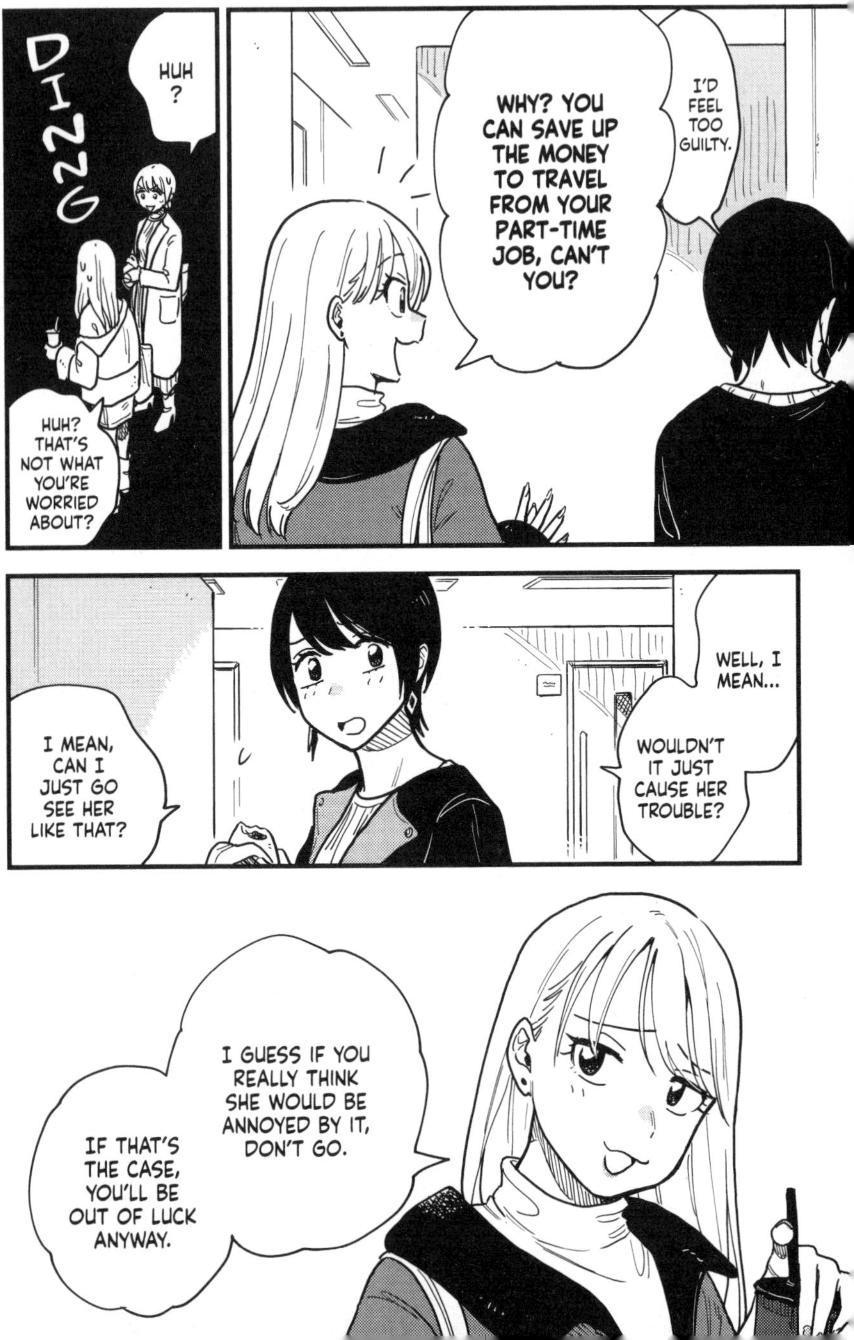
I'D FEEL TOO GUILTY.
WHY? YOU CAN SAVE UP THE MONEY TO TRAVEL FROM YOUR PART-TIME JOB, CAN'T YOU?
HUH ?
DING
HUH? THAT'S NOT WHAT YOU'RE WORRIED ABOUT?
WELL, I MEAN...
WOULDN'T IT JUST CAUSE HER TROUBLE?
I MEAN, CAN I JUST GO SEE HER LIKE THAT?
I GUESS IF YOU REALLY THINK SHE WOULD BE ANNOYED BY IT, DON'T GO.
IF THAT'S THE CASE, YOU'LL BE OUT OF LUCK ANYWAY.

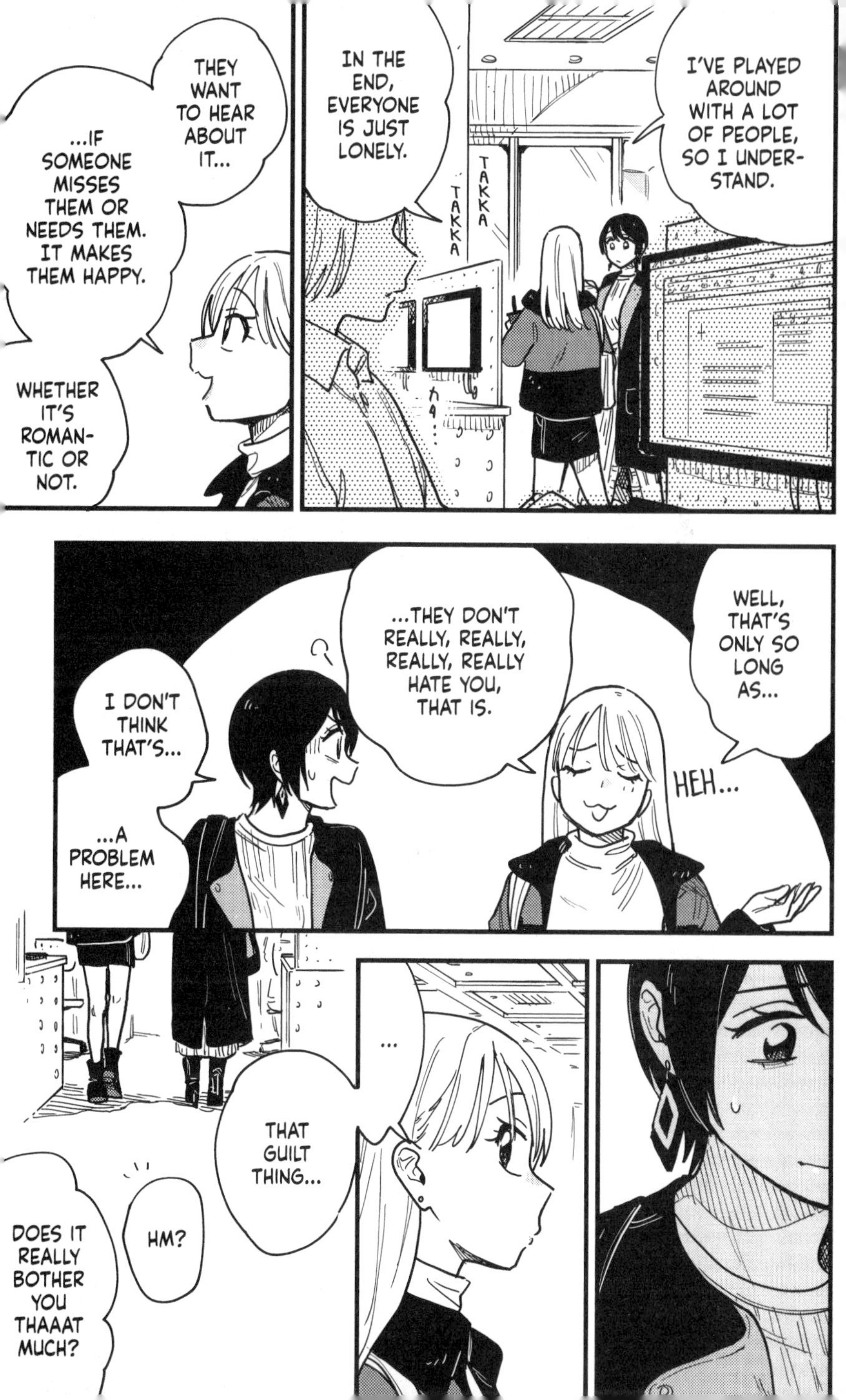
I'VE PLAYED AROUND WITH A LOT OF PEOPLE, SO I UNDERSTAND.
IN THE END, EVERYONE IS JUST LONELY.
TAKKA
TAKKA
THEY WANT TO HEAR ABOUT IT...
...IF SOMEONE MISSES THEM OR NEEDS THEM. IT MAKES THEM HAPPY.
WHETHER IT'S ROMANTIC OR NOT.
WELL, THAT'S ONLY SO LONG AS...
...THEY DON'T REALLY, REALLY, REALLY, REALLY HATE YOU, THAT IS.
HEH...
I DON'T THINK THAT'S...
...A PROBLEM HERE...
...
THAT GUILT THING...
HM?
DOES IT REALLY BOTHER YOU THAAAT MUCH?

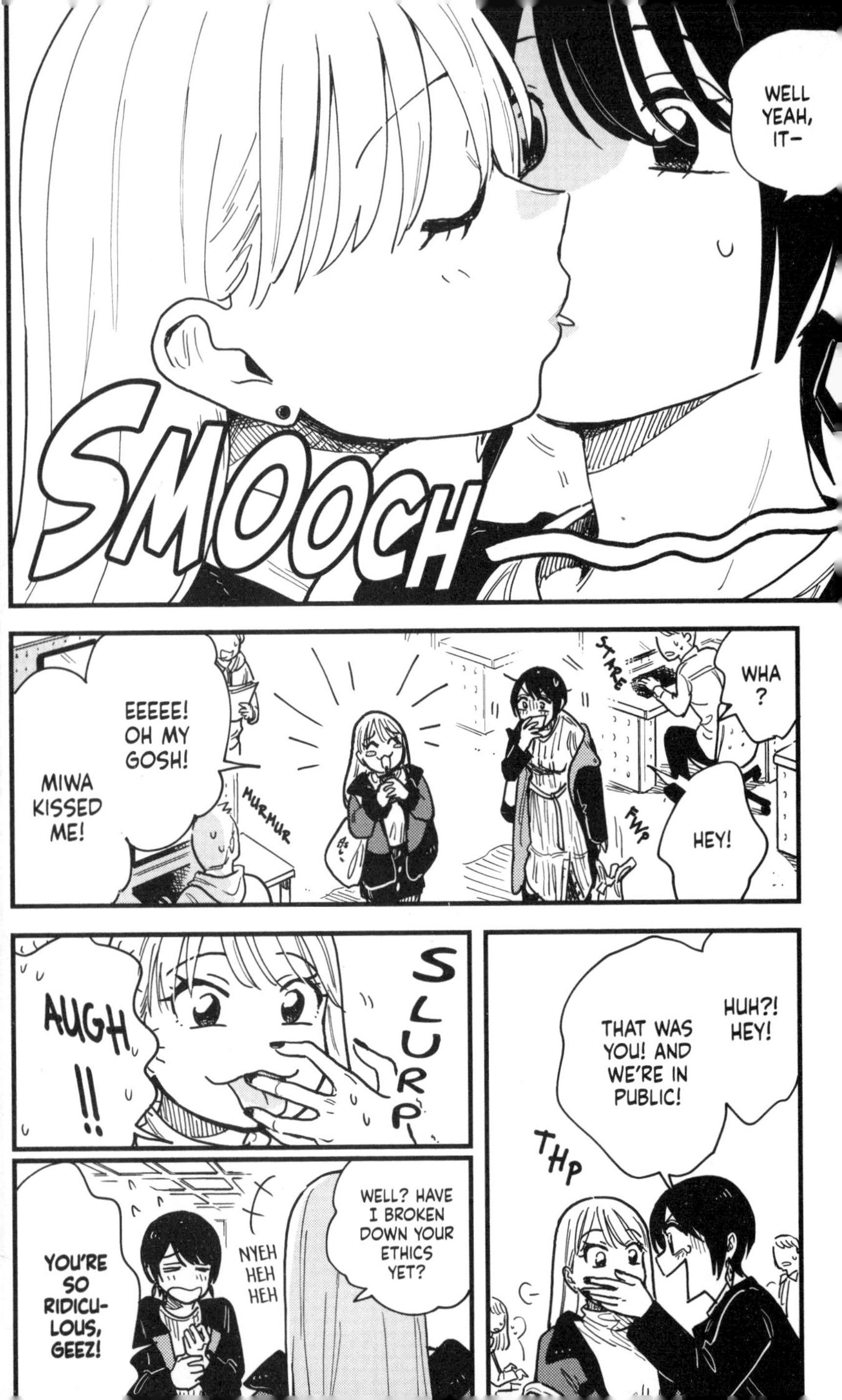

WELL YEAH, IT—
SMOOCH
WHA?
STARE
HEY!
FWP
EEEEE! OH MY GOSH!
MIWA KISSED ME!
MURMUR
HUH?! HEY!
THAT WAS YOU! AND WE'RE IN PUBLIC!
THP
SLURP
AUGH!!
WELL? HAVE I BROKEN DOWN YOUR ETHICS YET?
NYEH HEH HEH
YOU'RE SO RIDICULOUS, GEEZ!

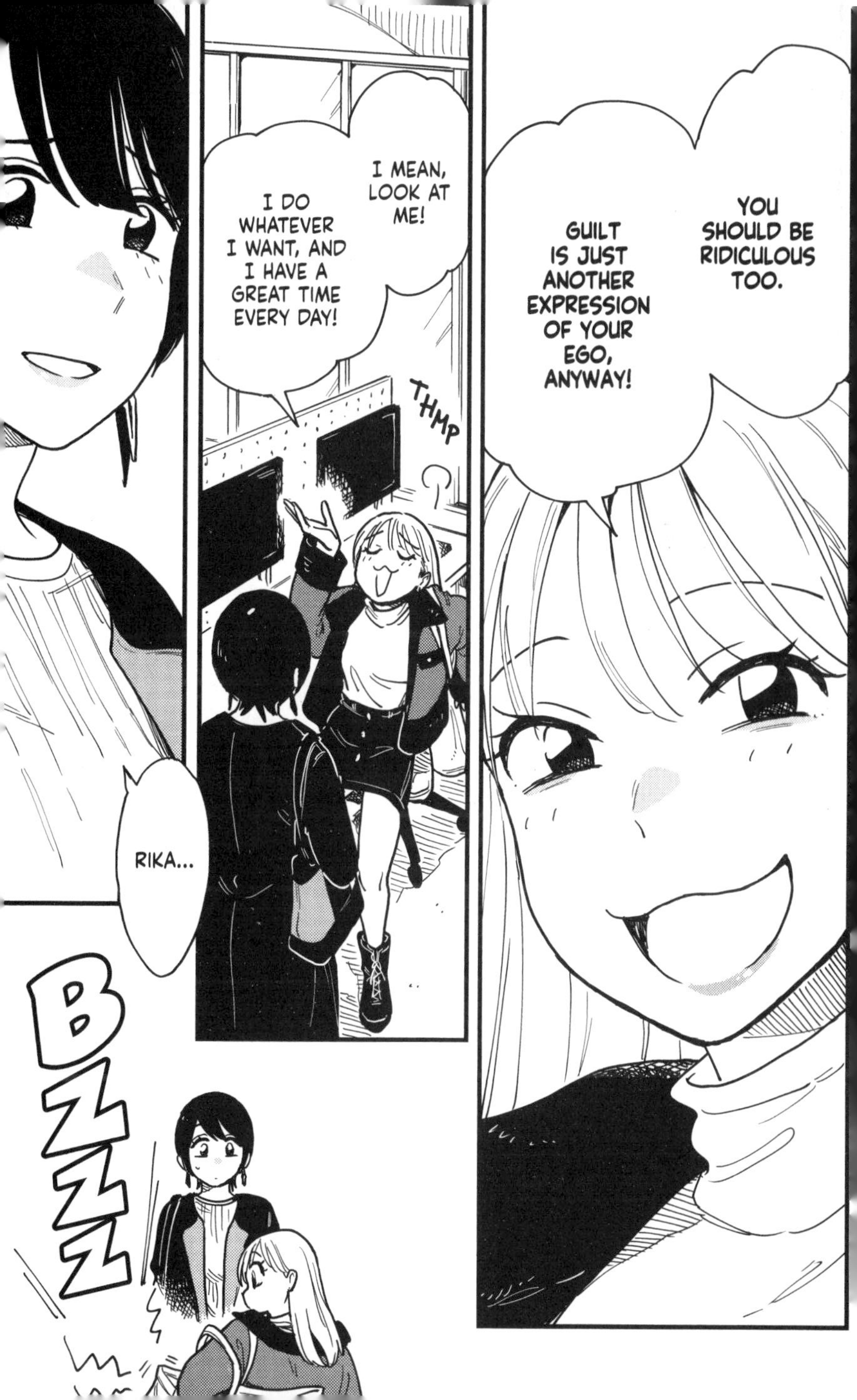
YOU SHOULD BE RIDICULOUS TOO.
GUILT IS JUST ANOTHER EXPRESSION OF YOUR EGO, ANYWAY!
I MEAN, LOOK AT ME!
I DO WHATEVER I WANT, AND I HAVE A GREAT TIME EVERY DAY!
THMP
RIKA...
BZZZ

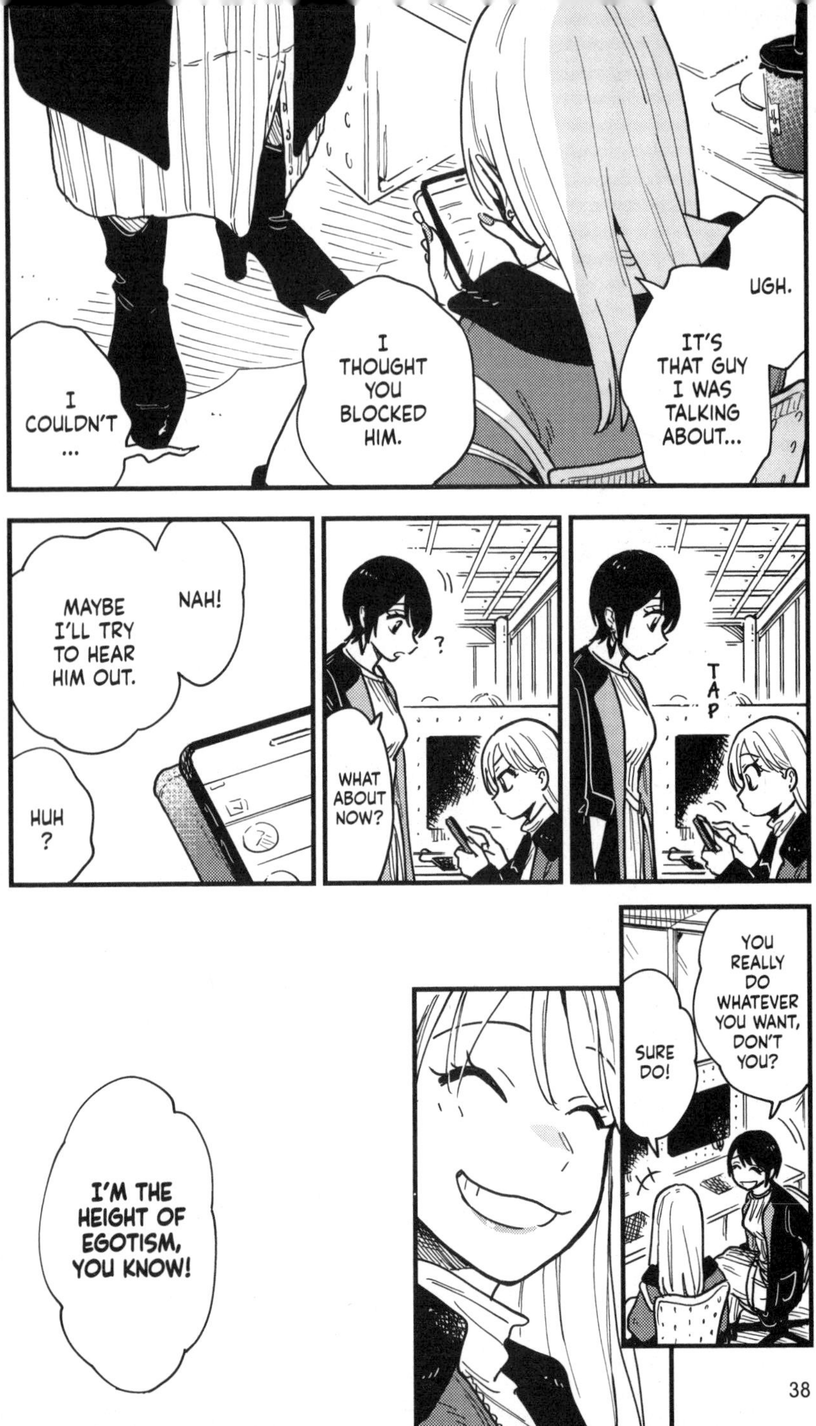
UGH.
IT'S THAT GUY I WAS TALKING ABOUT...
I THOUGHT YOU BLOCKED HIM.
I COULDN'T ...
TAP
?
WHAT ABOUT NOW?
NAH!
MAYBE I'LL TRY TO HEAR HIM OUT.
HUH ?
YOU REALLY DO WHATEVER YOU WANT, DON'T YOU?
SURE DO!
I'M THE HEIGHT OF EGOTISM, YOU KNOW!

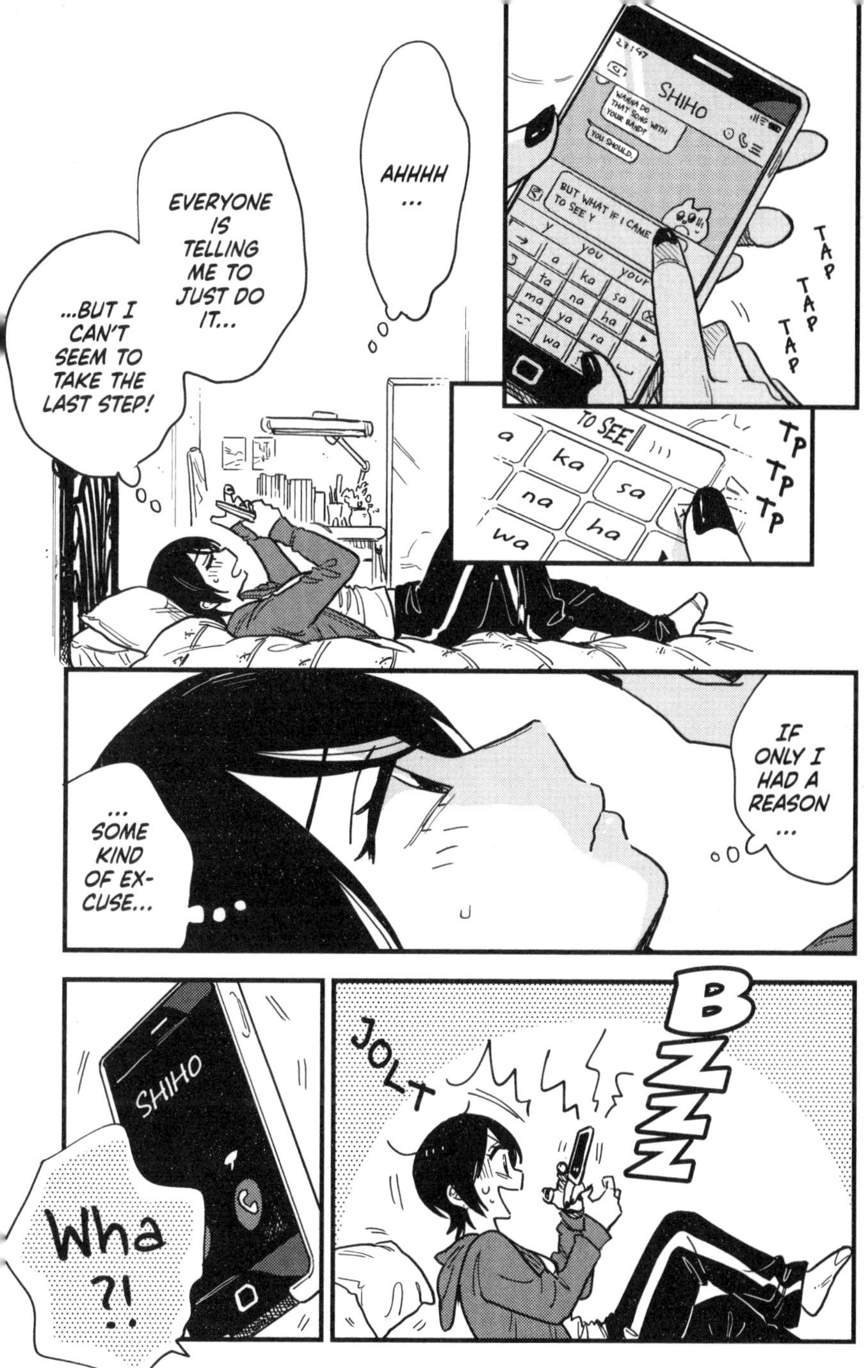
SHIHO
WANNA DO THAT SONG WITH YOUR BAND?
YOU SHOULD.
BUT WHAT IF I CAME TO SEE Y
TAP TAP TAP
TO SEE
TP TP TP
AHHHH...
EVERYONE IS TELLING ME TO JUST DO IT...
...BUT I CAN'T SEEM TO TAKE THE LAST STEP!
IF ONLY I HAD A REASON...
...SOME KIND OF EXCUSE...
BZZZ
JOLT
SHIHO
Wha?!

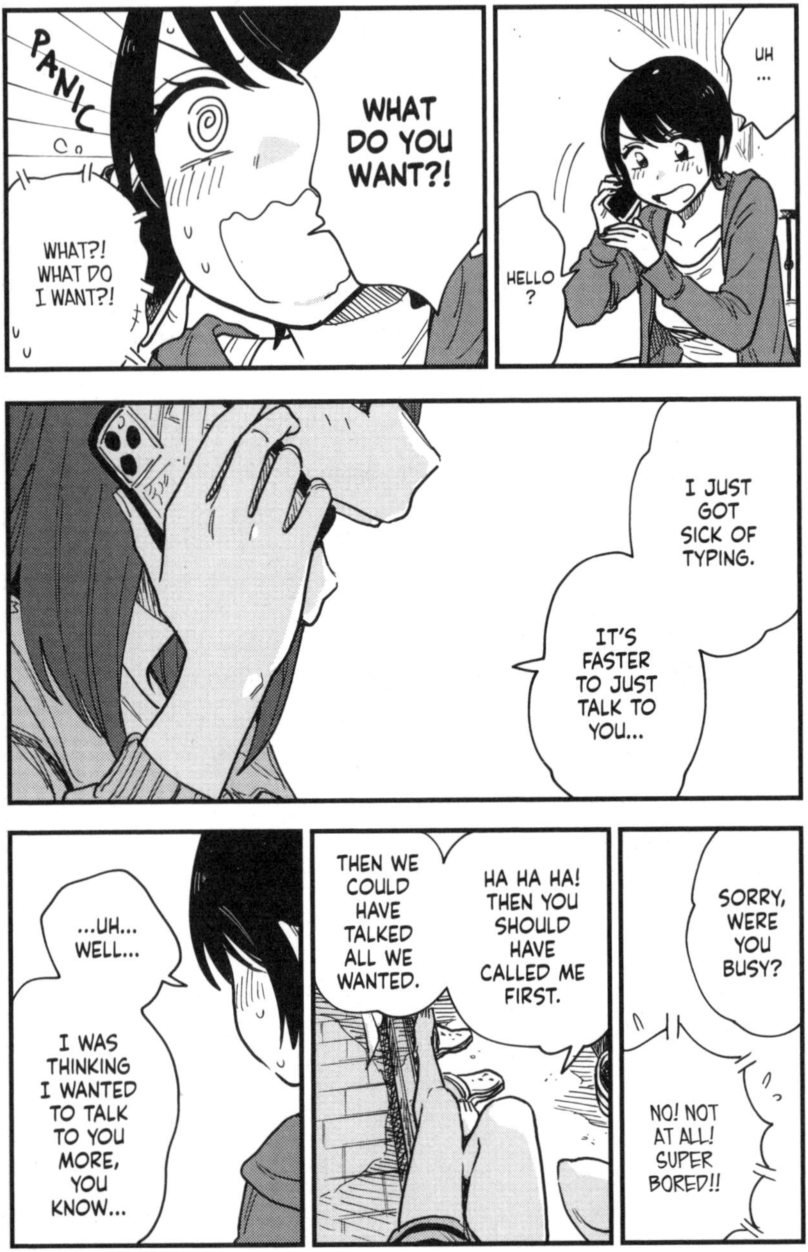
UH ...
HELLO ?
WHAT DO YOU WANT?!
PANIC
WHAT?! WHAT DO I WANT?!
I JUST GOT SICK OF TYPING.
IT'S FASTER TO JUST TALK TO YOU...
SORRY, WERE YOU BUSY?
NO! NOT AT ALL! SUPER BORED!!
HA HA HA! THEN YOU SHOULD HAVE CALLED ME FIRST.
THEN WE COULD HAVE TALKED ALL WE WANTED.
...UH... WELL...
I WAS THINKING I WANTED TO TALK TO YOU MORE, YOU KNOW...

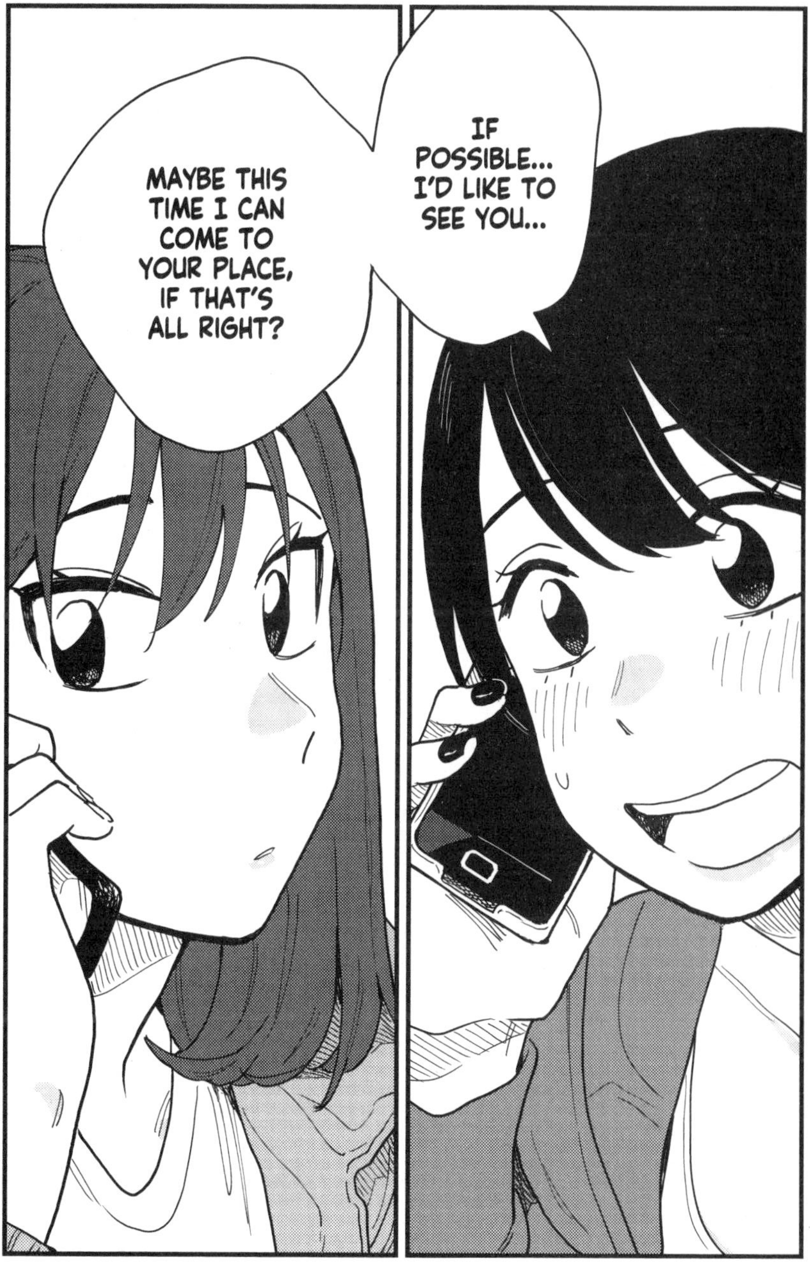
IF POSSIBLE... I'D LIKE TO SEE YOU...
MAYBE THIS TIME I CAN COME TO YOUR PLACE, IF THAT'S ALL RIGHT?

HOW DO WE RELATIONSHIP?

Chapter 39: Like a Roller Coaster

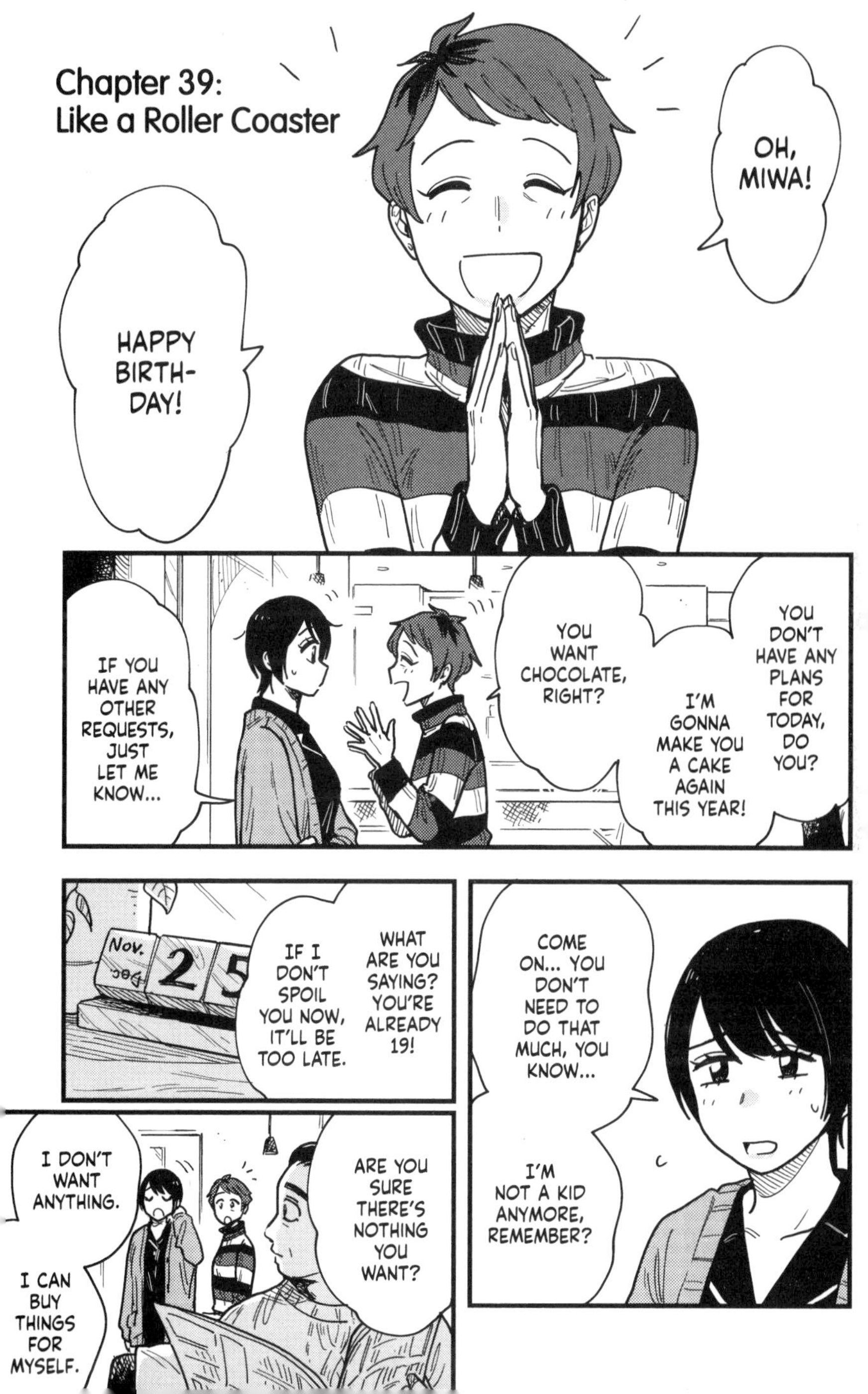
OH, MIWA!
HAPPY BIRTH-DAY!
YOU DON'T HAVE ANY PLANS FOR TODAY, DO YOU?
I'M GONNA MAKE YOU A CAKE AGAIN THIS YEAR!
YOU WANT CHOCOLATE, RIGHT?
IF YOU HAVE ANY OTHER REQUESTS, JUST LET ME KNOW...
COME ON... YOU DON'T NEED TO DO THAT MUCH, YOU KNOW...
I'M NOT A KID ANYMORE, REMEMBER?
Nov. 25
WHAT ARE YOU SAYING? YOU'RE ALREADY 19!
IF I DON'T SPOIL YOU NOW, IT'LL BE TOO LATE.
ARE YOU SURE THERE'S NOTHING YOU WANT?
I DON'T WANT ANYTHING.
I CAN BUY THINGS FOR MYSELF.

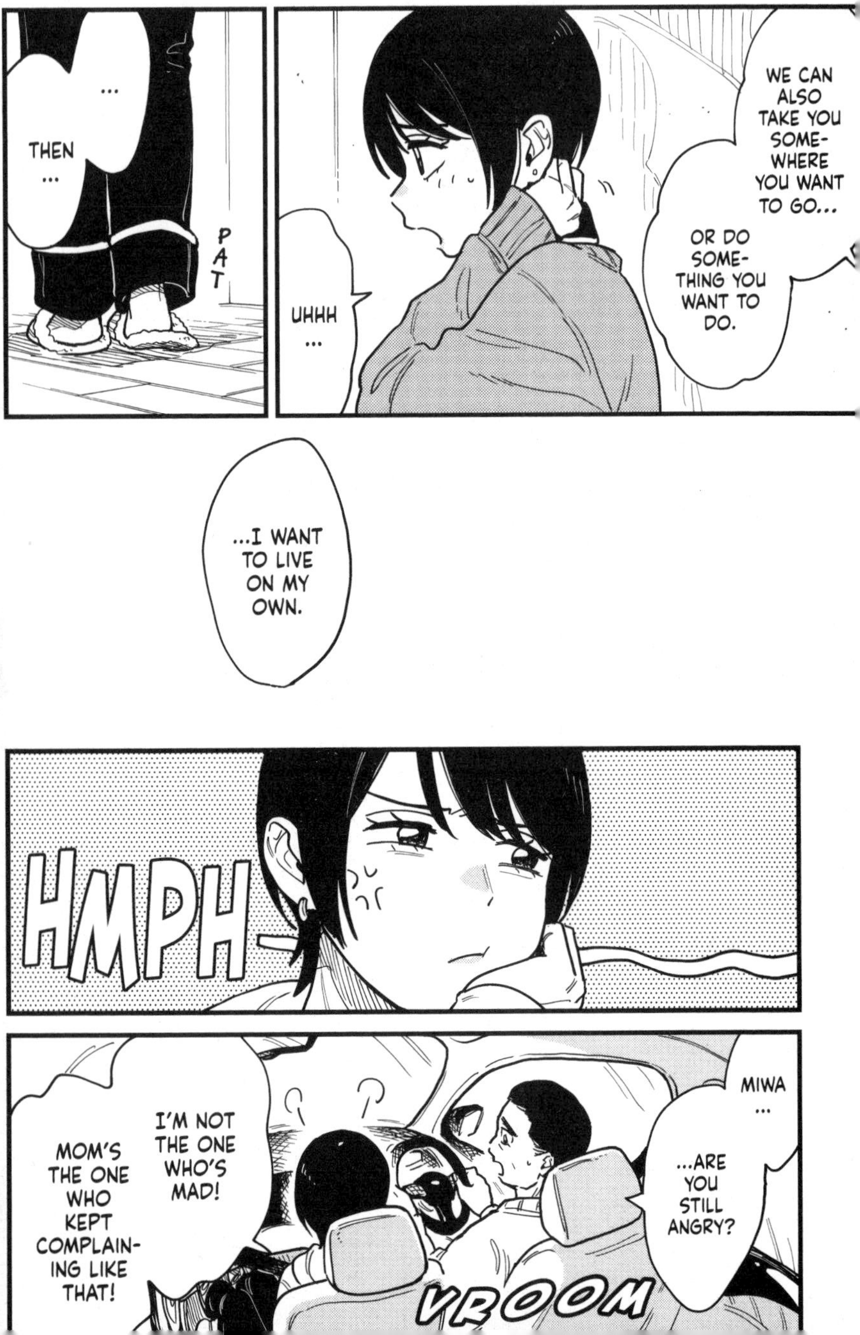
WE CAN ALSO TAKE YOU SOME-WHERE YOU WANT TO GO...
OR DO SOME-THING YOU WANT TO DO.
UHHH ...
...
THEN ...
PAT
...I WANT TO LIVE ON MY OWN.
HMPH
MIWA ...
...ARE YOU STILL ANGRY?
I'M NOT THE ONE WHO'S MAD!
MOM'S THE ONE WHO KEPT COMPLAIN-ING LIKE THAT!
VROOM

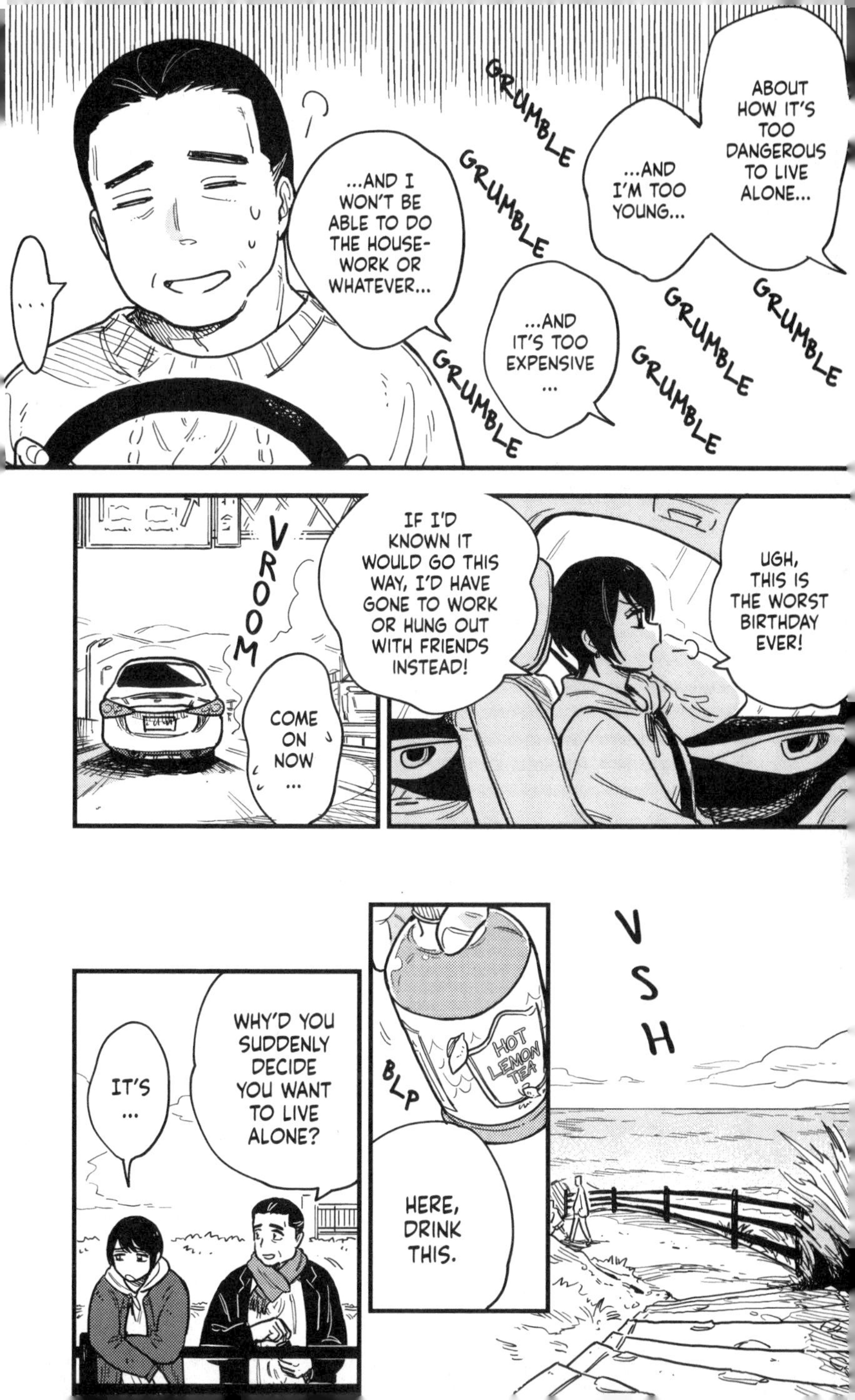
ABOUT HOW IT'S TOO DANGEROUS TO LIVE ALONE...
GRUMBLE
...AND I'M TOO YOUNG...
GRUMBLE
GRUMBLE
GRUMBLE
...AND IT'S TOO EXPENSIVE...
GRUMBLE
...AND I WON'T BE ABLE TO DO THE HOUSE-WORK OR WHATEVER...
GRUMBLE
GRUMBLE
...
UGH, THIS IS THE WORST BIRTHDAY EVER!
IF I'D KNOWN IT WOULD GO THIS WAY, I'D HAVE GONE TO WORK OR HUNG OUT WITH FRIENDS INSTEAD!
VROOM
COME ON NOW ...
VSH
BLP
HOT LEMON TEA
HERE, DRINK THIS.
WHY'D YOU SUDDENLY DECIDE YOU WANT TO LIVE ALONE?
IT'S ...

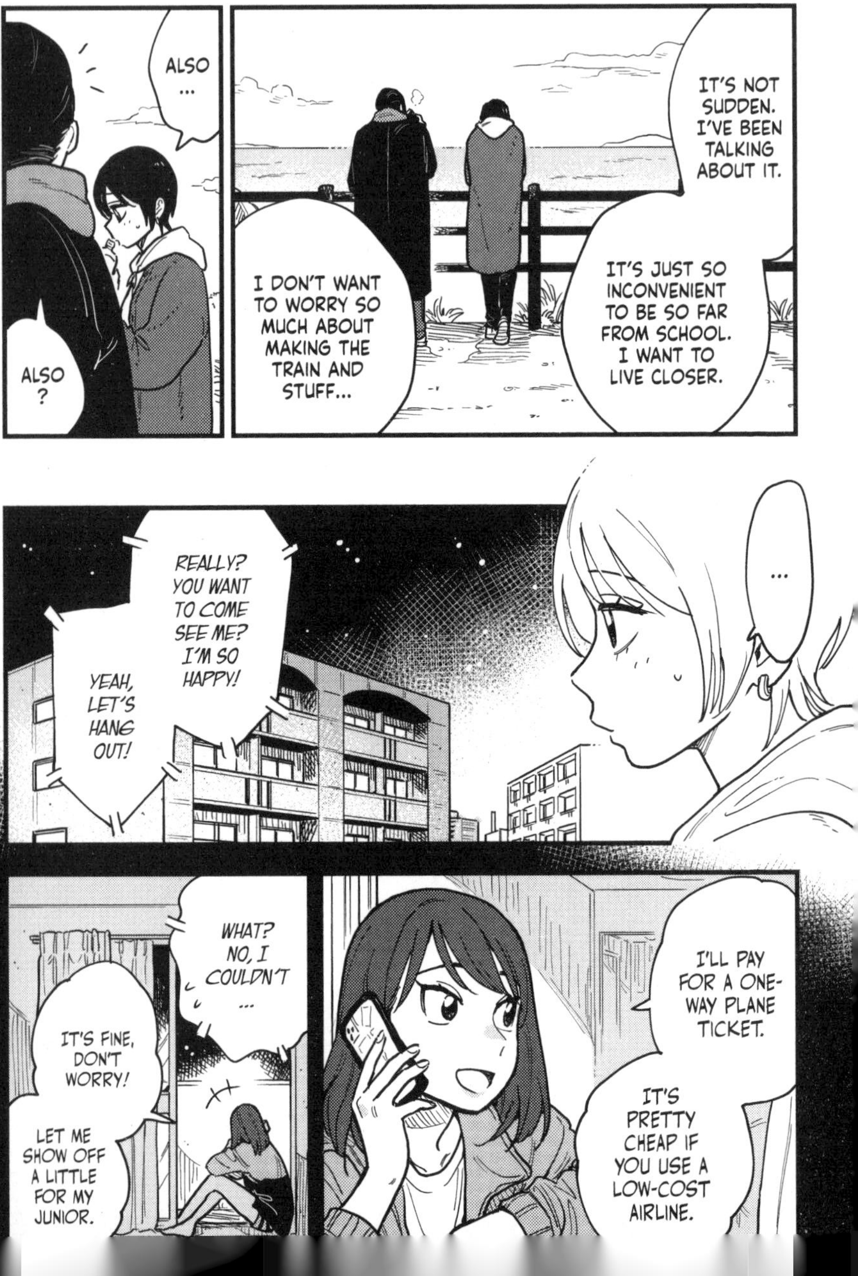
IT'S NOT SUDDEN. I'VE BEEN TALKING ABOUT IT.
IT'S JUST SO INCONVENIENT TO BE SO FAR FROM SCHOOL. I WANT TO LIVE CLOSER.
I DON'T WANT TO WORRY SO MUCH ABOUT MAKING THE TRAIN AND STUFF...
ALSO ...
ALSO ?
...
REALLY? YOU WANT TO COME SEE ME? I'M SO HAPPY!
YEAH, LET'S HANG OUT!
I'LL PAY FOR A ONE-WAY PLANE TICKET.
IT'S PRETTY CHEAP IF YOU USE A LOW-COST AIRLINE.
WHAT? NO, I COULDN'T ...
IT'S FINE, DON'T WORRY!
LET ME SHOW OFF A LITTLE FOR MY JUNIOR.

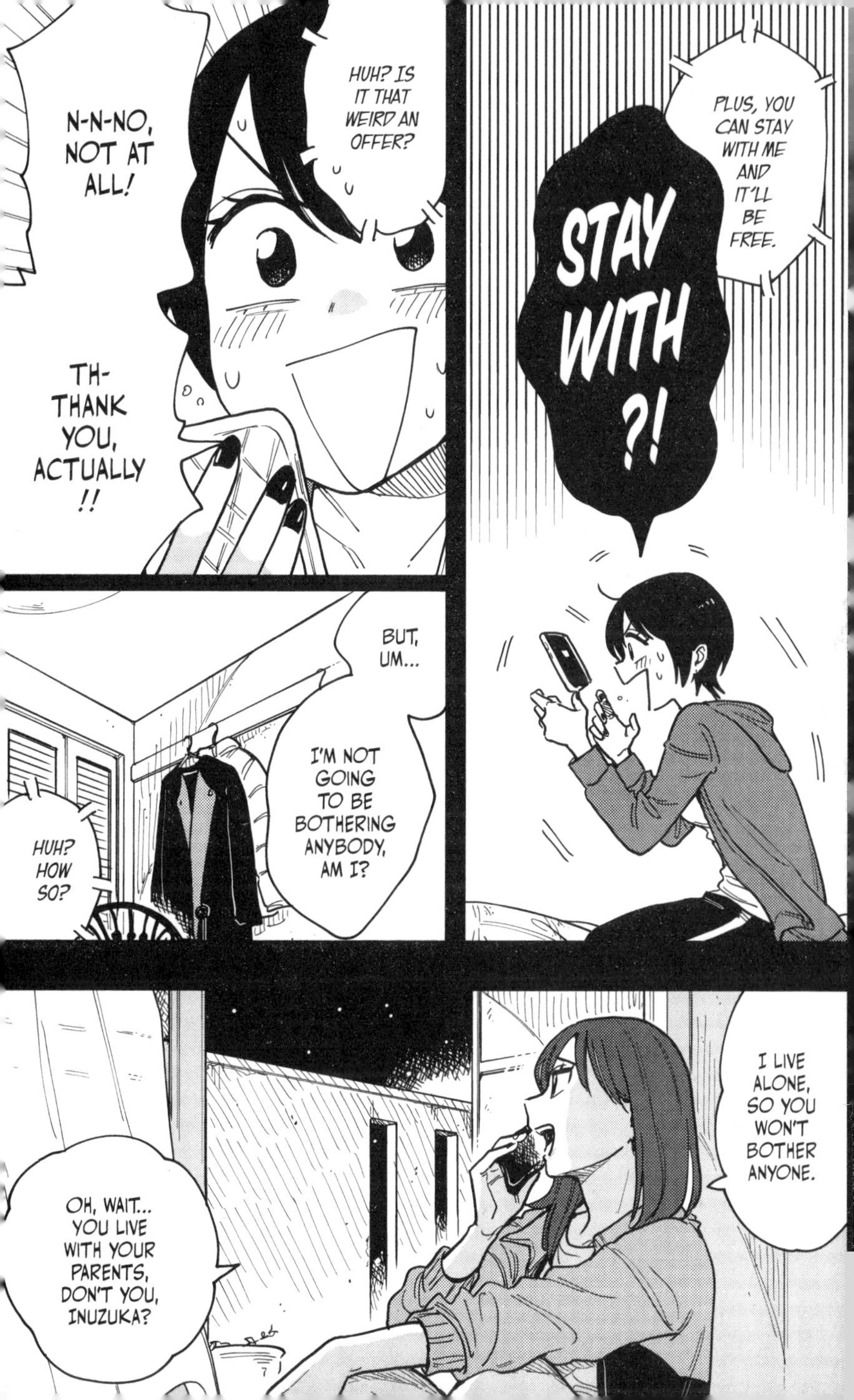
PLUS, YOU CAN STAY WITH ME AND IT'LL BE FREE.
STAY WITH ?!
HUH? IS IT THAT WEIRD AN OFFER?
N-N-NO, NOT AT ALL!
TH- THANK YOU, ACTUALLY !!
BUT, UM...
I'M NOT GOING TO BE BOTHERING ANYBODY, AM I?
HUH? HOW SO?
I LIVE ALONE, SO YOU WON'T BOTHER ANYONE.
OH, WAIT... YOU LIVE WITH YOUR PARENTS, DON'T YOU, INUZUKA?

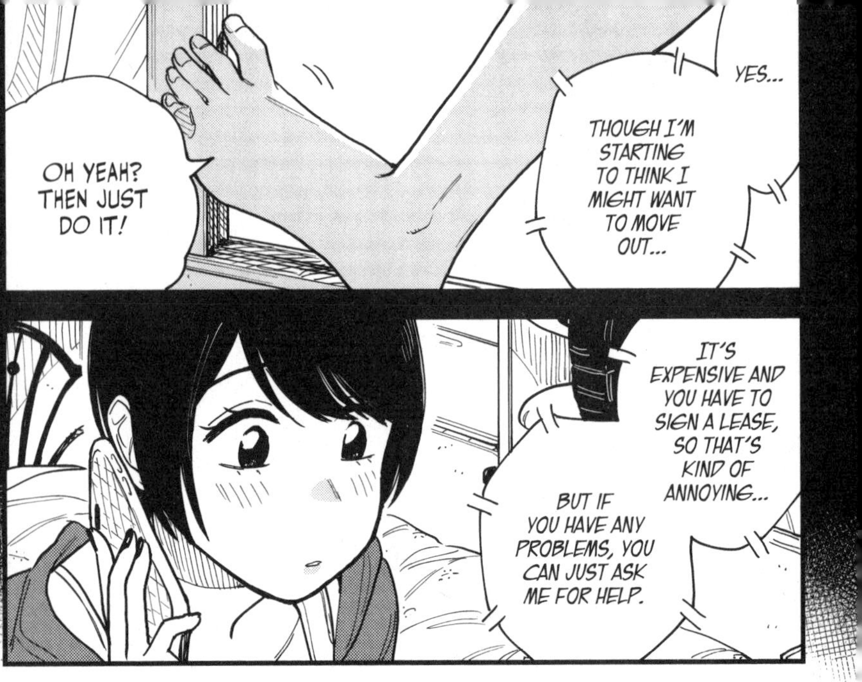
YES...
THOUGH I'M STARTING TO THINK I MIGHT WANT TO MOVE OUT...
OH YEAH? THEN JUST DO IT!
IT'S EXPENSIVE AND YOU HAVE TO SIGN A LEASE, SO THAT'S KIND OF ANNOYING...
BUT IF YOU HAVE ANY PROBLEMS, YOU CAN JUST ASK ME FOR HELP.

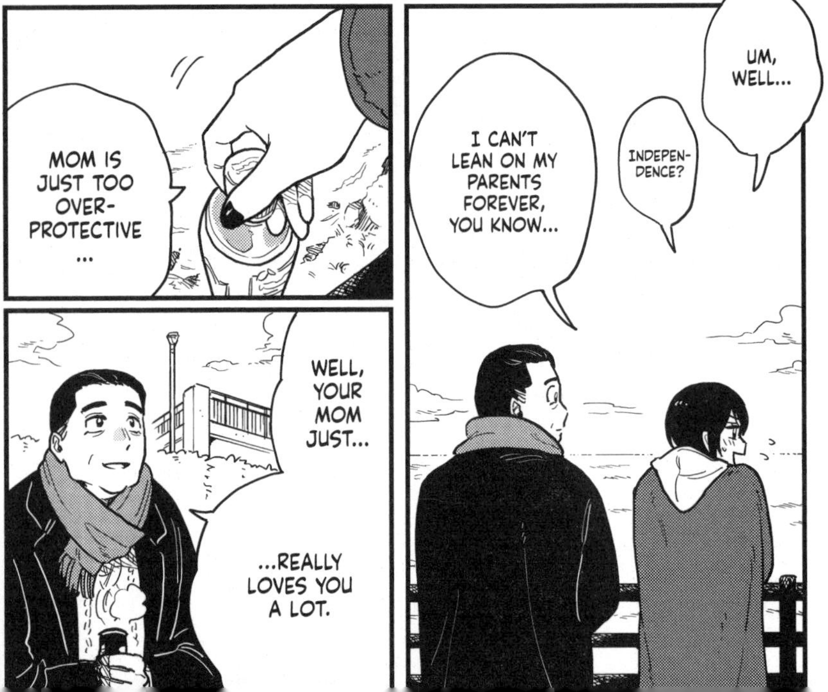
UM, WELL...
INDEPEN-DENCE?
I CAN'T LEAN ON MY PARENTS FOREVER, YOU KNOW...
MOM IS JUST TOO OVER-PROTECTIVE...
WELL, YOUR MOM JUST...
...REALLY LOVES YOU A LOT.

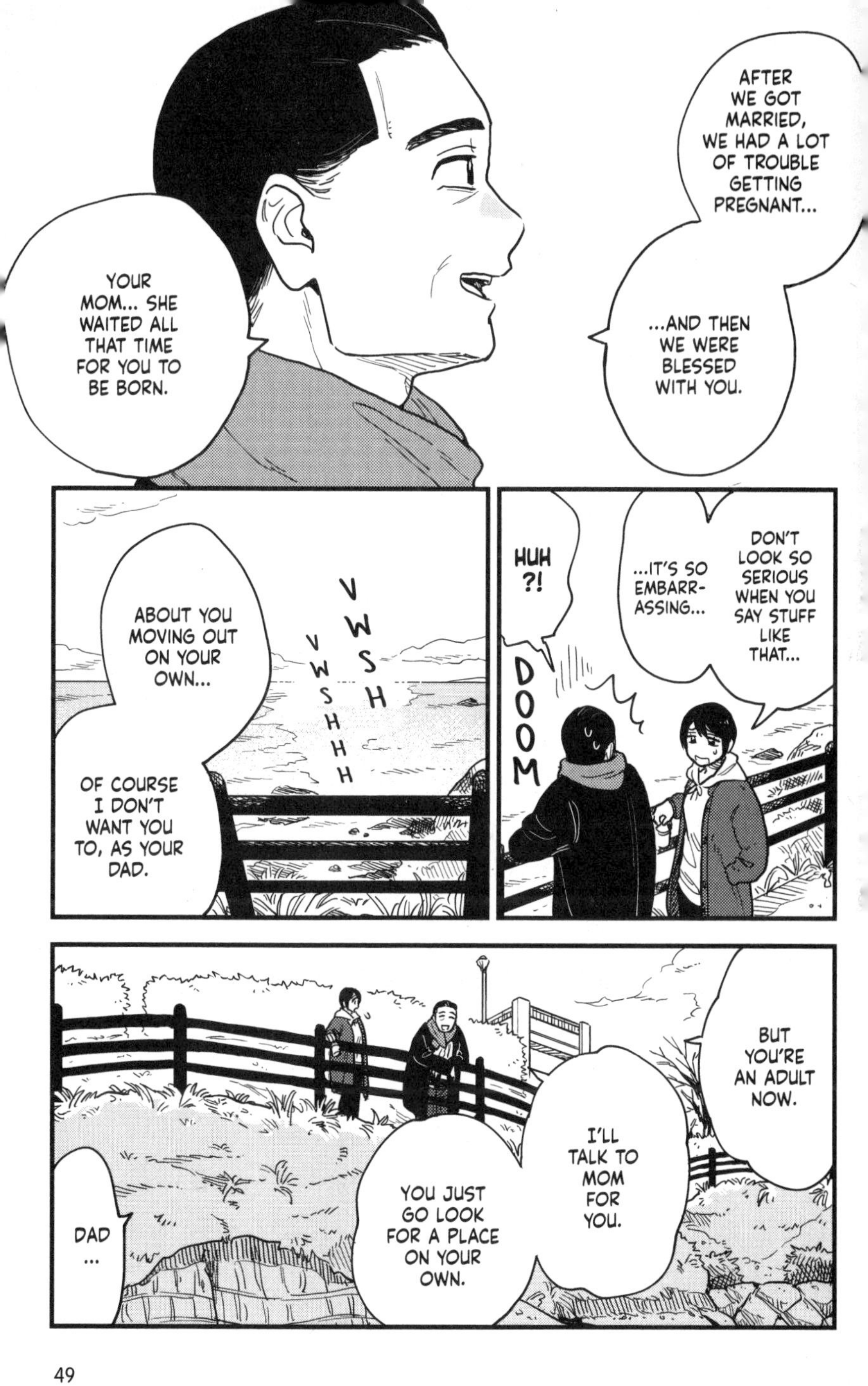
AFTER WE GOT MARRIED, WE HAD A LOT OF TROUBLE GETTING PREGNANT...
...AND THEN WE WERE BLESSED WITH YOU.
YOUR MOM... SHE WAITED ALL THAT TIME FOR YOU TO BE BORN.
DON'T LOOK SO SERIOUS WHEN YOU SAY STUFF LIKE THAT...
...IT'S SO EMBARR-ASSING...
HUH?!
DOOOM
VWSH
VWSHHH
ABOUT YOU MOVING OUT ON YOUR OWN...
OF COURSE I DON'T WANT YOU TO, AS YOUR DAD.
BUT YOU'RE AN ADULT NOW.
I'LL TALK TO MOM FOR YOU.
YOU JUST GO LOOK FOR A PLACE ON YOUR OWN.
DAD...

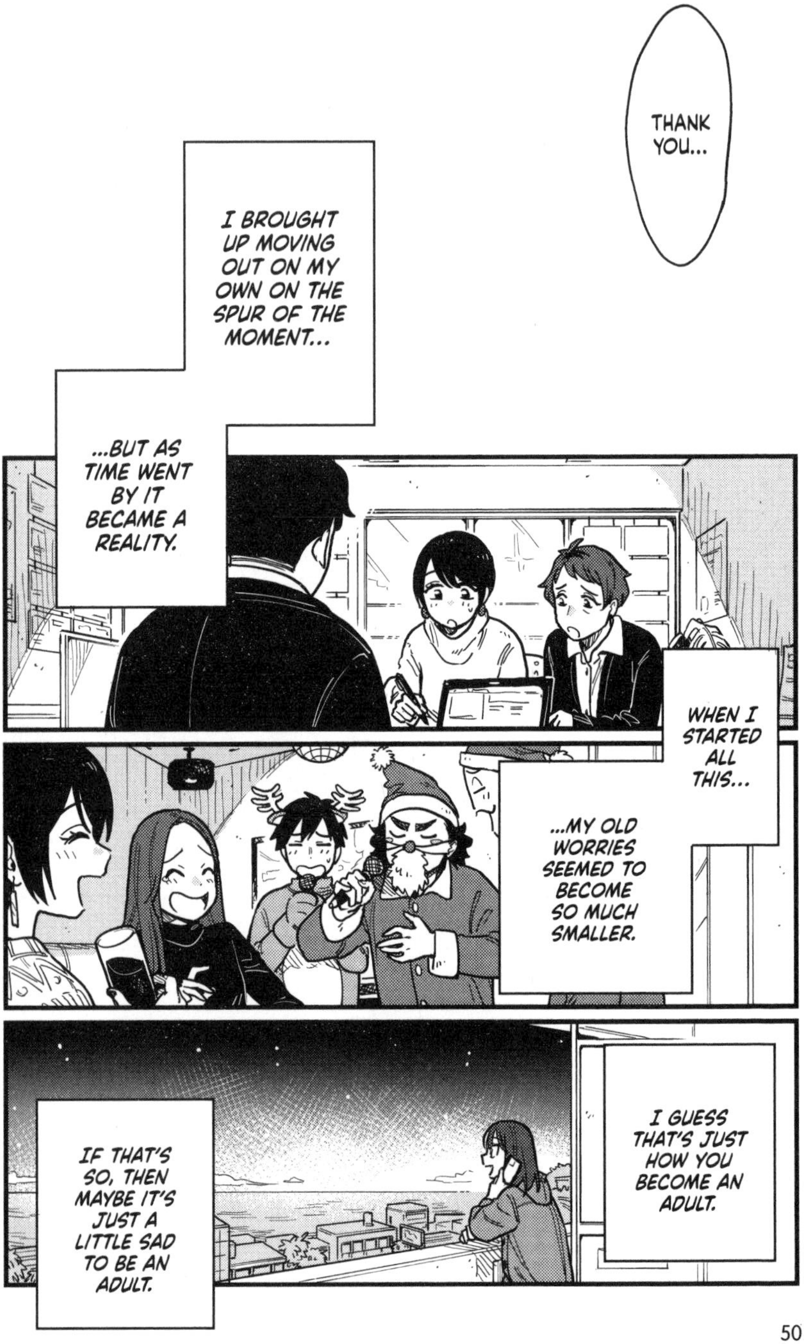
THANK YOU...
I BROUGHT UP MOVING OUT ON MY OWN ON THE SPUR OF THE MOMENT...
...BUT AS TIME WENT BY IT BECAME A REALITY.
WHEN I STARTED ALL THIS...
...MY OLD WORRIES SEEMED TO BECOME SO MUCH SMALLER.
I GUESS THAT'S JUST HOW YOU BECOME AN ADULT.
IF THAT'S SO, THEN MAYBE IT'S JUST A LITTLE SAD TO BE AN ADULT.

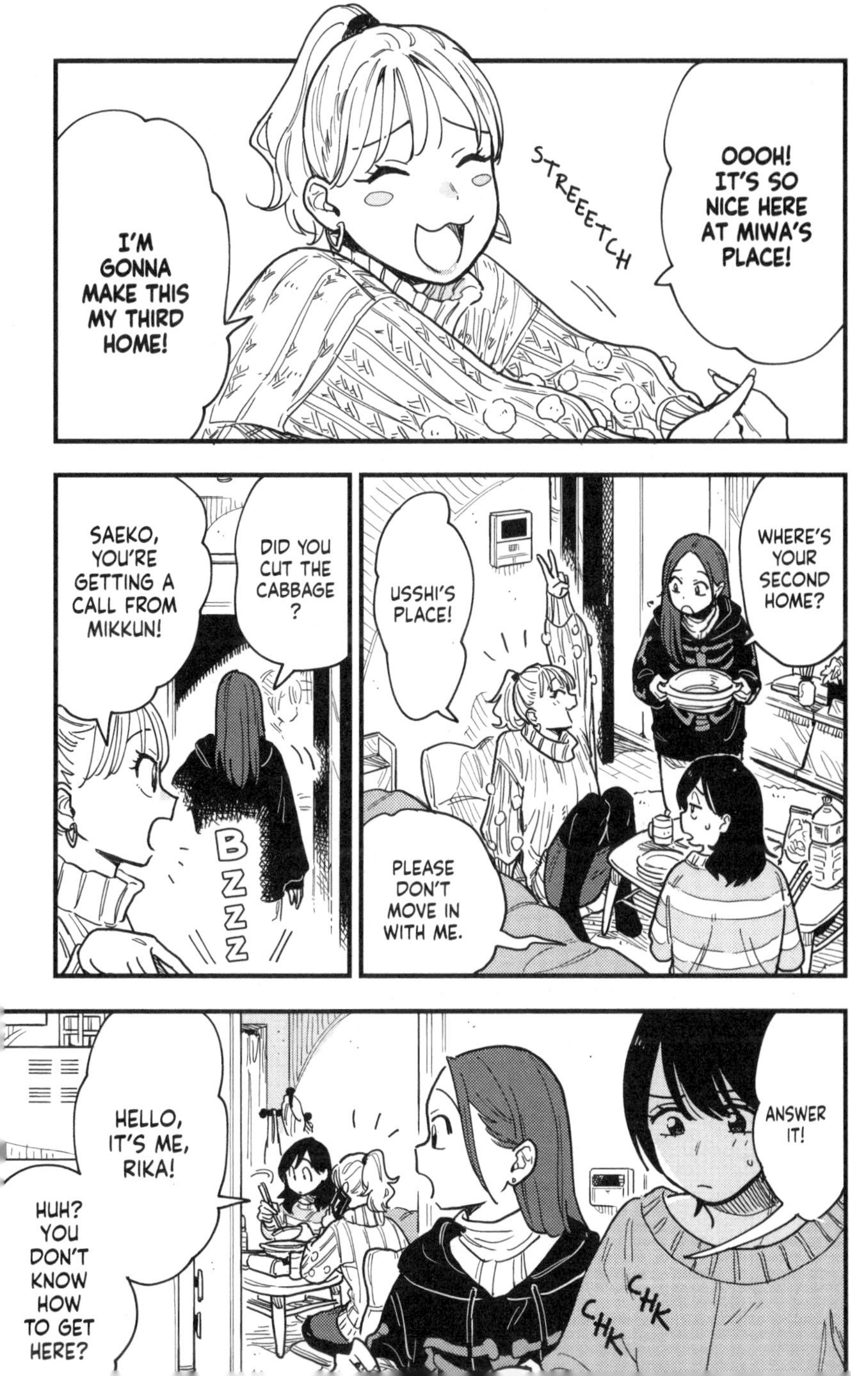
OOOH! IT'S SO NICE HERE AT MIWA'S PLACE!
STREEEETCH
I'M GONNA MAKE THIS MY THIRD HOME!
WHERE'S YOUR SECOND HOME?
USSHI'S PLACE!
PLEASE DON'T MOVE IN WITH ME.
DID YOU CUT THE CABBAGE?
SAEKO, YOU'RE GETTING A CALL FROM MIKKUN!
BZZZ
ANSWER IT!
CHK CHK
HELLO, IT'S ME, RIKA!
HUH? YOU DON'T KNOW HOW TO GET HERE?

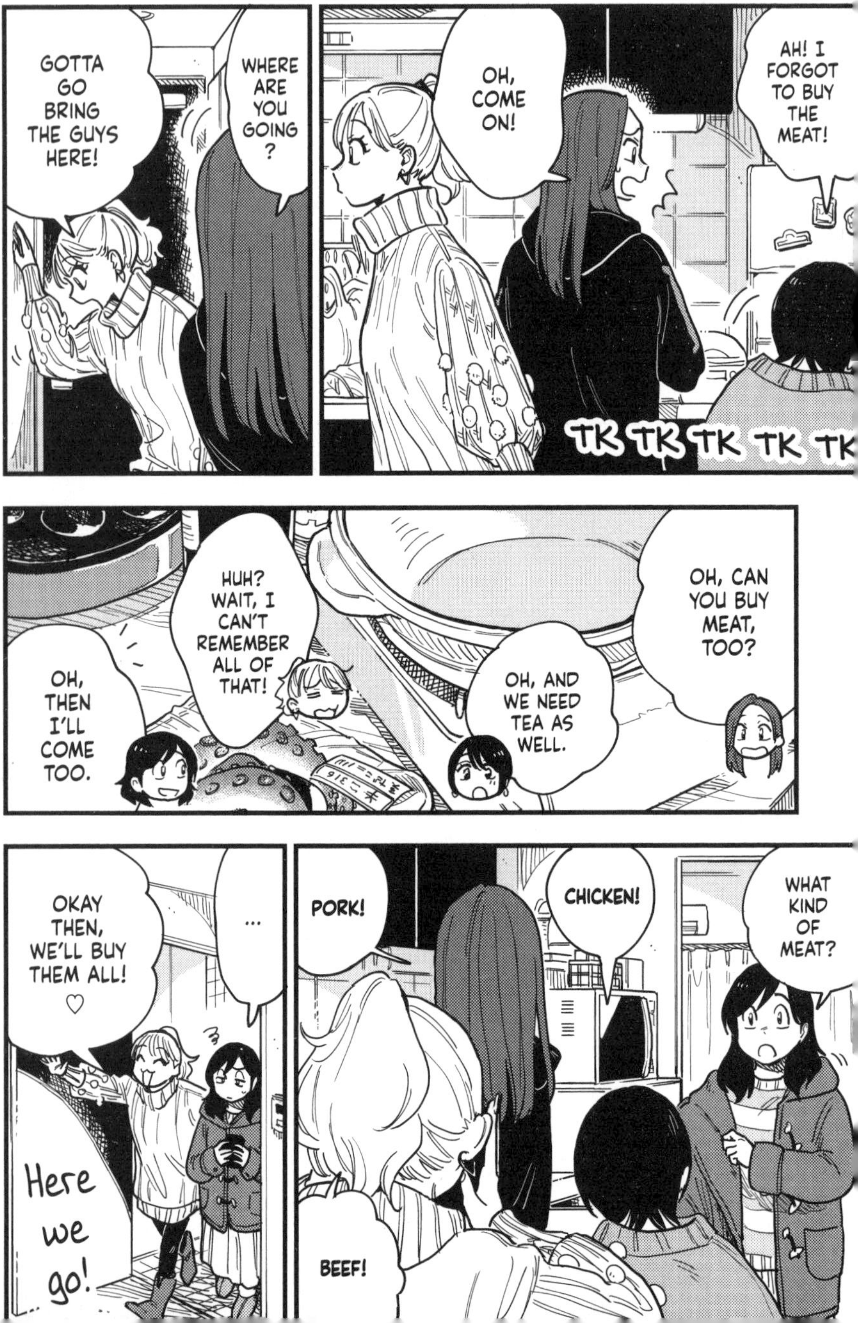
AH! I FORGOT TO BUY THE MEAT!
OH, COME ON!
TK TK TK TK TK
WHERE ARE YOU GOING?
GOTTA GO BRING THE GUYS HERE!
OH, CAN YOU BUY MEAT, TOO?
OH, AND WE NEED TEA AS WELL.
HUH? WAIT, I CAN'T REMEMBER ALL OF THAT!
OH, THEN I'LL COME TOO.
WHAT KIND OF MEAT?
CHICKEN!
PORK!
BEEF!
...
OKAY THEN, WE'LL BUY THEM ALL! ♡
Here we go!

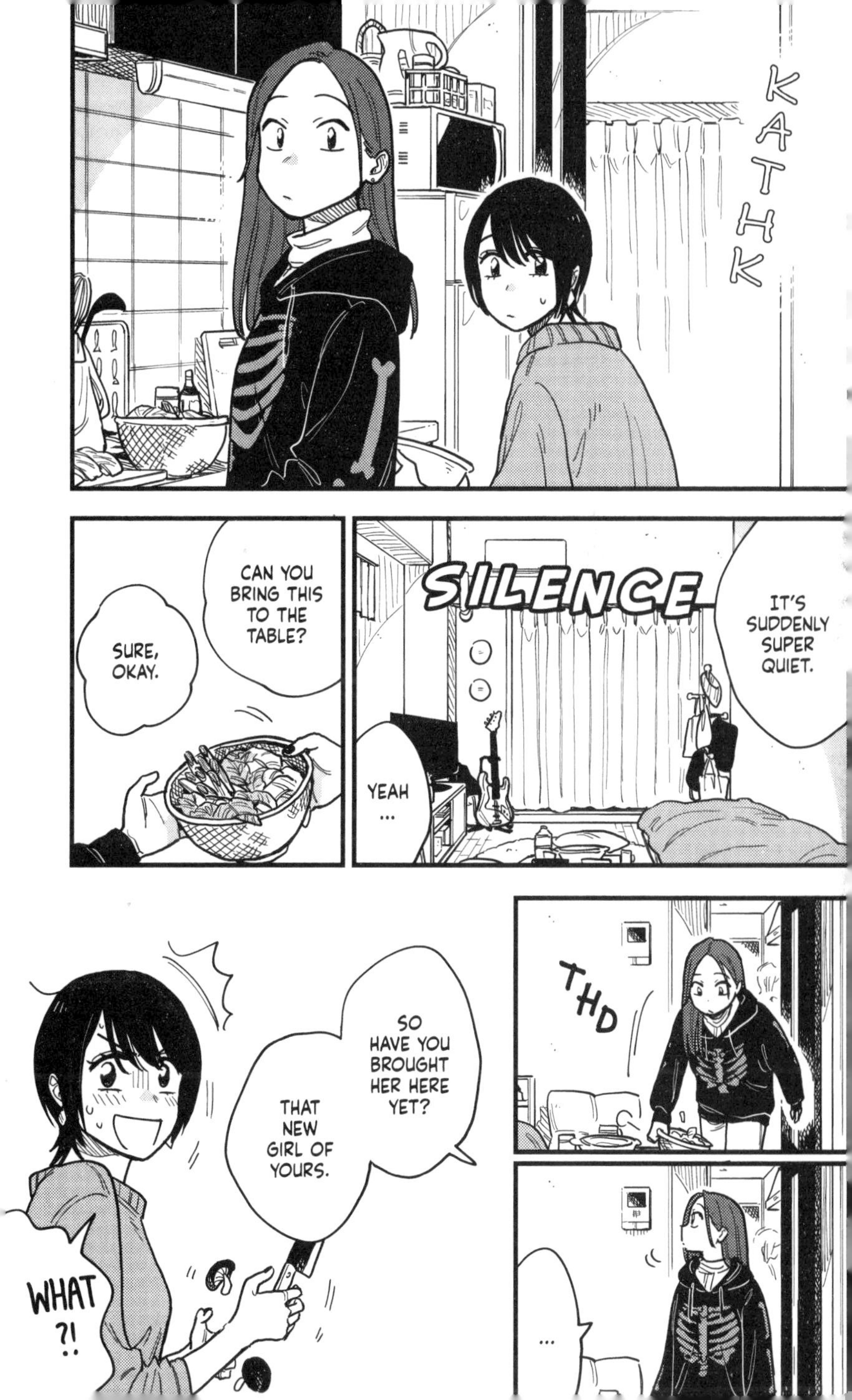
KATHK
IT'S SUDDENLY SUPER QUIET.
SILENCE
YEAH ...
CAN YOU BRING THIS TO THE TABLE?
SURE, OKAY.
THD
...
SO HAVE YOU BROUGHT HER HERE YET?
THAT NEW GIRL OF YOURS.
WHAT ?!

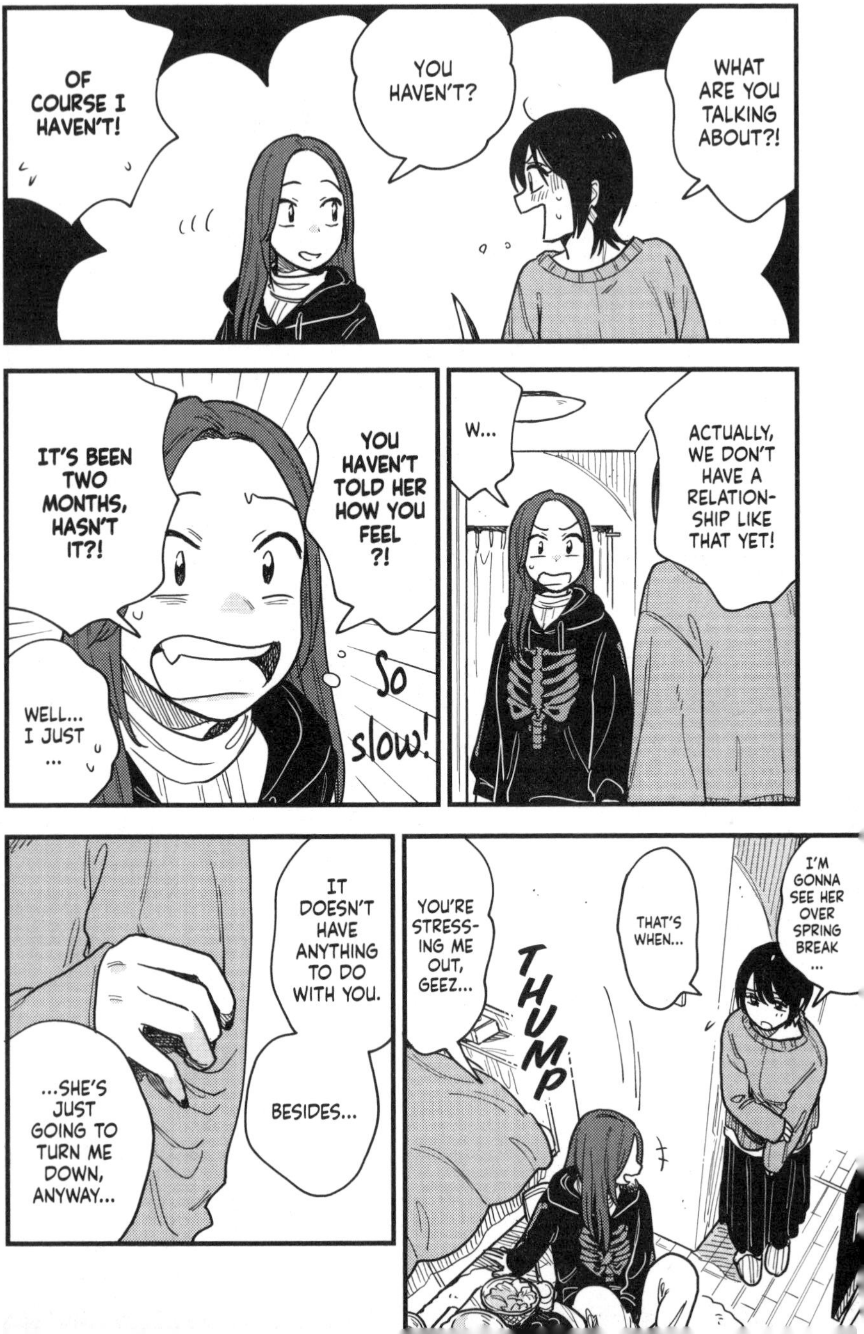
WHAT ARE YOU TALKING ABOUT?!
YOU HAVEN'T?
OF COURSE I HAVEN'T!
ACTUALLY, WE DON'T HAVE A RELATIONSHIP LIKE THAT YET!
W...
YOU HAVEN'T TOLD HER HOW YOU FEEL ?!
IT'S BEEN TWO MONTHS, HASN'T IT?!
So slow!
WELL... I JUST ...
I'M GONNA SEE HER OVER SPRING BREAK ...
THAT'S WHEN...
THUMP
YOU'RE STRESSING ME OUT, GEEZ...
IT DOESN'T HAVE ANYTHING TO DO WITH YOU.
BESIDES...
...SHE'S JUST GOING TO TURN ME DOWN, ANYWAY...

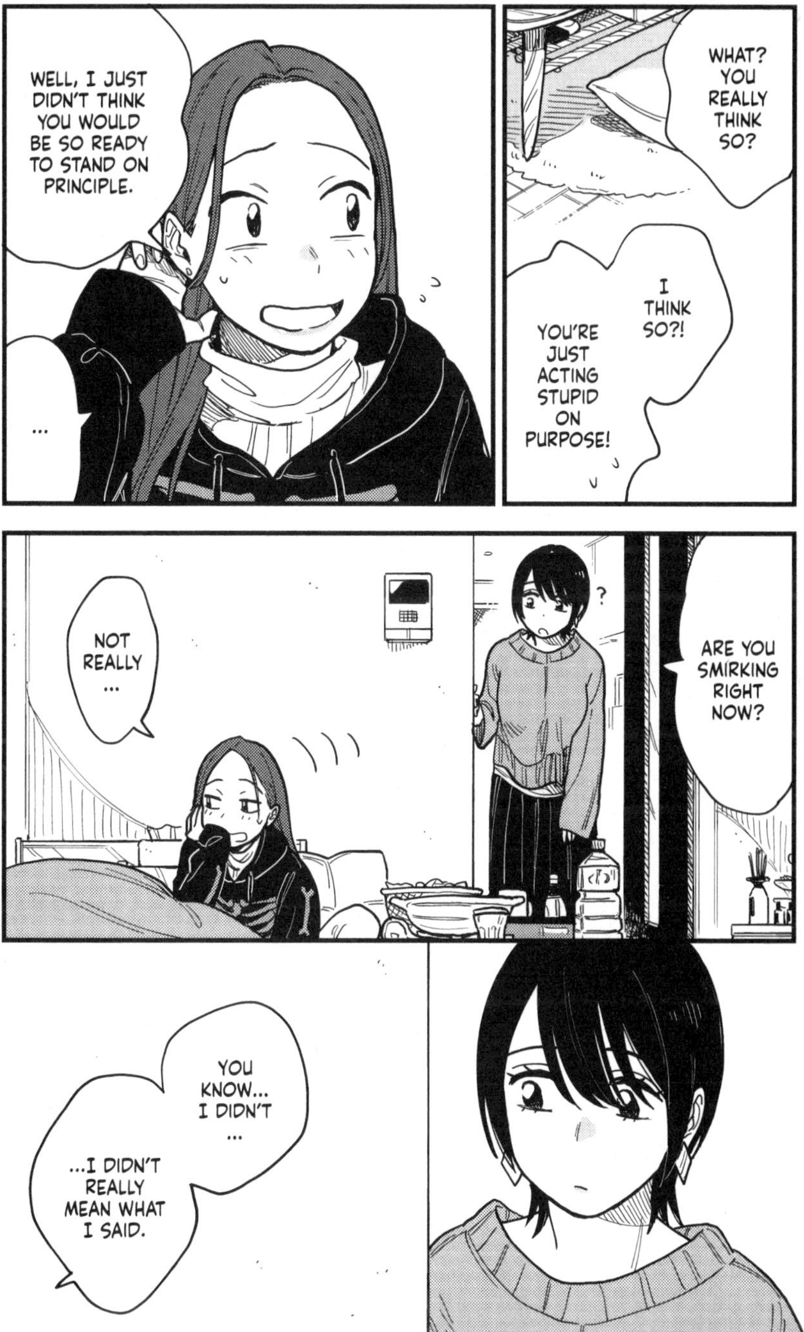
WHAT? YOU REALLY THINK SO?
I THINK SO?!
YOU'RE JUST ACTING STUPID ON PURPOSE!
WELL, I JUST DIDN'T THINK YOU WOULD BE SO READY TO STAND ON PRINCIPLE.
...
ARE YOU SMIRKING RIGHT NOW?
NOT REALLY ...
YOU KNOW... I DIDN'T ...
...I DIDN'T REALLY MEAN WHAT I SAID.

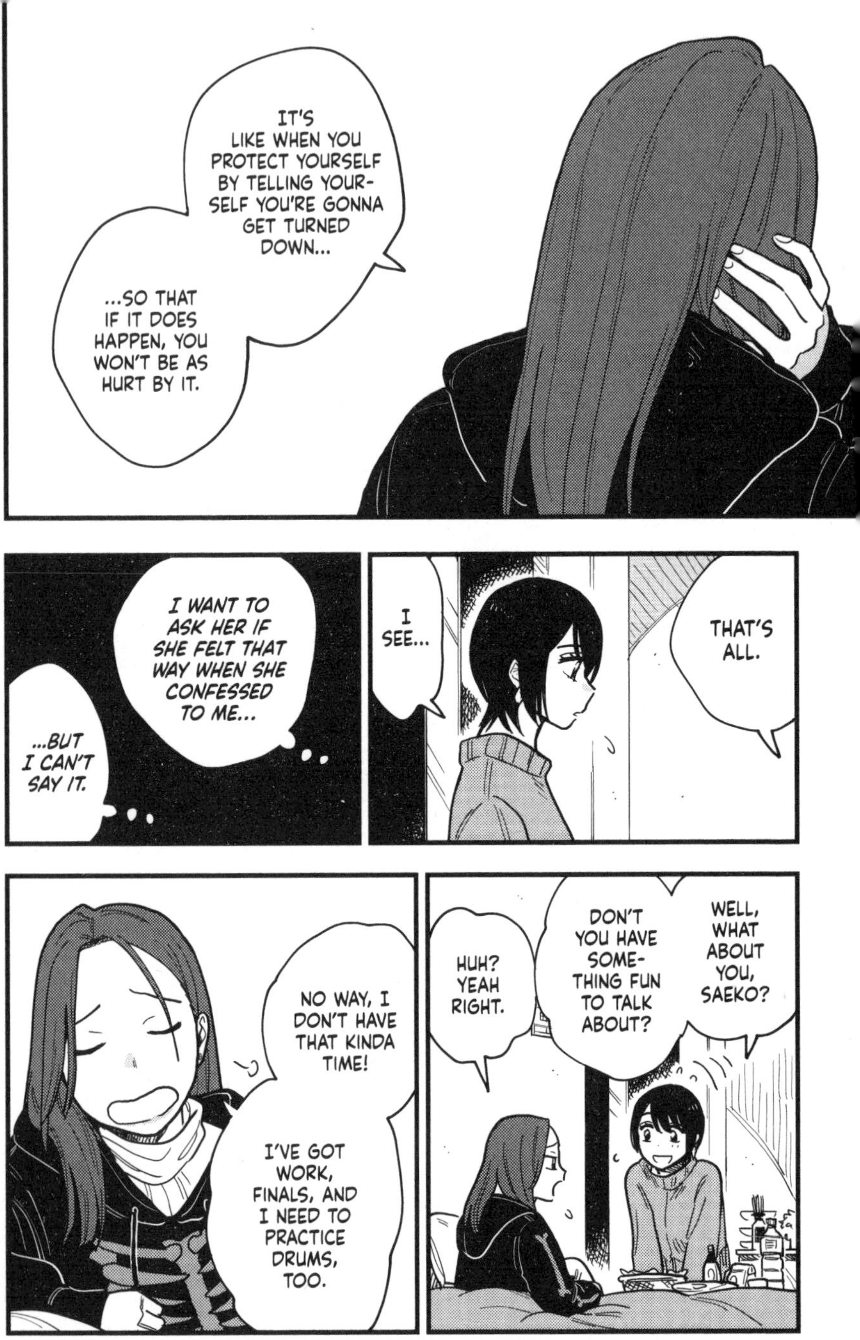
IT'S LIKE WHEN YOU PROTECT YOURSELF BY TELLING YOURSELF YOU'RE GONNA GET TURNED DOWN...
...SO THAT IF IT DOES HAPPEN, YOU WON'T BE AS HURT BY IT.
THAT'S ALL.
I SEE...
I WANT TO ASK HER IF SHE FELT THAT WAY WHEN SHE CONFESSED TO ME...
...BUT I CAN'T SAY IT.
WELL, WHAT ABOUT YOU, SAEKO?
DON'T YOU HAVE SOMETHING FUN TO TALK ABOUT?
HUH? YEAH RIGHT.
NO WAY, I DON'T HAVE THAT KINDA TIME!
I'VE GOT WORK, FINALS, AND I NEED TO PRACTICE DRUMS, TOO.

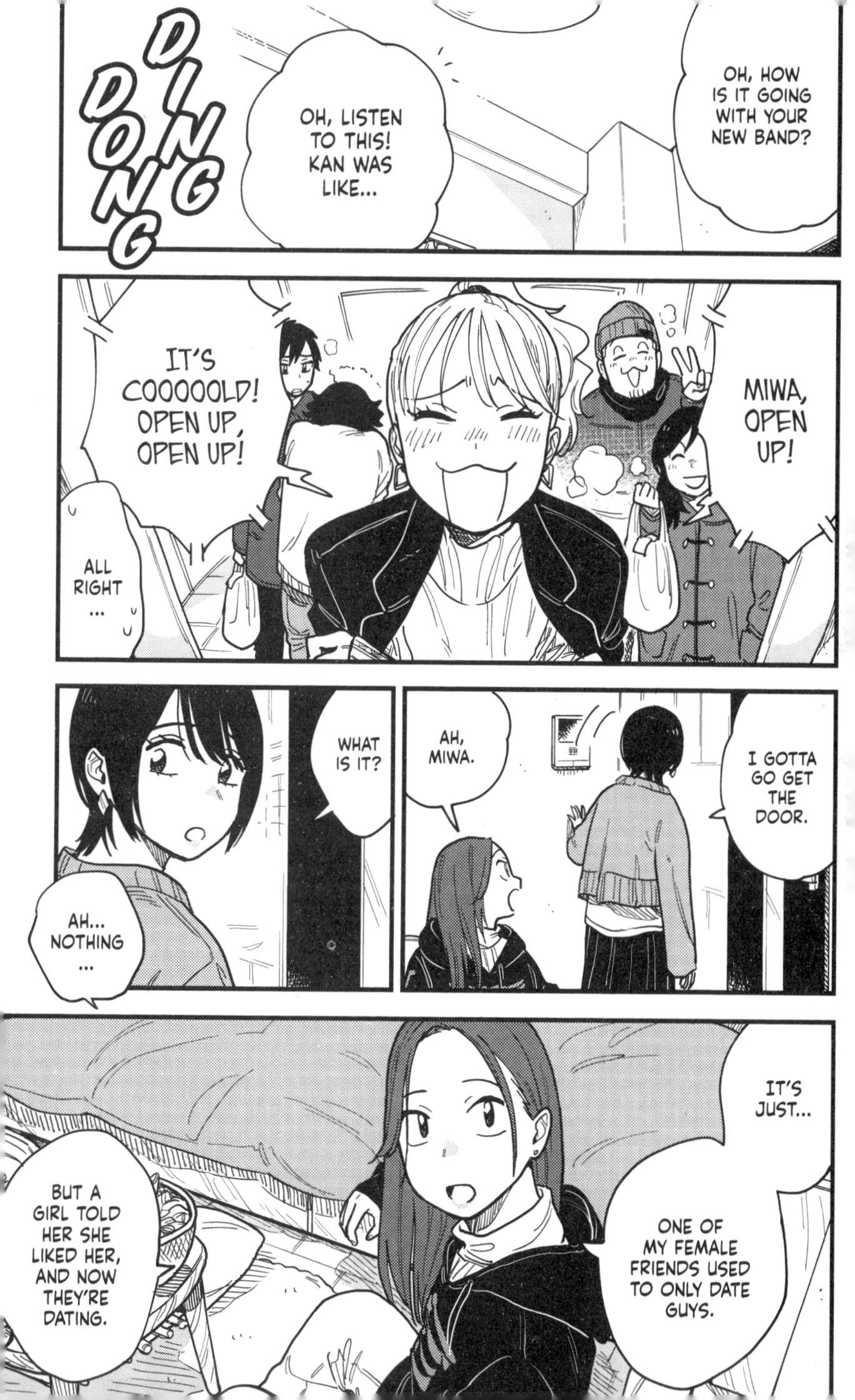
OH, HOW IS IT GOING WITH YOUR NEW BAND?
OH, LISTEN TO THIS! KAN WAS LIKE...
DING DONG
MIWA, OPEN UP!
IT'S COOOOOLD! OPEN UP, OPEN UP!
ALL RIGHT ...
I GOTTA GO GET THE DOOR.
AH, MIWA.
WHAT IS IT?
AH... NOTHING ...
IT'S JUST...
ONE OF MY FEMALE FRIENDS USED TO ONLY DATE GUYS.
BUT A GIRL TOLD HER SHE LIKED HER, AND NOW THEY'RE DATING.

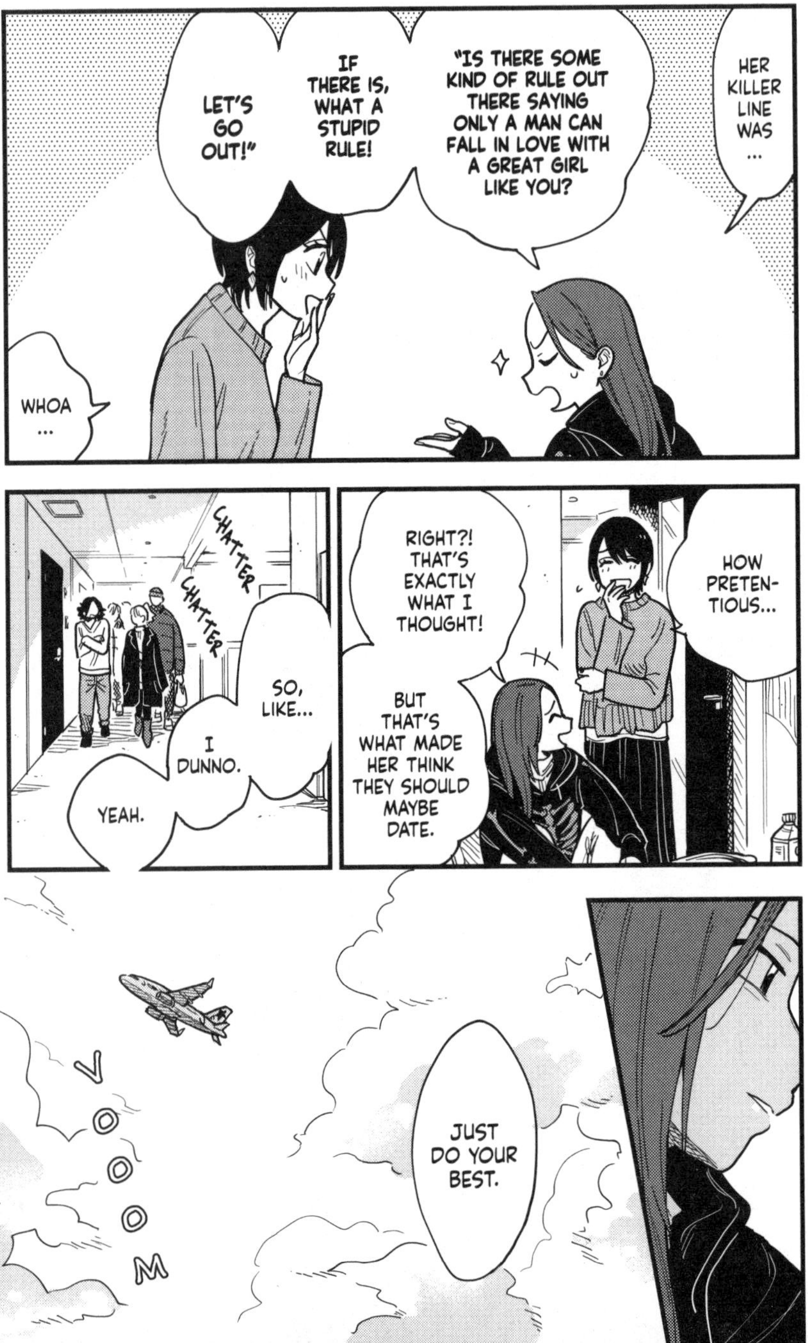
HER KILLER LINE WAS ...
"IS THERE SOME KIND OF RULE OUT THERE SAYING ONLY A MAN CAN FALL IN LOVE WITH A GREAT GIRL LIKE YOU?
IF THERE IS, WHAT A STUPID RULE!
LET'S GO OUT!"
WHOA ...
HOW PRETEN-TIOUS...
RIGHT?! THAT'S EXACTLY WHAT I THOUGHT!
BUT THAT'S WHAT MADE HER THINK THEY SHOULD MAYBE DATE.
CHATTER CHATTER
SO, LIKE...
I DUNNO.
YEAH.
JUST DO YOUR BEST.
VOOOOM

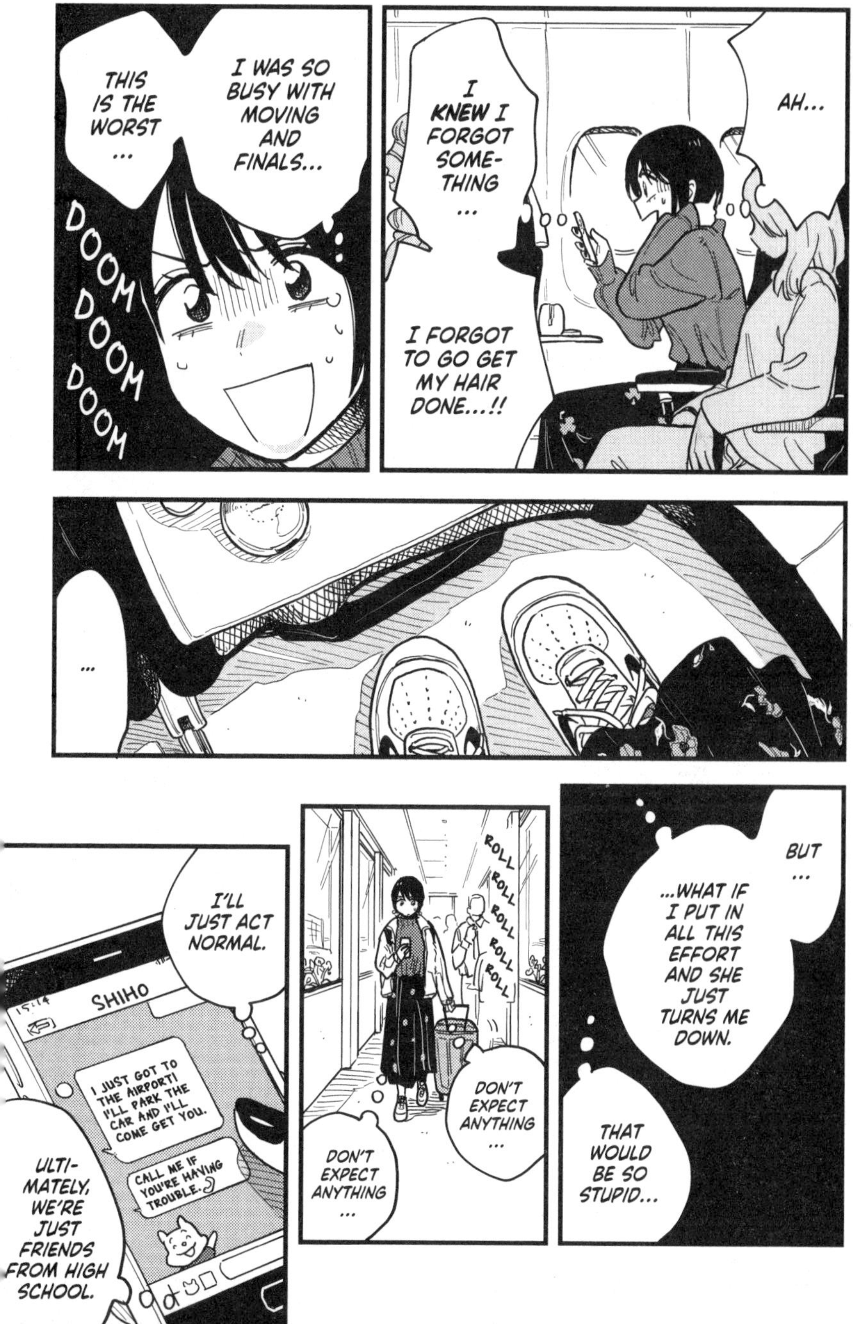
AH...
I KNEW I FORGOT SOME-THING...
I FORGOT TO GO GET MY HAIR DONE...!!
I WAS SO BUSY WITH MOVING AND FINALS...
THIS IS THE WORST...
DOOM DOOM DOOM DOOM
...
BUT...
...WHAT IF I PUT IN ALL THIS EFFORT AND SHE JUST TURNS ME DOWN.
THAT WOULD BE SO STUPID...
ROLL ROLL ROLL ROLL ROLL ROLL
DON'T EXPECT ANYTHING...
DON'T EXPECT ANYTHING...
I'LL JUST ACT NORMAL.
15:14
SHIHO
I JUST GOT TO THE AIRPORT! I'LL PARK THE CAR AND I'LL COME GET YOU.
CALL ME IF YOU'RE HAVING TROUBLE.
ULTI-MATELY, WE'RE JUST FRIENDS FROM HIGH SCHOOL.

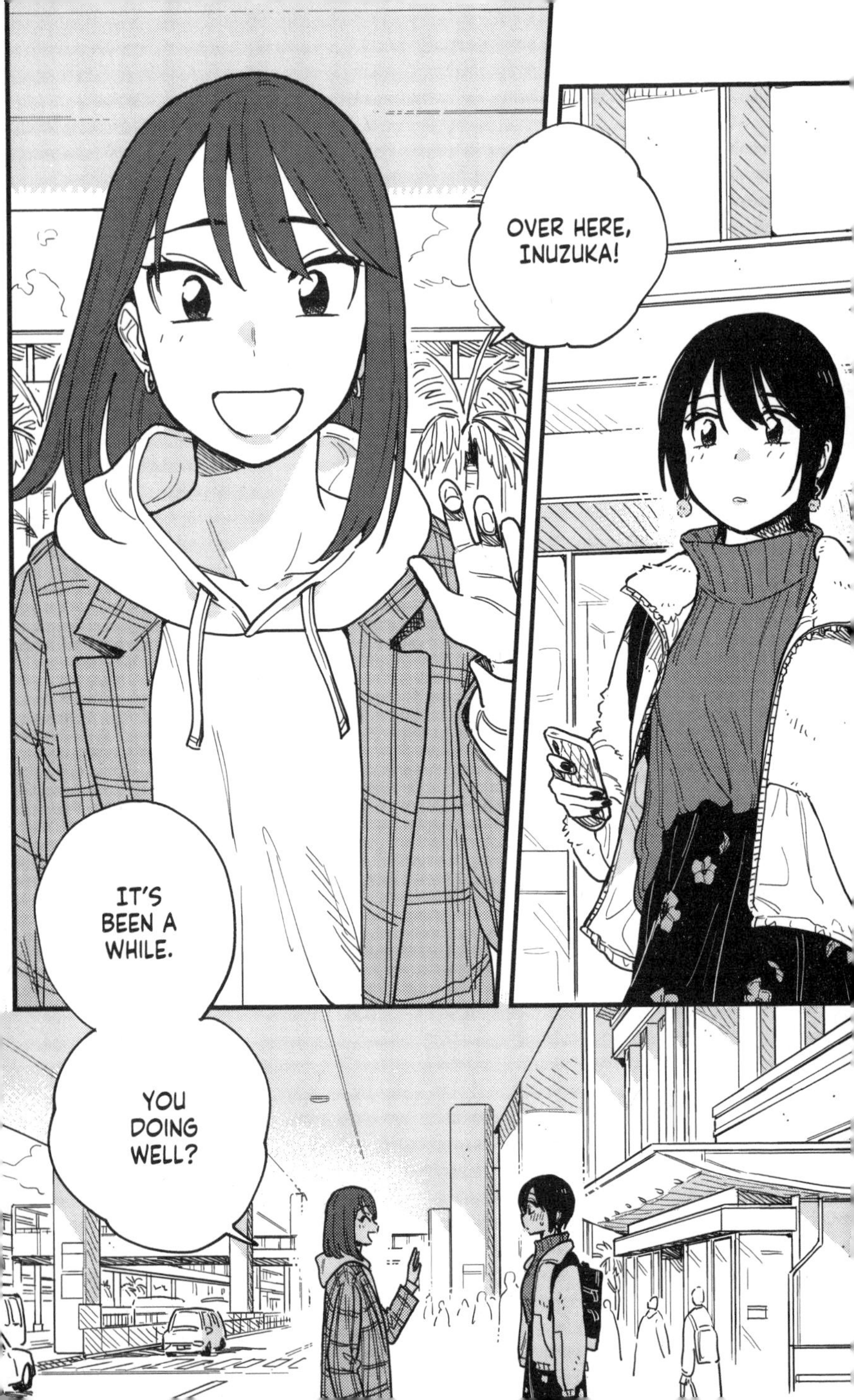
OVER HERE, INUZUKA!
IT'S BEEN A WHILE.
YOU DOING WELL?

HOW DO WE
RELATIONSHIP?

HOW DO WE RELATIONSHIP?

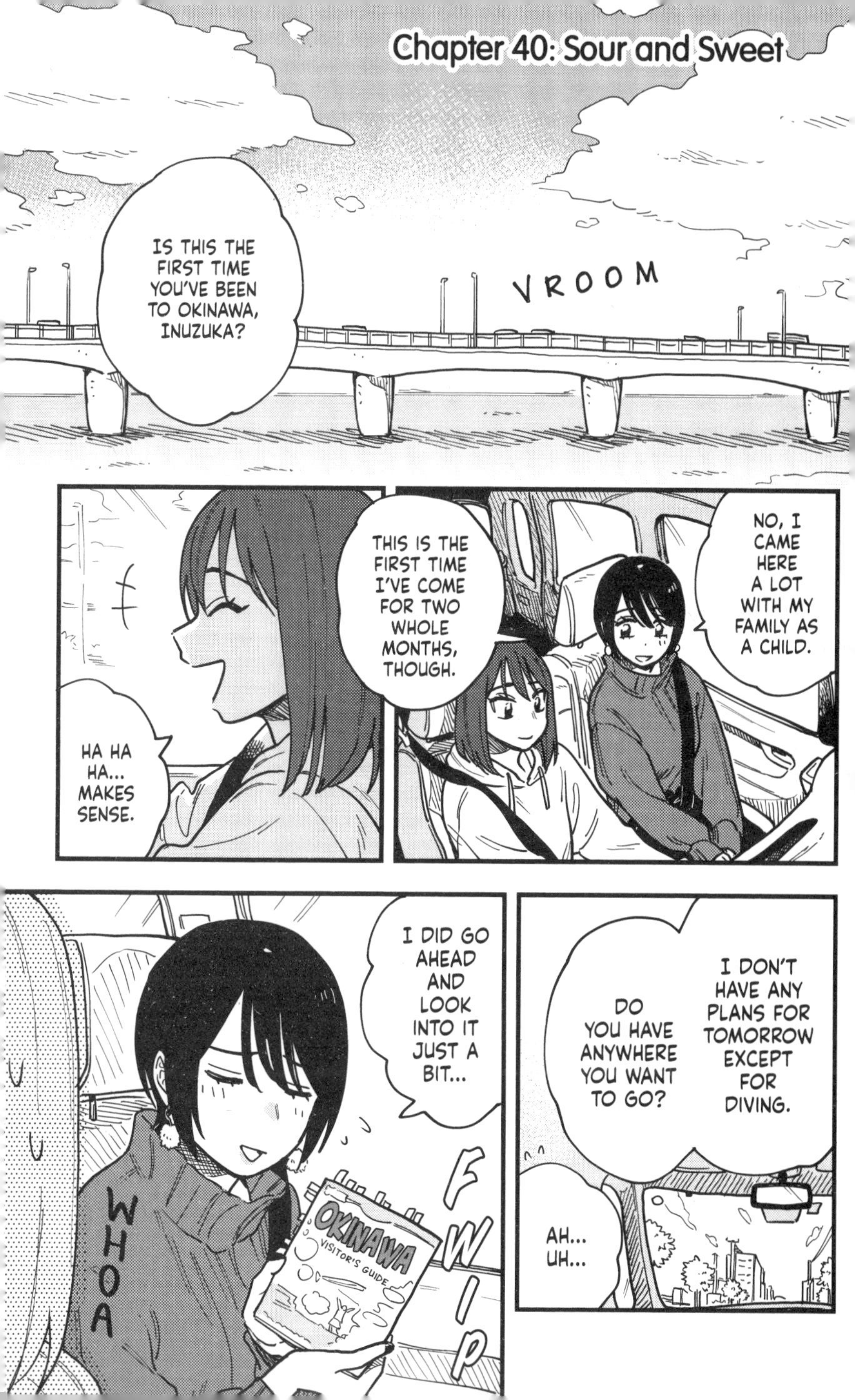
Chapter 40: Sour and Sweet
IS THIS THE FIRST TIME YOU'VE BEEN TO OKINAWA, INUZUKA?
VROOM
NO, I CAME HERE A LOT WITH MY FAMILY AS A CHILD.
THIS IS THE FIRST TIME I'VE COME FOR TWO WHOLE MONTHS, THOUGH.
HA HA HA... MAKES SENSE.
I DON'T HAVE ANY PLANS FOR TOMORROW EXCEPT FOR DIVING.
DO YOU HAVE ANYWHERE YOU WANT TO GO?
AH... UH...
I DID GO AHEAD AND LOOK INTO IT JUST A BIT...
FWIP
WHOA
OKINAWA VISITOR'S GUIDE

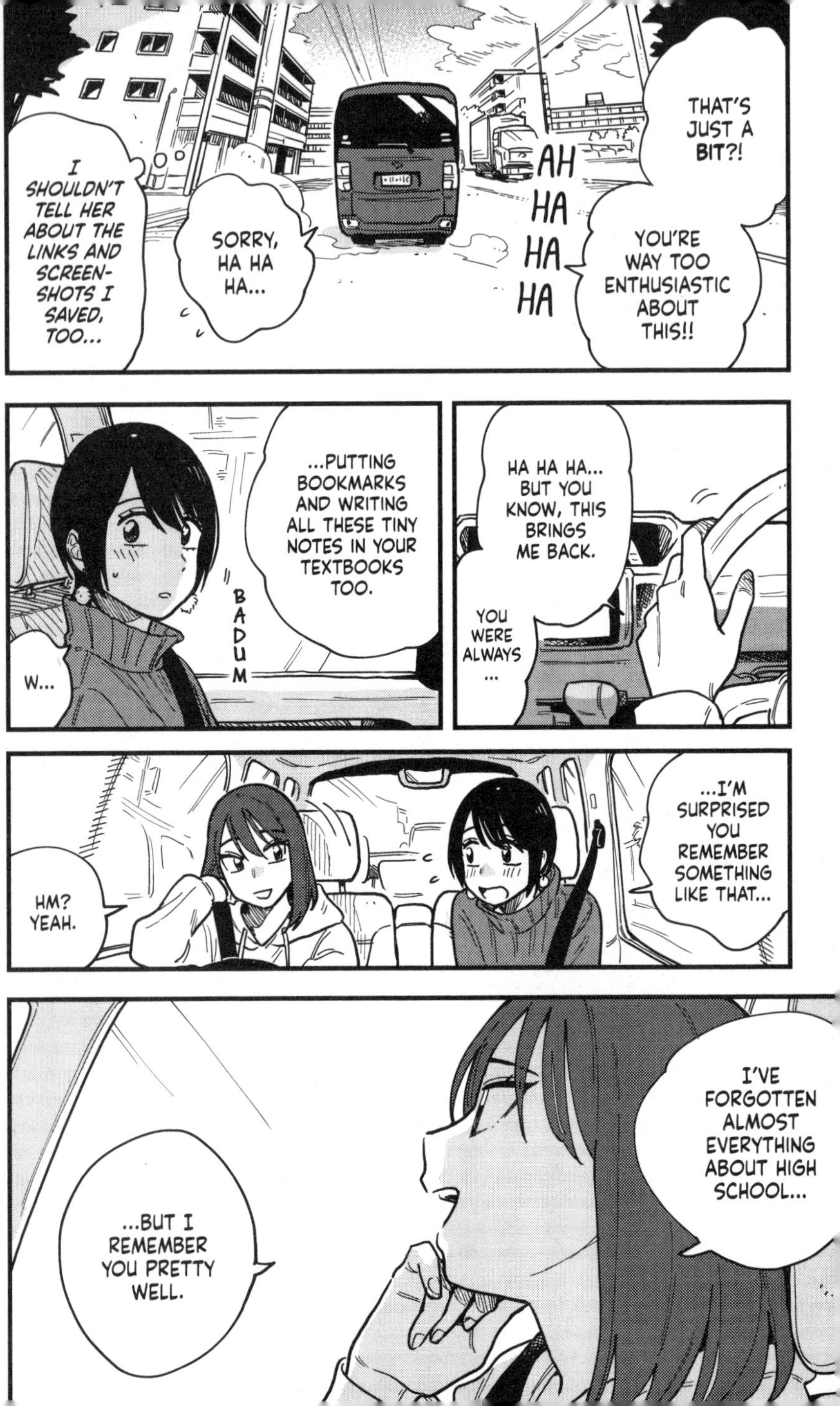
THAT'S JUST A BIT?!
YOU'RE WAY TOO ENTHUSIASTIC ABOUT THIS!!
AH HA HA HA
SORRY, HA HA HA...
I SHOULDN'T TELL HER ABOUT THE LINKS AND SCREEN-SHOTS I SAVED, TOO...
HA HA HA... BUT YOU KNOW, THIS BRINGS ME BACK.
YOU WERE ALWAYS ...
...PUTTING BOOKMARKS AND WRITING ALL THESE TINY NOTES IN YOUR TEXTBOOKS TOO.
BADUM
W...
...I'M SURPRISED YOU REMEMBER SOMETHING LIKE THAT...
HM? YEAH.
I'VE FORGOTTEN ALMOST EVERYTHING ABOUT HIGH SCHOOL...
...BUT I REMEMBER YOU PRETTY WELL.

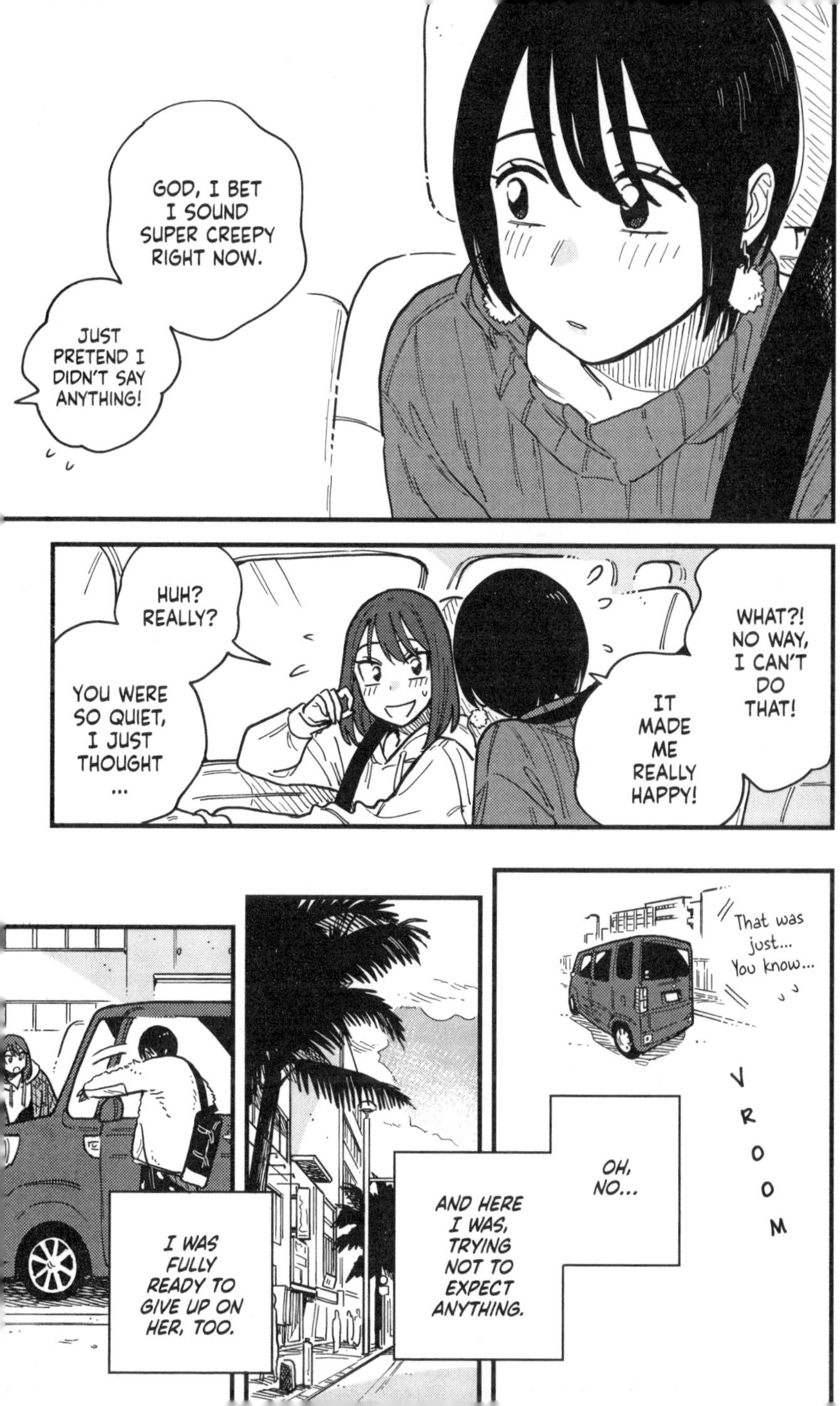
GOD, I BET I SOUND SUPER CREEPY RIGHT NOW.
JUST PRETEND I DIDN'T SAY ANYTHING!
WHAT?! NO WAY, I CAN'T DO THAT!
IT MADE ME REALLY HAPPY!
HUH? REALLY?
YOU WERE SO QUIET, I JUST THOUGHT ...
That was just... You know...
VROOM
OH, NO...
AND HERE I WAS, TRYING NOT TO EXPECT ANYTHING.
I WAS FULLY READY TO GIVE UP ON HER, TOO.

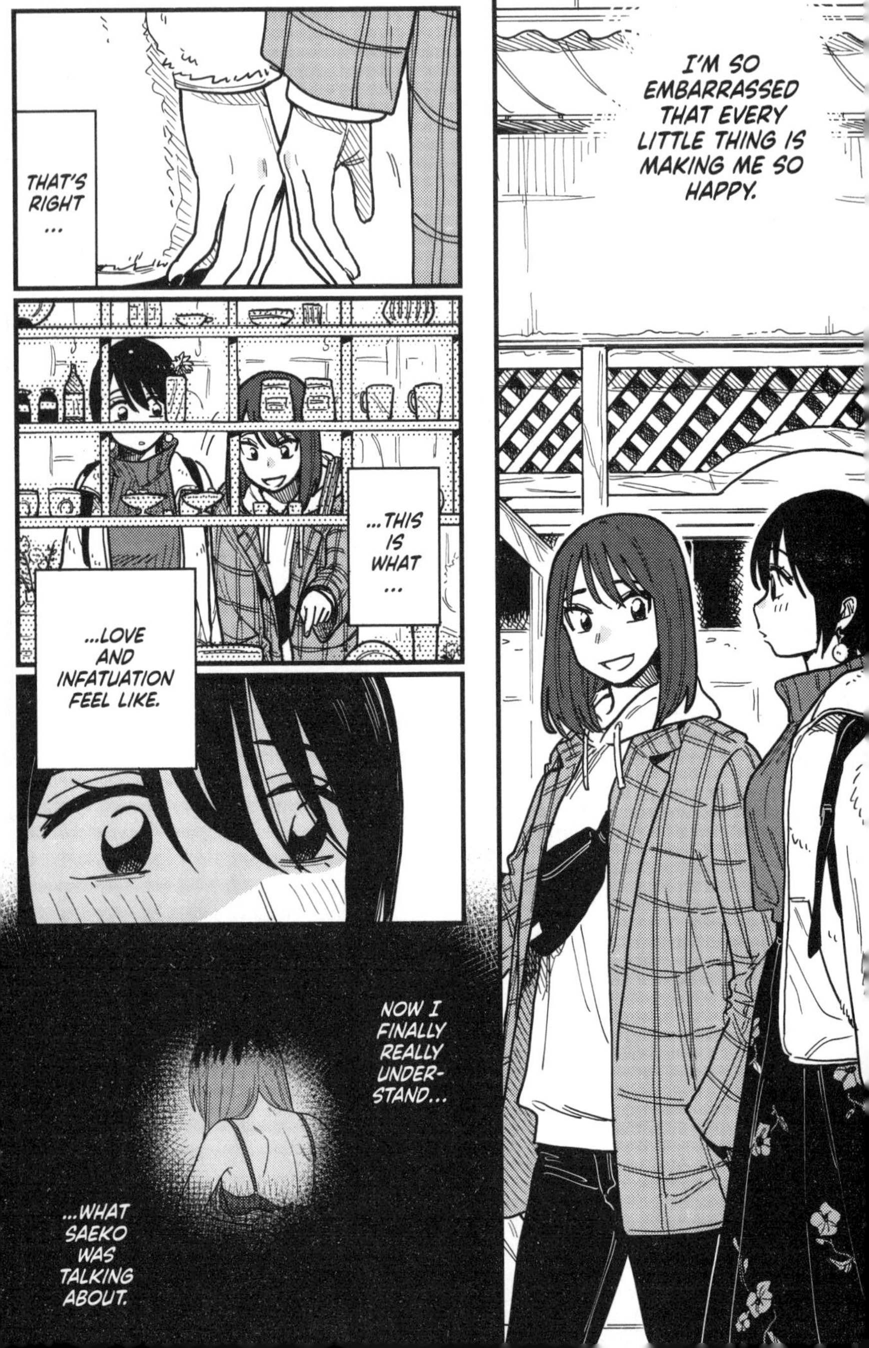
I'M SO EMBARRASSED THAT EVERY LITTLE THING IS MAKING ME SO HAPPY.
THAT'S RIGHT ...
...THIS IS WHAT ...
...LOVE AND INFATUATION FEEL LIKE.
NOW I FINALLY REALLY UNDER-STAND...
...WHAT SAEKO WAS TALKING ABOUT.

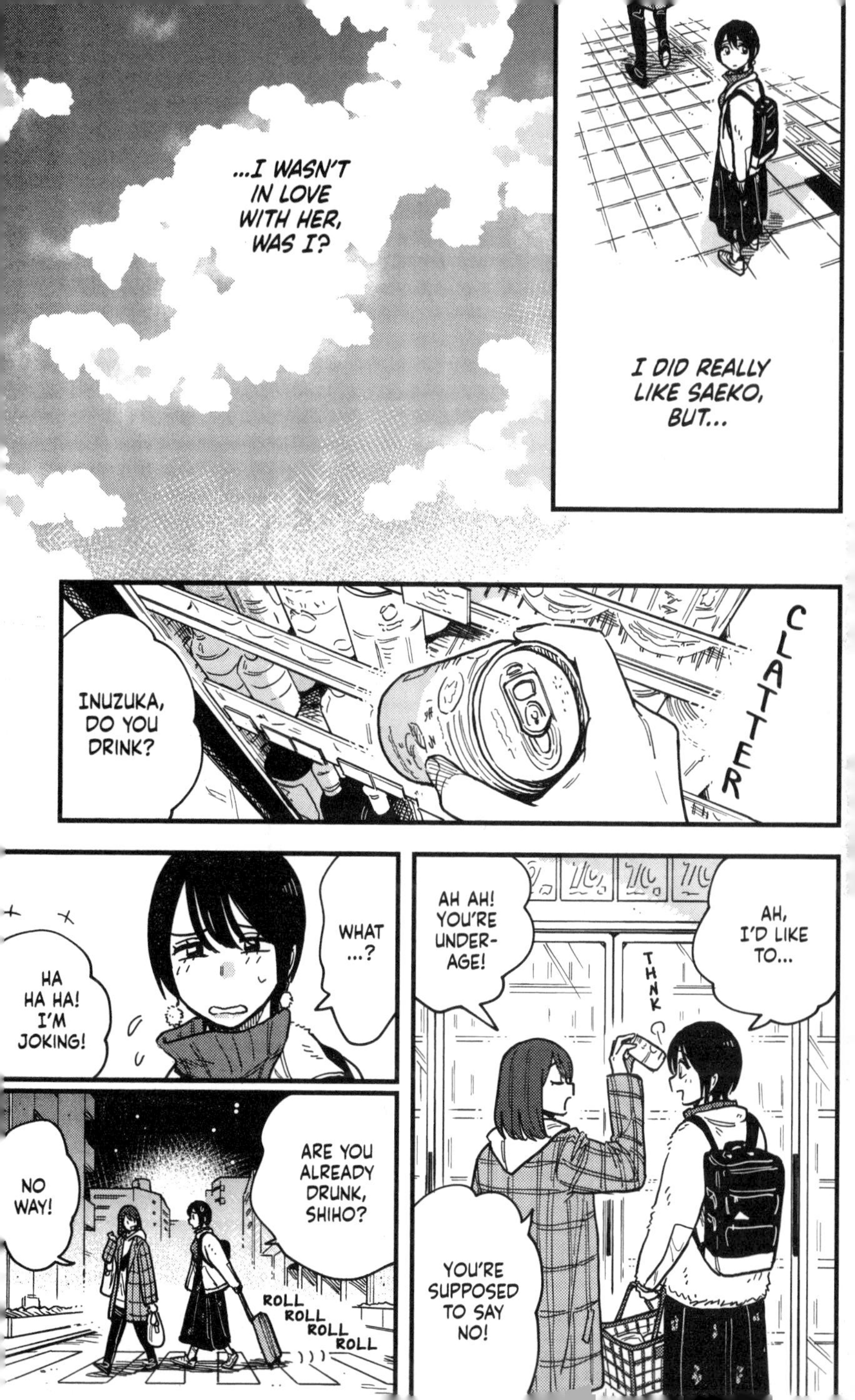
I DID REALLY LIKE SAEKO, BUT...
...I WASN'T IN LOVE WITH HER, WAS I?
CLATTER
INUZUKA, DO YOU DRINK?
AH, I'D LIKE TO...
THNK
AH AH! YOU'RE UNDER-AGE!
YOU'RE SUPPOSED TO SAY NO!
WHAT ...?
HA HA HA! I'M JOKING!
ARE YOU ALREADY DRUNK, SHIHO?
NO WAY!
ROLL ROLL ROLL ROLL

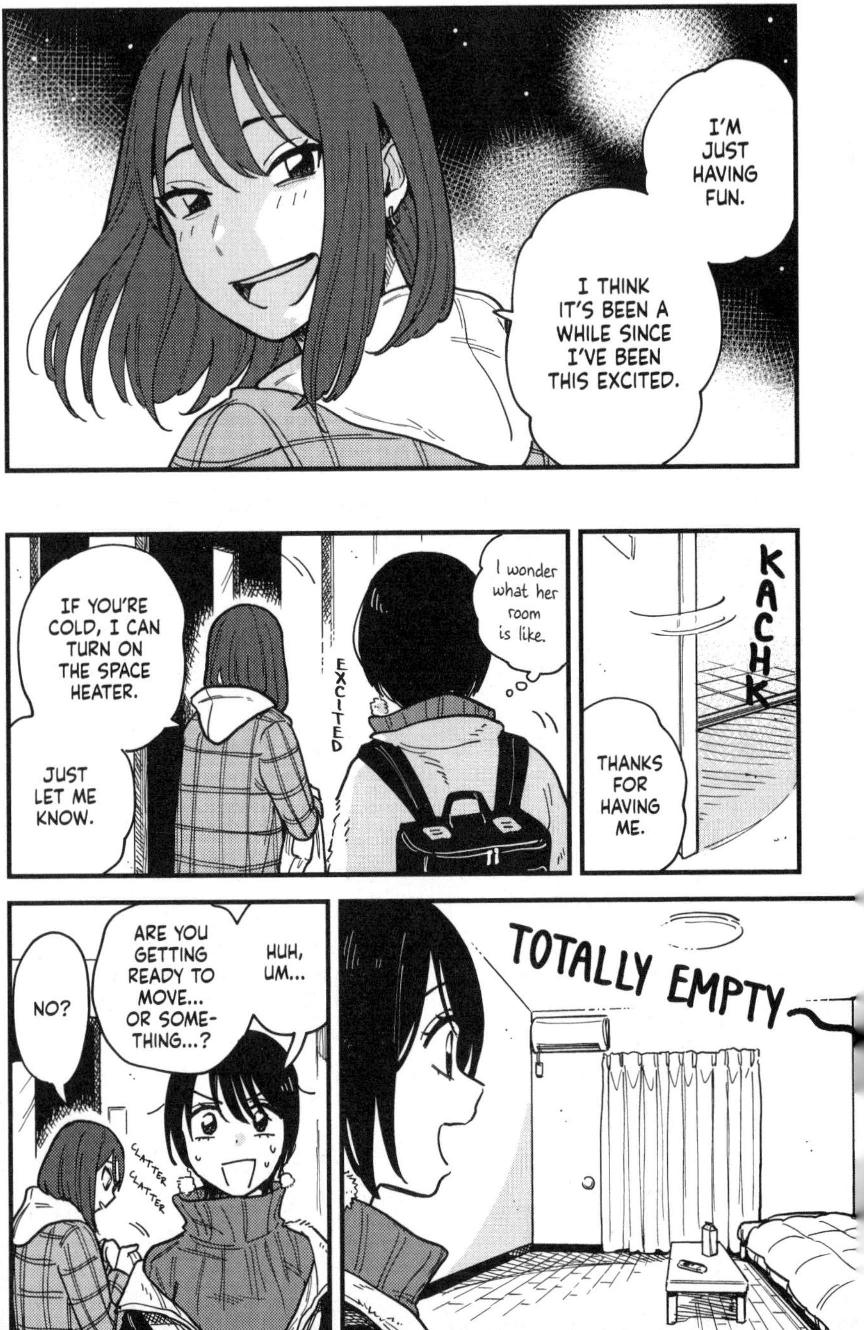
I'M JUST HAVING FUN.
I THINK IT'S BEEN A WHILE SINCE I'VE BEEN THIS EXCITED.
KACHK
THANKS FOR HAVING ME.
I wonder what her room is like.
EXCITED
IF YOU'RE COLD, I CAN TURN ON THE SPACE HEATER.
JUST LET ME KNOW.
TOTALLY EMPTY
HUH, UM...
ARE YOU GETTING READY TO MOVE... OR SOME-THING...?
NO?
CLATTER CLATTER

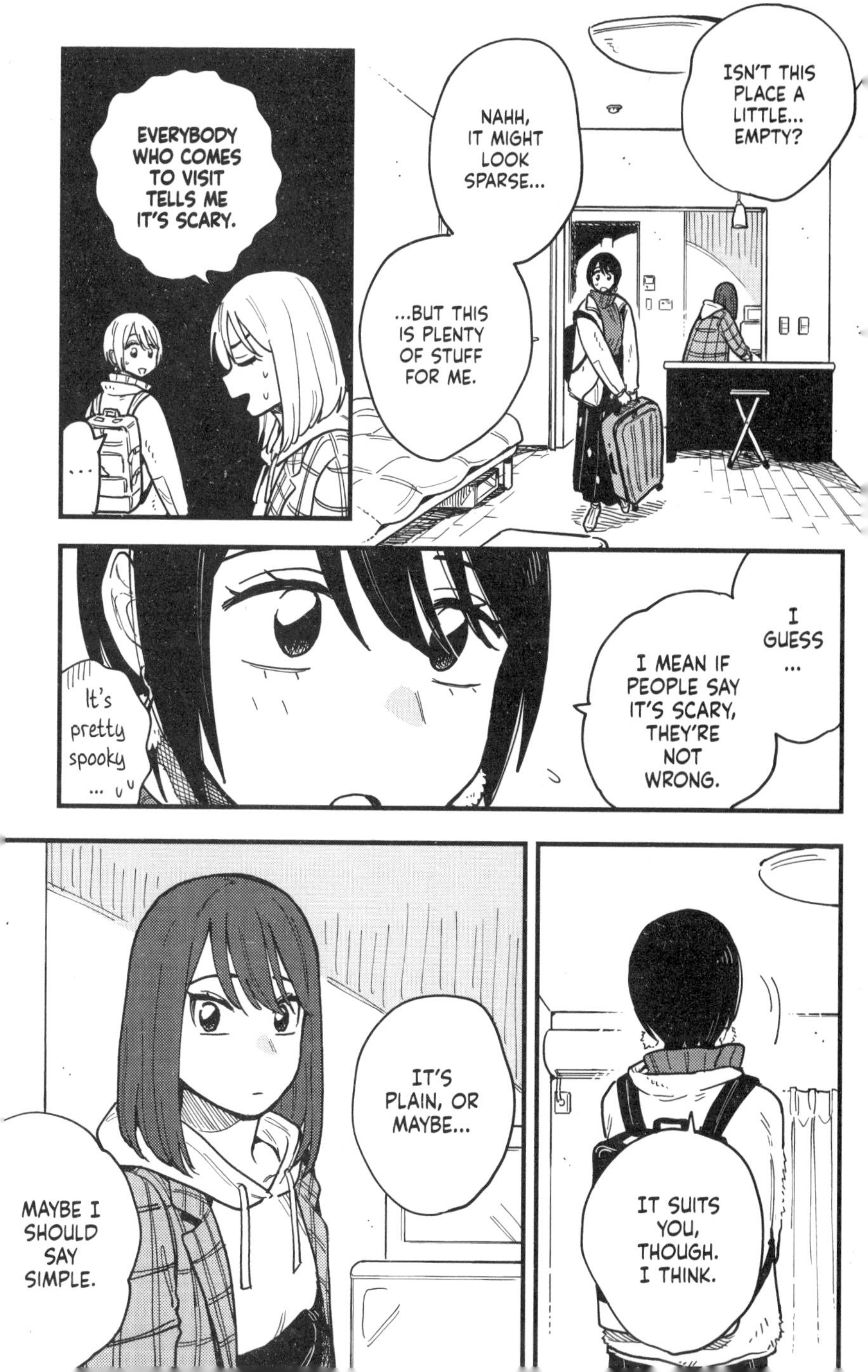
ISN'T THIS PLACE A LITTLE... EMPTY?
NAHH, IT MIGHT LOOK SPARSE...
...BUT THIS IS PLENTY OF STUFF FOR ME.
EVERYBODY WHO COMES TO VISIT TELLS ME IT'S SCARY.
...
I GUESS...
I MEAN IF PEOPLE SAY IT'S SCARY, THEY'RE NOT WRONG.
It's pretty spooky...
IT SUITS YOU, THOUGH. I THINK.
IT'S PLAIN, OR MAYBE...
MAYBE I SHOULD SAY SIMPLE.

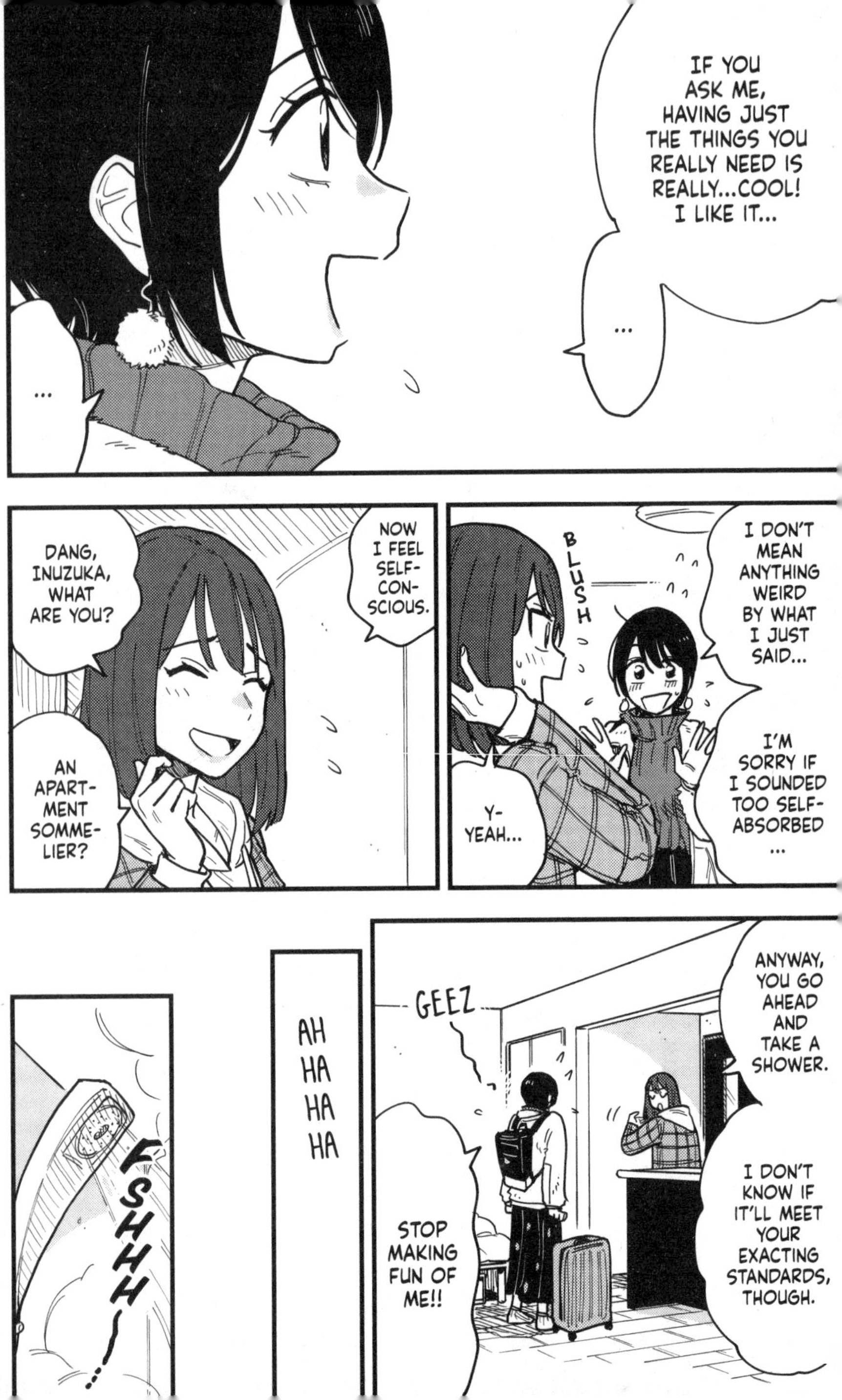
IF YOU ASK ME, HAVING JUST THE THINGS YOU REALLY NEED IS REALLY...COOL! I LIKE IT...
...
...
I DON'T MEAN ANYTHING WEIRD BY WHAT I JUST SAID...
BLUSH
I'M SORRY IF I SOUNDED TOO SELF-ABSORBED ...
Y-YEAH...
NOW I FEEL SELF-CONSCIOUS.
DANG, INUZUKA, WHAT ARE YOU?
AN APARTMENT SOMMELIER?
ANYWAY, YOU GO AHEAD AND TAKE A SHOWER.
GEEZ
I DON'T KNOW IF IT'LL MEET YOUR EXACTING STANDARDS, THOUGH.
STOP MAKING FUN OF ME!!
AH HA HA HA
FSHHH...

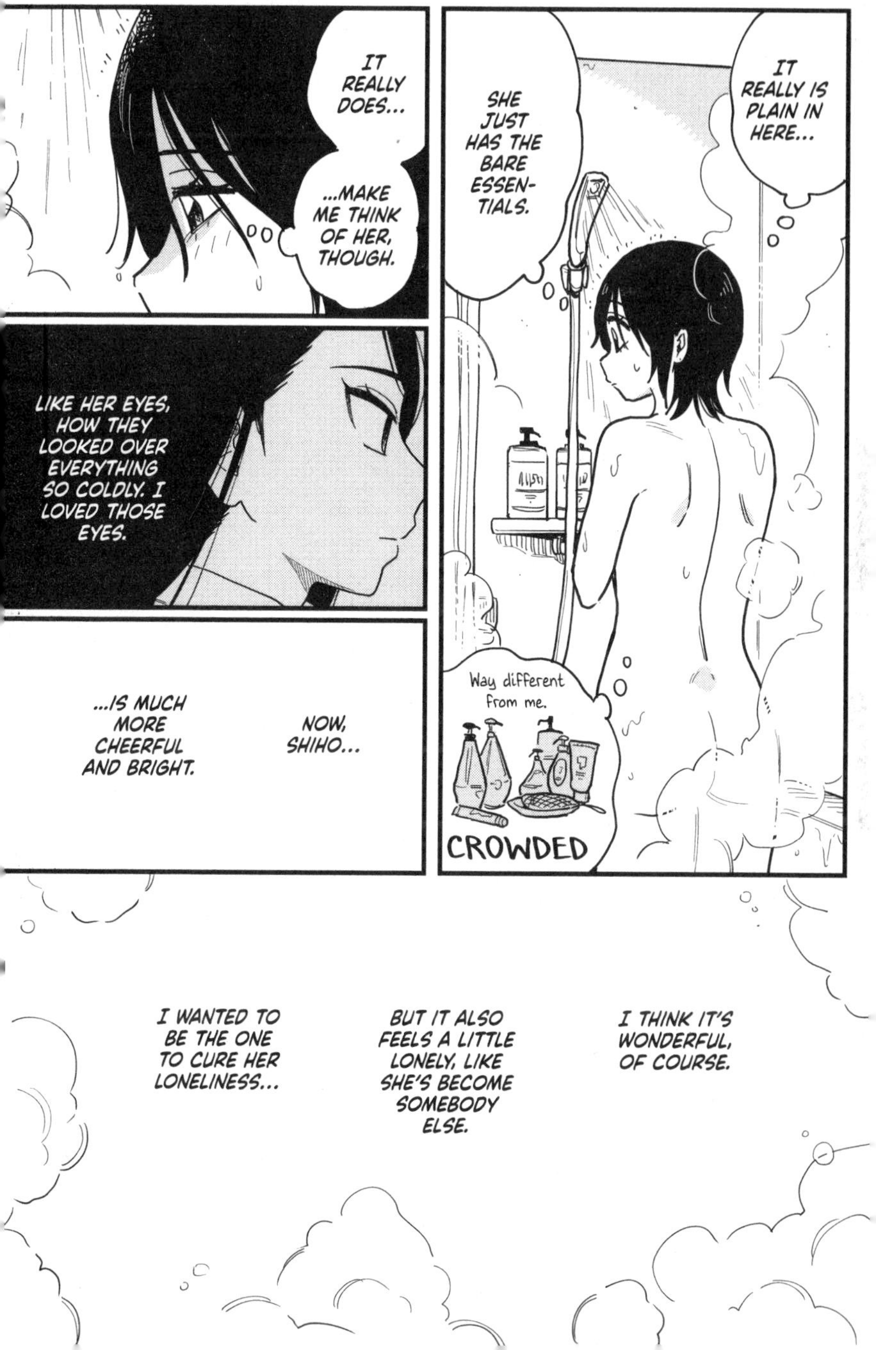
IT REALLY IS PLAIN IN HERE...
SHE JUST HAS THE BARE ESSEN-TIALS.
Way different from me.
CROWDED
IT REALLY DOES...
...MAKE ME THINK OF HER, THOUGH.
LIKE HER EYES, HOW THEY LOOKED OVER EVERYTHING SO COLDLY. I LOVED THOSE EYES.
NOW, SHIHO...
...IS MUCH MORE CHEERFUL AND BRIGHT.
I THINK IT'S WONDERFUL, OF COURSE.
BUT IT ALSO FEELS A LITTLE LONELY, LIKE SHE'S BECOME SOMEBODY ELSE.
I WANTED TO BE THE ONE TO CURE HER LONELINESS...

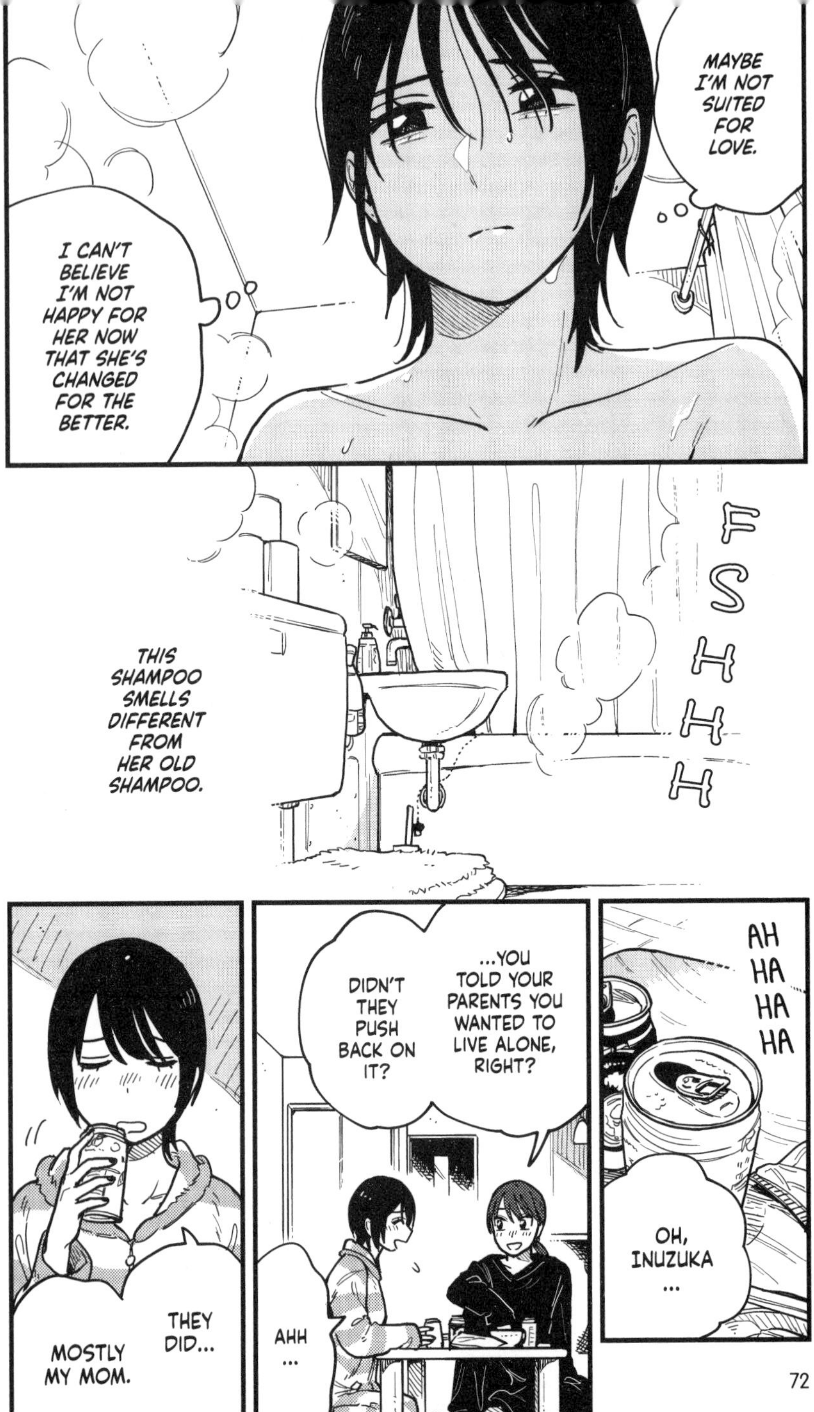
MAYBE I'M NOT SUITED FOR LOVE.
I CAN'T BELIEVE I'M NOT HAPPY FOR HER NOW THAT SHE'S CHANGED FOR THE BETTER.
FSHHH
THIS SHAMPOO SMELLS DIFFERENT FROM HER OLD SHAMPOO.
AH HA HA HA
OH, INUZUKA...
...YOU TOLD YOUR PARENTS YOU WANTED TO LIVE ALONE, RIGHT?
DIDN'T THEY PUSH BACK ON IT?
AHH...
THEY DID...
MOSTLY MY MOM.

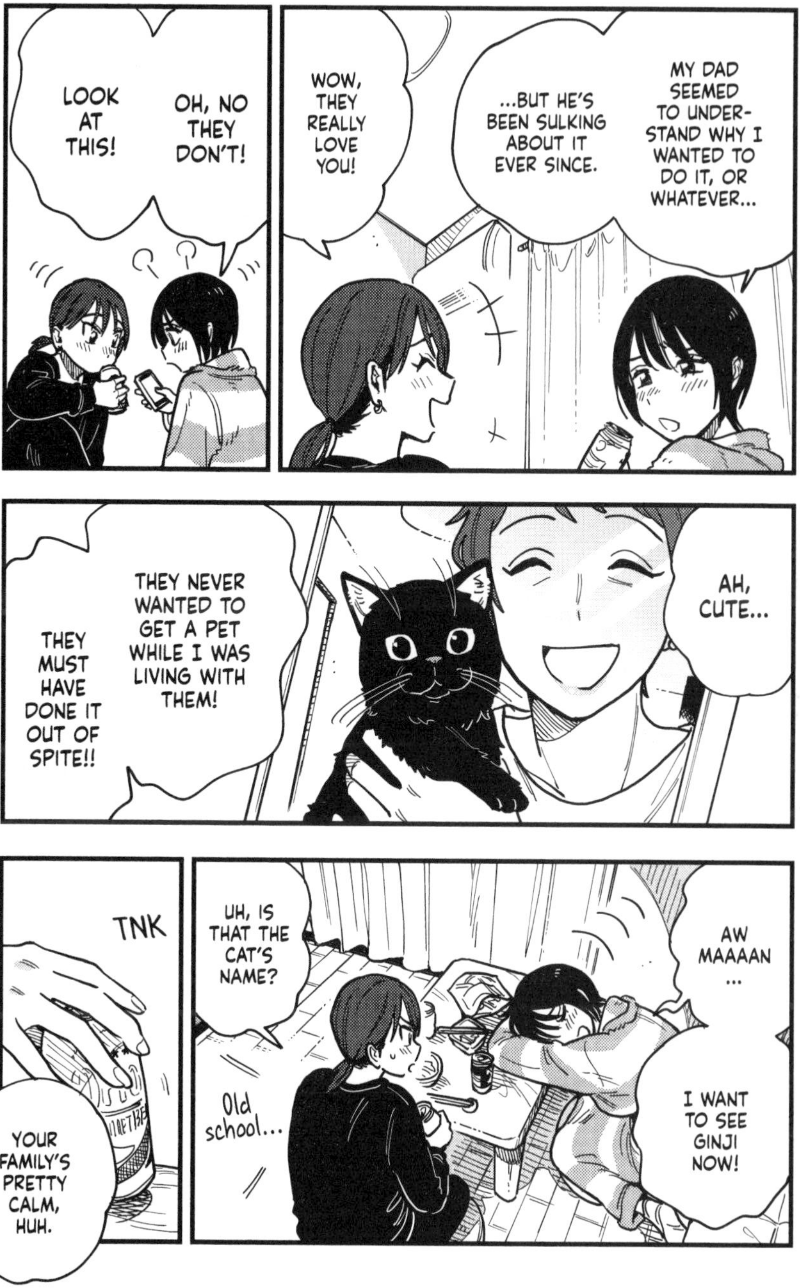
MY DAD SEEMED TO UNDERSTAND WHY I WANTED TO DO IT, OR WHATEVER...
...BUT HE'S BEEN SULKING ABOUT IT EVER SINCE.
WOW, THEY REALLY LOVE YOU!
OH, NO THEY DON'T!
LOOK AT THIS!
AH, CUTE...
THEY NEVER WANTED TO GET A PET WHILE I WAS LIVING WITH THEM!
THEY MUST HAVE DONE IT OUT OF SPITE!!
AW MAAAAN ...
I WANT TO SEE GINJI NOW!
UH, IS THAT THE CAT'S NAME?
Old school...
TNK
YOUR FAMILY'S PRETTY CALM, HUH.

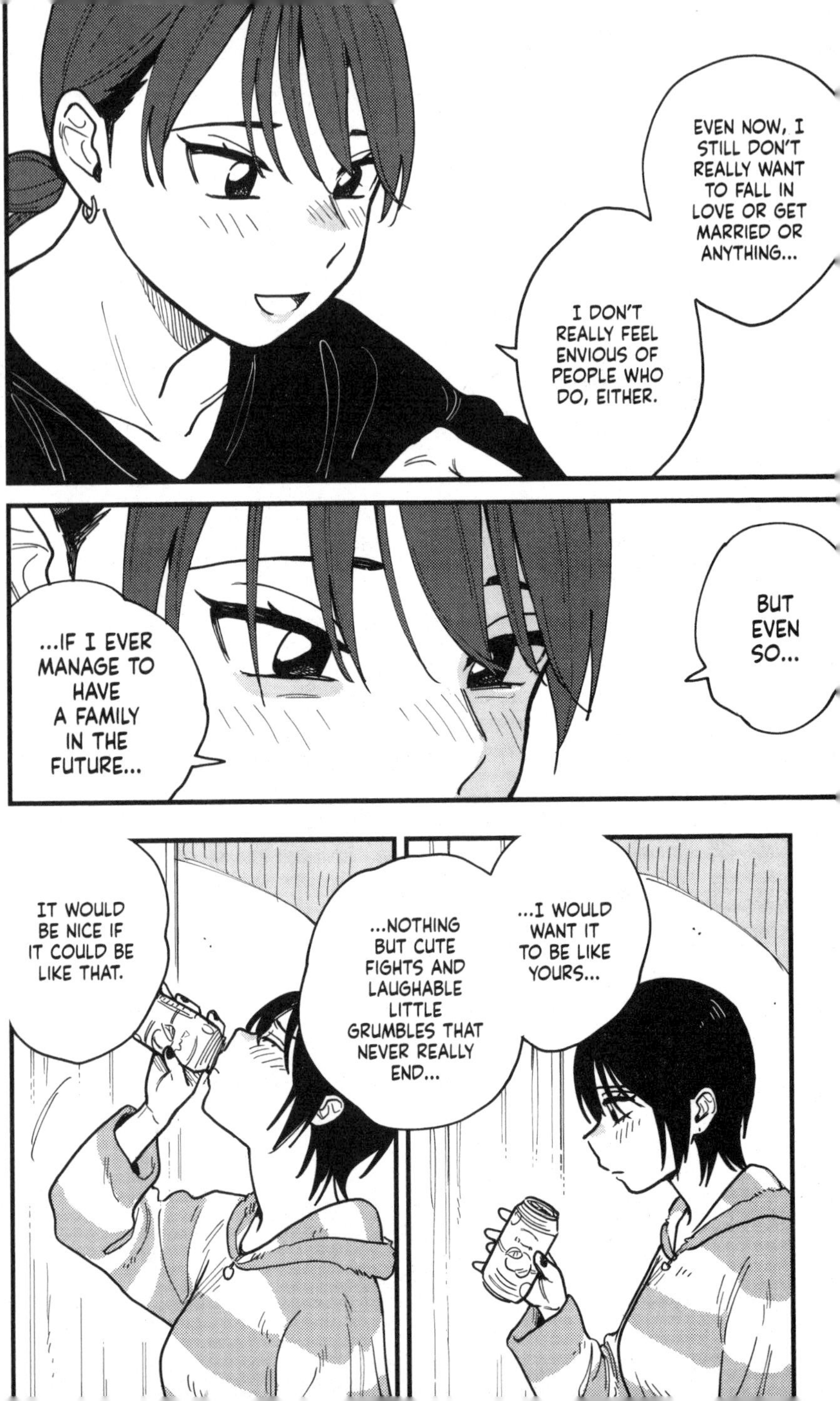
EVEN NOW, I STILL DON'T REALLY WANT TO FALL IN LOVE OR GET MARRIED OR ANYTHING...
I DON'T REALLY FEEL ENVIOUS OF PEOPLE WHO DO, EITHER.
BUT EVEN SO...
...IF I EVER MANAGE TO HAVE A FAMILY IN THE FUTURE...
...I WOULD WANT IT TO BE LIKE YOURS...
...NOTHING BUT CUTE FIGHTS AND LAUGHABLE LITTLE GRUMBLES THAT NEVER REALLY END...
IT WOULD BE NICE IF IT COULD BE LIKE THAT.

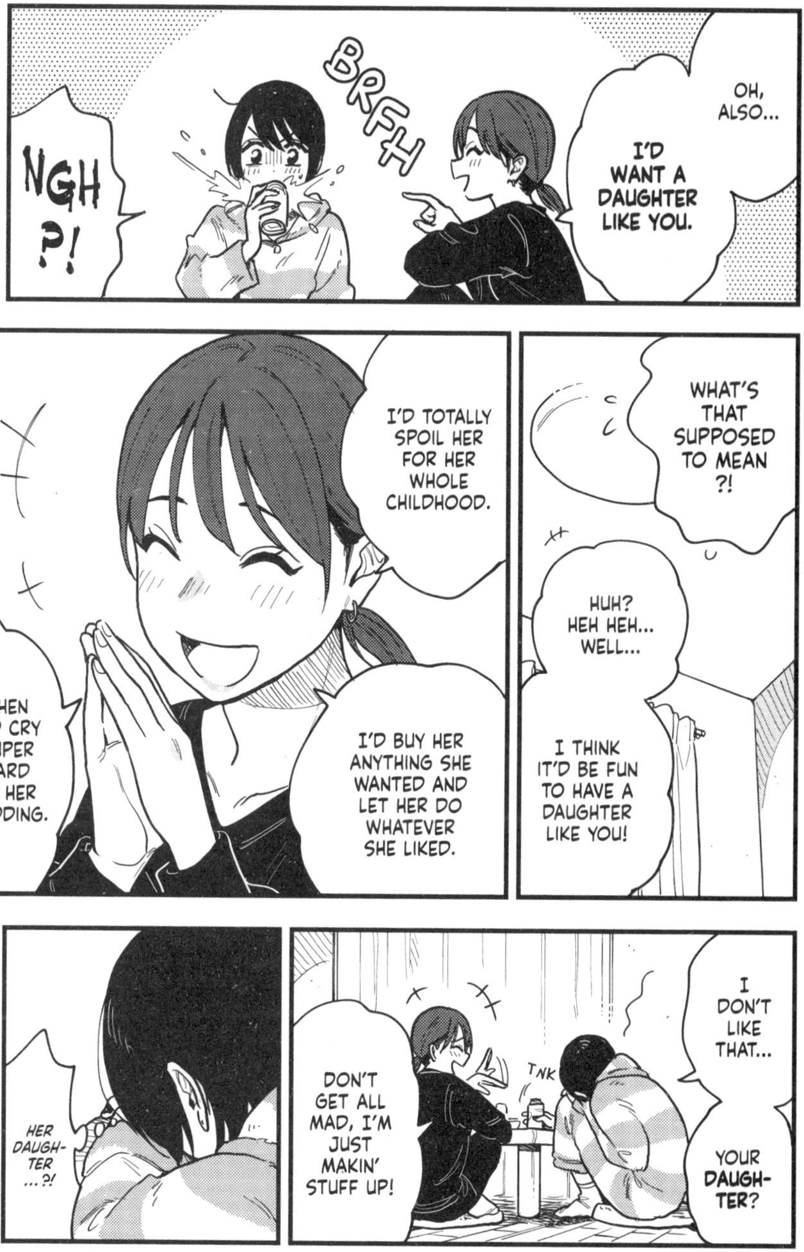
OH, ALSO...
I'D WANT A DAUGHTER LIKE YOU.
BRFH
NGH ?!
WHAT'S THAT SUPPOSED TO MEAN ?!
HUH? HEH HEH... WELL...
I THINK IT'D BE FUN TO HAVE A DAUGHTER LIKE YOU!
I'D TOTALLY SPOIL HER FOR HER WHOLE CHILDHOOD.
I'D BUY HER ANYTHING SHE WANTED AND LET HER DO WHATEVER SHE LIKED.
THEN I'D CRY SUPER HARD AT HER WEDDING.
I DON'T LIKE THAT...
YOUR DAUGHTER?
TNK
DON'T GET ALL MAD, I'M JUST MAKIN' STUFF UP!
HER DAUGHTER ...?!

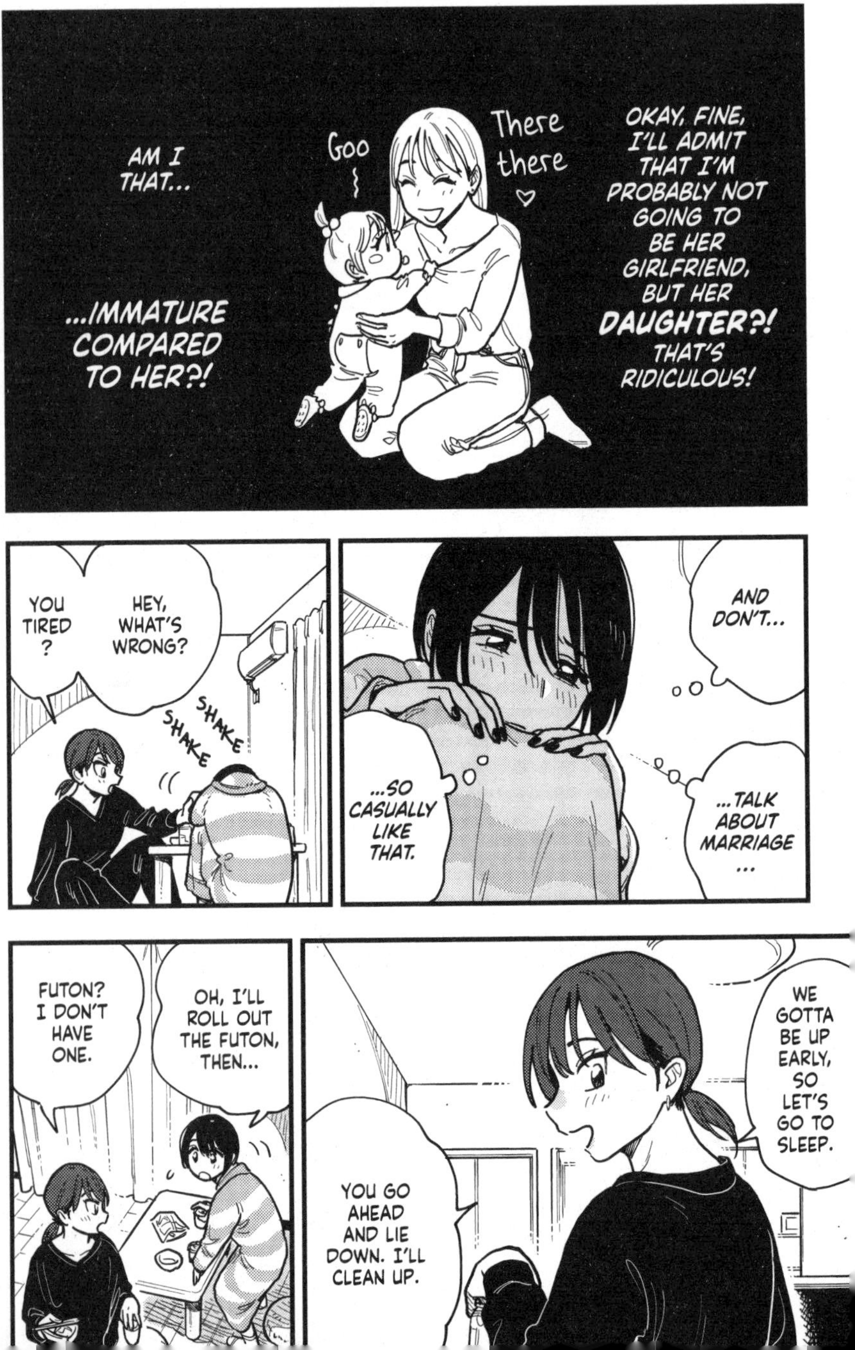
OKAY, FINE, I'LL ADMIT THAT I'M PROBABLY NOT GOING TO BE HER GIRLFRIEND, BUT HER DAUGHTER?! THAT'S RIDICULOUS!
There there ♡
Goo
AM I THAT...
...IMMATURE COMPARED TO HER?!
AND DON'T...
...TALK ABOUT MARRIAGE...
...SO CASUALLY LIKE THAT.
HEY, WHAT'S WRONG?
YOU TIRED?
SHAKE SHAKE
WE GOTTA BE UP EARLY, SO LET'S GO TO SLEEP.
YOU GO AHEAD AND LIE DOWN. I'LL CLEAN UP.
OH, I'LL ROLL OUT THE FUTON, THEN...
FUTON? I DON'T HAVE ONE.

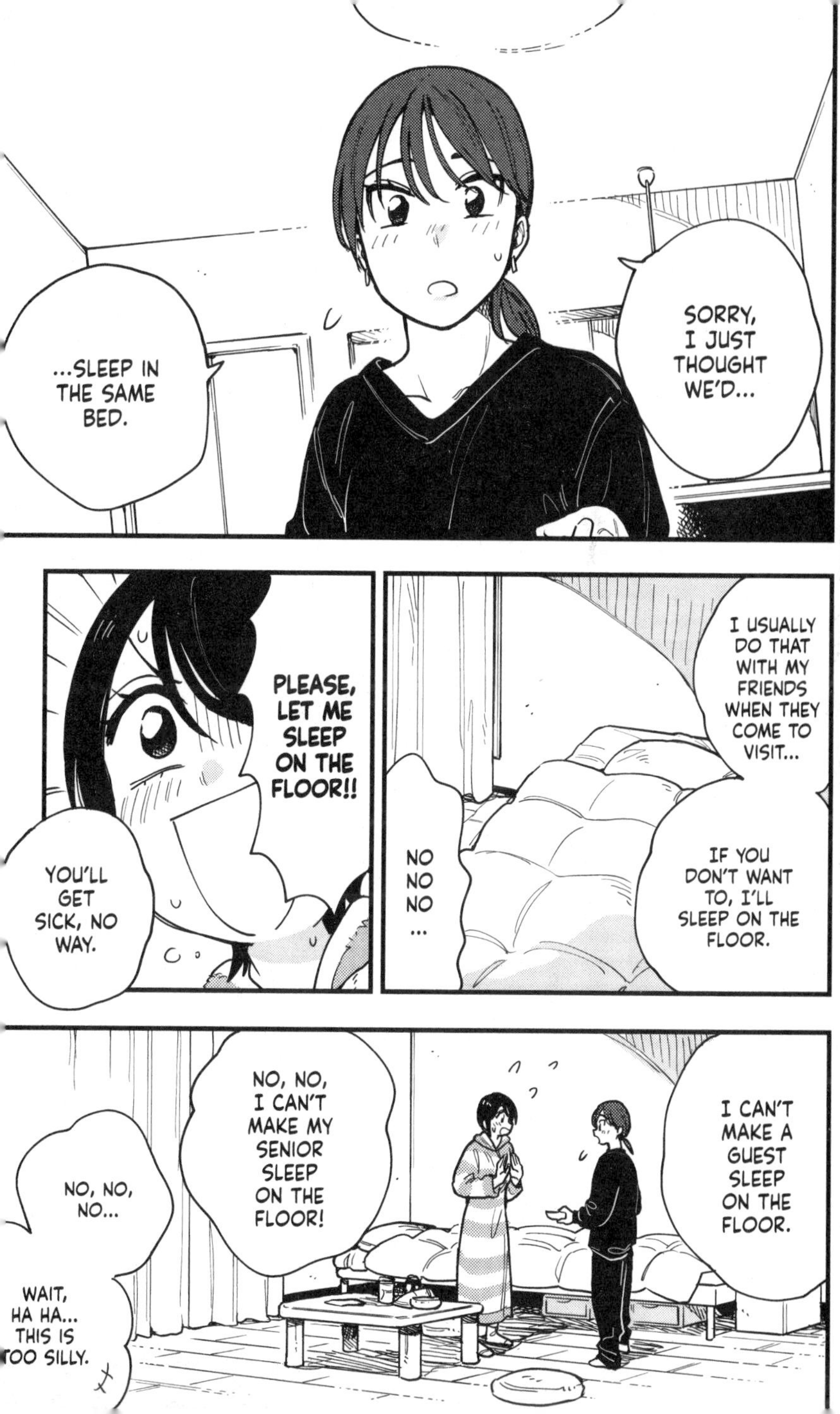
SORRY, I JUST THOUGHT WE'D...
...SLEEP IN THE SAME BED.
I USUALLY DO THAT WITH MY FRIENDS WHEN THEY COME TO VISIT...
IF YOU DON'T WANT TO, I'LL SLEEP ON THE FLOOR.
NO NO NO ...
PLEASE, LET ME SLEEP ON THE FLOOR!!
YOU'LL GET SICK, NO WAY.
I CAN'T MAKE A GUEST SLEEP ON THE FLOOR.
NO, NO, I CAN'T MAKE MY SENIOR SLEEP ON THE FLOOR!
NO, NO, NO...
WAIT, HA HA... THIS IS TOO SILLY.

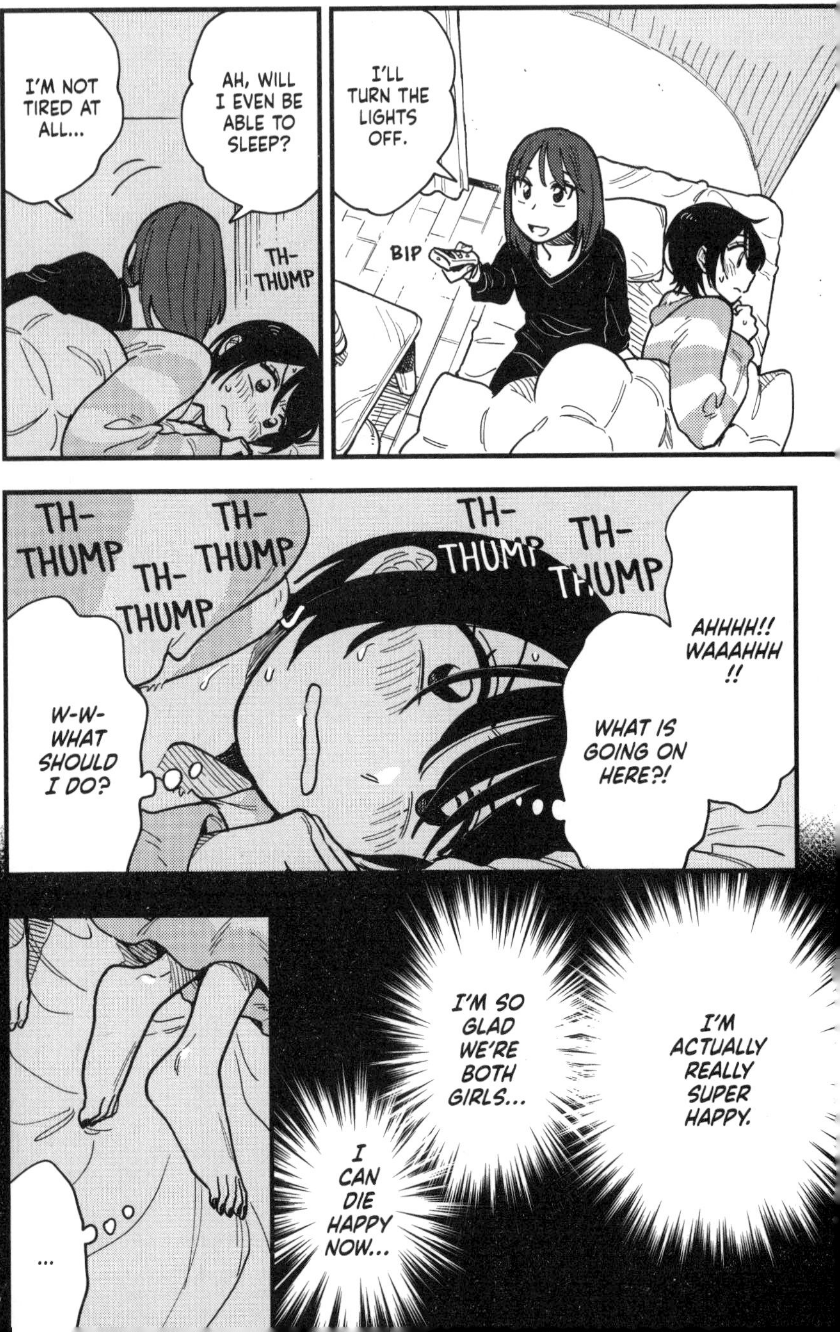
I'LL TURN THE LIGHTS OFF.
BIP
AH, WILL I EVEN BE ABLE TO SLEEP?
I'M NOT TIRED AT ALL...
TH-THUMP
TH-THUMP
TH-THUMP
AHHHH!! WAAAHHH !!
WHAT IS GOING ON HERE?!
TH-THUMP
TH-THUMP
TH-THUMP
W-W-WHAT SHOULD I DO?
I'M ACTUALLY REALLY SUPER HAPPY.
I'M SO GLAD WE'RE BOTH GIRLS...
I CAN DIE HAPPY NOW...
...

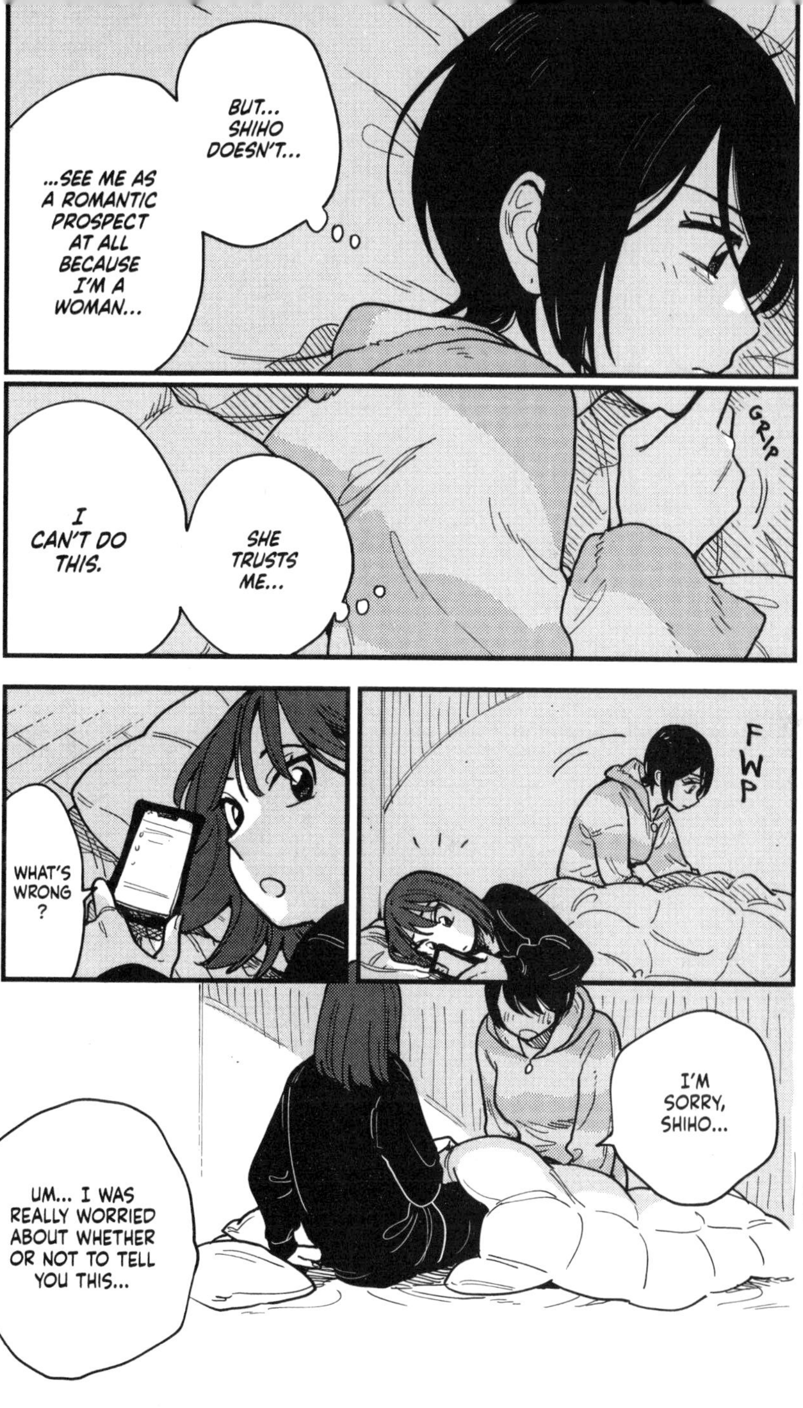

BUT... SHIHO DOESN'T...
...SEE ME AS A ROMANTIC PROSPECT AT ALL BECAUSE I'M A WOMAN...
GRIP
SHE TRUSTS ME...
I CAN'T DO THIS.
FWP
WHAT'S WRONG?
I'M SORRY, SHIHO...
UM... I WAS REALLY WORRIED ABOUT WHETHER OR NOT TO TELL YOU THIS...

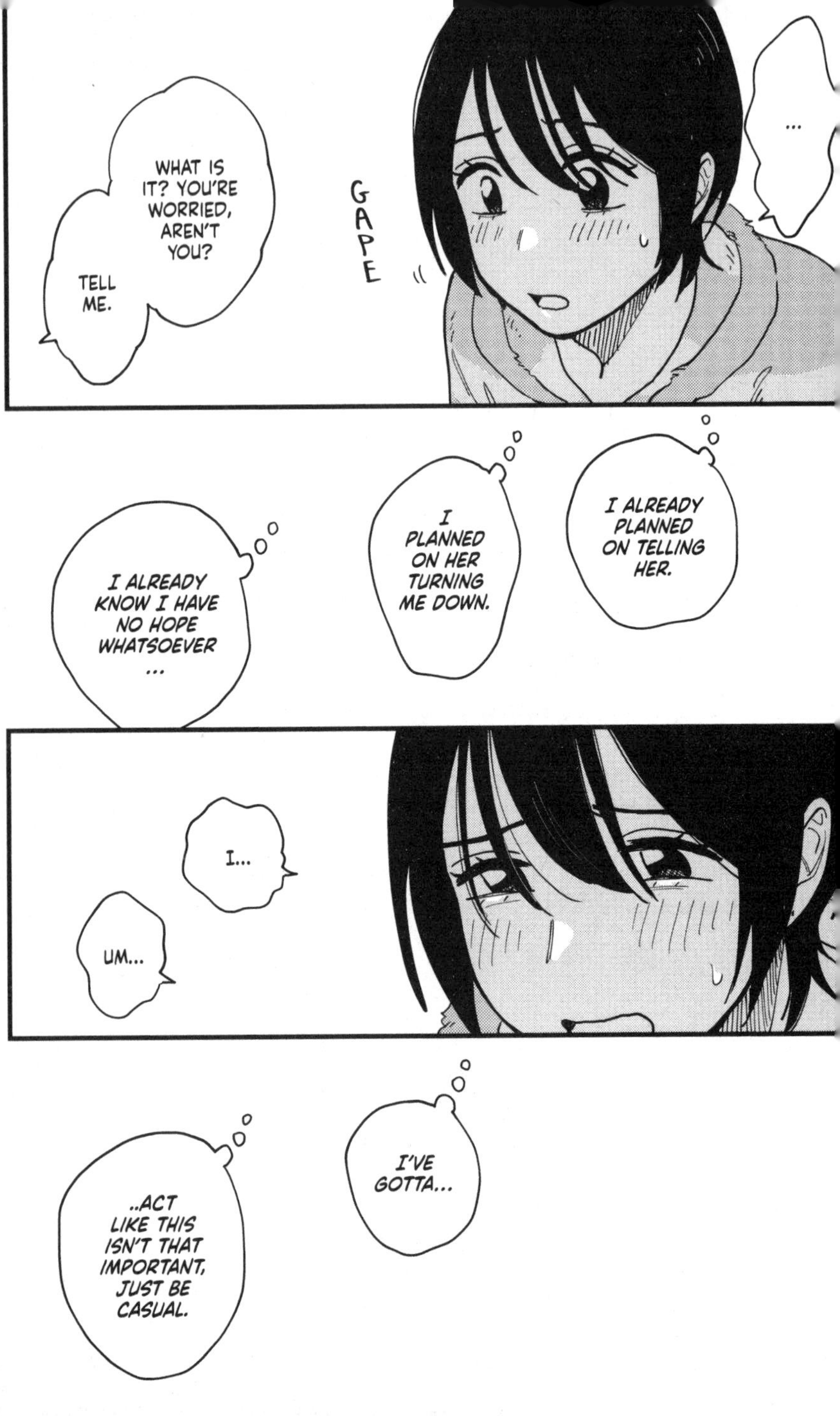
...
GAPE
WHAT IS IT? YOU'RE WORRIED, AREN'T YOU?
TELL ME.
I ALREADY PLANNED ON TELLING HER.
I PLANNED ON HER TURNING ME DOWN.
I ALREADY KNOW I HAVE NO HOPE WHATSOEVER ...
I...
UM...
I'VE GOTTA...
..ACT LIKE THIS ISN'T THAT IMPORTANT, JUST BE CASUAL.

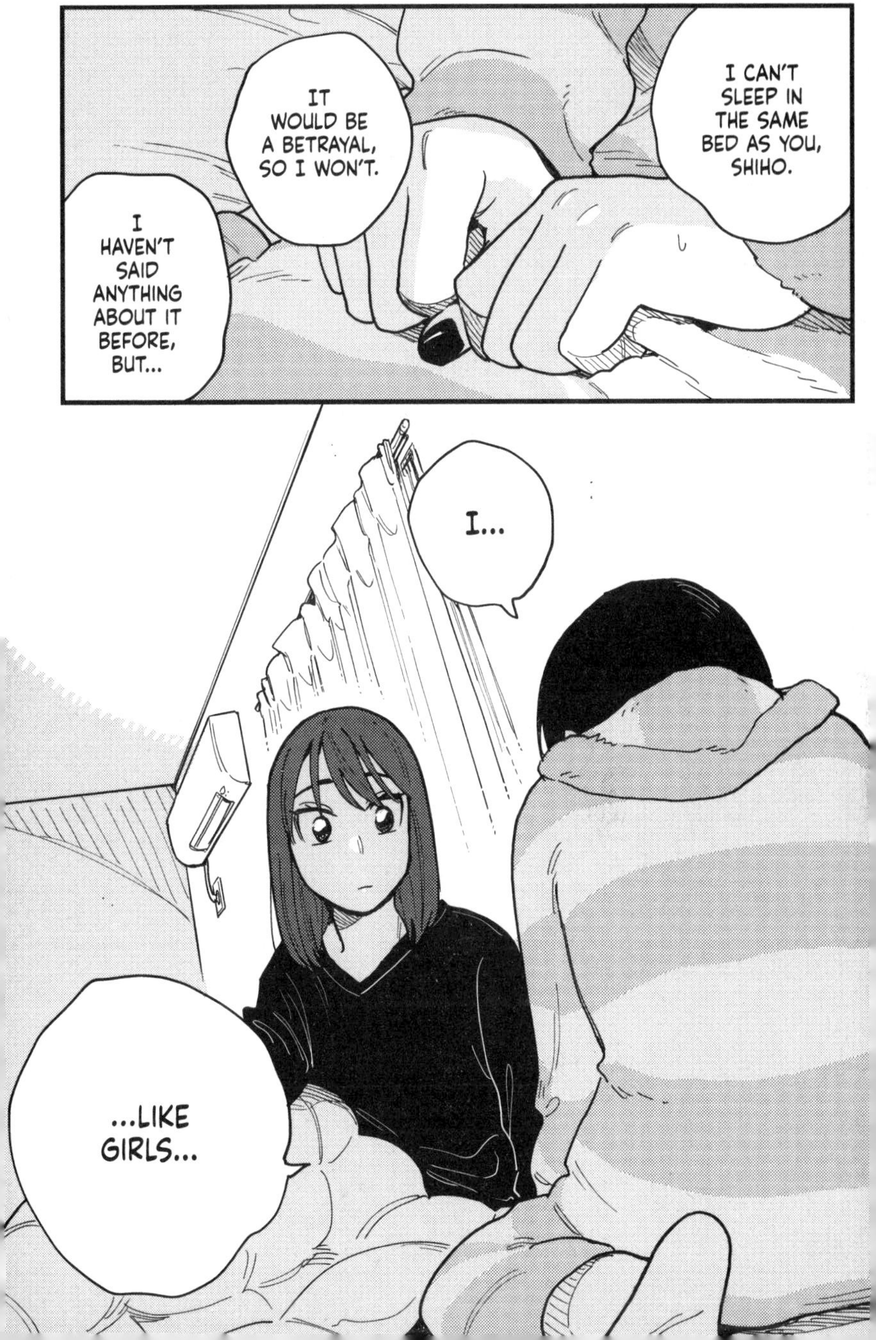
I CAN'T SLEEP IN THE SAME BED AS YOU, SHIHO.
IT WOULD BE A BETRAYAL, SO I WON'T.
I HAVEN'T SAID ANYTHING ABOUT IT BEFORE, BUT...
I...
...LIKE GIRLS...

HOW DO WE RELATIONSHIP?

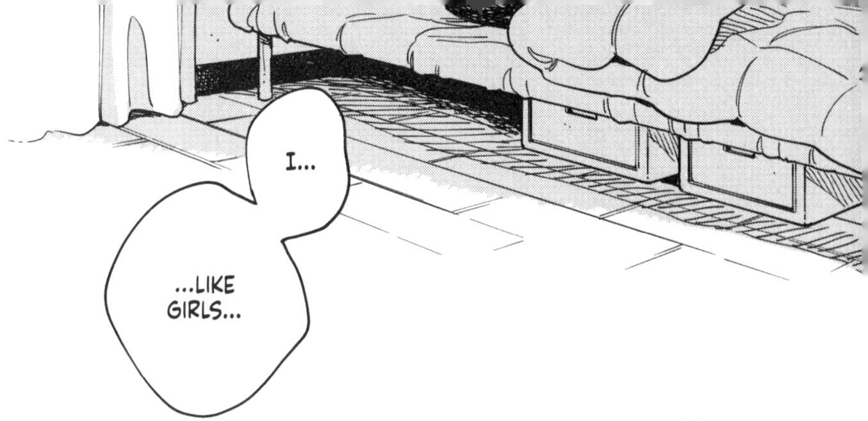
I...
...LIKE GIRLS...

Chapter 41: Fickle Heart

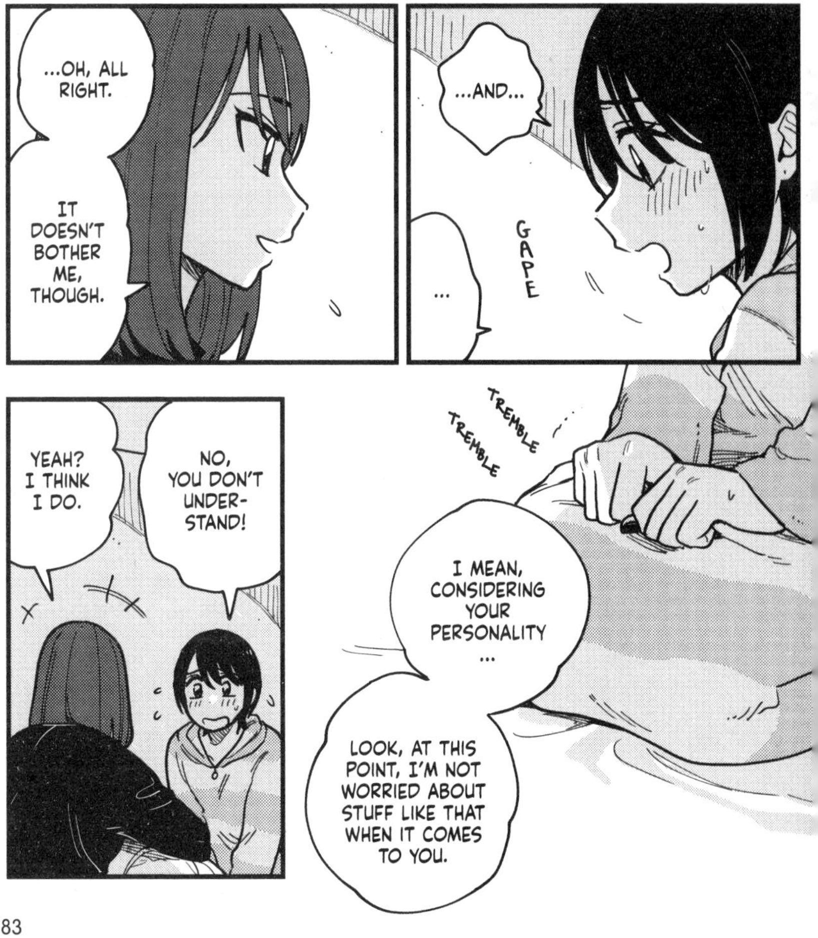
...AND...
GAPE
...
...OH, ALL RIGHT.
IT DOESN'T BOTHER ME, THOUGH.
TREMBLE
TREMBLE
I MEAN, CONSIDERING YOUR PERSONALITY ...
LOOK, AT THIS POINT, I'M NOT WORRIED ABOUT STUFF LIKE THAT WHEN IT COMES TO YOU.
NO, YOU DON'T UNDER-STAND!
YEAH? I THINK I DO.

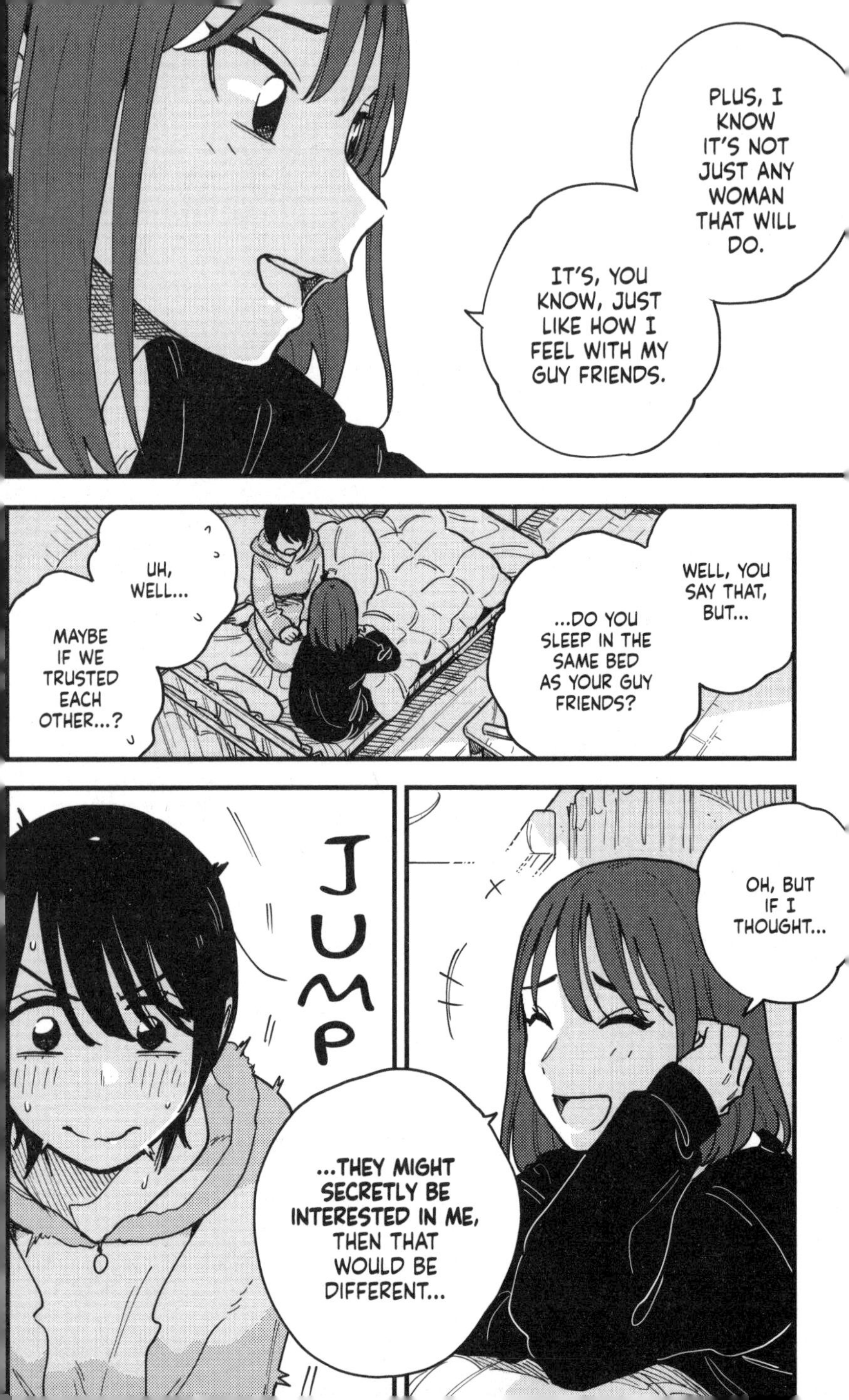
PLUS, I KNOW IT'S NOT JUST ANY WOMAN THAT WILL DO.
IT'S, YOU KNOW, JUST LIKE HOW I FEEL WITH MY GUY FRIENDS.
WELL, YOU SAY THAT, BUT...
...DO YOU SLEEP IN THE SAME BED AS YOUR GUY FRIENDS?
UH, WELL...
MAYBE IF WE TRUSTED EACH OTHER...?
OH, BUT IF I THOUGHT...
...THEY MIGHT SECRETLY BE INTERESTED IN ME, THEN THAT WOULD BE DIFFERENT...
JUMP

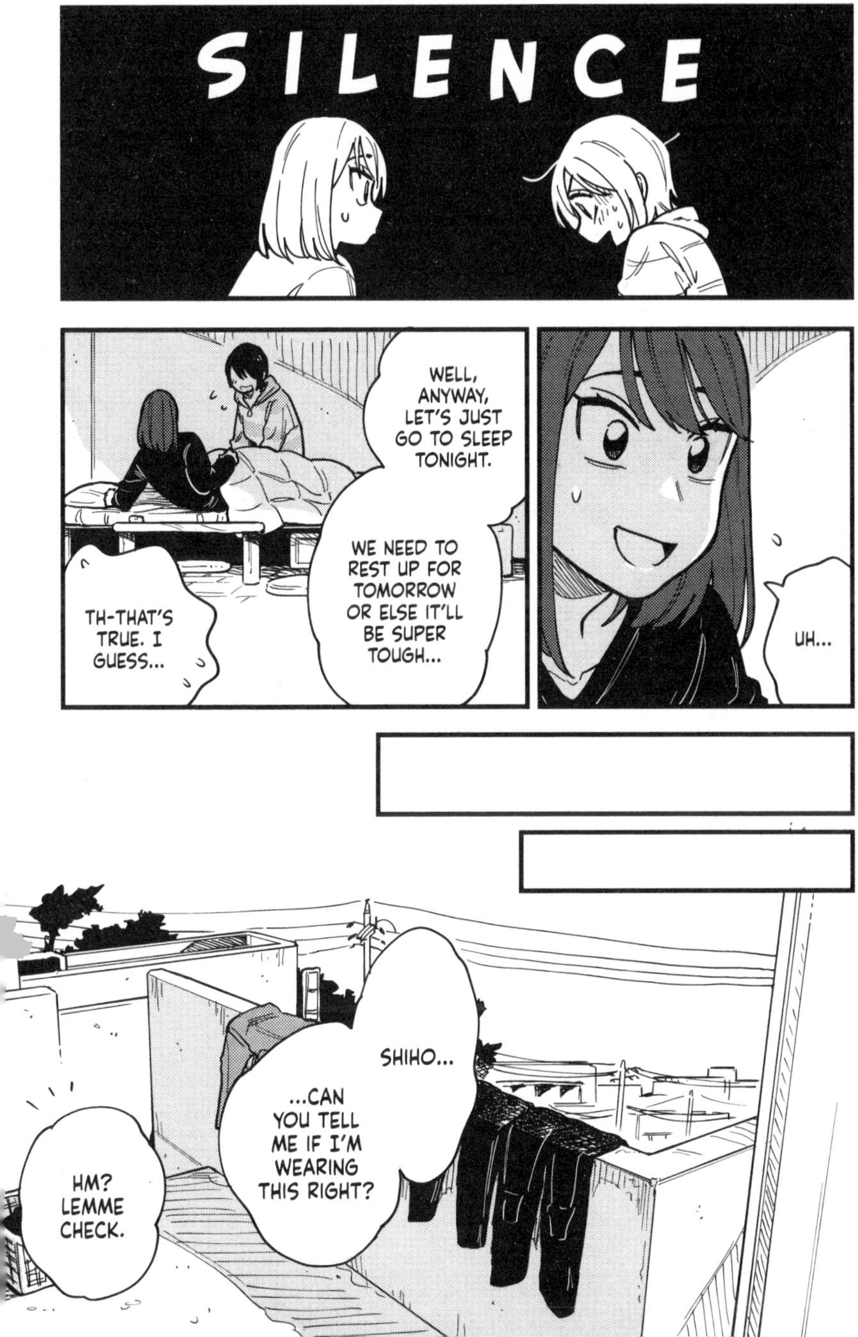
SILENCE
UH...
WELL, ANYWAY, LET'S JUST GO TO SLEEP TONIGHT.
WE NEED TO REST UP FOR TOMORROW OR ELSE IT'LL BE SUPER TOUGH...
TH-THAT'S TRUE. I GUESS...
SHIHO...
...CAN YOU TELL ME IF I'M WEARING THIS RIGHT?
HM? LEMME CHECK.

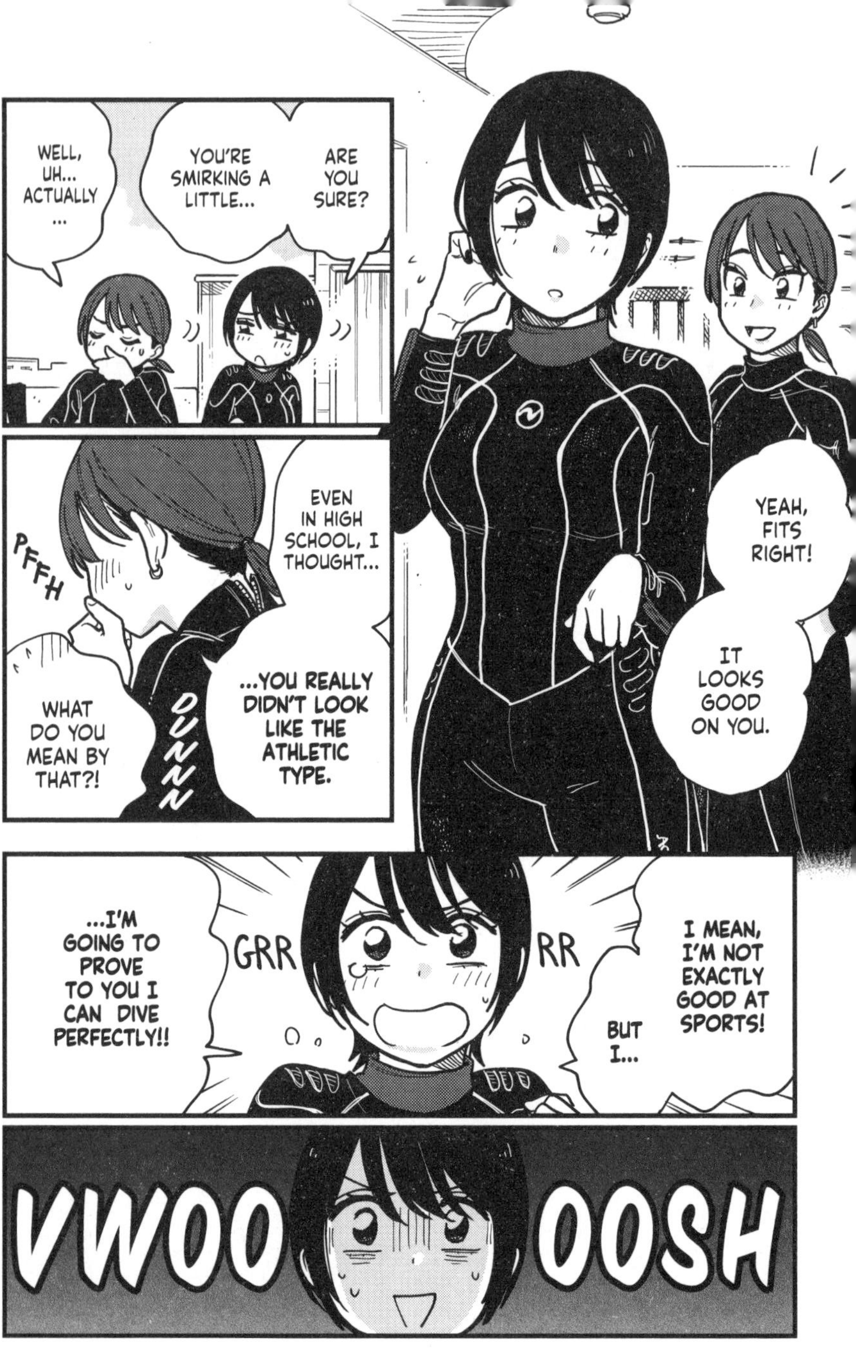
YEAH, FITS RIGHT!
IT LOOKS GOOD ON YOU.
ARE YOU SURE?
YOU'RE SMIRKING A LITTLE...
WELL, UH... ACTUALLY ...
EVEN IN HIGH SCHOOL, I THOUGHT...
...YOU REALLY DIDN'T LOOK LIKE THE ATHLETIC TYPE.
PFFH
DUNNN
WHAT DO YOU MEAN BY THAT?!
I MEAN, I'M NOT EXACTLY GOOD AT SPORTS!
BUT I...
GRR
RR
...I'M GOING TO PROVE TO YOU I CAN DIVE PERFECTLY!!
VWOO
OOSH

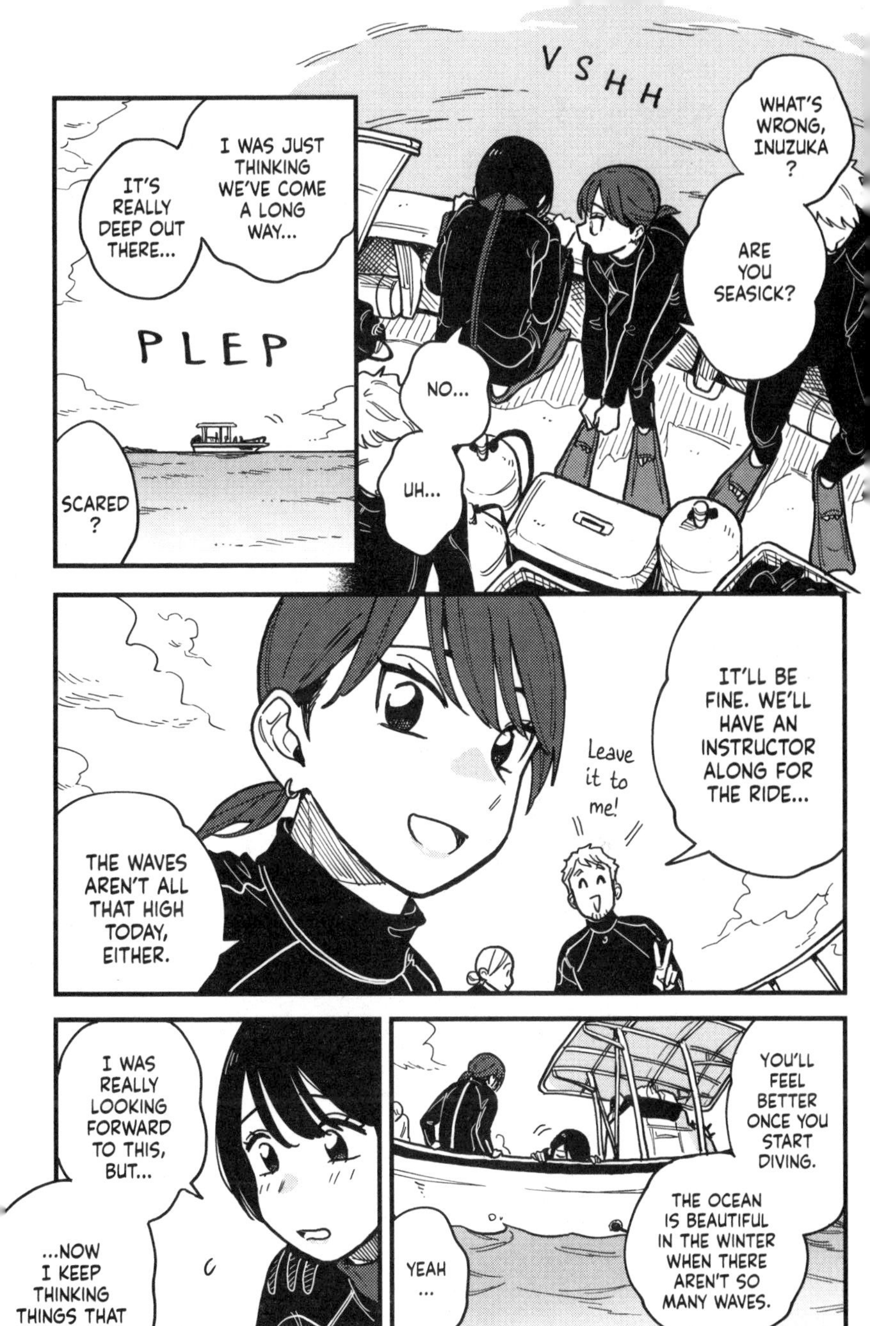
VSHH
WHAT'S WRONG, INUZUKA?
ARE YOU SEASICK?
NO...
UH...
I WAS JUST THINKING WE'VE COME A LONG WAY...
IT'S REALLY DEEP OUT THERE...
PLEP
SCARED?
IT'LL BE FINE. WE'LL HAVE AN INSTRUCTOR ALONG FOR THE RIDE...
Leave it to me!
THE WAVES AREN'T ALL THAT HIGH TODAY, EITHER.
YOU'LL FEEL BETTER ONCE YOU START DIVING.
THE OCEAN IS BEAUTIFUL IN THE WINTER WHEN THERE AREN'T SO MANY WAVES.
YEAH...
I WAS REALLY LOOKING FORWARD TO THIS, BUT...
...NOW I KEEP THINKING THINGS THAT WORRY ME.

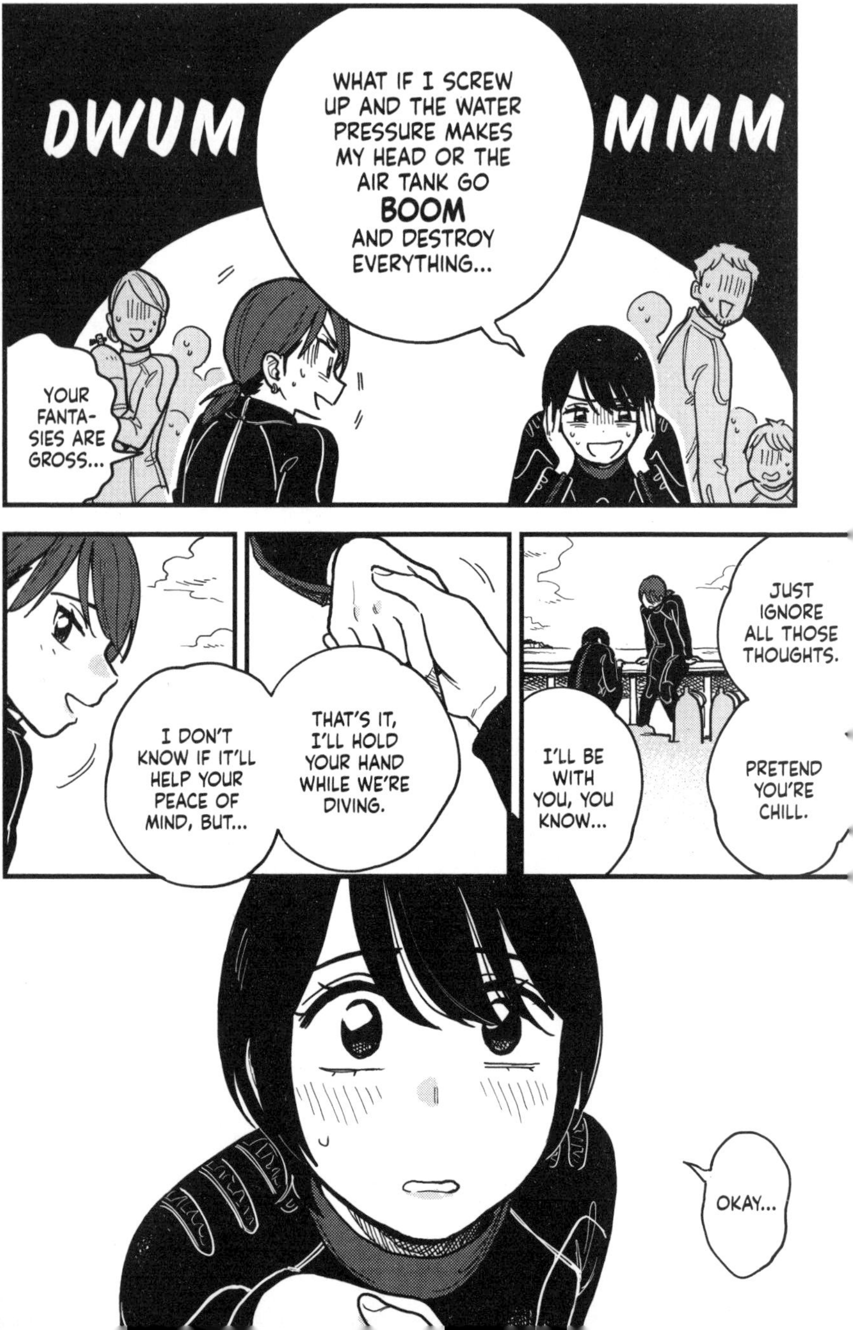
DWUM MMM
WHAT IF I SCREW UP AND THE WATER PRESSURE MAKES MY HEAD OR THE AIR TANK GO BOOM AND DESTROY EVERYTHING...
YOUR FANTA-SIES ARE GROSS...
JUST IGNORE ALL THOSE THOUGHTS.
PRETEND YOU'RE CHILL.
I'LL BE WITH YOU, YOU KNOW...
THAT'S IT, I'LL HOLD YOUR HAND WHILE WE'RE DIVING.
I DON'T KNOW IF IT'LL HELP YOUR PEACE OF MIND, BUT...
OKAY...

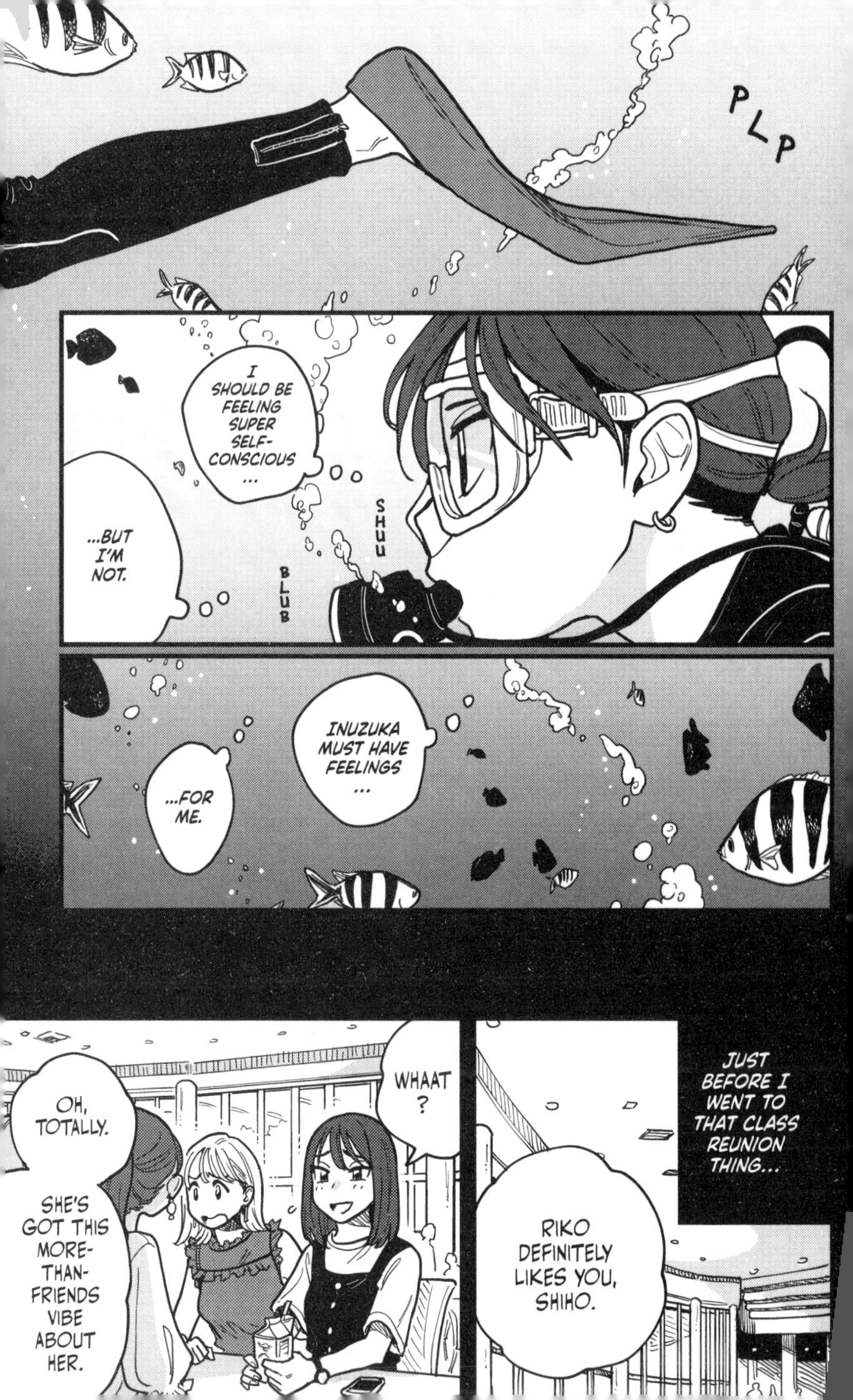
PLP
I SHOULD BE FEELING SUPER SELF-CONSCIOUS...
SHUU
BLUB
...BUT I'M NOT.
INUZUKA MUST HAVE FEELINGS...
...FOR ME.
JUST BEFORE I WENT TO THAT CLASS REUNION THING...
RIKO DEFINITELY LIKES YOU, SHIHO.
WHAAT?
OH, TOTALLY.
SHE'S GOT THIS MORE-THAN-FRIENDS VIBE ABOUT HER.

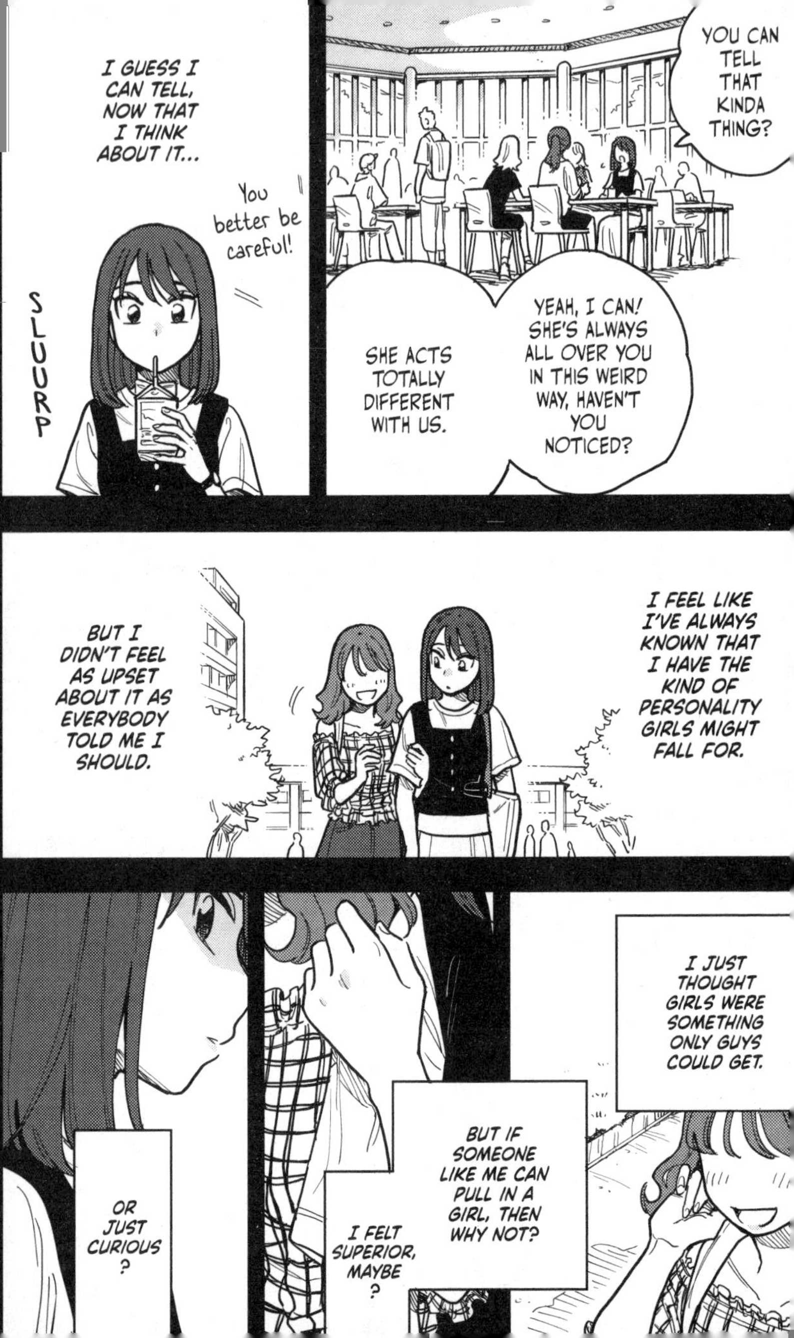
YOU CAN TELL THAT KINDA THING?
YEAH, I CAN! SHE'S ALWAYS ALL OVER YOU IN THIS WEIRD WAY, HAVEN'T YOU NOTICED?
SHE ACTS TOTALLY DIFFERENT WITH US.
I GUESS I CAN TELL, NOW THAT I THINK ABOUT IT...
You better be careful!
SLUURP
I FEEL LIKE I'VE ALWAYS KNOWN THAT I HAVE THE KIND OF PERSONALITY GIRLS MIGHT FALL FOR.
BUT I DIDN'T FEEL AS UPSET ABOUT IT AS EVERYBODY TOLD ME I SHOULD.
I JUST THOUGHT GIRLS WERE SOMETHING ONLY GUYS COULD GET.
BUT IF SOMEONE LIKE ME CAN PULL IN A GIRL, THEN WHY NOT?
I FELT SUPERIOR, MAYBE?
OR JUST CURIOUS?

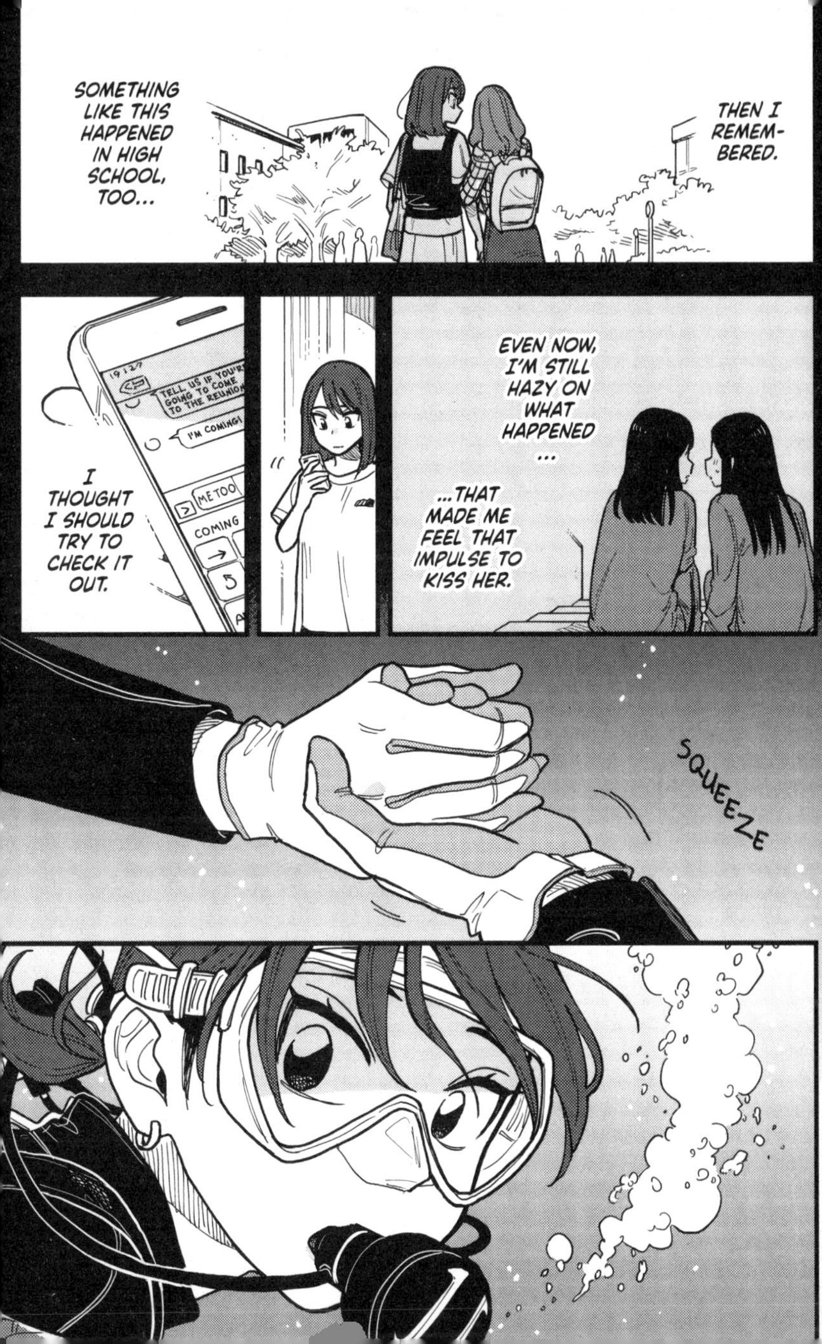
THEN I REMEMBERED.
SOMETHING LIKE THIS HAPPENED IN HIGH SCHOOL, TOO...
EVEN NOW, I'M STILL HAZY ON WHAT HAPPENED...
...THAT MADE ME FEEL THAT IMPULSE TO KISS HER.
TELL US IF YOU'RE GOING TO COME TO THE REUNION
I'M COMING!
ME TOO
COMING
I THOUGHT I SHOULD TRY TO CHECK IT OUT.
SQUEEZE

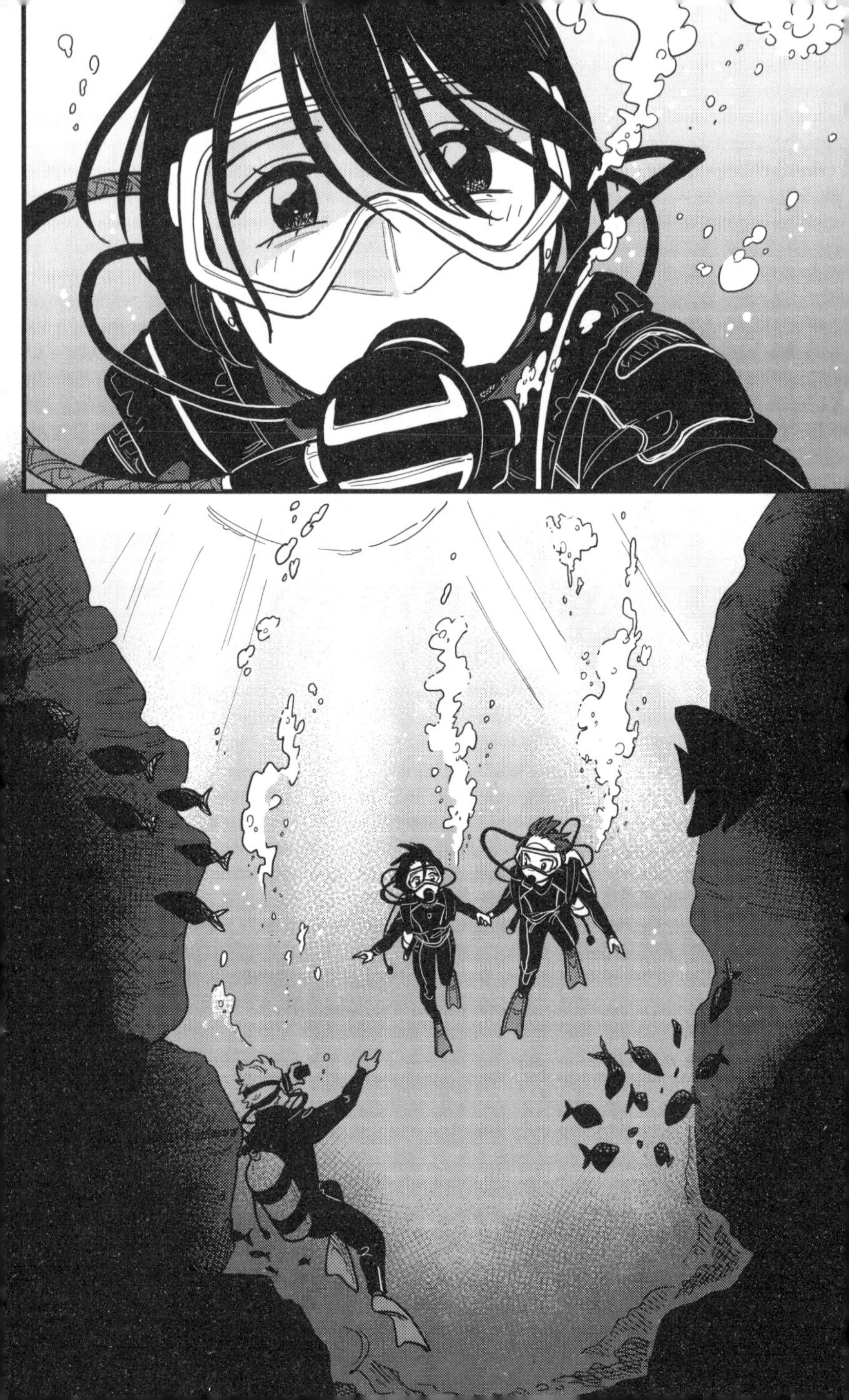

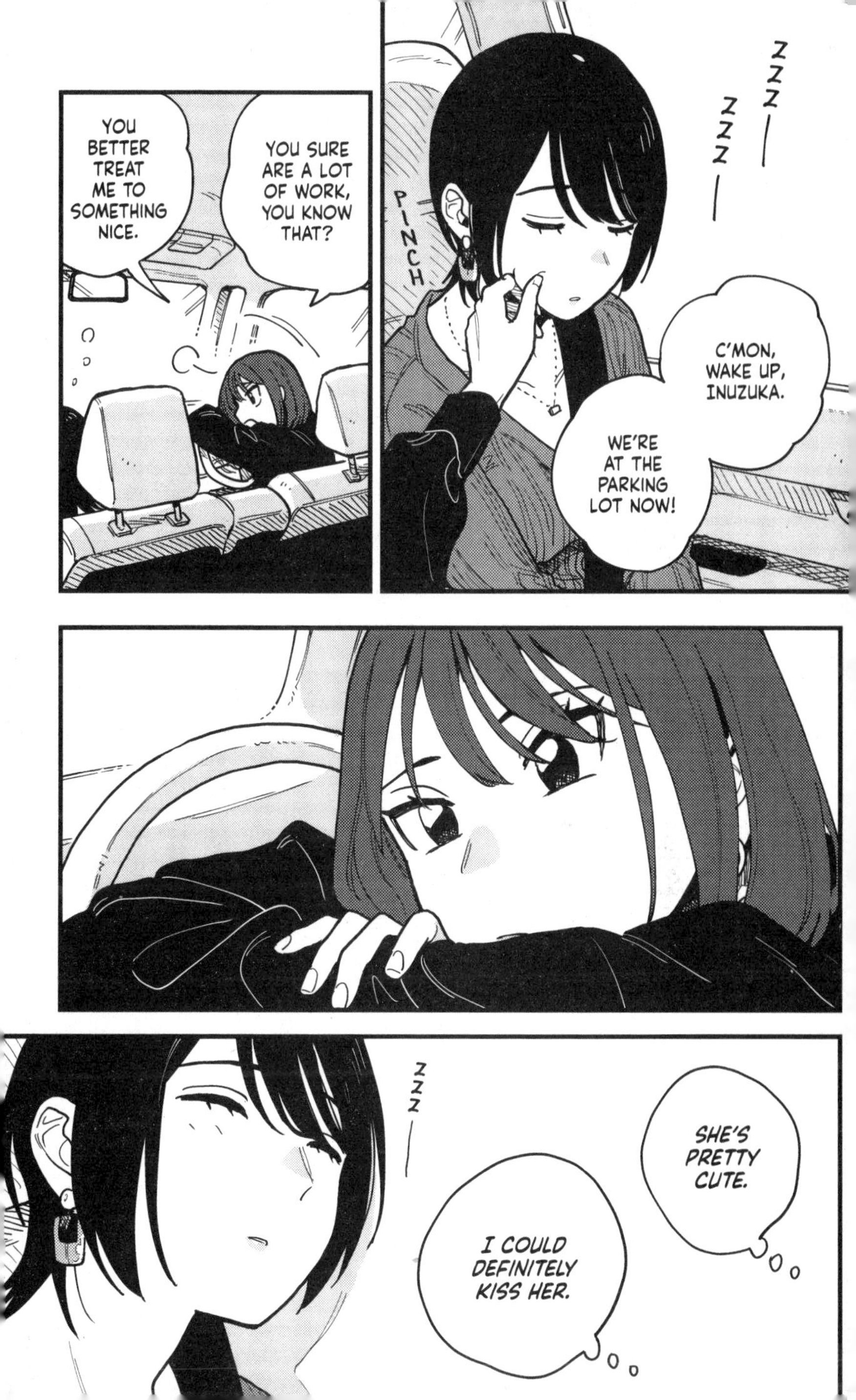
ZZZ— ZZZ—
PINCH
C'MON, WAKE UP, INUZUKA.
WE'RE AT THE PARKING LOT NOW!
YOU SURE ARE A LOT OF WORK, YOU KNOW THAT?
YOU BETTER TREAT ME TO SOMETHING NICE.
ZZZ—
SHE'S PRETTY CUTE.
I COULD DEFINITELY KISS HER.

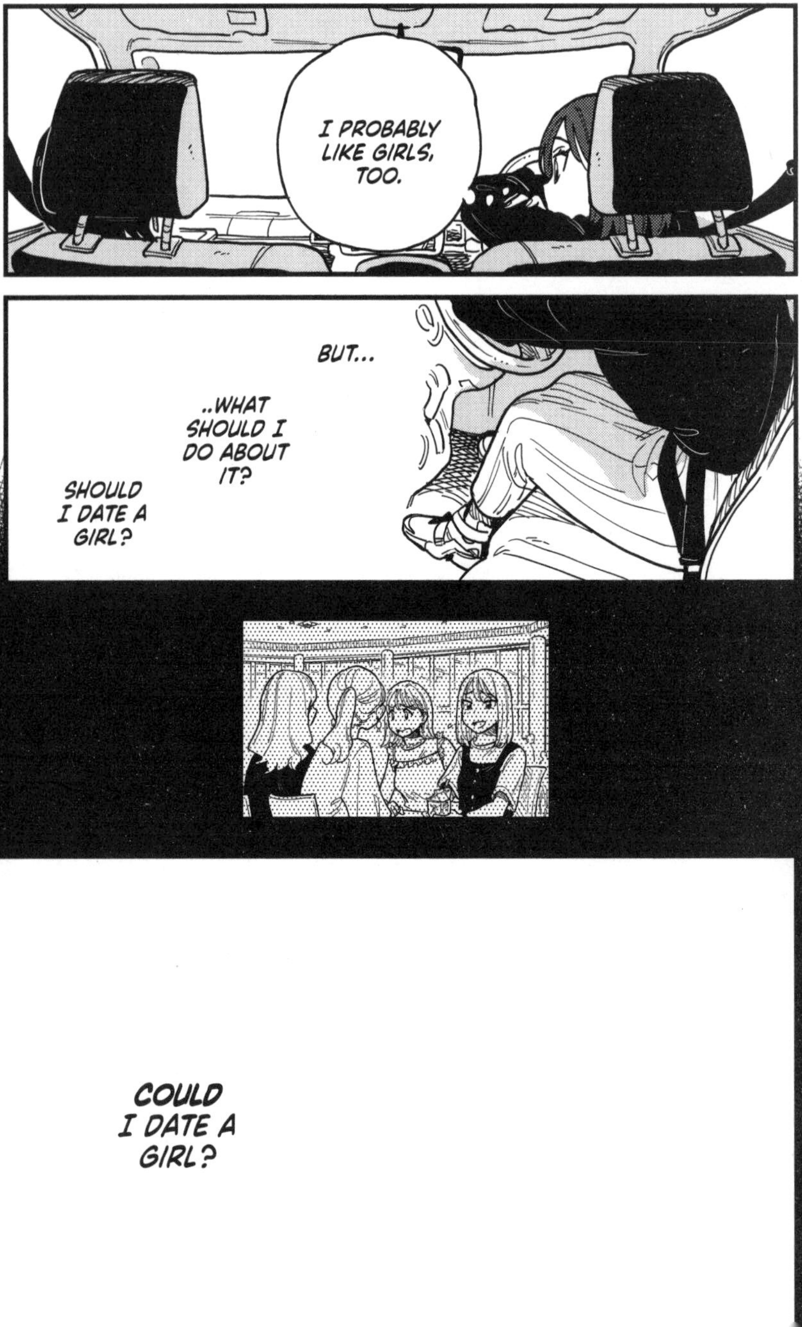
I PROBABLY LIKE GIRLS, TOO.
BUT...
..WHAT SHOULD I DO ABOUT IT?
SHOULD I DATE A GIRL?
COULD I DATE A GIRL?

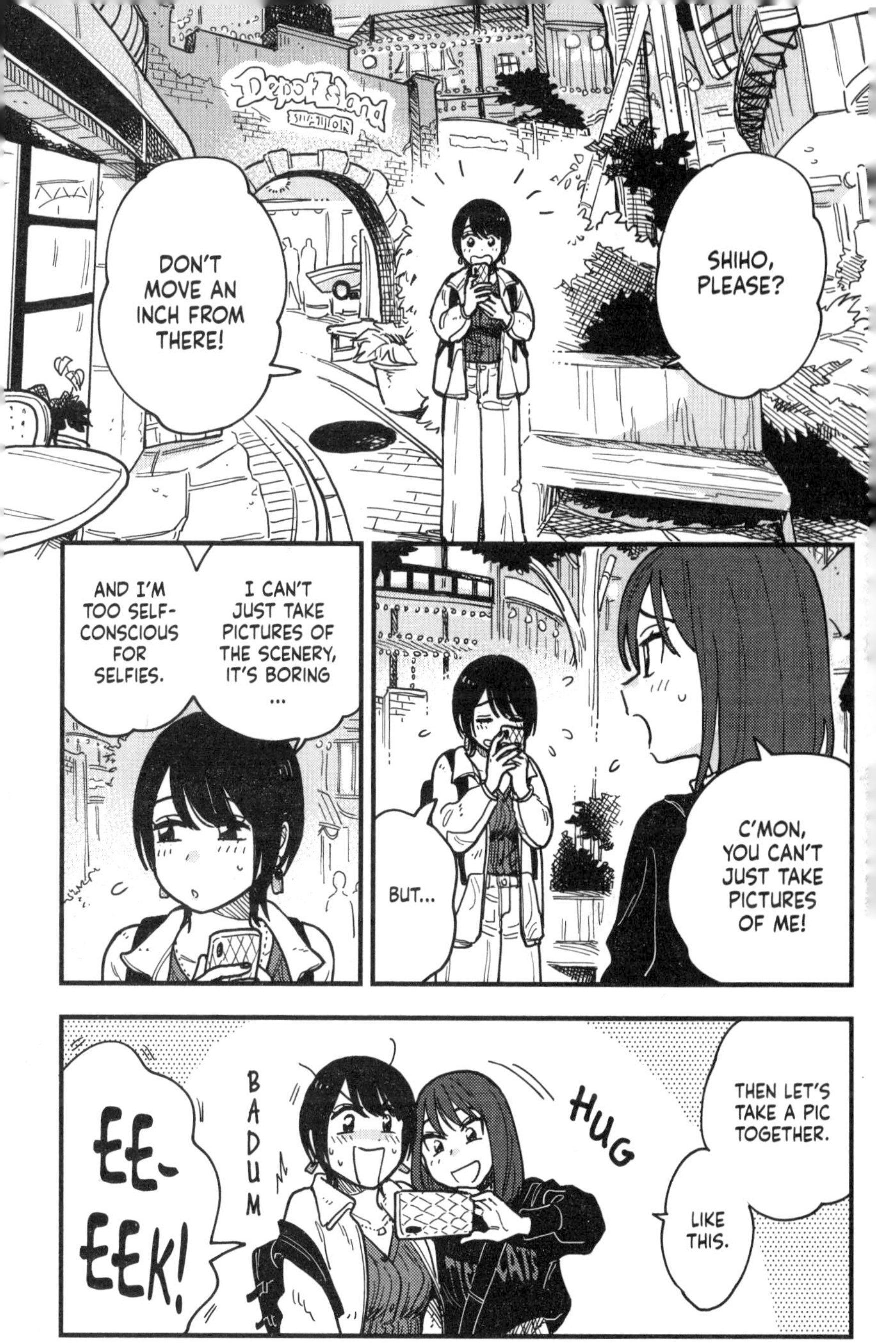
Depot Island
SHIHO, PLEASE?
DON'T MOVE AN INCH FROM THERE!
C'MON, YOU CAN'T JUST TAKE PICTURES OF ME!
BUT...
I CAN'T JUST TAKE PICTURES OF THE SCENERY, IT'S BORING ...
AND I'M TOO SELF-CONSCIOUS FOR SELFIES.
THEN LET'S TAKE A PIC TOGETHER.
LIKE THIS.
HUG
BADUM
EE-EEK!

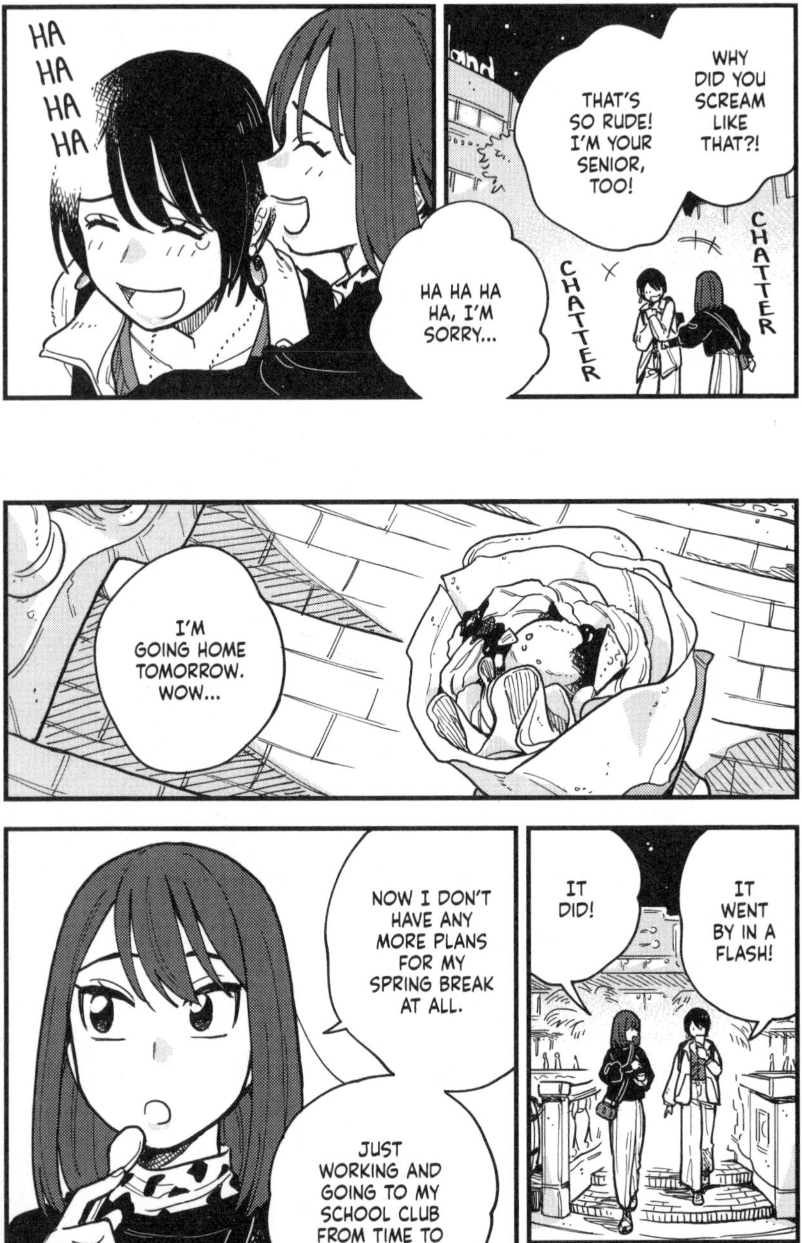
WHY DID YOU SCREAM LIKE THAT?!
THAT'S SO RUDE! I'M YOUR SENIOR, TOO!
CHATTER
CHATTER
HA HA HA HA
HA HA HA HA, I'M SORRY...
I'M GOING HOME TOMORROW. WOW...
IT WENT BY IN A FLASH!
IT DID!
NOW I DON'T HAVE ANY MORE PLANS FOR MY SPRING BREAK AT ALL.
JUST WORKING AND GOING TO MY SCHOOL CLUB FROM TIME TO TIME...

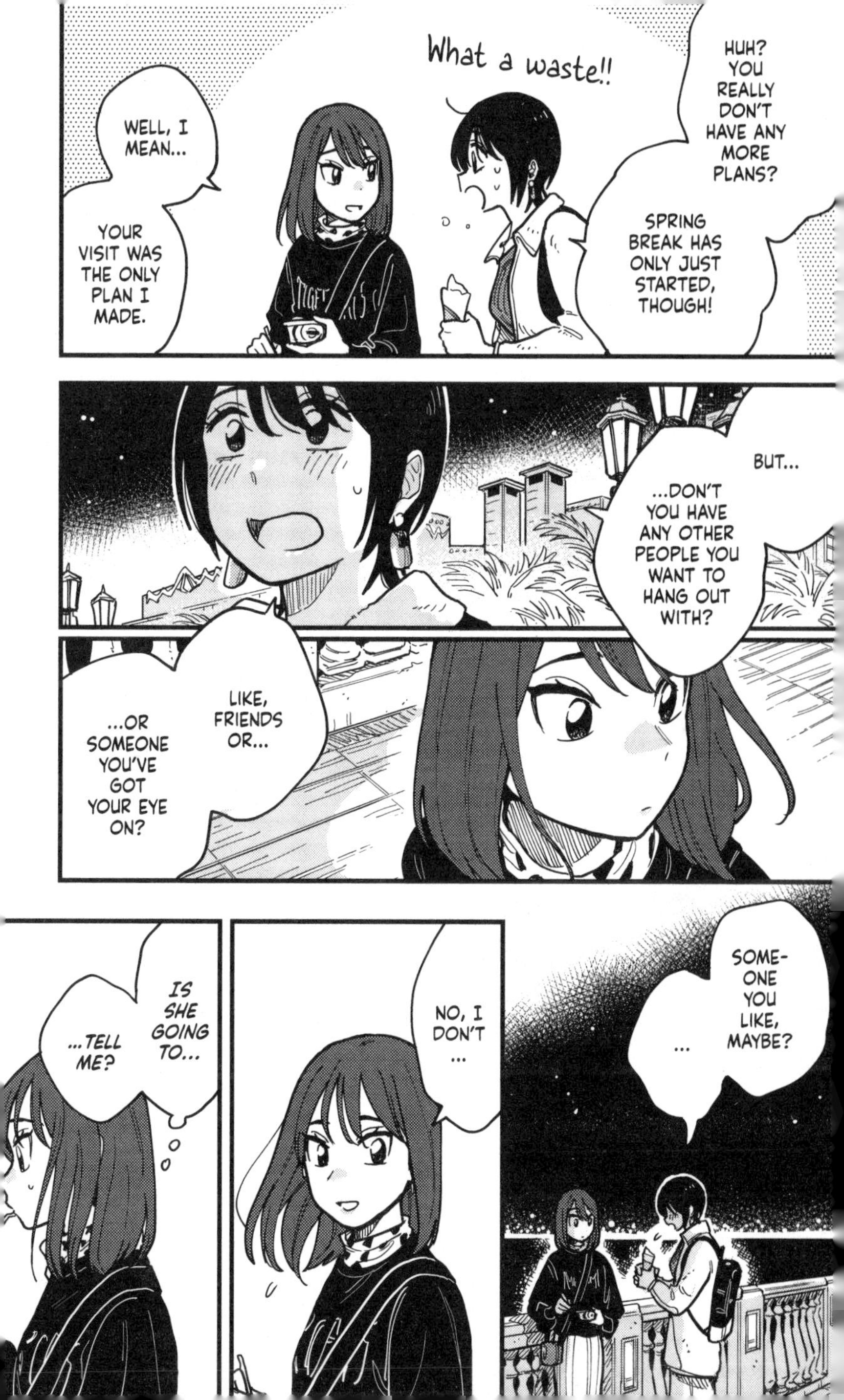
HUH? YOU REALLY DON'T HAVE ANY MORE PLANS?
What a waste!!
SPRING BREAK HAS ONLY JUST STARTED, THOUGH!
WELL, I MEAN...
YOUR VISIT WAS THE ONLY PLAN I MADE.
BUT...
...DON'T YOU HAVE ANY OTHER PEOPLE YOU WANT TO HANG OUT WITH?
LIKE, FRIENDS OR...
...OR SOMEONE YOU'VE GOT YOUR EYE ON?
SOME-ONE YOU LIKE, MAYBE?
...
NO, I DON'T ...
IS SHE GOING TO...
...TELL ME?

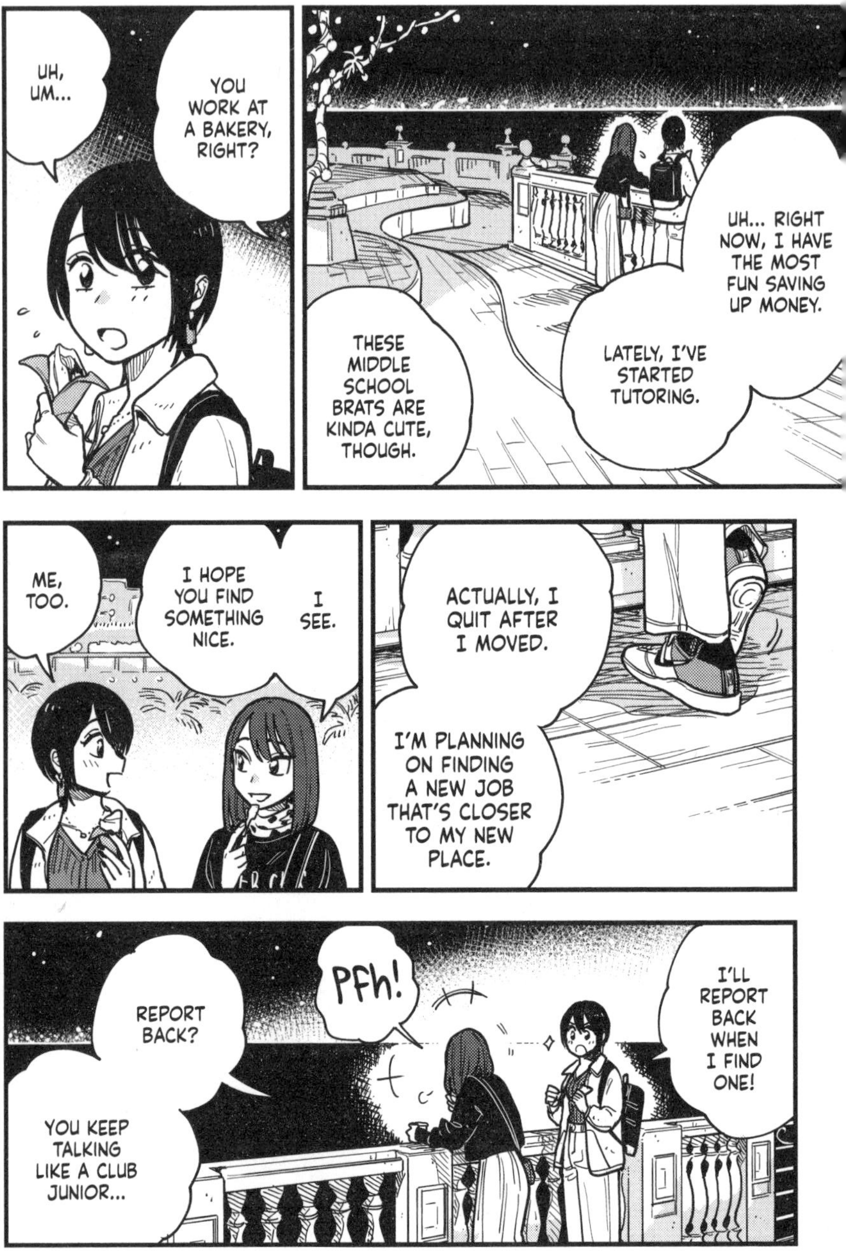
UH... RIGHT NOW, I HAVE THE MOST FUN SAVING UP MONEY.
LATELY, I'VE STARTED TUTORING.
THESE MIDDLE SCHOOL BRATS ARE KINDA CUTE, THOUGH.
YOU WORK AT A BAKERY, RIGHT?
UH, UM...
ACTUALLY, I QUIT AFTER I MOVED.
I'M PLANNING ON FINDING A NEW JOB THAT'S CLOSER TO MY NEW PLACE.
I SEE.
I HOPE YOU FIND SOMETHING NICE.
ME, TOO.
I'LL REPORT BACK WHEN I FIND ONE!
Pfh!
REPORT BACK?
YOU KEEP TALKING LIKE A CLUB JUNIOR...

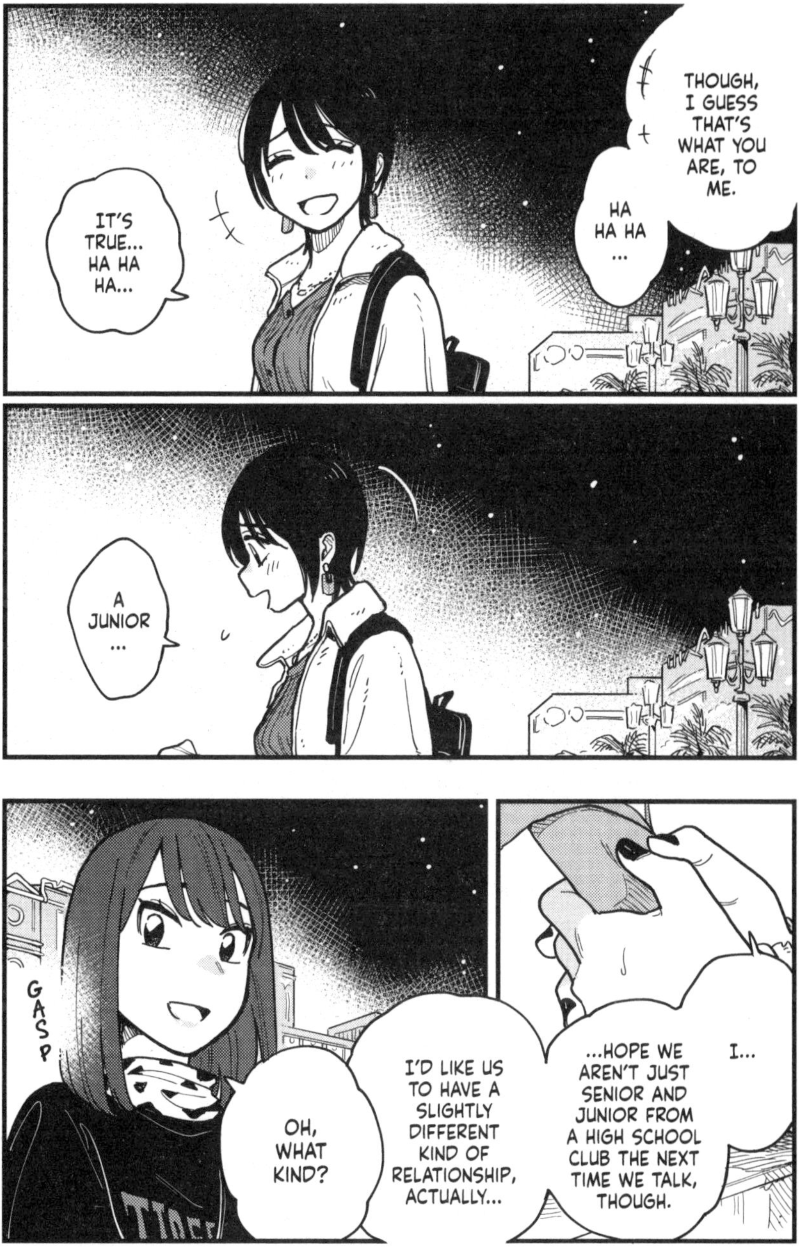
THOUGH, I GUESS THAT'S WHAT YOU ARE, TO ME.
HA HA HA ...
IT'S TRUE... HA HA HA...
A JUNIOR ...
I...
...HOPE WE AREN'T JUST SENIOR AND JUNIOR FROM A HIGH SCHOOL CLUB THE NEXT TIME WE TALK, THOUGH.
I'D LIKE US TO HAVE A SLIGHTLY DIFFERENT KIND OF RELATIONSHIP, ACTUALLY...
OH, WHAT KIND?
GASP

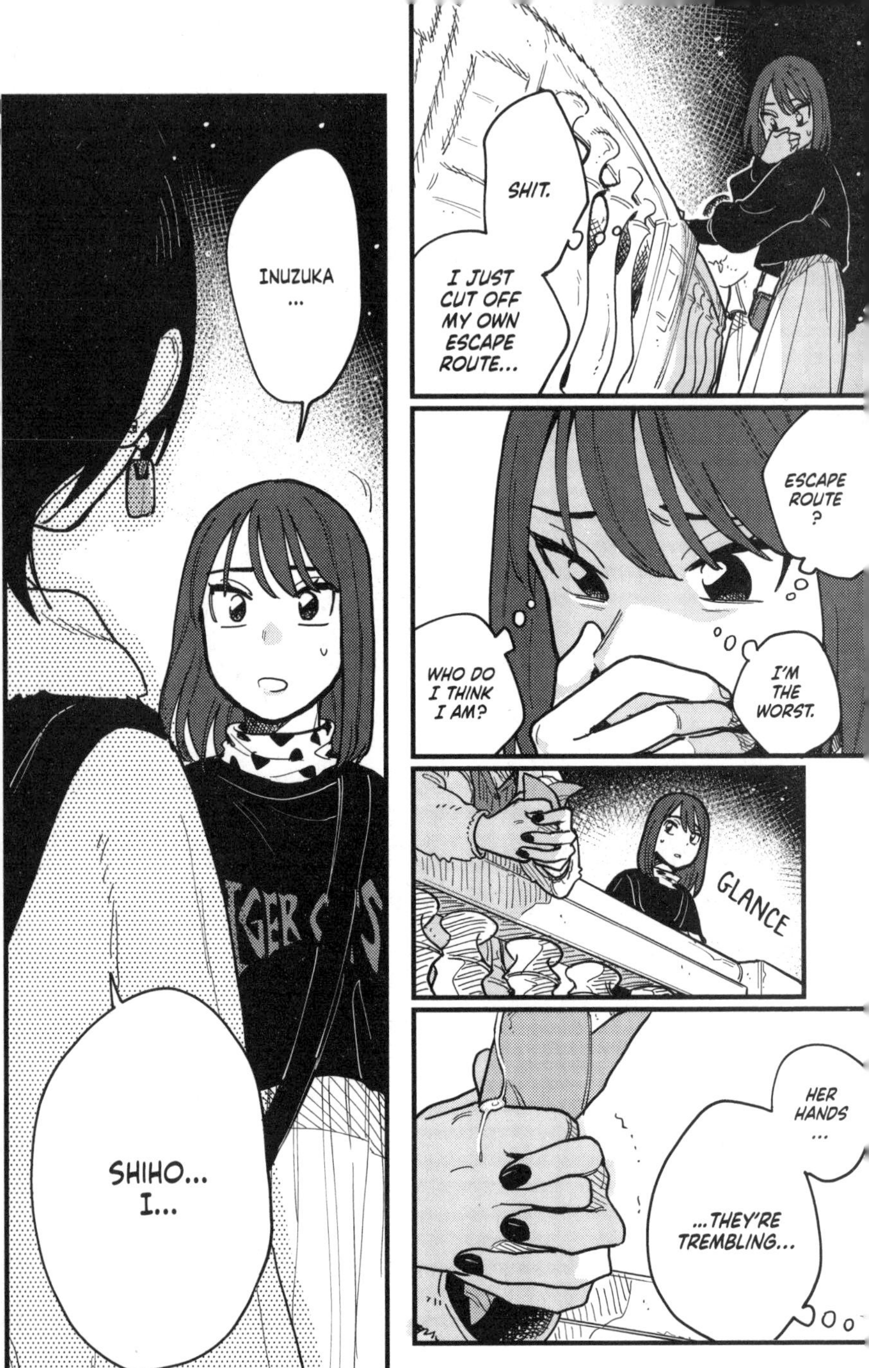

SHIT.
I JUST CUT OFF MY OWN ESCAPE ROUTE...
ESCAPE ROUTE?
I'M THE WORST.
WHO DO I THINK I AM?
GLANCE
HER HANDS...
...THEY'RE TREMBLING...
INUZUKA...
SHIHO... I...

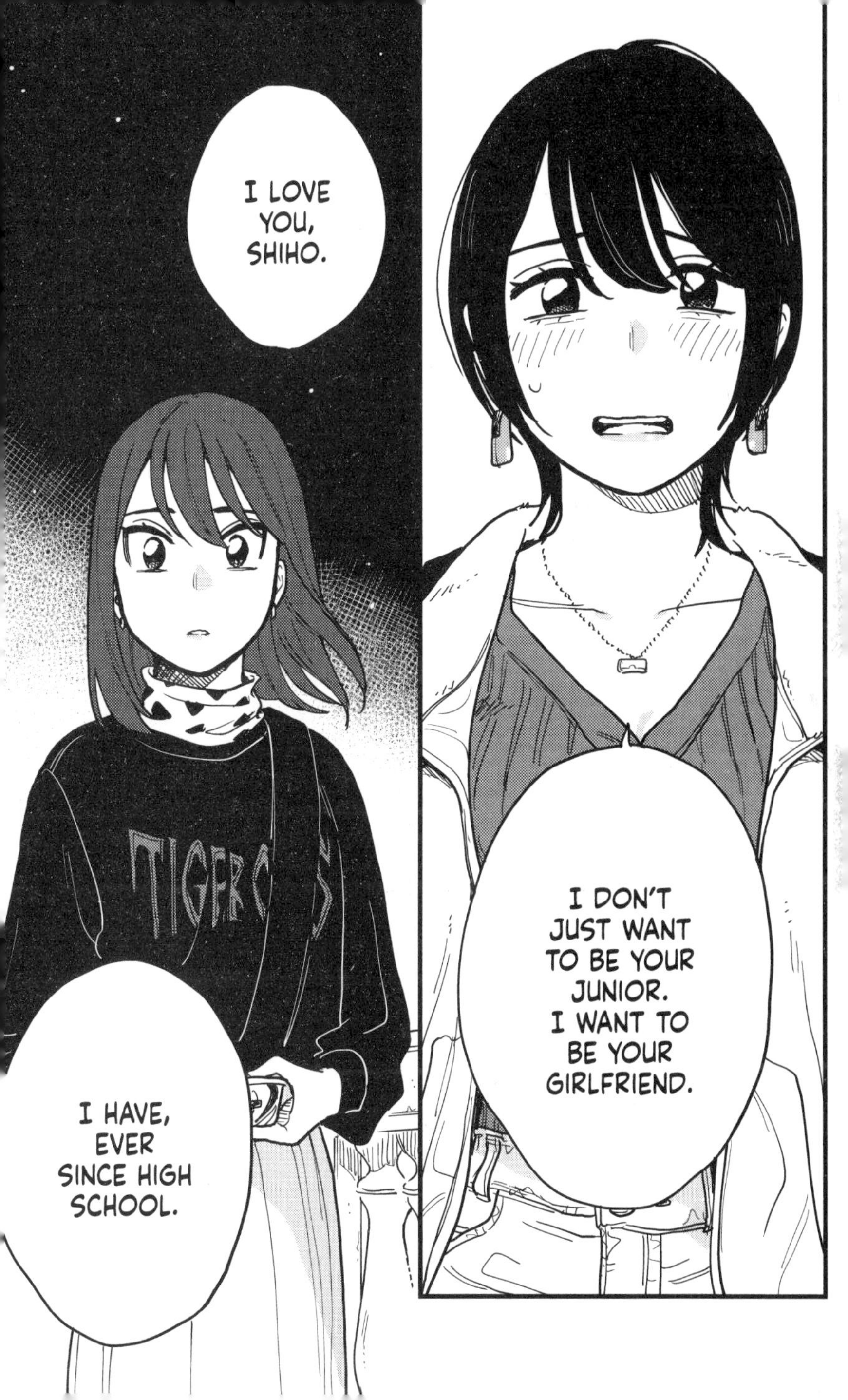
I DON'T JUST WANT TO BE YOUR JUNIOR. I WANT TO BE YOUR GIRLFRIEND.
I LOVE YOU, SHIHO.
I HAVE, EVER SINCE HIGH SCHOOL.

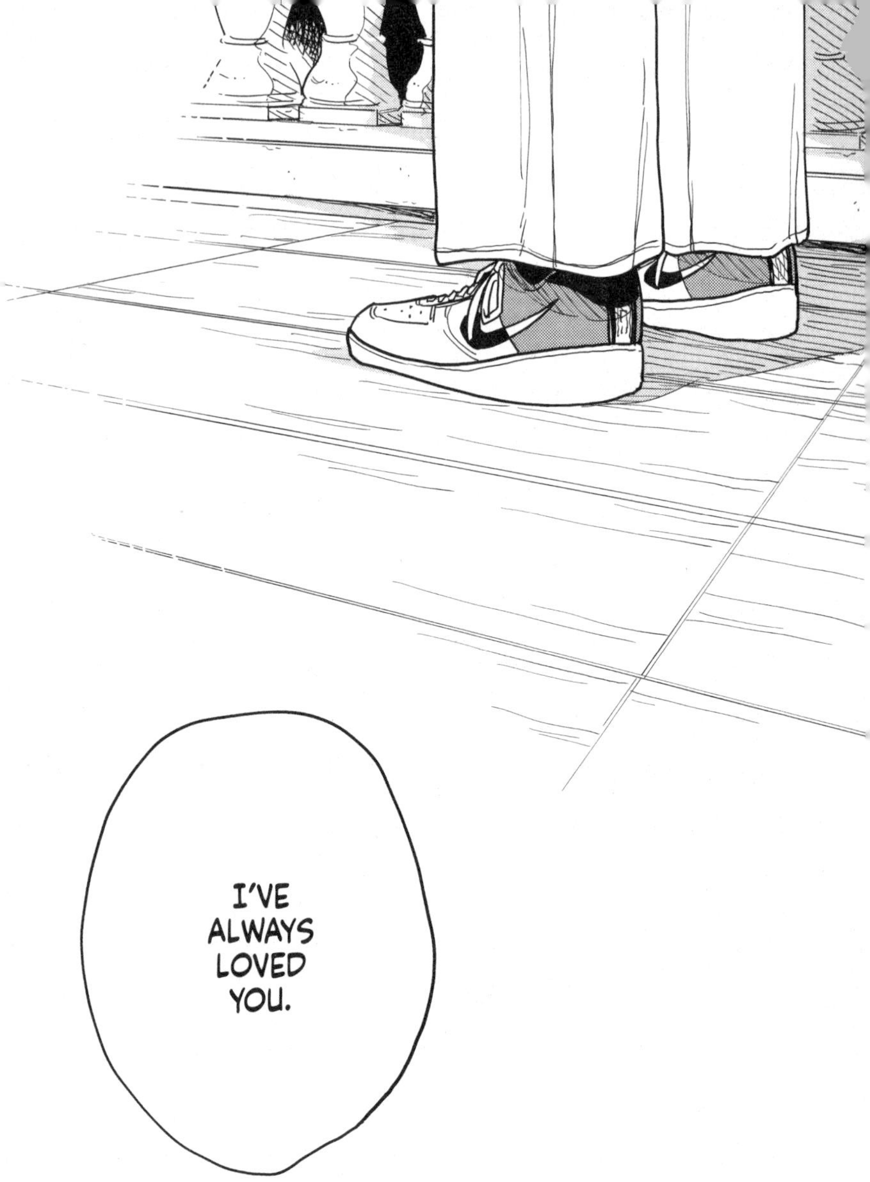
I'VE ALWAYS LOVED YOU.

How Do We
Relationship?

How Do We Relationship?

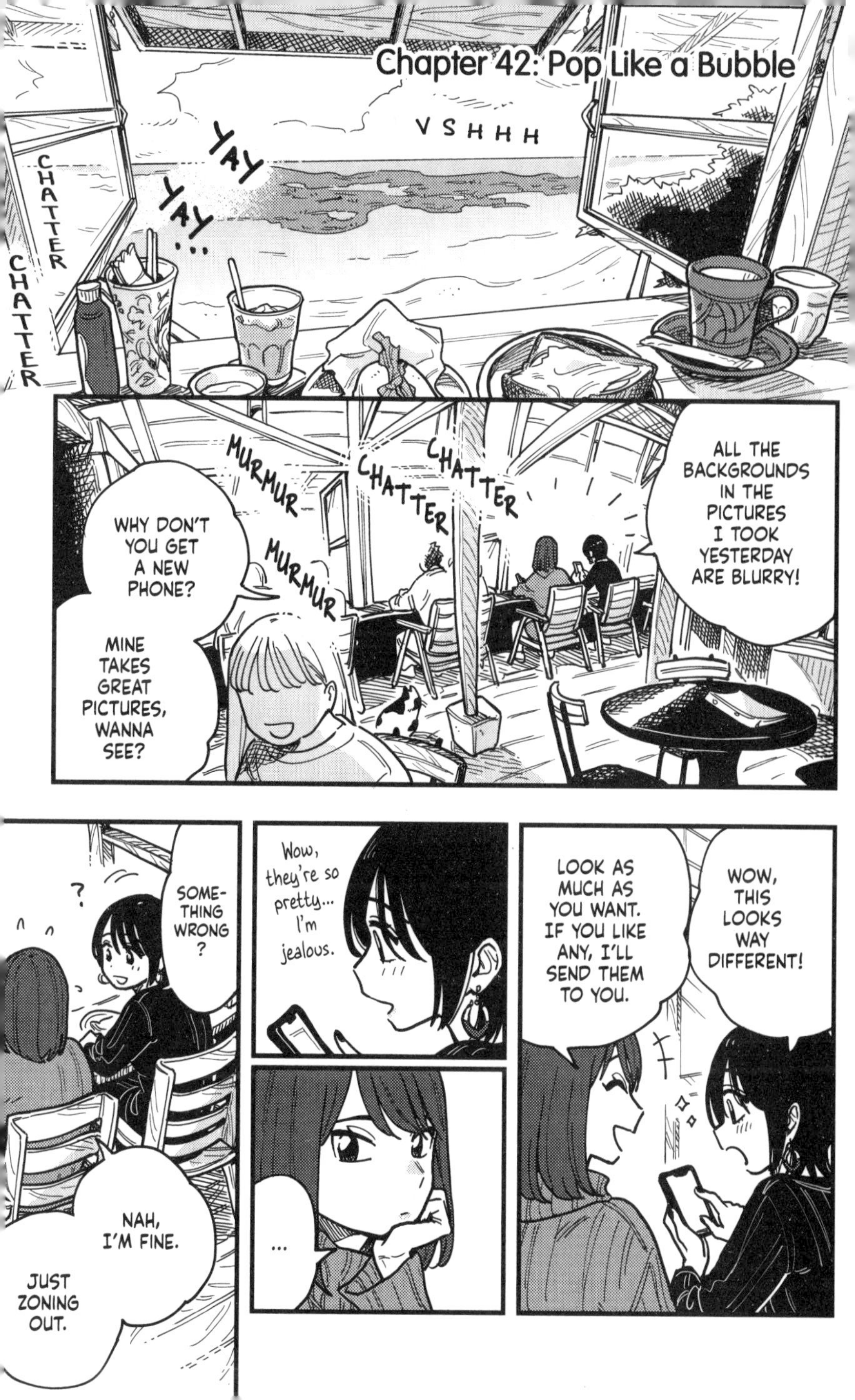
Chapter 42: Pop Like a Bubble
VSHHHH
YAY YAY...
CHATTER CHATTER
ALL THE BACKGROUNDS IN THE PICTURES I TOOK YESTERDAY ARE BLURRY!
CHATTER CHATTER
MURMUR MURMUR
WHY DON'T YOU GET A NEW PHONE?
MINE TAKES GREAT PICTURES, WANNA SEE?
WOW, THIS LOOKS WAY DIFFERENT!
LOOK AS MUCH AS YOU WANT. IF YOU LIKE ANY, I'LL SEND THEM TO YOU.
Wow, they're so pretty... I'm jealous.
...
SOME-THING WRONG?
?
NAH, I'M FINE.
JUST ZONING OUT.

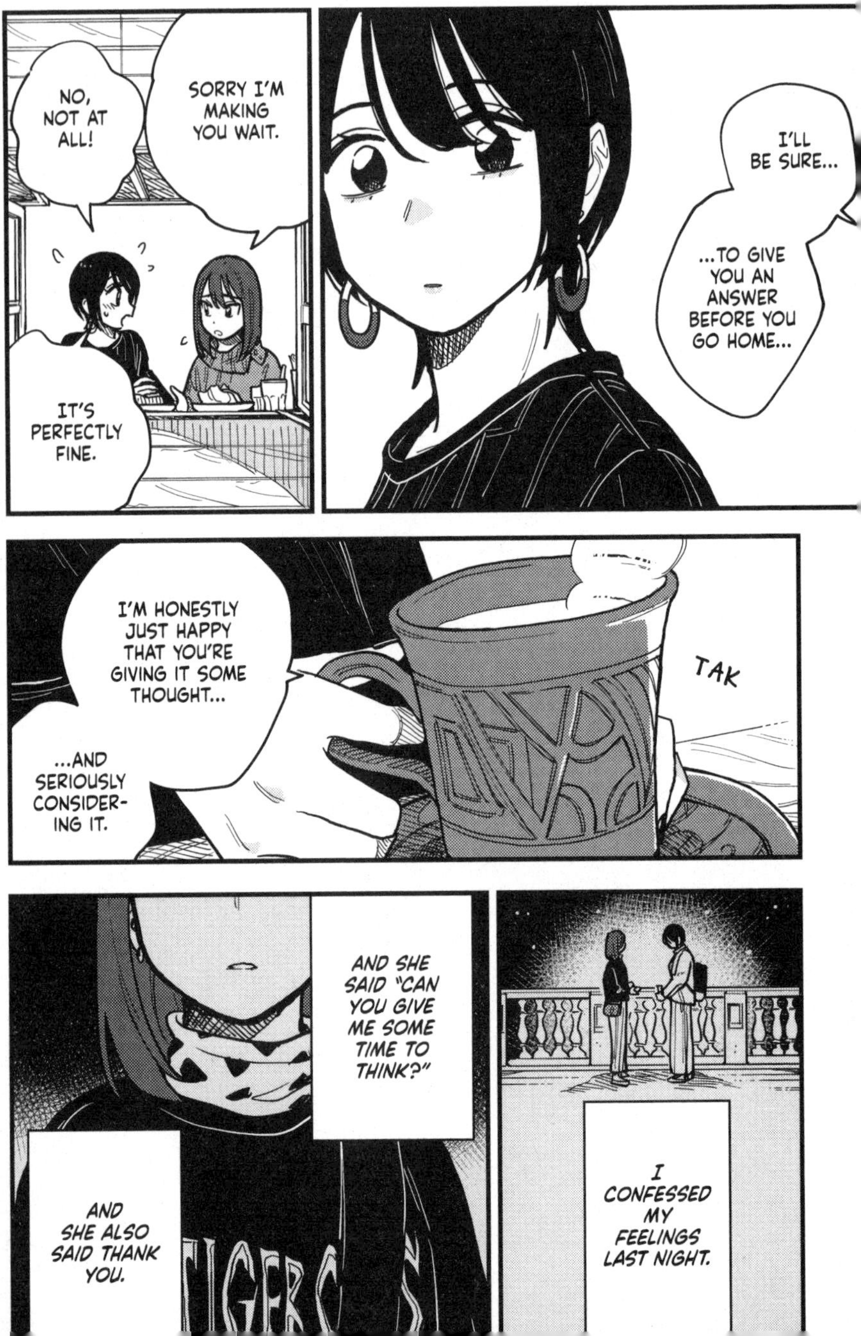
I'LL BE SURE...
...TO GIVE YOU AN ANSWER BEFORE YOU GO HOME...
SORRY I'M MAKING YOU WAIT.
NO, NOT AT ALL!
IT'S PERFECTLY FINE.
TAK
I'M HONESTLY JUST HAPPY THAT YOU'RE GIVING IT SOME THOUGHT...
...AND SERIOUSLY CONSIDER-ING IT.
I CONFESSED MY FEELINGS LAST NIGHT.
AND SHE SAID "CAN YOU GIVE ME SOME TIME TO THINK?"
AND SHE ALSO SAID THANK YOU.

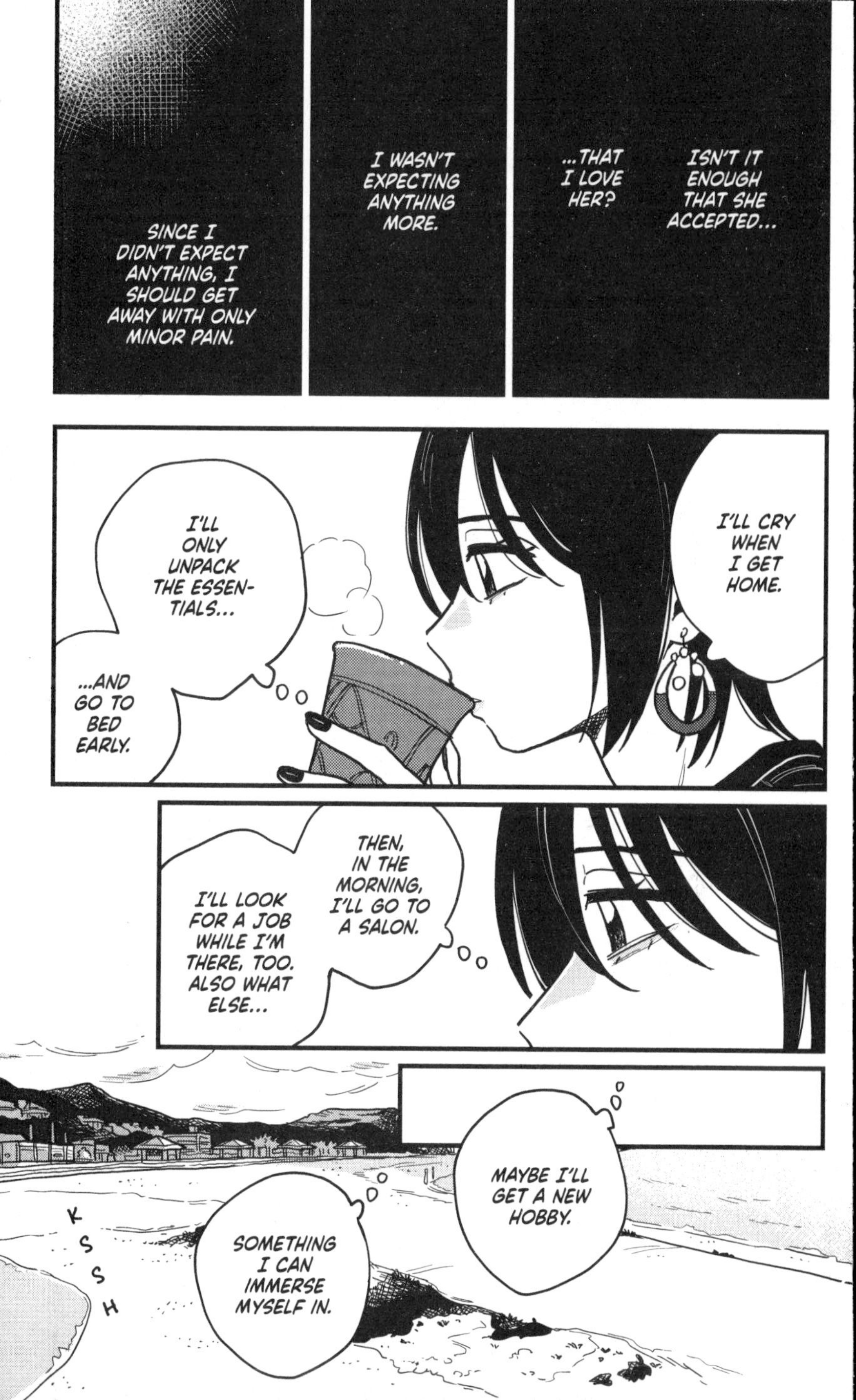
ISN'T IT ENOUGH THAT SHE ACCEPTED...
...THAT I LOVE HER?
I WASN'T EXPECTING ANYTHING MORE.
SINCE I DIDN'T EXPECT ANYTHING, I SHOULD GET AWAY WITH ONLY MINOR PAIN.
I'LL CRY WHEN I GET HOME.
I'LL ONLY UNPACK THE ESSEN-TIALS...
...AND GO TO BED EARLY.
THEN, IN THE MORNING, I'LL GO TO A SALON.
I'LL LOOK FOR A JOB WHILE I'M THERE, TOO. ALSO WHAT ELSE...
MAYBE I'LL GET A NEW HOBBY.
SOMETHING I CAN IMMERSE MYSELF IN.
KSSH

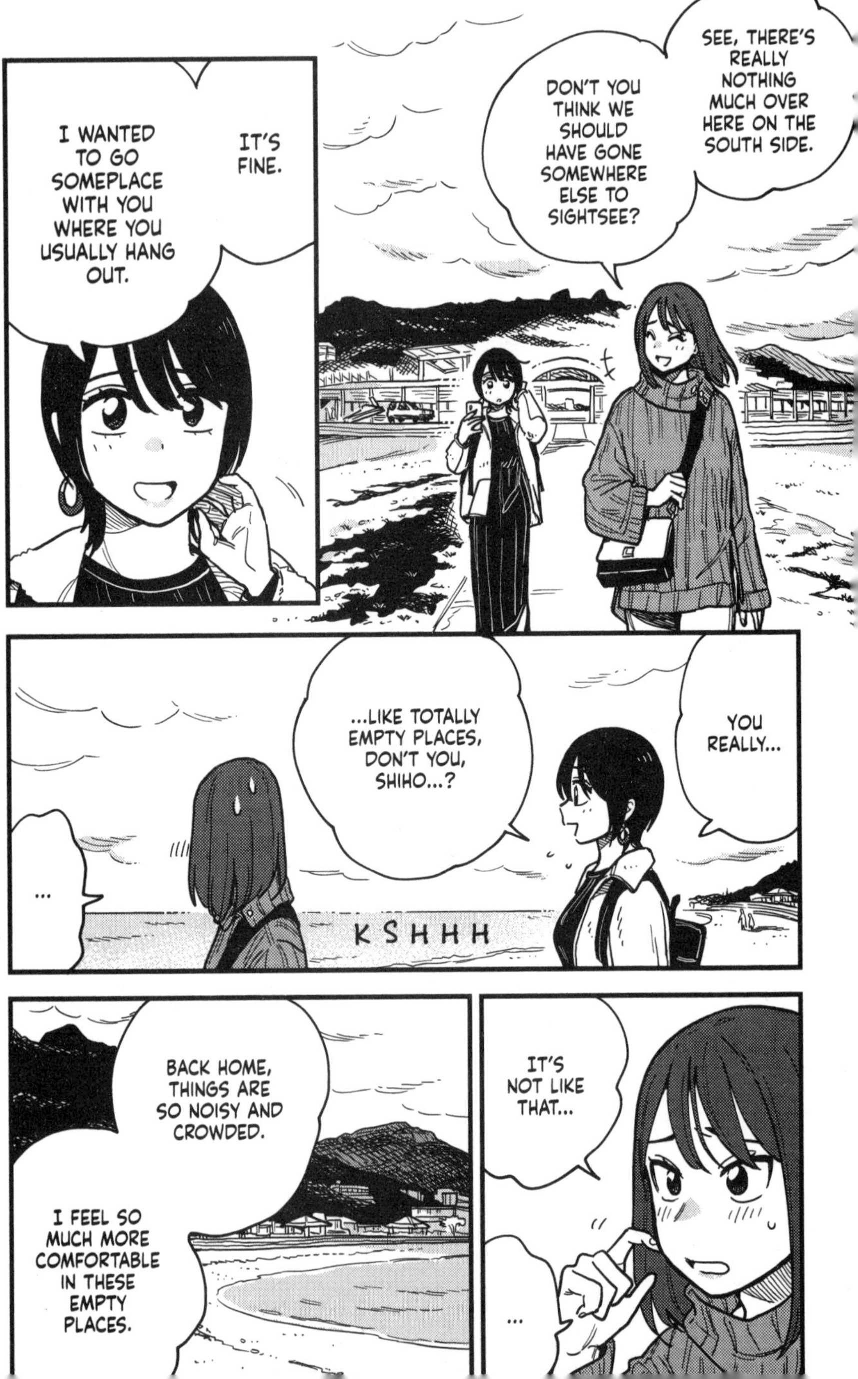
SEE, THERE'S REALLY NOTHING MUCH OVER HERE ON THE SOUTH SIDE.
DON'T YOU THINK WE SHOULD HAVE GONE SOMEWHERE ELSE TO SIGHTSEE?
IT'S FINE.
I WANTED TO GO SOMEPLACE WITH YOU WHERE YOU USUALLY HANG OUT.
YOU REALLY...
...LIKE TOTALLY EMPTY PLACES, DON'T YOU, SHIHO...?
KSHHH
...
IT'S NOT LIKE THAT...
...
BACK HOME, THINGS ARE SO NOISY AND CROWDED.
I FEEL SO MUCH MORE COMFORTABLE IN THESE EMPTY PLACES.

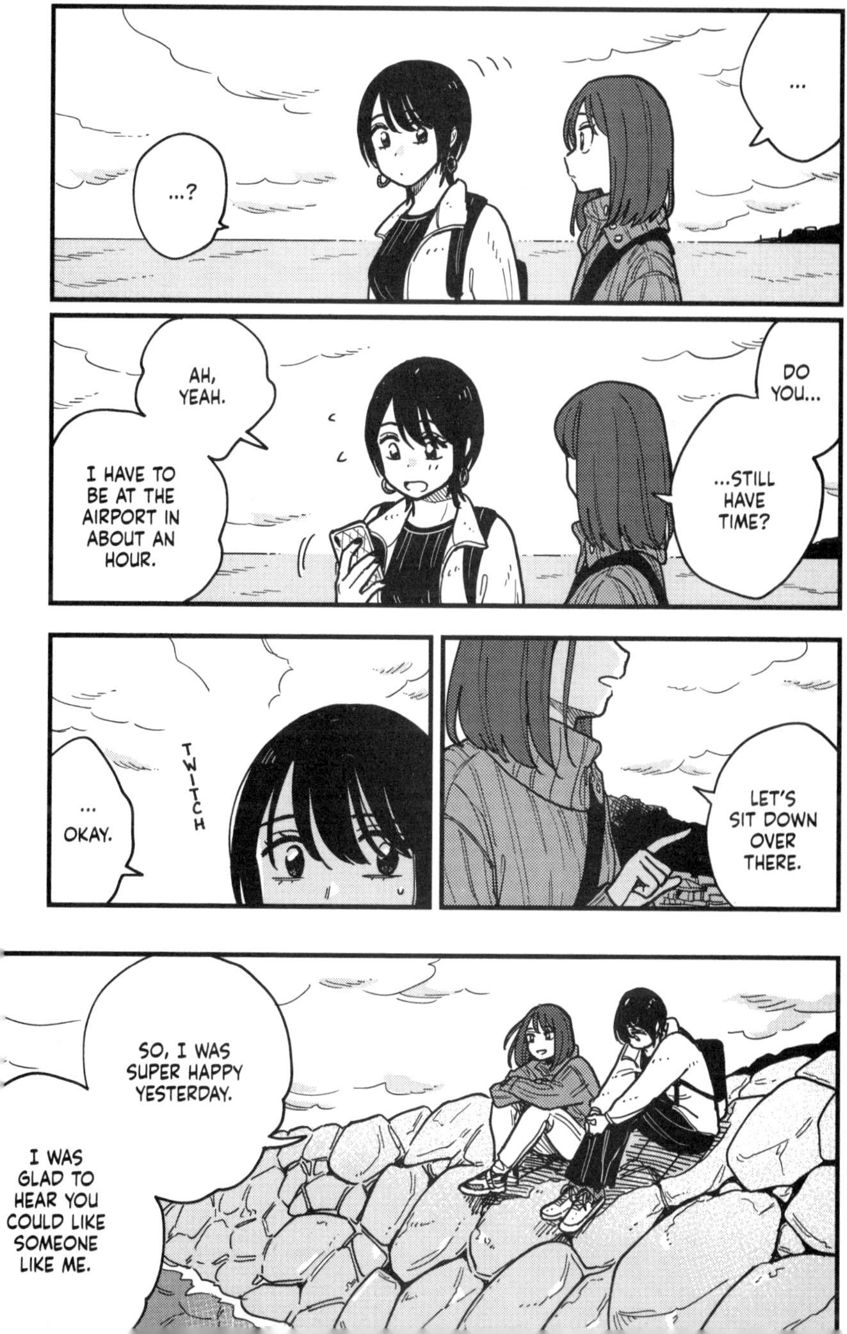
...
...?
DO YOU...
...STILL HAVE TIME?
AH, YEAH.
I HAVE TO BE AT THE AIRPORT IN ABOUT AN HOUR.
LET'S SIT DOWN OVER THERE.
TWITCH
... OKAY.
SO, I WAS SUPER HAPPY YESTERDAY.
I WAS GLAD TO HEAR YOU COULD LIKE SOMEONE LIKE ME.

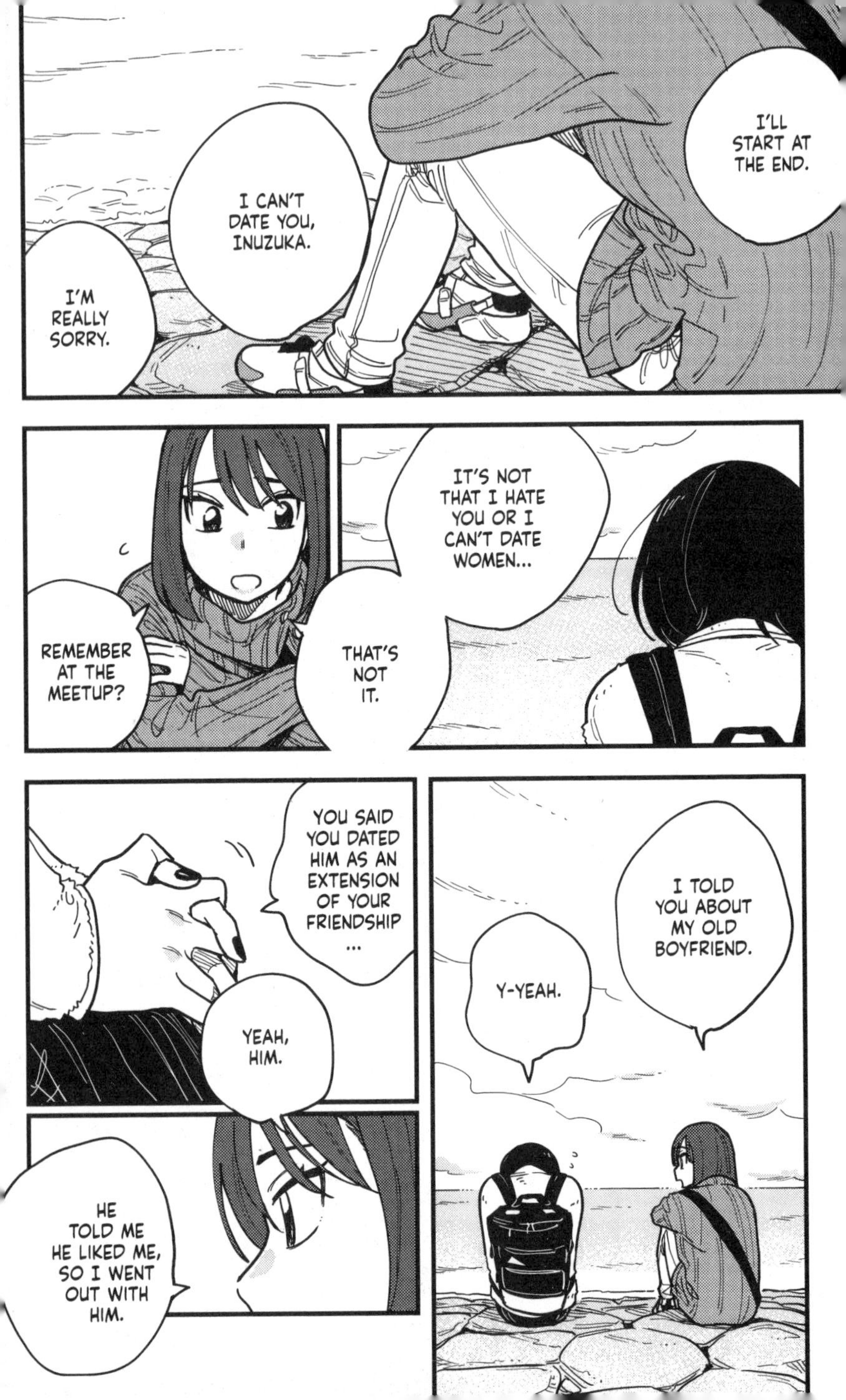
I'LL START AT THE END.
I CAN'T DATE YOU, INUZUKA.
I'M REALLY SORRY.
IT'S NOT THAT I HATE YOU OR I CAN'T DATE WOMEN...
THAT'S NOT IT.
REMEMBER AT THE MEETUP?
I TOLD YOU ABOUT MY OLD BOYFRIEND.
Y-YEAH.
YOU SAID YOU DATED HIM AS AN EXTENSION OF YOUR FRIENDSHIP ...
YEAH, HIM.
HE TOLD ME HE LIKED ME, SO I WENT OUT WITH HIM.

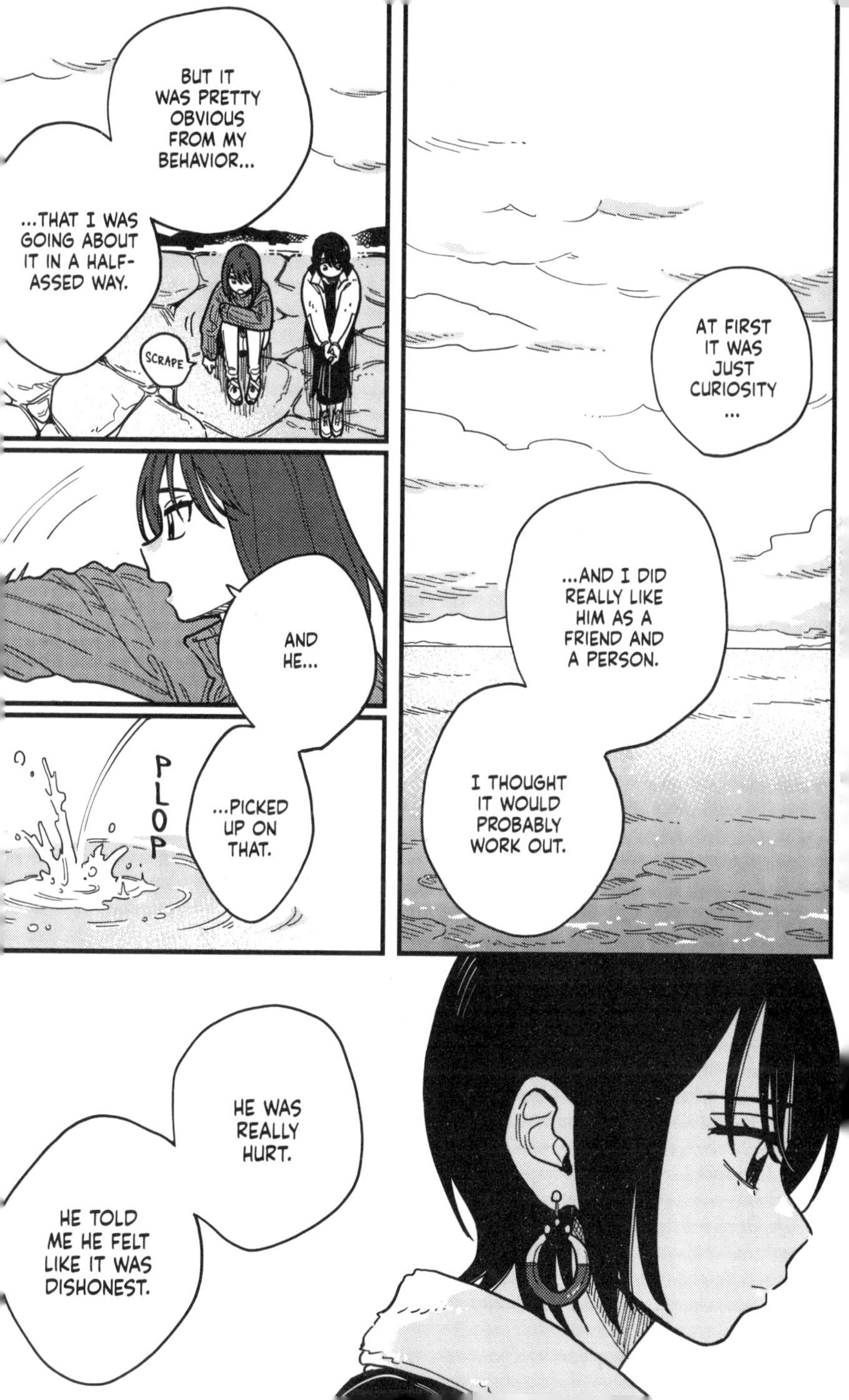
AT FIRST IT WAS JUST CURIOSITY ...
...AND I DID REALLY LIKE HIM AS A FRIEND AND A PERSON.
I THOUGHT IT WOULD PROBABLY WORK OUT.
BUT IT WAS PRETTY OBVIOUS FROM MY BEHAVIOR...
...THAT I WAS GOING ABOUT IT IN A HALF-ASSED WAY.
SCRAPE
AND HE...
...PICKED UP ON THAT.
PLOP
HE WAS REALLY HURT.
HE TOLD ME HE FELT LIKE IT WAS DISHONEST.

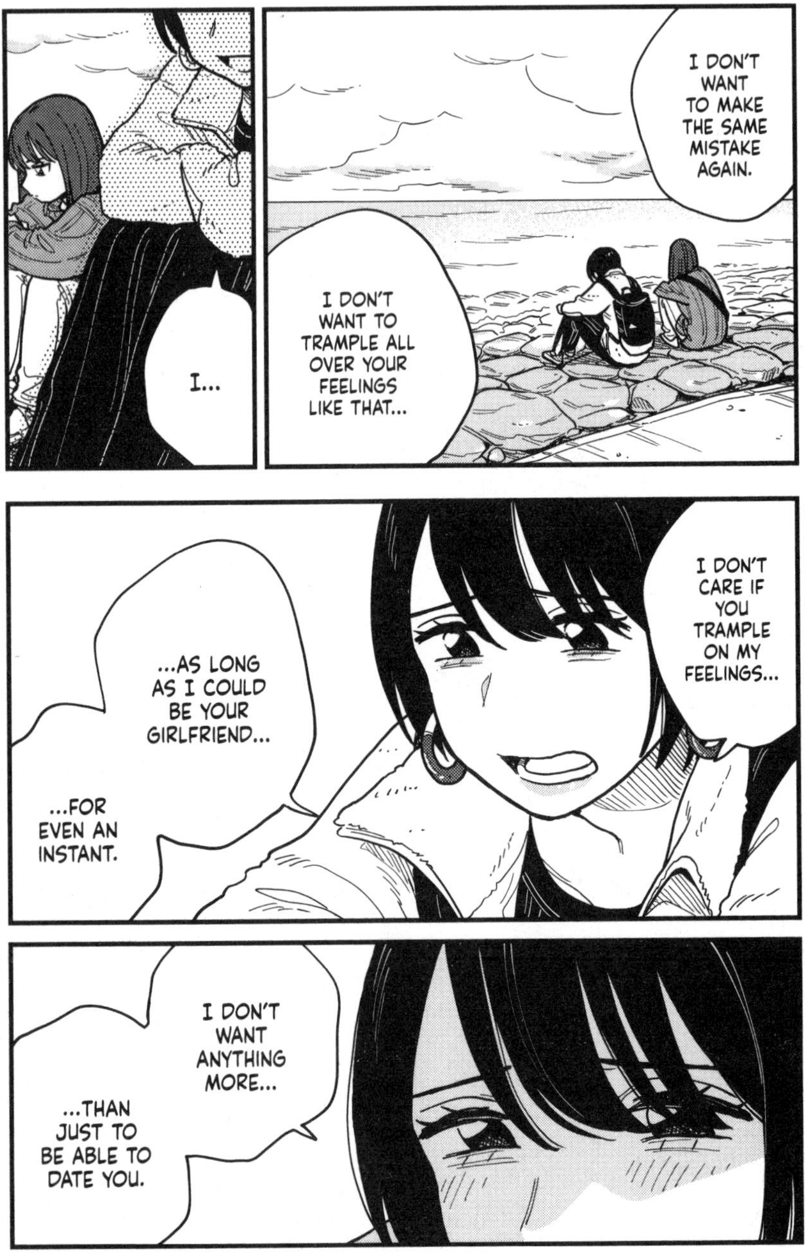
I DON'T WANT TO MAKE THE SAME MISTAKE AGAIN.
I DON'T WANT TO TRAMPLE ALL OVER YOUR FEELINGS LIKE THAT...
I...
I DON'T CARE IF YOU TRAMPLE ON MY FEELINGS...
...AS LONG AS I COULD BE YOUR GIRLFRIEND...
...FOR EVEN AN INSTANT.
I DON'T WANT ANYTHING MORE...
...THAN JUST TO BE ABLE TO DATE YOU.

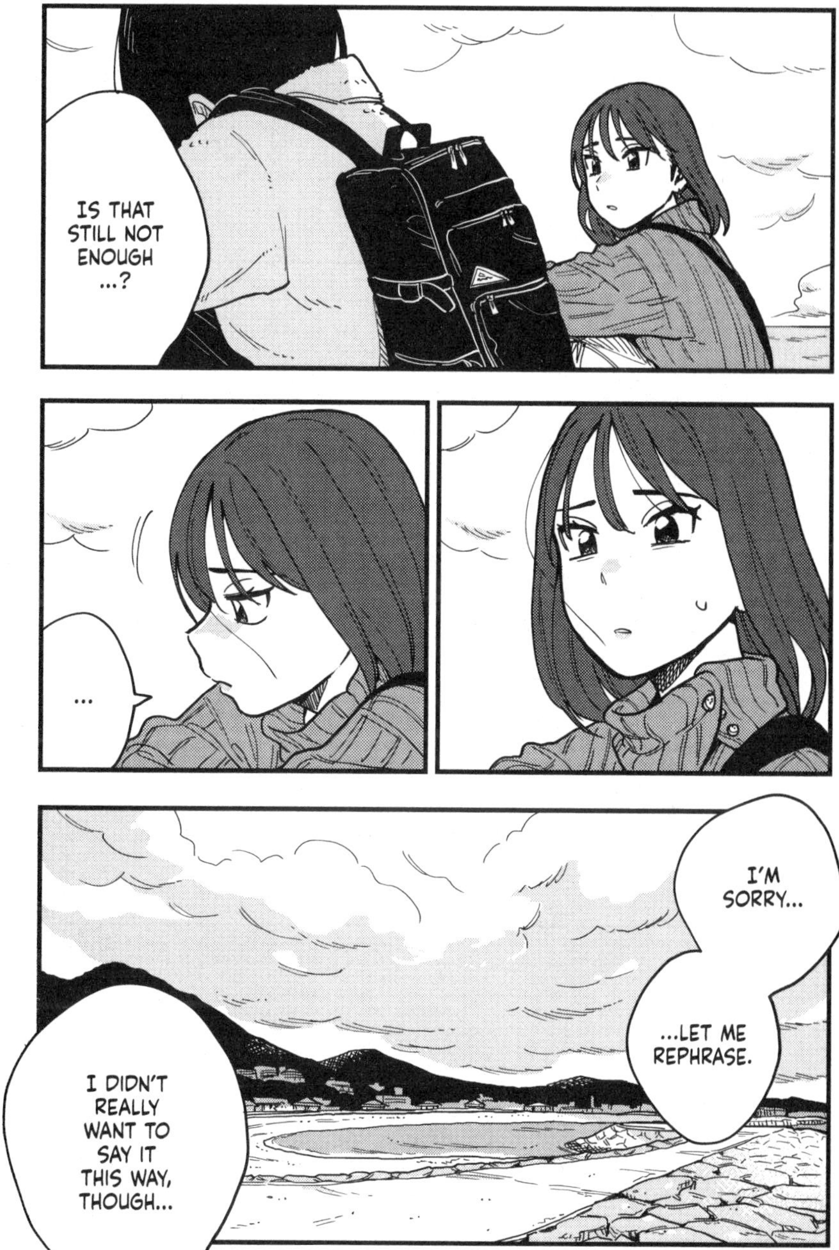
IS THAT STILL NOT ENOUGH ...?
...
I'M SORRY...
...LET ME REPHRASE.
I DIDN'T REALLY WANT TO SAY IT THIS WAY, THOUGH...

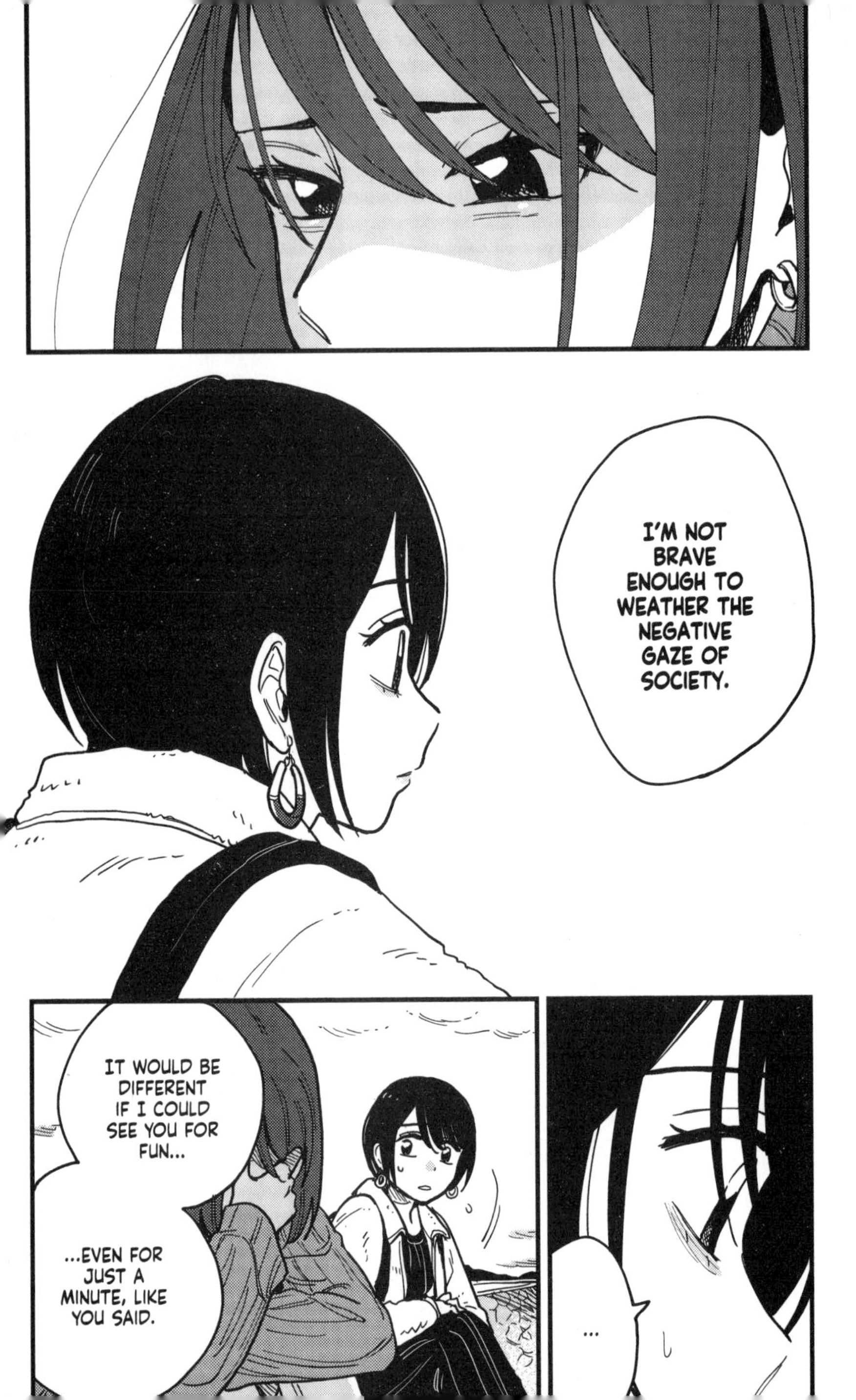
I'M NOT BRAVE ENOUGH TO WEATHER THE NEGATIVE GAZE OF SOCIETY.
...
IT WOULD BE DIFFERENT IF I COULD SEE YOU FOR FUN...
...EVEN FOR JUST A MINUTE, LIKE YOU SAID.

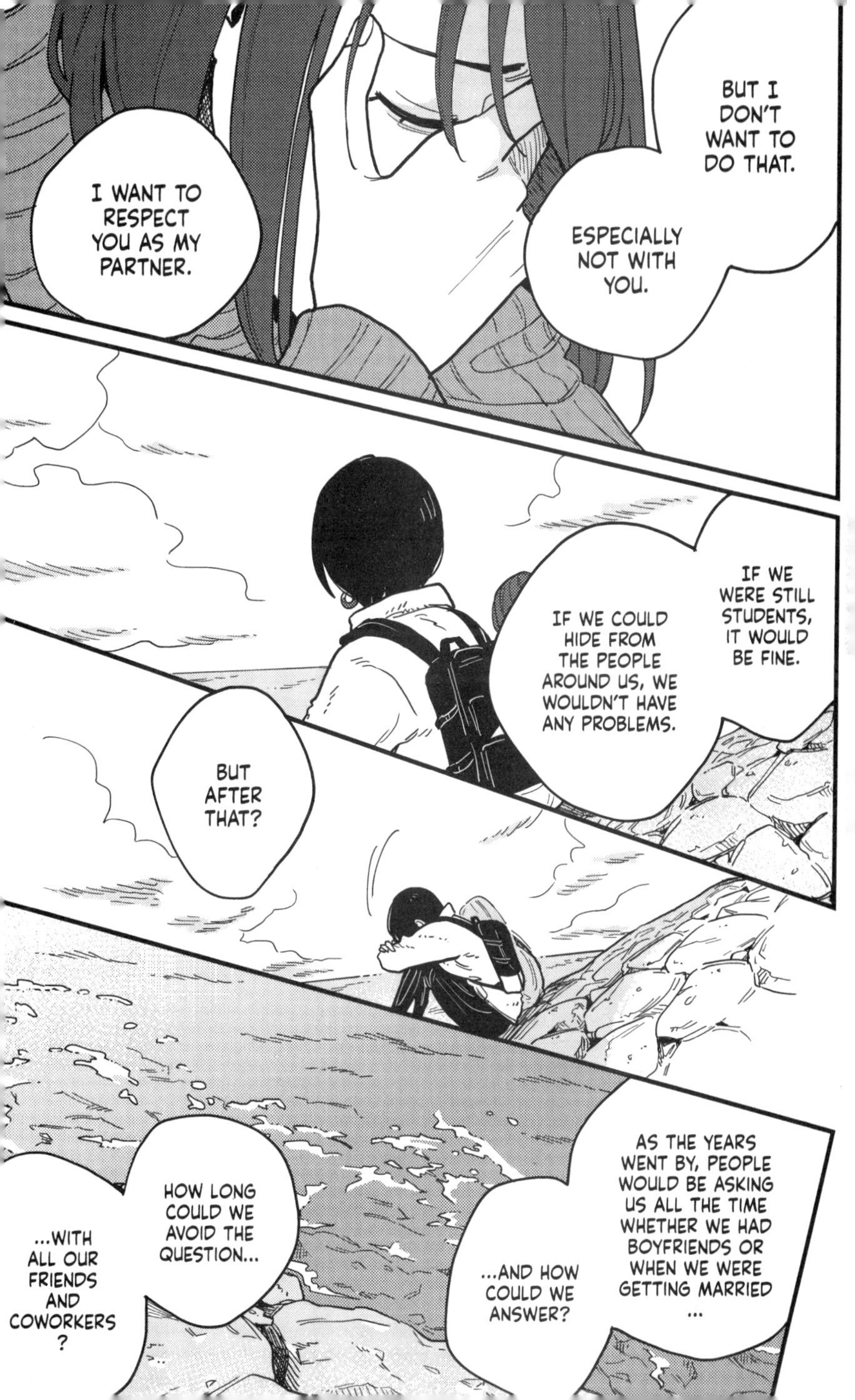
BUT I DON'T WANT TO DO THAT.
ESPECIALLY NOT WITH YOU.
I WANT TO RESPECT YOU AS MY PARTNER.
IF WE WERE STILL STUDENTS, IT WOULD BE FINE.
IF WE COULD HIDE FROM THE PEOPLE AROUND US, WE WOULDN'T HAVE ANY PROBLEMS.
BUT AFTER THAT?
AS THE YEARS WENT BY, PEOPLE WOULD BE ASKING US ALL THE TIME WHETHER WE HAD BOYFRIENDS OR WHEN WE WERE GETTING MARRIED ...
...AND HOW COULD WE ANSWER?
HOW LONG COULD WE AVOID THE QUESTION...
...WITH ALL OUR FRIENDS AND COWORKERS ?

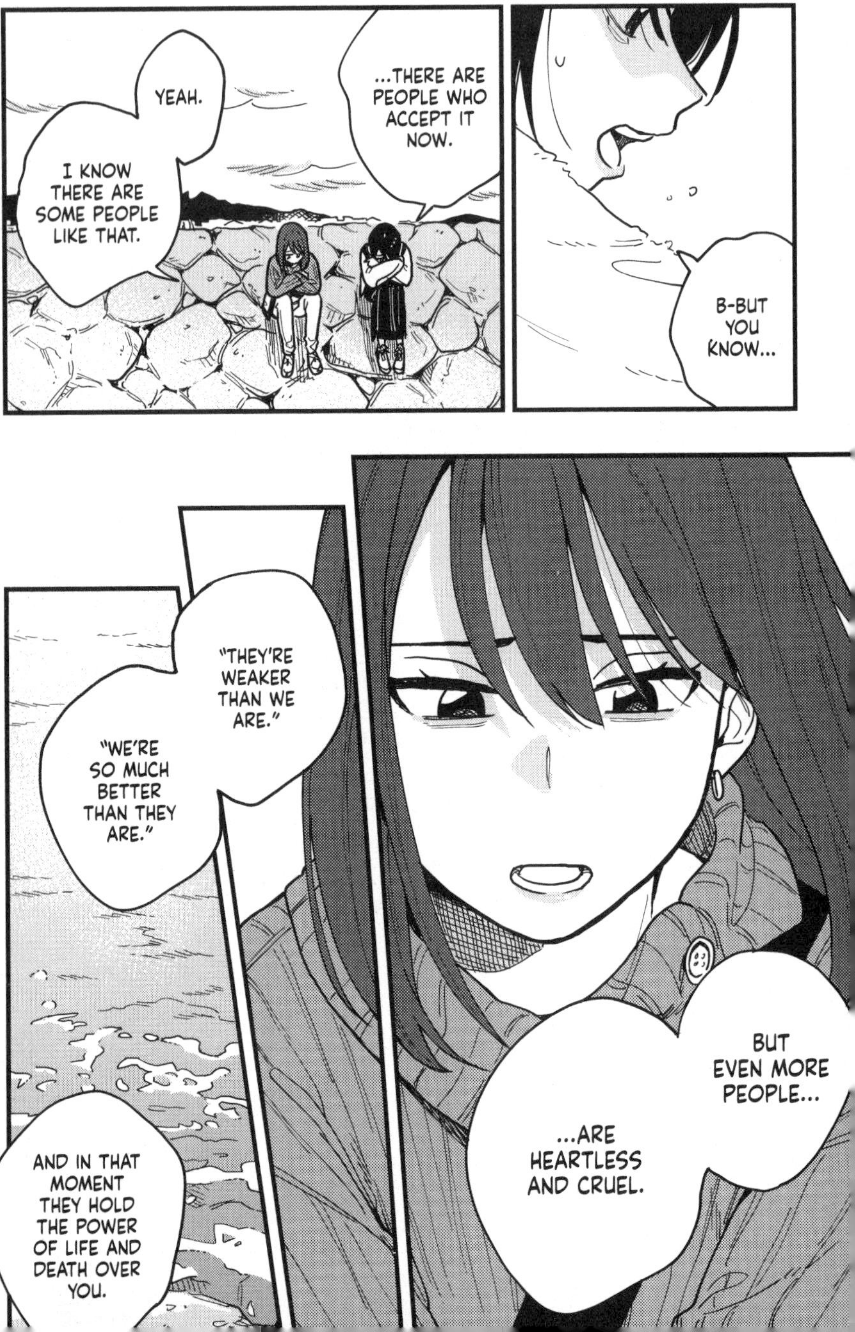
B-BUT YOU KNOW...
...THERE ARE PEOPLE WHO ACCEPT IT NOW.
YEAH.
I KNOW THERE ARE SOME PEOPLE LIKE THAT.
BUT EVEN MORE PEOPLE...
...ARE HEARTLESS AND CRUEL.
"THEY'RE WEAKER THAN WE ARE."
"WE'RE SO MUCH BETTER THAN THEY ARE."
AND IN THAT MOMENT THEY HOLD THE POWER OF LIFE AND DEATH OVER YOU.

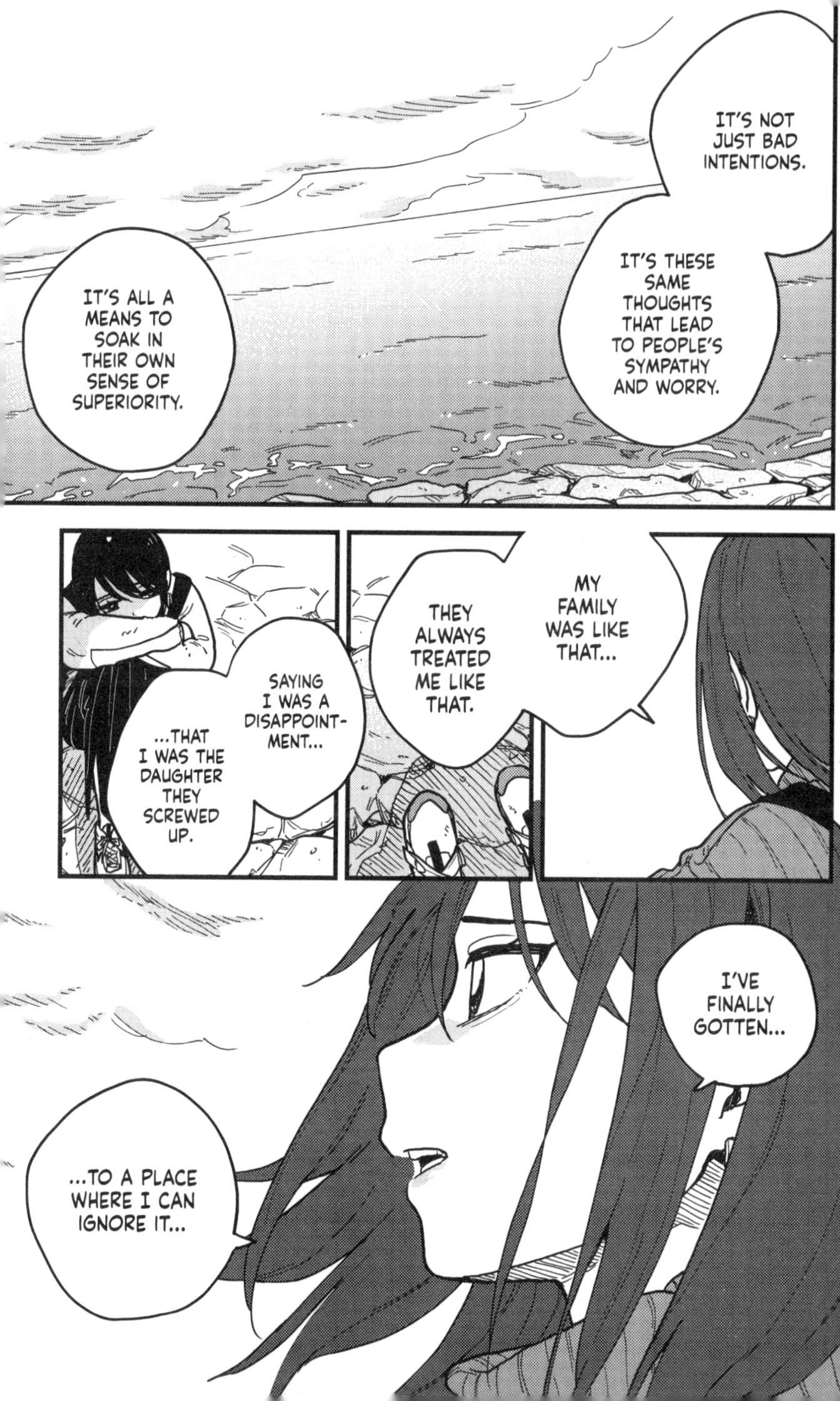
IT'S NOT JUST BAD INTENTIONS.
IT'S THESE SAME THOUGHTS THAT LEAD TO PEOPLE'S SYMPATHY AND WORRY.
IT'S ALL A MEANS TO SOAK IN THEIR OWN SENSE OF SUPERIORITY.
MY FAMILY WAS LIKE THAT...
THEY ALWAYS TREATED ME LIKE THAT.
SAYING I WAS A DISAPPOINT-MENT...
...THAT I WAS THE DAUGHTER THEY SCREWED UP.
I'VE FINALLY GOTTEN...
...TO A PLACE WHERE I CAN IGNORE IT...

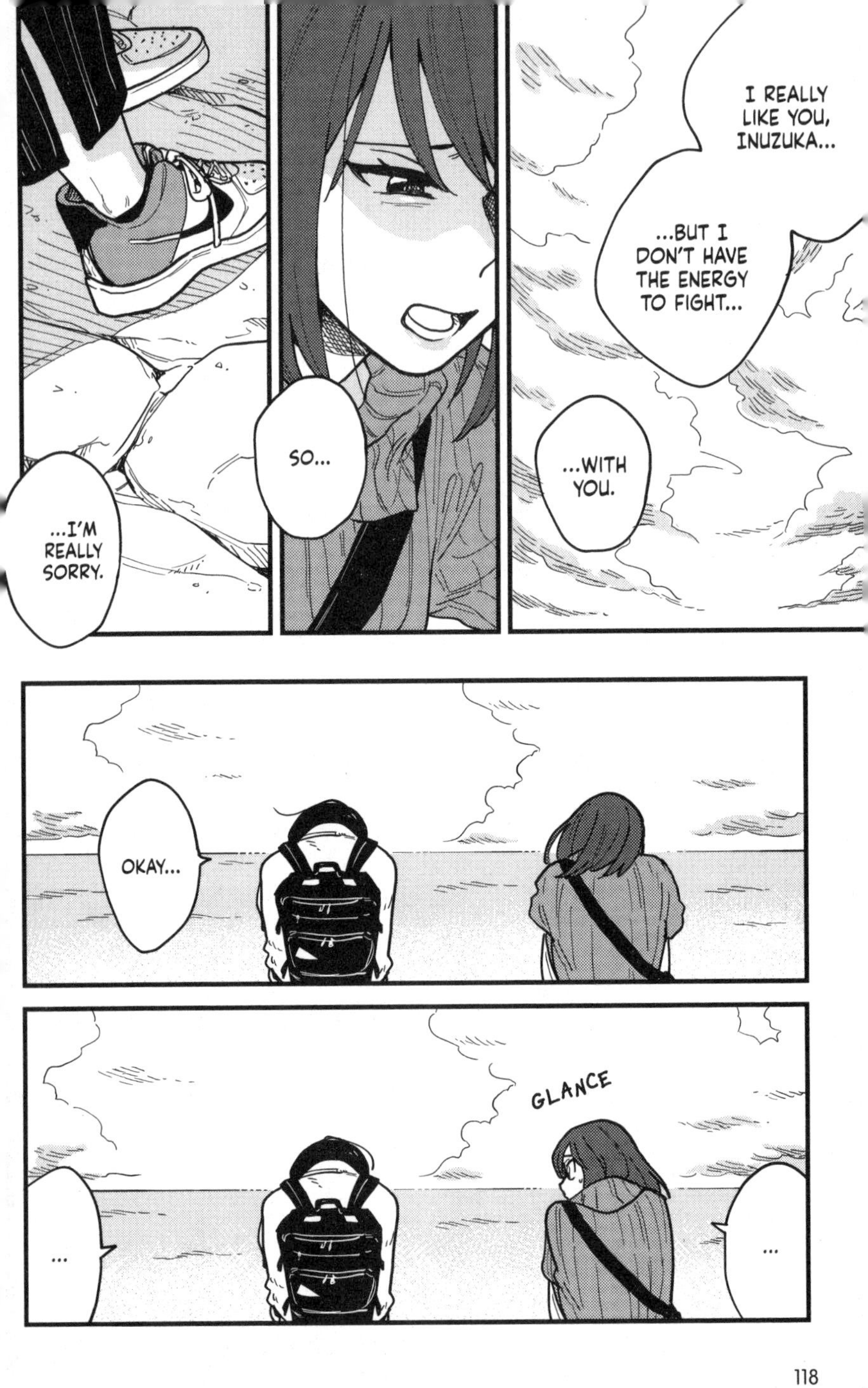
I REALLY LIKE YOU, INUZUKA...
...BUT I DON'T HAVE THE ENERGY TO FIGHT...
...WITH YOU.
SO...
...I'M REALLY SORRY.
OKAY...
GLANCE
...
...

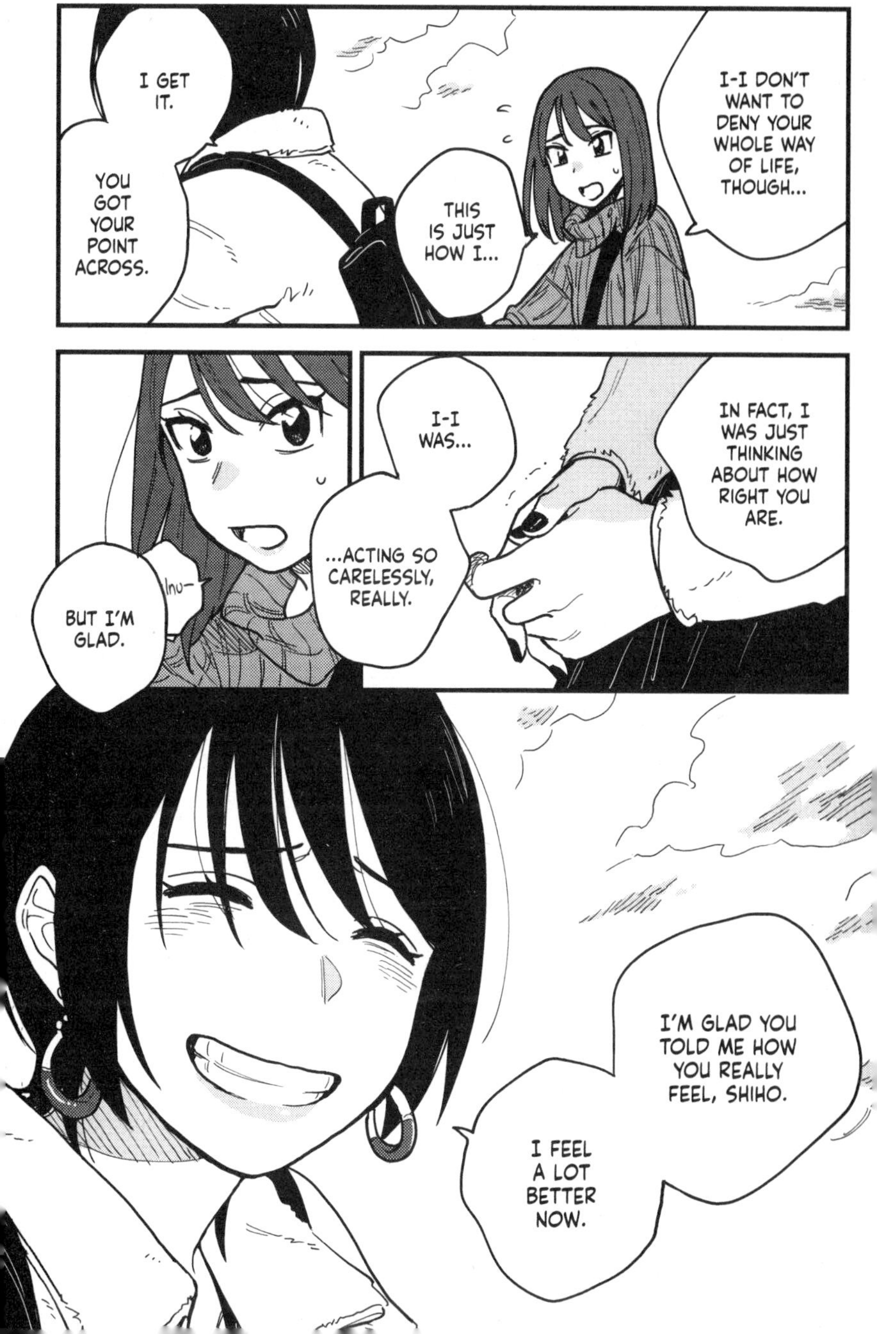
I-I DON'T WANT TO DENY YOUR WHOLE WAY OF LIFE, THOUGH...
THIS IS JUST HOW I...
I GET IT.
YOU GOT YOUR POINT ACROSS.
IN FACT, I WAS JUST THINKING ABOUT HOW RIGHT YOU ARE.
I-I WAS...
...ACTING SO CARELESSLY, REALLY.
Inu-
BUT I'M GLAD.
I'M GLAD YOU TOLD ME HOW YOU REALLY FEEL, SHIHO.
I FEEL A LOT BETTER NOW.

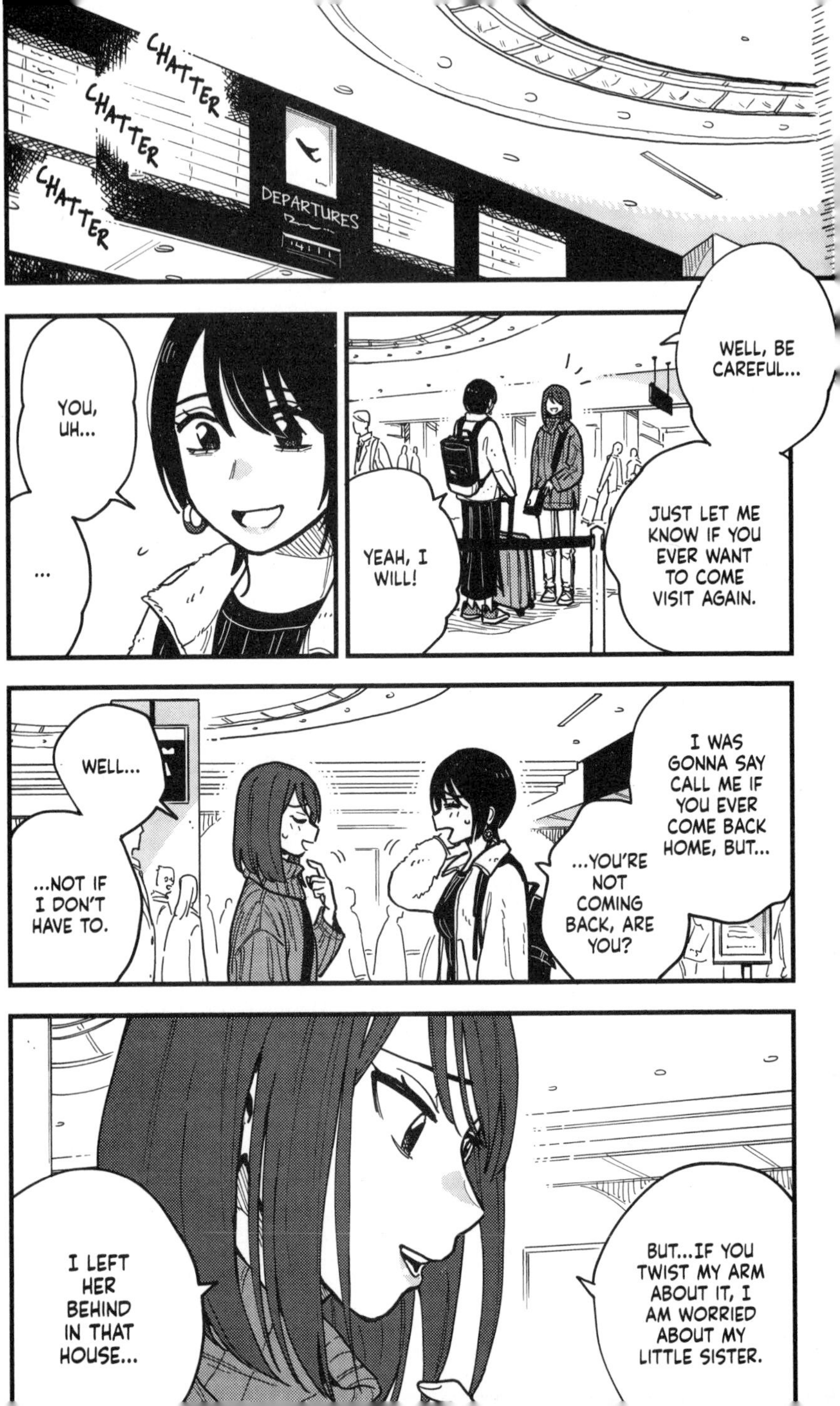
CHATTER
CHATTER
CHATTER
DEPARTURES
WELL, BE CAREFUL...
JUST LET ME KNOW IF YOU EVER WANT TO COME VISIT AGAIN.
YEAH, I WILL!
YOU, UH...
...
I WAS GONNA SAY CALL ME IF YOU EVER COME BACK HOME, BUT...
...YOU'RE NOT COMING BACK, ARE YOU?
WELL...
...NOT IF I DON'T HAVE TO.
BUT...IF YOU TWIST MY ARM ABOUT IT, I AM WORRIED ABOUT MY LITTLE SISTER.
I LEFT HER BEHIND IN THAT HOUSE...

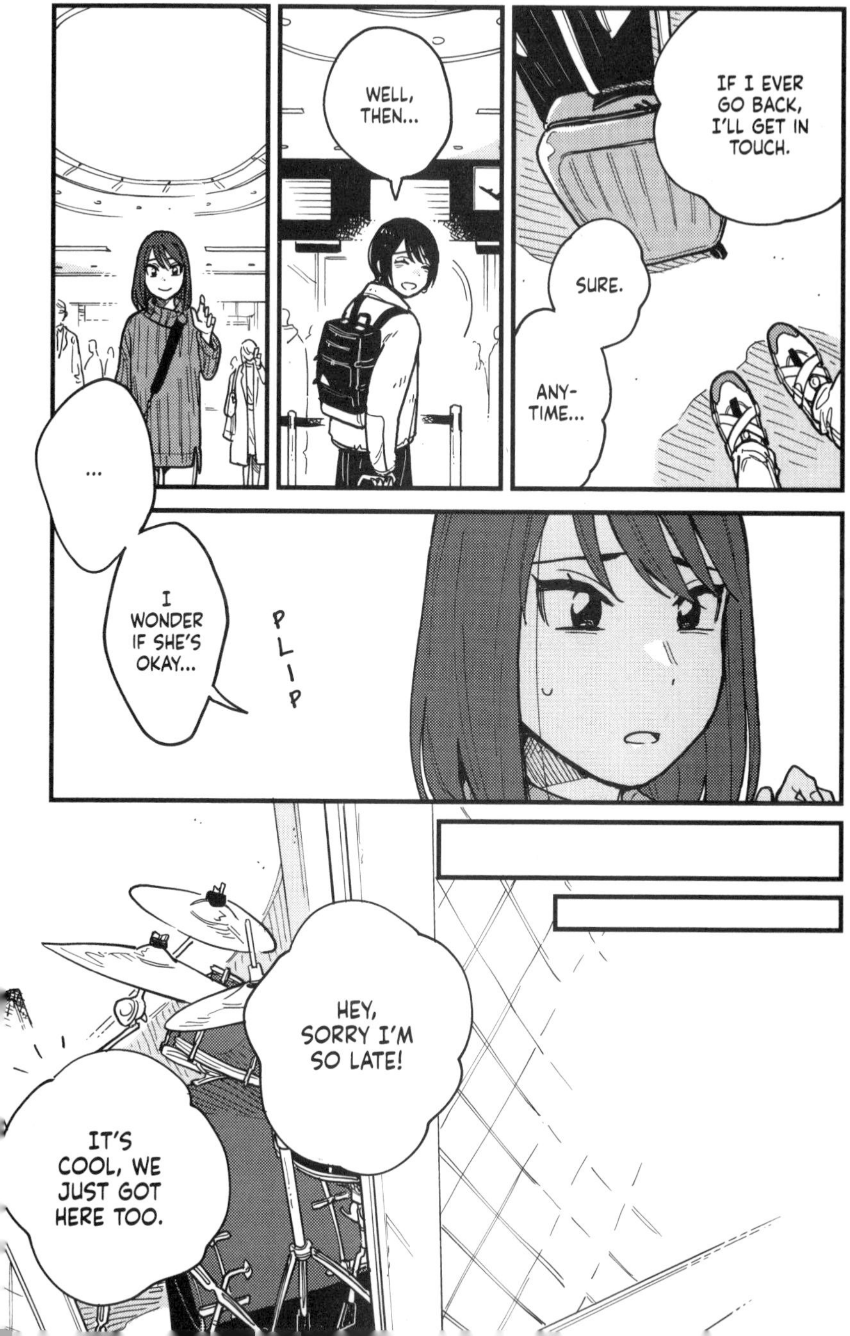
IF I EVER GO BACK, I'LL GET IN TOUCH.
SURE.
ANY-TIME...
WELL, THEN...
...
I WONDER IF SHE'S OKAY...
PLIP
HEY, SORRY I'M SO LATE!
IT'S COOL, WE JUST GOT HERE TOO.

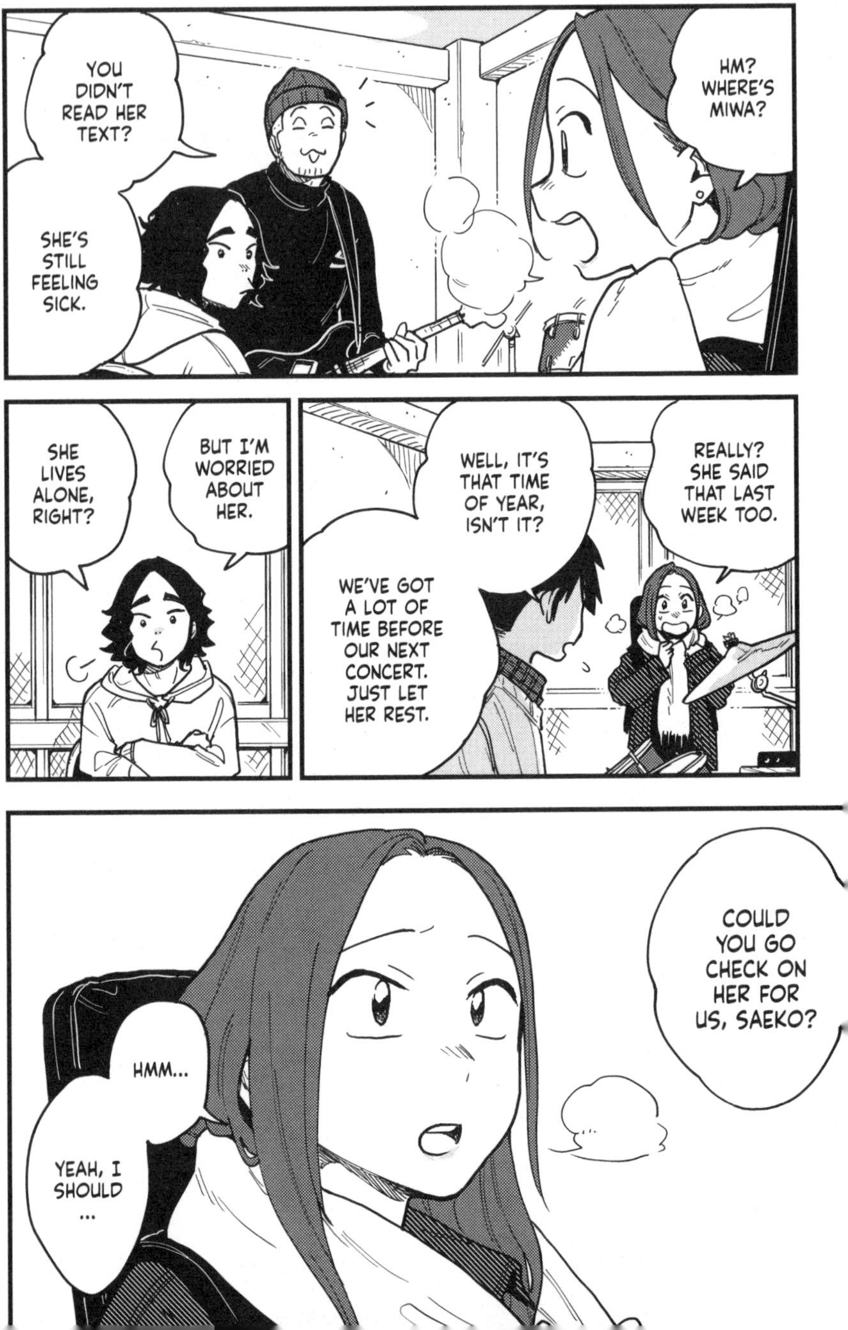
HM? WHERE'S MIWA?
YOU DIDN'T READ HER TEXT?
SHE'S STILL FEELING SICK.
REALLY? SHE SAID THAT LAST WEEK TOO.
WELL, IT'S THAT TIME OF YEAR, ISN'T IT?
WE'VE GOT A LOT OF TIME BEFORE OUR NEXT CONCERT. JUST LET HER REST.
BUT I'M WORRIED ABOUT HER.
SHE LIVES ALONE, RIGHT?
COULD YOU GO CHECK ON HER FOR US, SAEKO?
...
HMM...
YEAH, I SHOULD ...

How Do We RELATIONSHIP?

HOW DO WE RELATIONSHIP?

Chapter 43: Trampling in with Dirty Feet

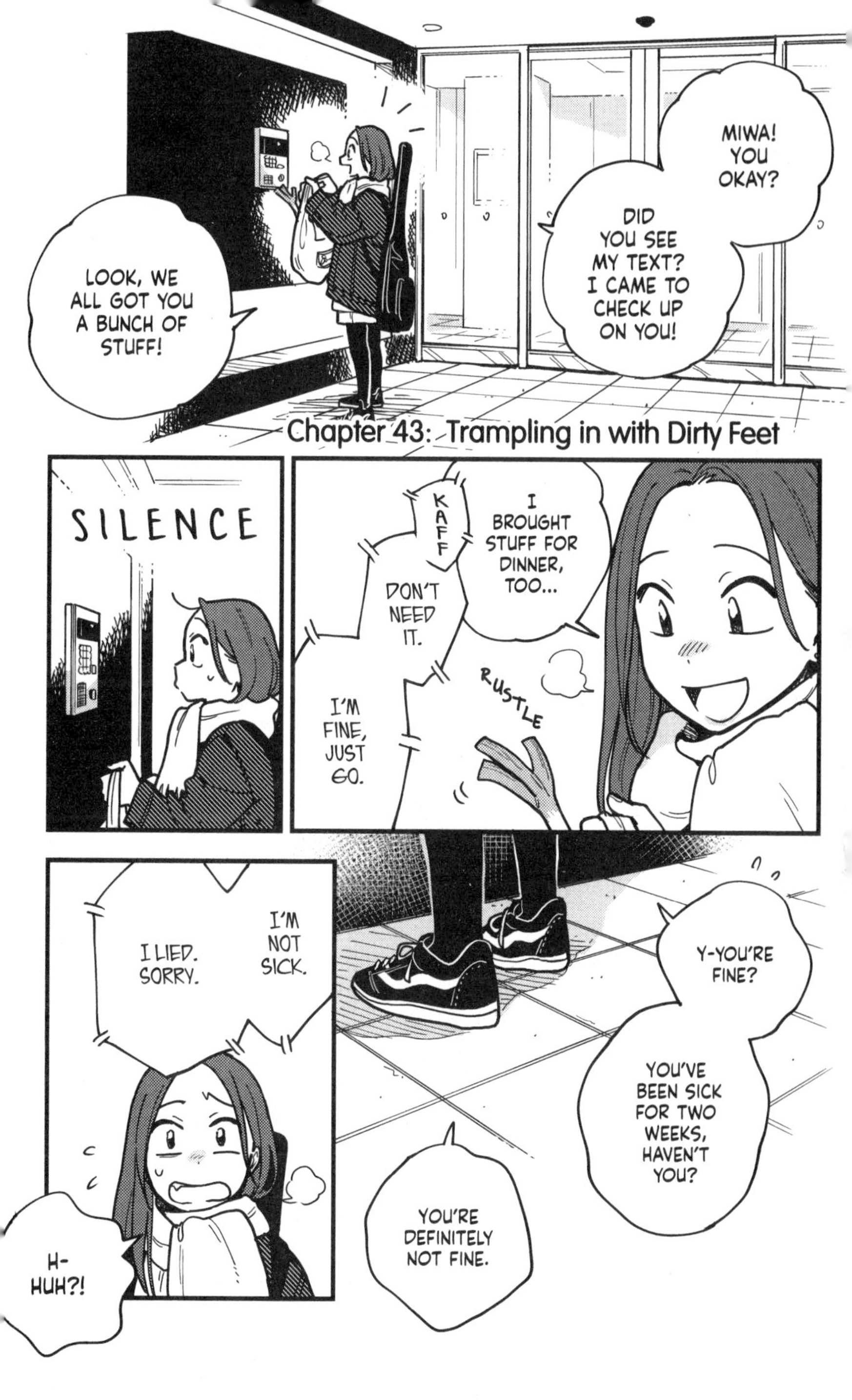
MIWA! YOU OKAY?
DID YOU SEE MY TEXT? I CAME TO CHECK UP ON YOU!
LOOK, WE ALL GOT YOU A BUNCH OF STUFF!
I BROUGHT STUFF FOR DINNER, TOO...
RUSTLE
KAFF
DON'T NEED IT.
I'M FINE, JUST GO.
SILENCE
Y-YOU'RE FINE?
YOU'VE BEEN SICK FOR TWO WEEKS, HAVEN'T YOU?
YOU'RE DEFINITELY NOT FINE.
I'M NOT SICK.
I LIED. SORRY.
H-HUH?!

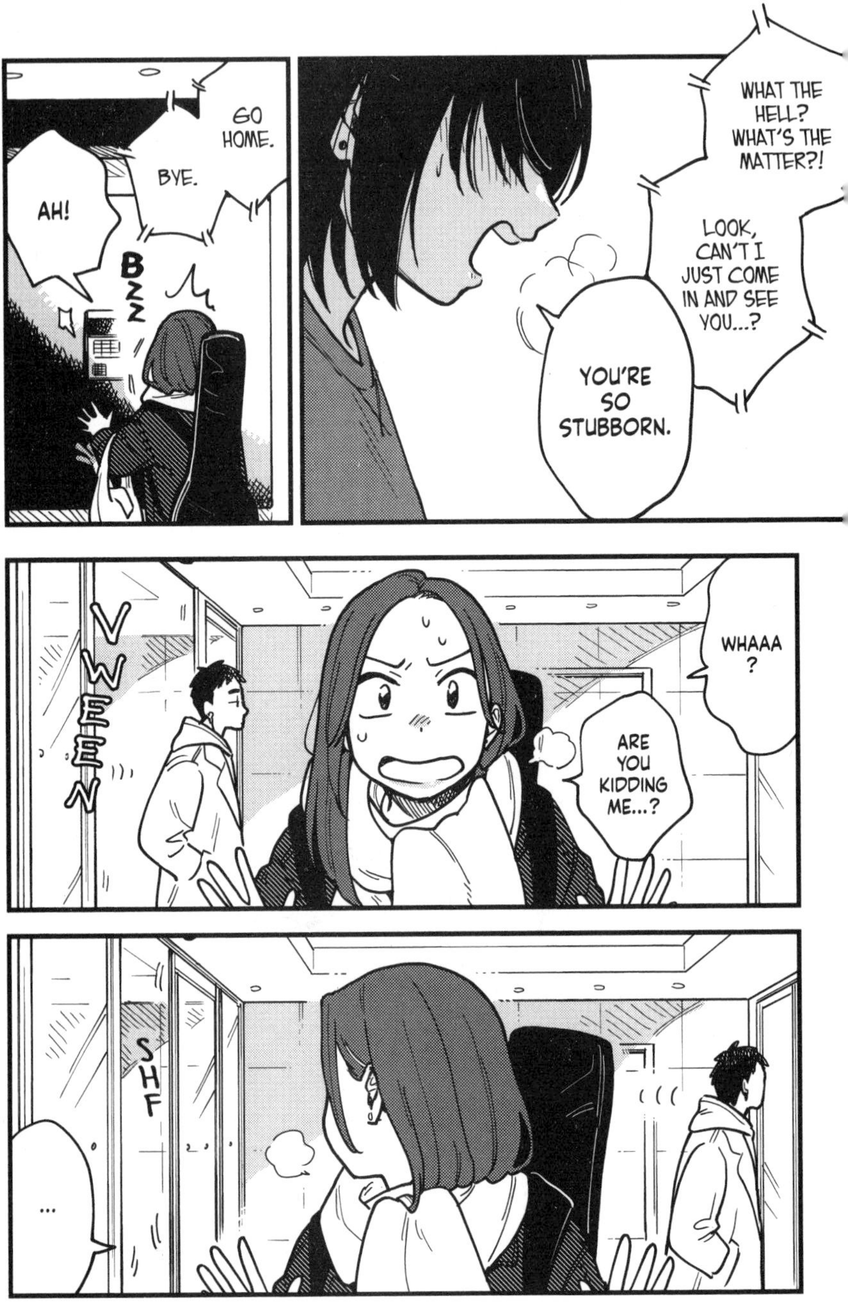
WHAT THE HELL? WHAT'S THE MATTER?!
LOOK, CAN'T I JUST COME IN AND SEE YOU...?
YOU'RE SO STUBBORN.
GO HOME.
BYE.
AH!
BZZ
WHAAA?
ARE YOU KIDDING ME...?
VWEEN
SHF
...

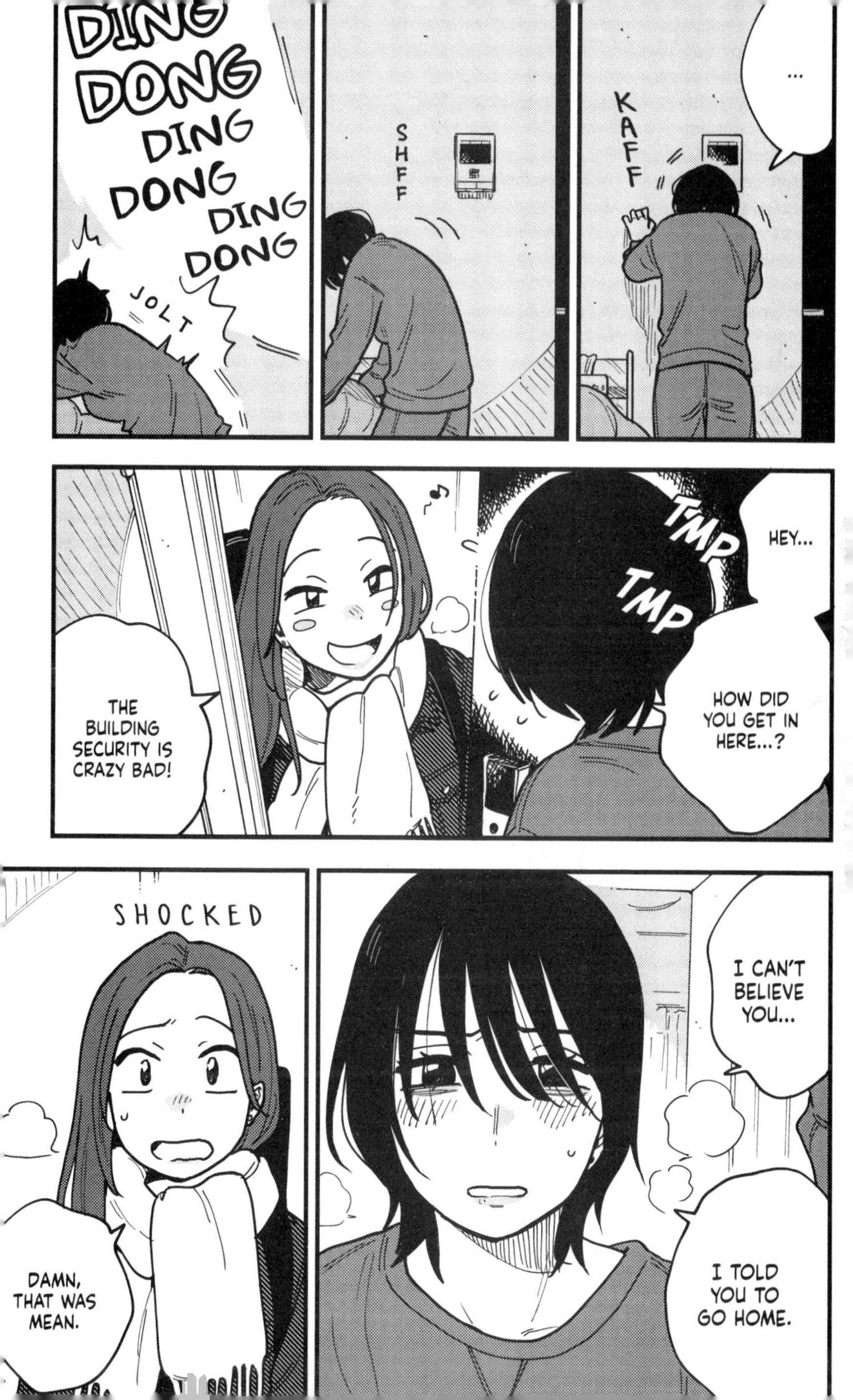
...
KAFF
SHFF
DING DONG
DING DONG
DING DONG
JOLT
HEY...
TMP TMP
HOW DID YOU GET IN HERE...?
THE BUILDING SECURITY IS CRAZY BAD!
I CAN'T BELIEVE YOU...
I TOLD YOU TO GO HOME.
SHOCKED
DAMN, THAT WAS MEAN.

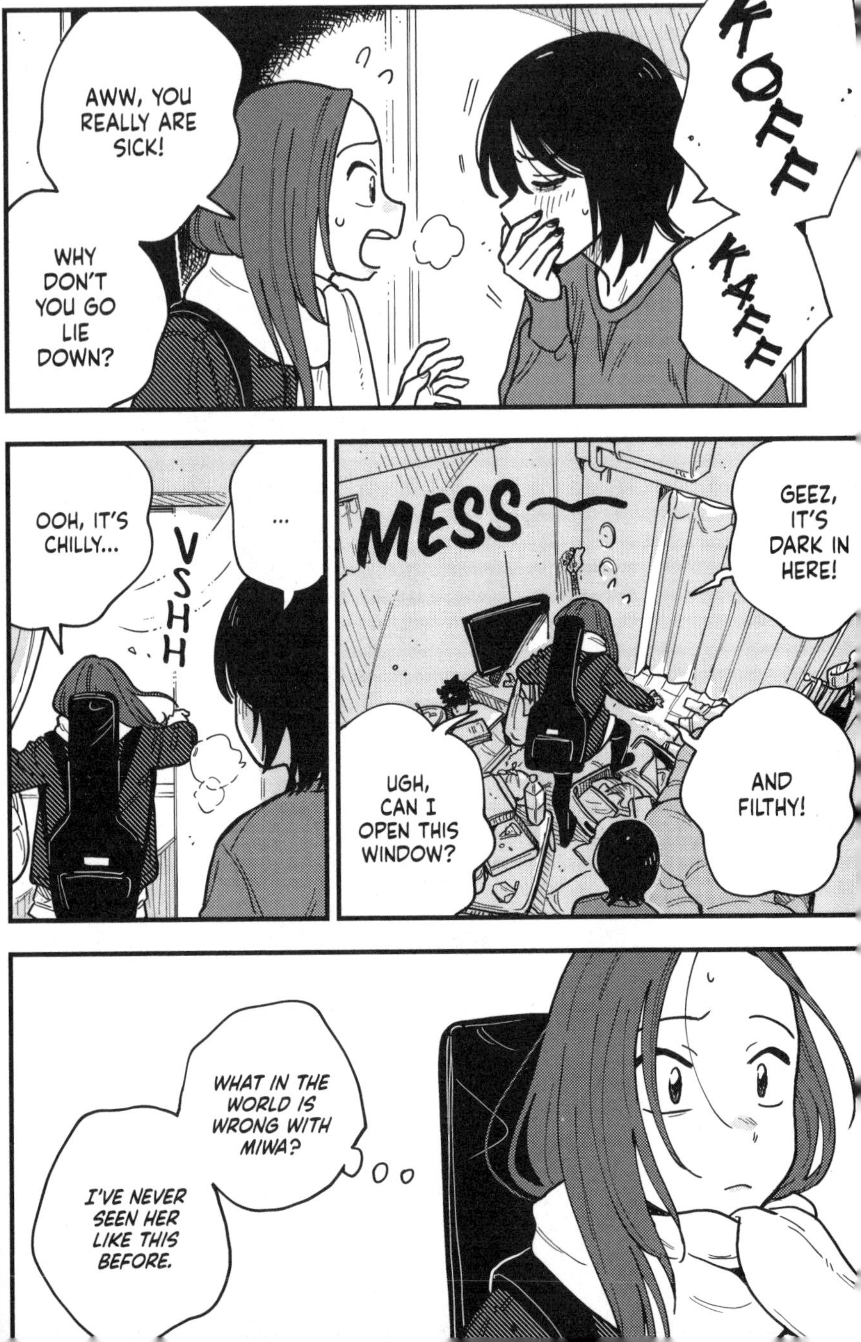
KOFF
KAFF
AWW, YOU REALLY ARE SICK!
WHY DON'T YOU GO LIE DOWN?
GEEZ, IT'S DARK IN HERE!
MESS~
AND FILTHY!
UGH, CAN I OPEN THIS WINDOW?
...
VSHH
OOH, IT'S CHILLY...
WHAT IN THE WORLD IS WRONG WITH MIWA?
I'VE NEVER SEEN HER LIKE THIS BEFORE.

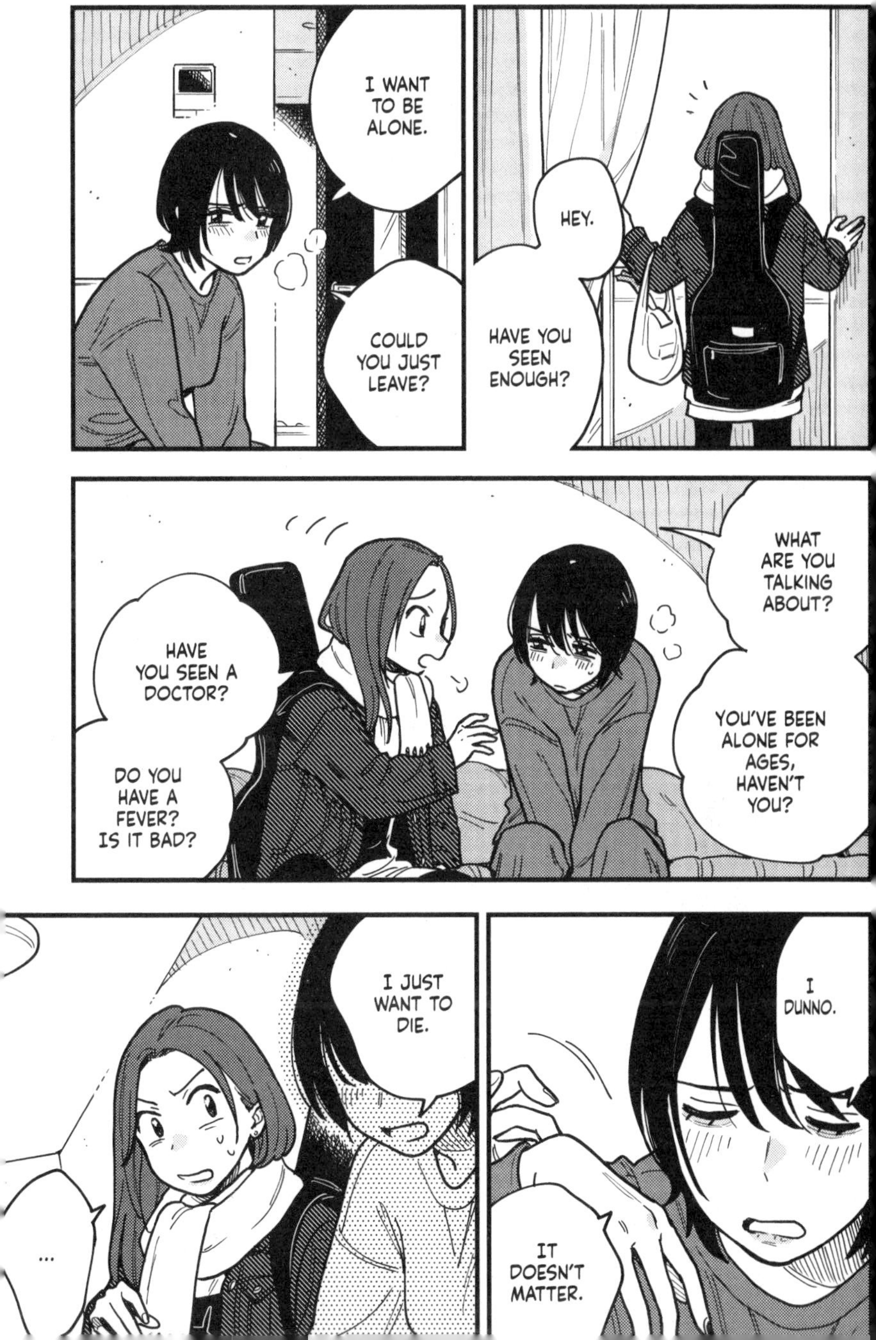
HEY.
HAVE YOU SEEN ENOUGH?
I WANT TO BE ALONE.
COULD YOU JUST LEAVE?
WHAT ARE YOU TALKING ABOUT?
YOU'VE BEEN ALONE FOR AGES, HAVEN'T YOU?
HAVE YOU SEEN A DOCTOR?
DO YOU HAVE A FEVER? IS IT BAD?
I DUNNO.
IT DOESN'T MATTER.
I JUST WANT TO DIE.
...

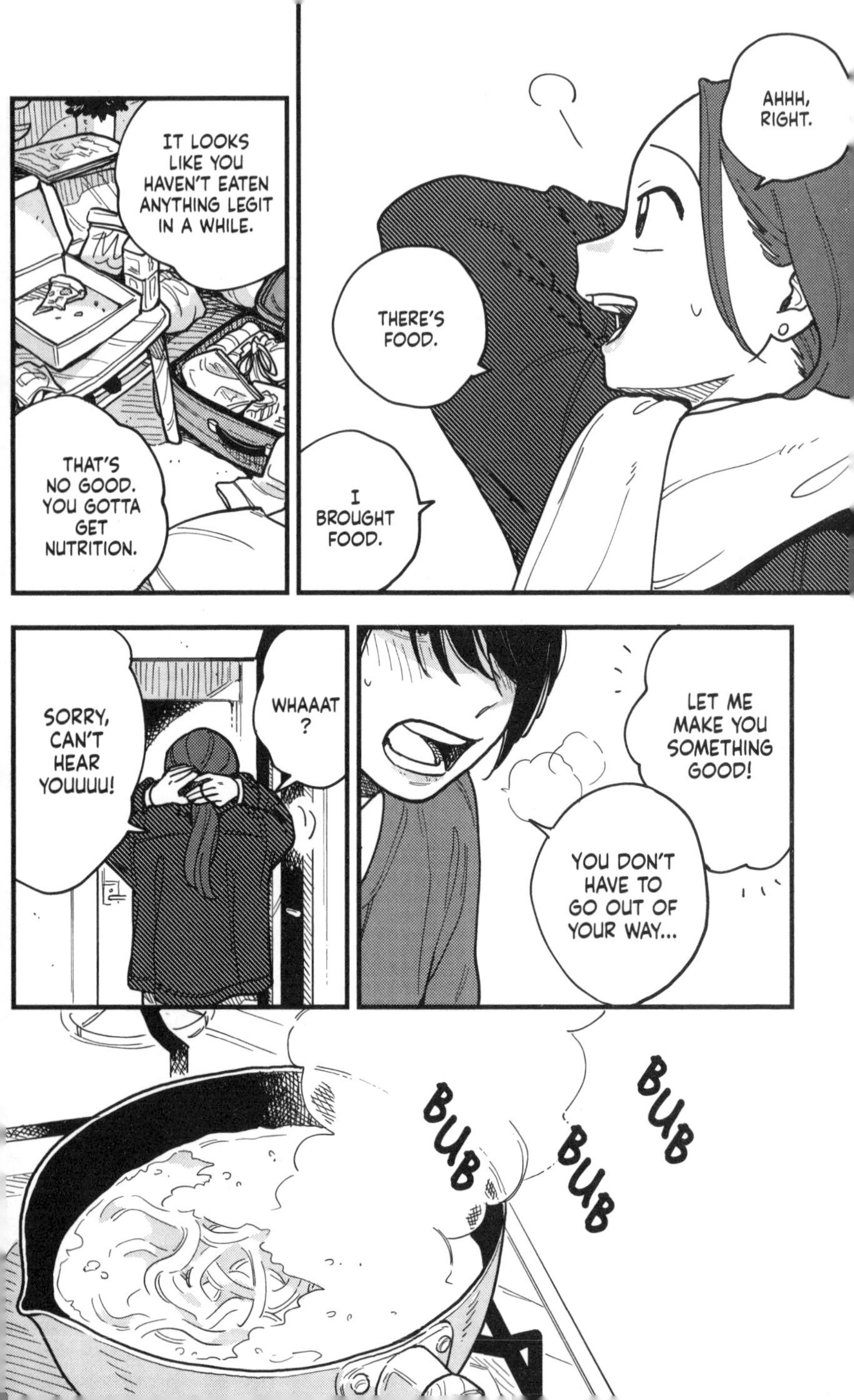
AHHH, RIGHT.
THERE'S FOOD.
I BROUGHT FOOD.
IT LOOKS LIKE YOU HAVEN'T EATEN ANYTHING LEGIT IN A WHILE.
THAT'S NO GOOD. YOU GOTTA GET NUTRITION.
LET ME MAKE YOU SOMETHING GOOD!
YOU DON'T HAVE TO GO OUT OF YOUR WAY...
WHAAAT?
SORRY, CAN'T HEAR YOUUUU!
BUB
BUB
BUB

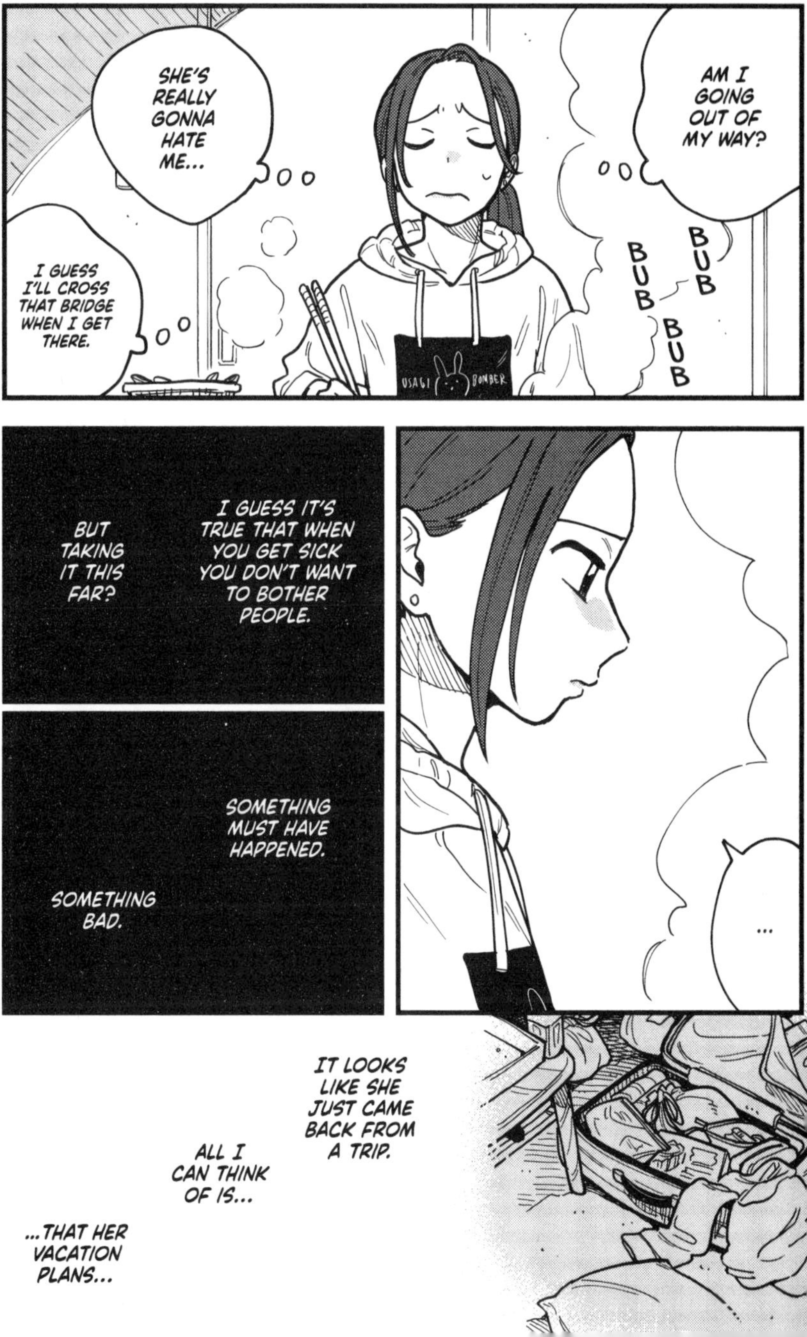
AM I GOING OUT OF MY WAY?
BUB BUB
BUB BUB
SHE'S REALLY GONNA HATE ME...
I GUESS I'LL CROSS THAT BRIDGE WHEN I GET THERE.
...
I GUESS IT'S TRUE THAT WHEN YOU GET SICK YOU DON'T WANT TO BOTHER PEOPLE.
BUT TAKING IT THIS FAR?
SOMETHING MUST HAVE HAPPENED.
SOMETHING BAD.
USAGI BOMBER
IT LOOKS LIKE SHE JUST CAME BACK FROM A TRIP.
ALL I CAN THINK OF IS...
...THAT HER VACATION PLANS...

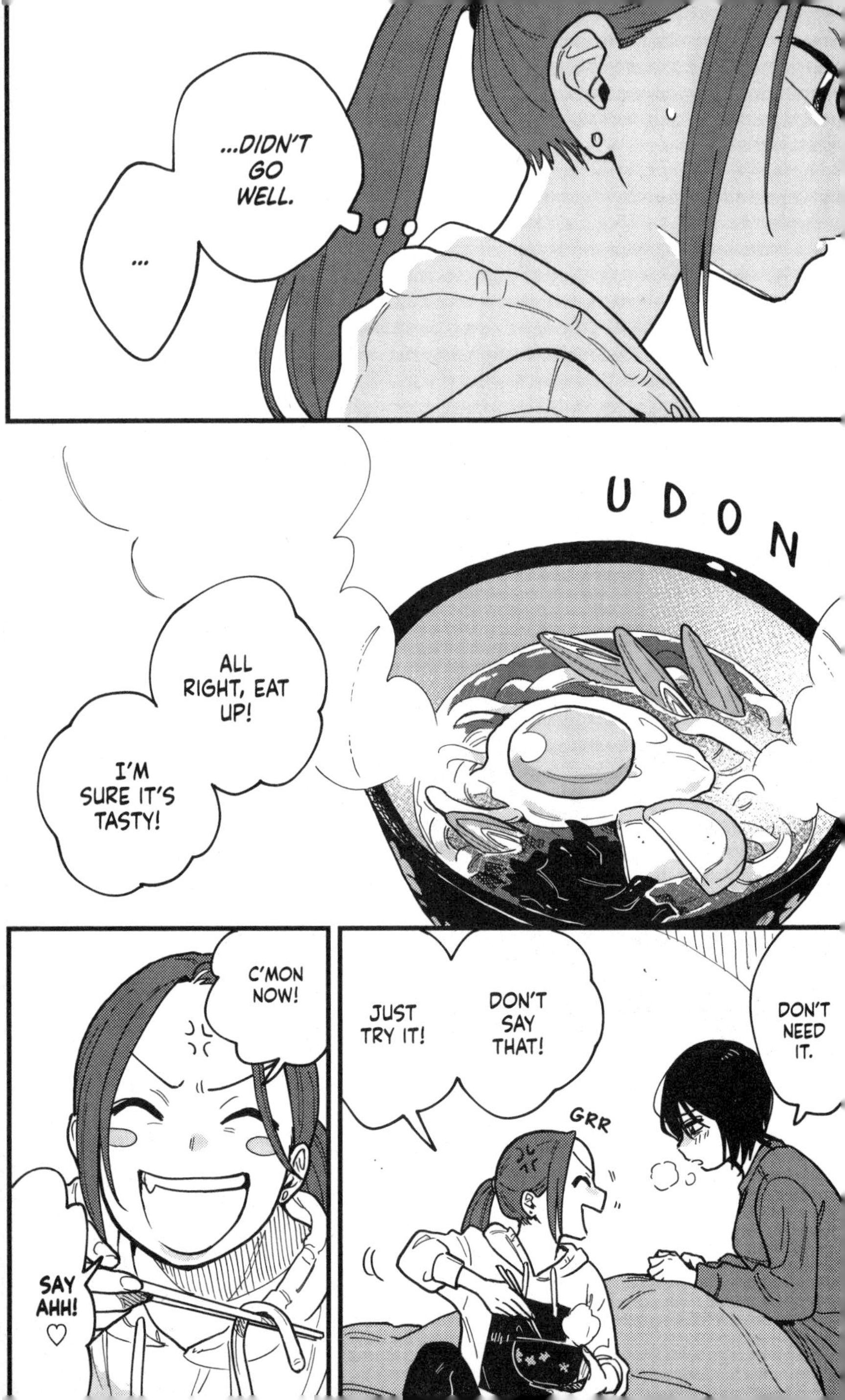
...DIDN'T GO WELL.
...
UDON
ALL RIGHT, EAT UP!
I'M SURE IT'S TASTY!
DON'T NEED IT.
DON'T SAY THAT!
JUST TRY IT!
GRR
C'MON NOW!
SAY AHH! ♡

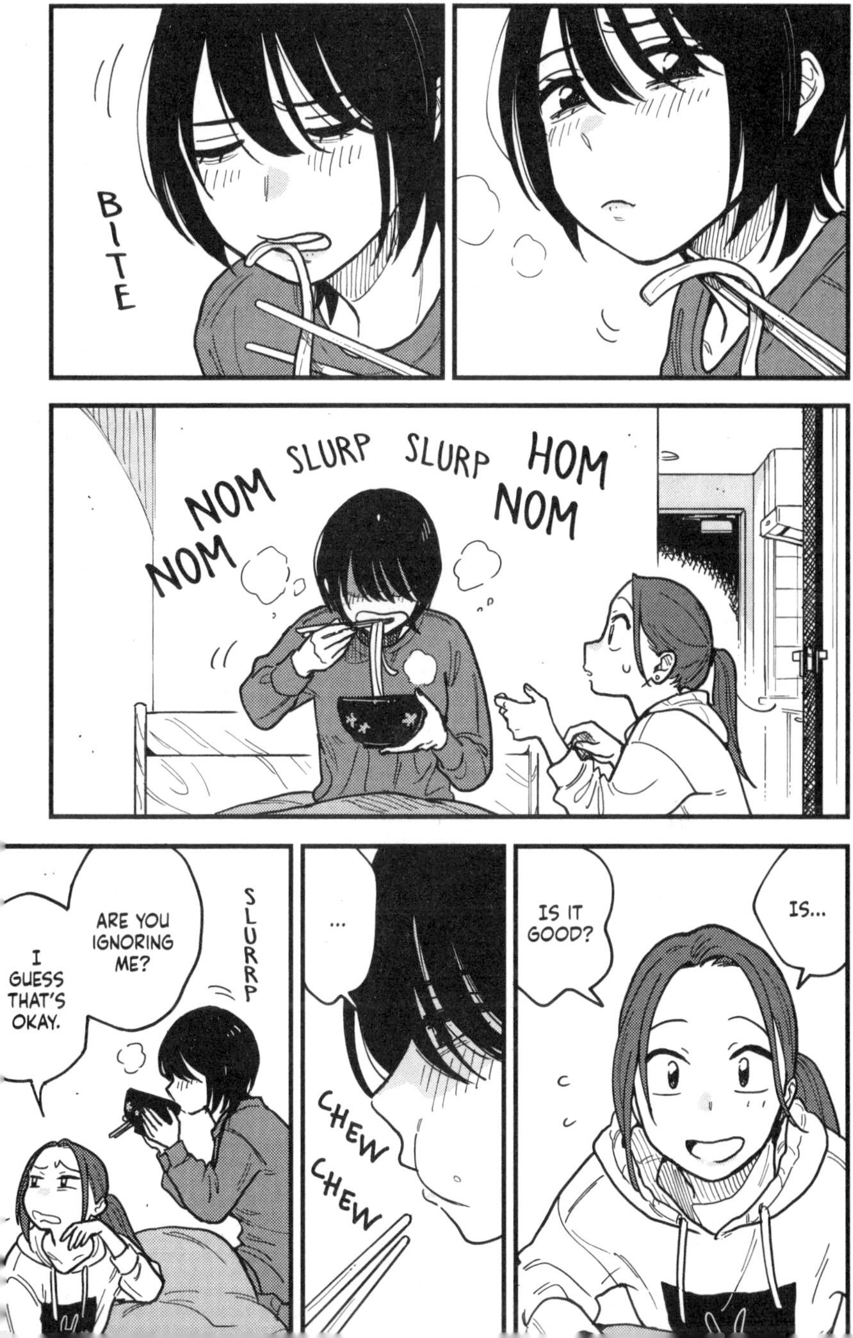
BITE
HOM NOM
SLURP
SLURP
NOM NOM
IS...
IS IT GOOD?
...
CHEW
CHEW
SLURRP
ARE YOU IGNORING ME?
I GUESS THAT'S OKAY.

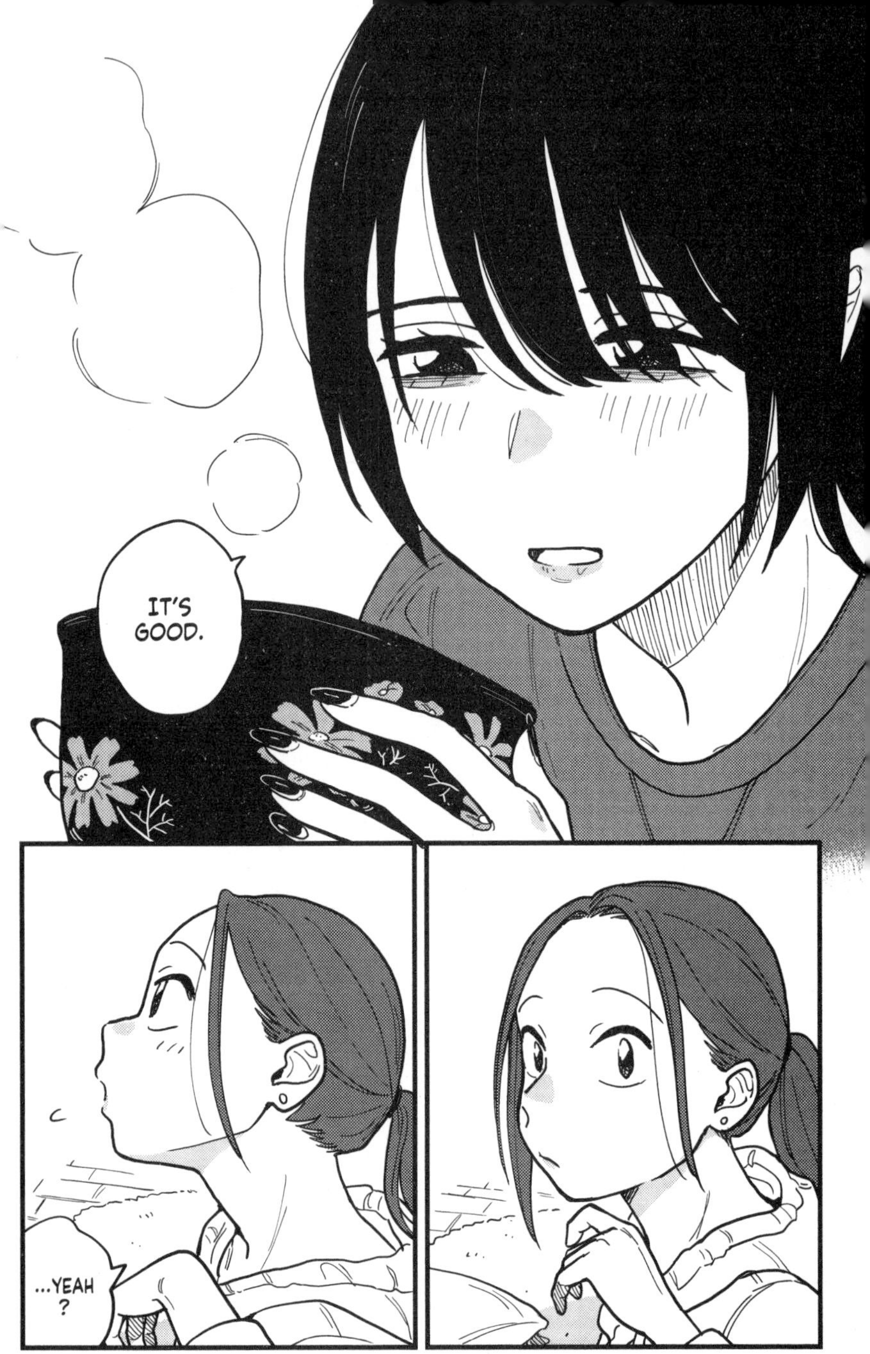
IT'S GOOD.
...YEAH ?

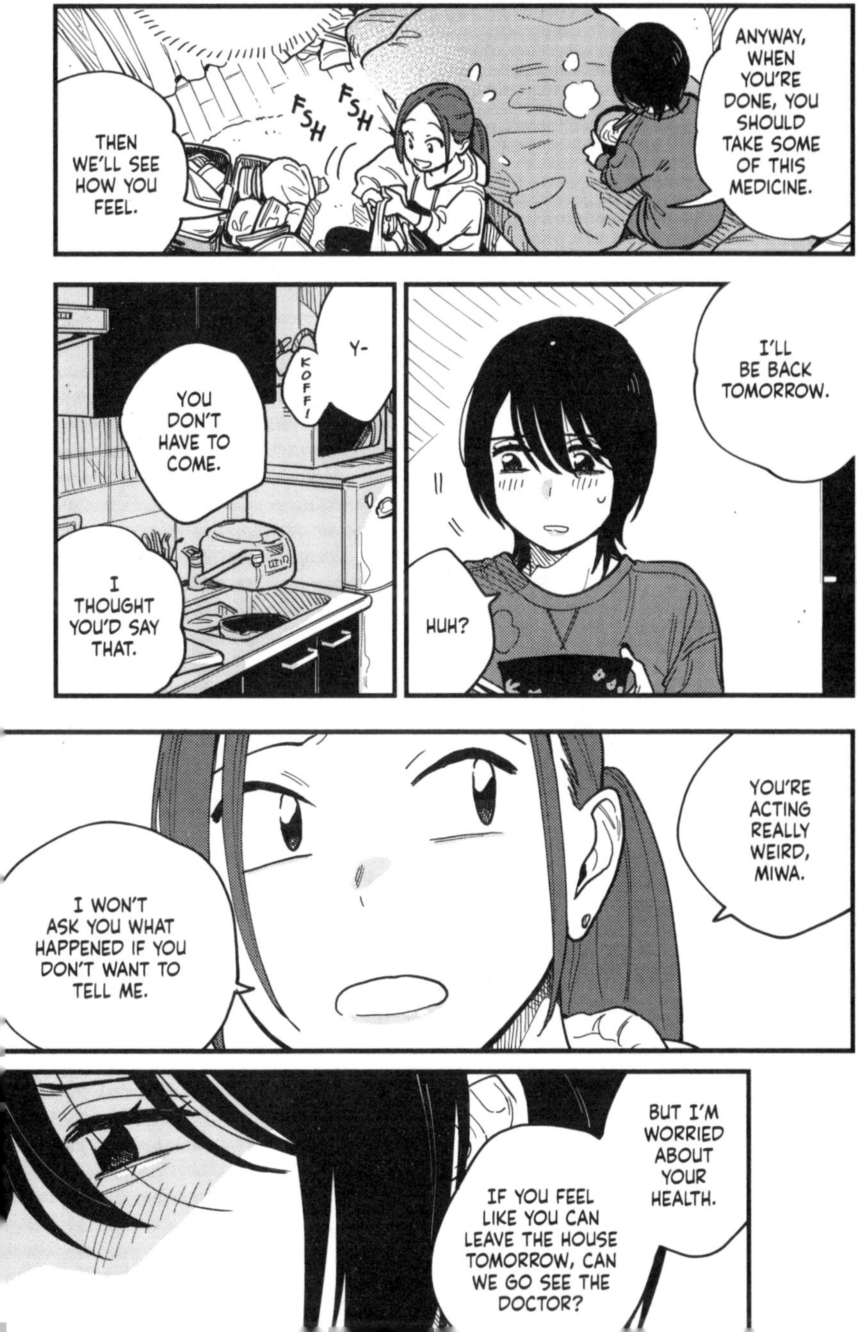
ANYWAY, WHEN YOU'RE DONE, YOU SHOULD TAKE SOME OF THIS MEDICINE.
FSH
FSH
THEN WE'LL SEE HOW YOU FEEL.
I'LL BE BACK TOMORROW.
HUH?
Y-
KOFF!
YOU DON'T HAVE TO COME.
I THOUGHT YOU'D SAY THAT.
YOU'RE ACTING REALLY WEIRD, MIWA.
I WON'T ASK YOU WHAT HAPPENED IF YOU DON'T WANT TO TELL ME.
BUT I'M WORRIED ABOUT YOUR HEALTH.
IF YOU FEEL LIKE YOU CAN LEAVE THE HOUSE TOMORROW, CAN WE GO SEE THE DOCTOR?

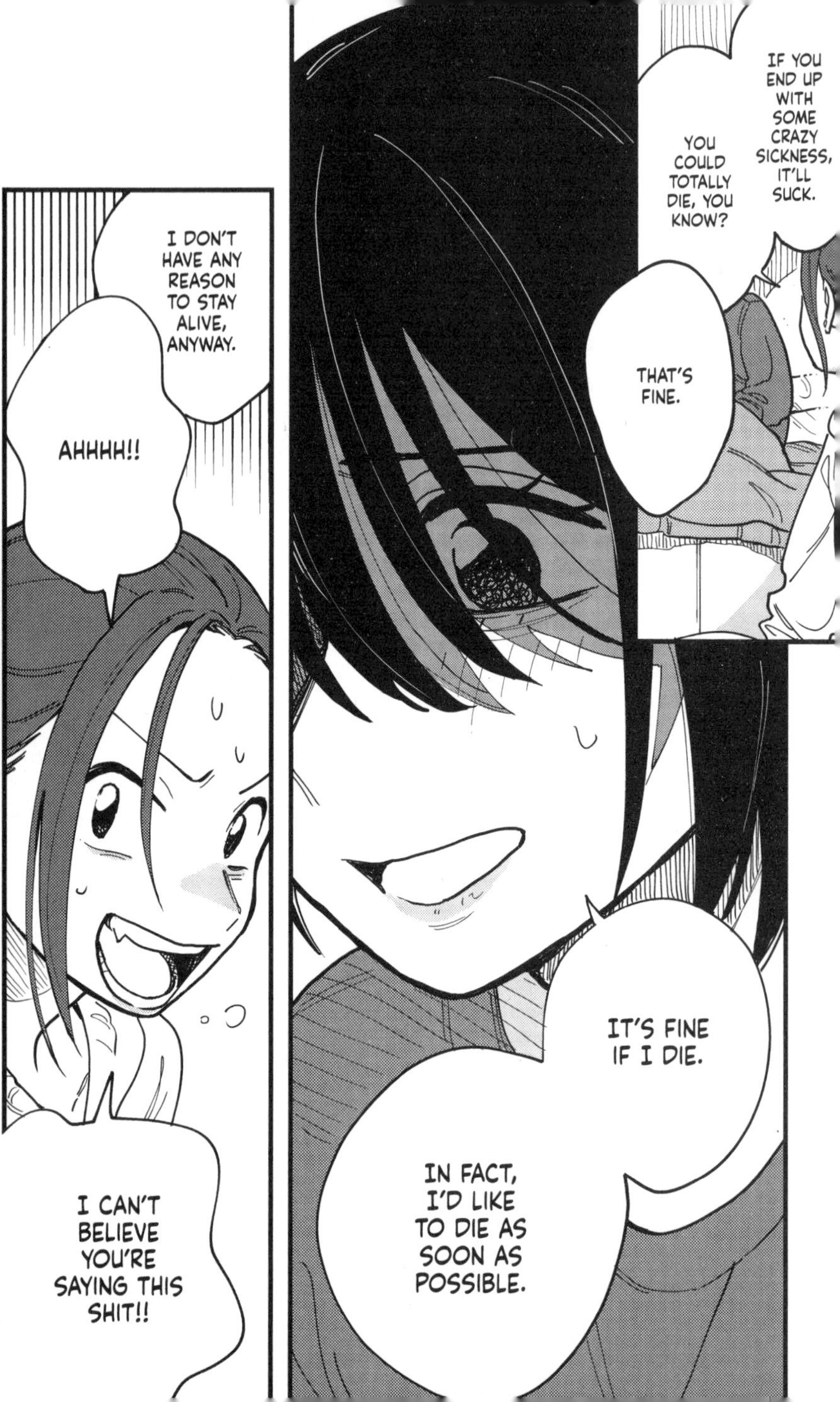
IF YOU END UP WITH SOME CRAZY SICKNESS, IT'LL SUCK.
YOU COULD TOTALLY DIE, YOU KNOW?
THAT'S FINE.
IT'S FINE IF I DIE.
IN FACT, I'D LIKE TO DIE AS SOON AS POSSIBLE.
I DON'T HAVE ANY REASON TO STAY ALIVE, ANYWAY.
AHHHH!!
I CAN'T BELIEVE YOU'RE SAYING THIS SHIT!!

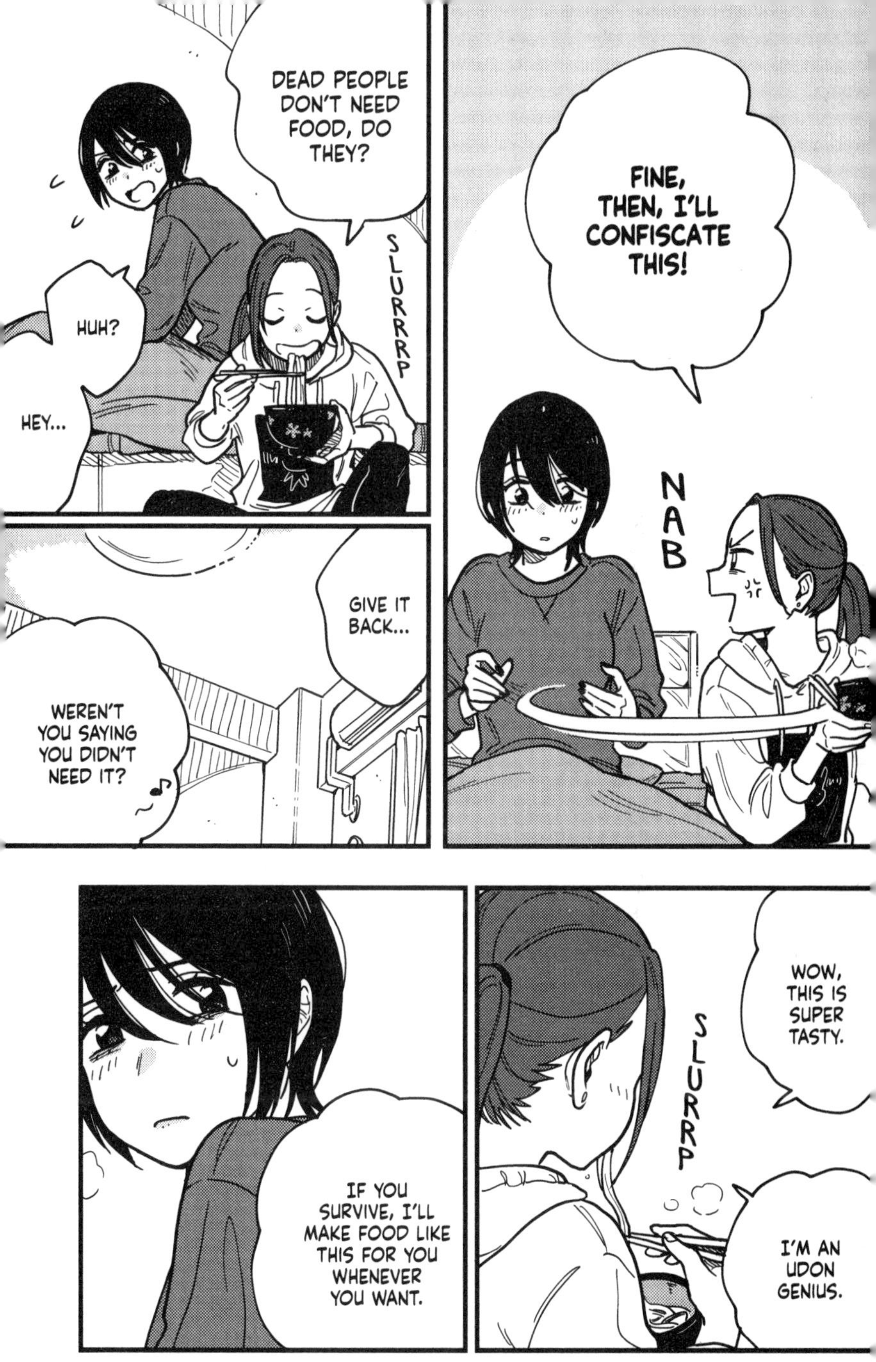
FINE, THEN, I'LL CONFISCATE THIS!
NAB
DEAD PEOPLE DON'T NEED FOOD, DO THEY?
SLURRRP
HUH?
HEY...
GIVE IT BACK...
WEREN'T YOU SAYING YOU DIDN'T NEED IT?
WOW, THIS IS SUPER TASTY.
SLURRP
I'M AN UDON GENIUS.
IF YOU SURVIVE, I'LL MAKE FOOD LIKE THIS FOR YOU WHENEVER YOU WANT.

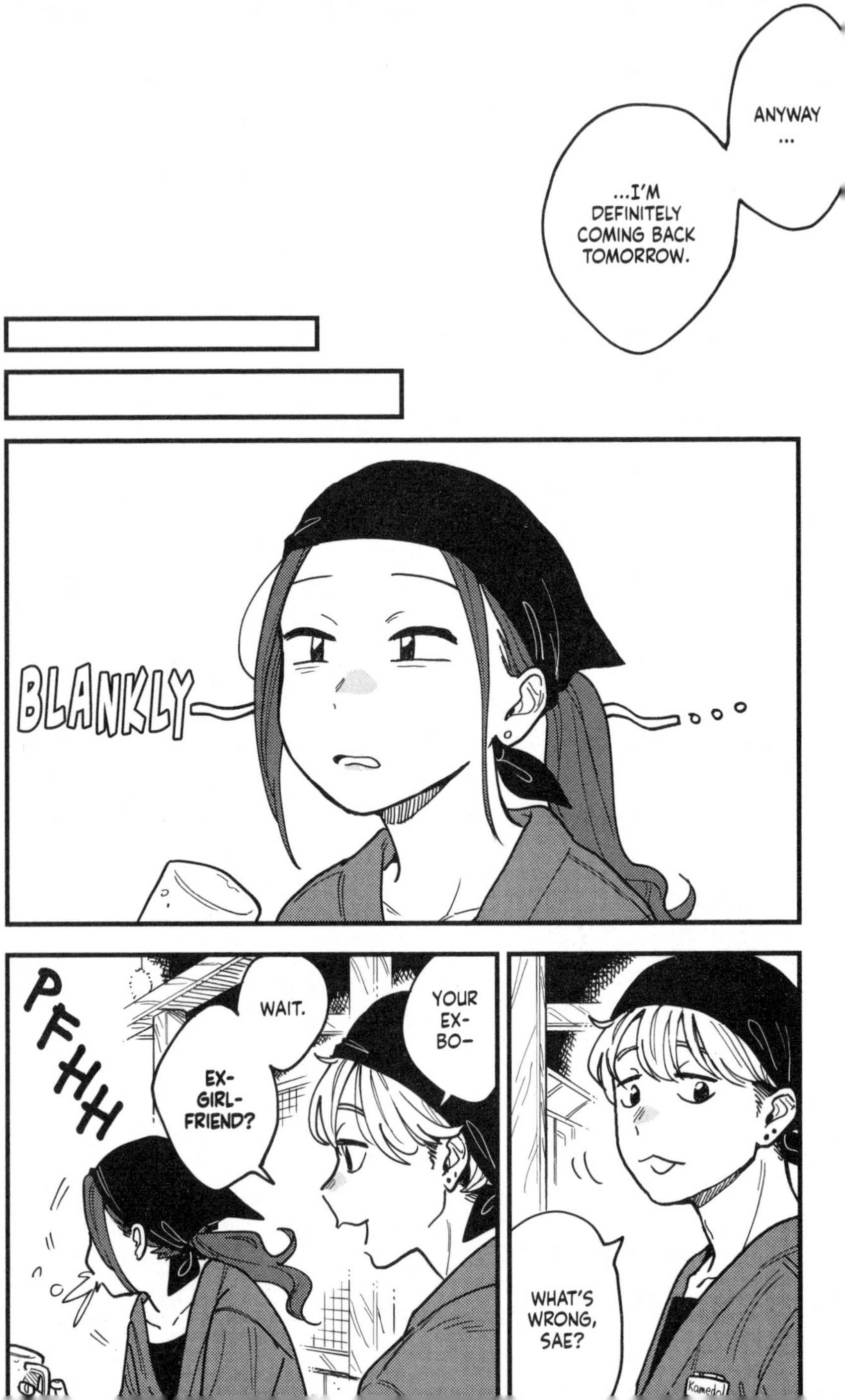
ANYWAY ...
...I'M DEFINITELY COMING BACK TOMORROW.
BLANKLY
WHAT'S WRONG, SAE?
YOUR EX-BO-
WAIT.
EX-GIRL-FRIEND?
PFHH

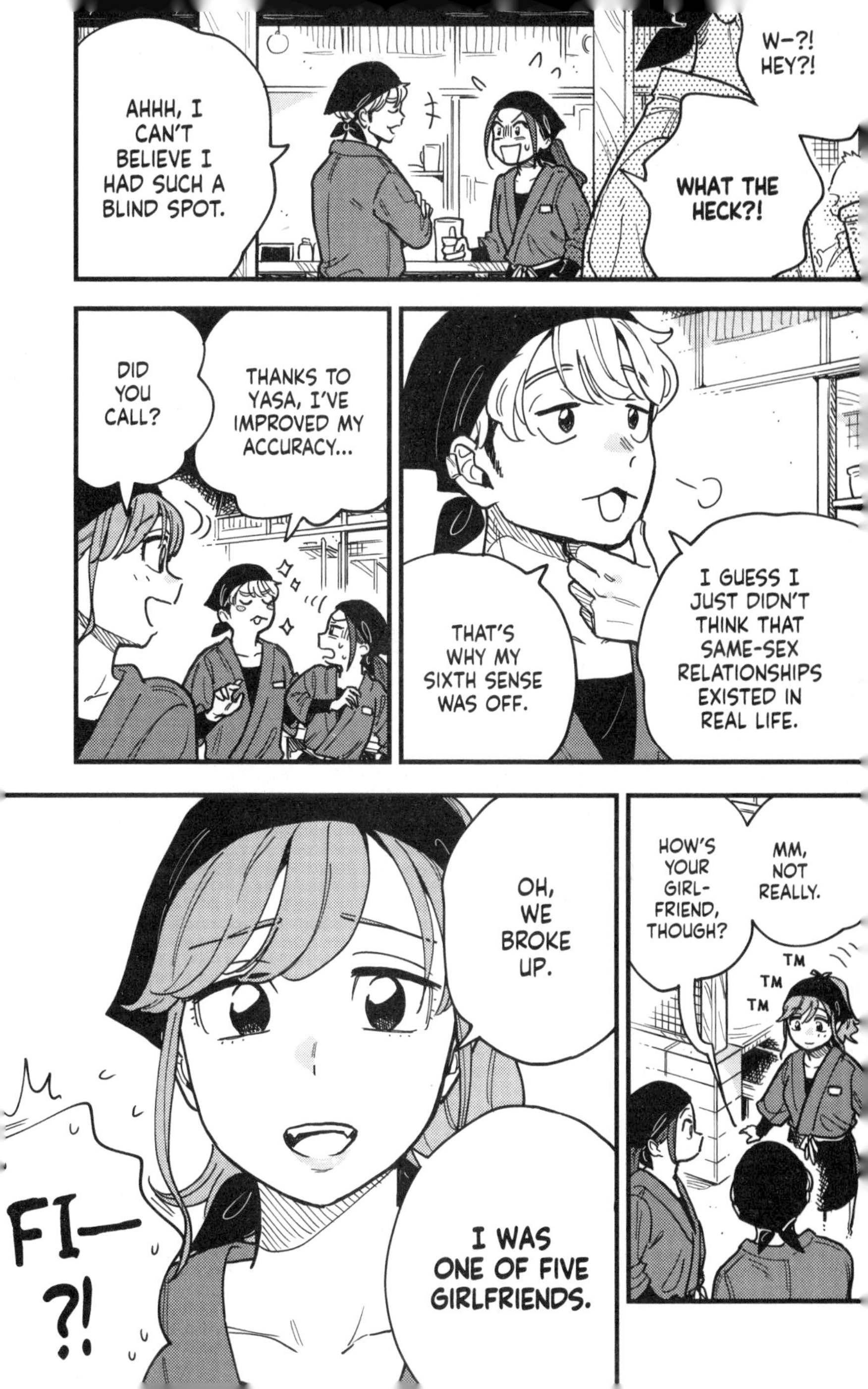
W—?! HEY?!
WHAT THE HECK?!
AHHH, I CAN'T BELIEVE I HAD SUCH A BLIND SPOT.
I GUESS I JUST DIDN'T THINK THAT SAME-SEX RELATIONSHIPS EXISTED IN REAL LIFE.
THAT'S WHY MY SIXTH SENSE WAS OFF.
THANKS TO YASA, I'VE IMPROVED MY ACCURACY...
DID YOU CALL?
MM, NOT REALLY.
HOW'S YOUR GIRL-FRIEND, THOUGH?
TM
TM
TM
OH, WE BROKE UP.
I WAS ONE OF FIVE GIRLFRIENDS.
FI— ?!

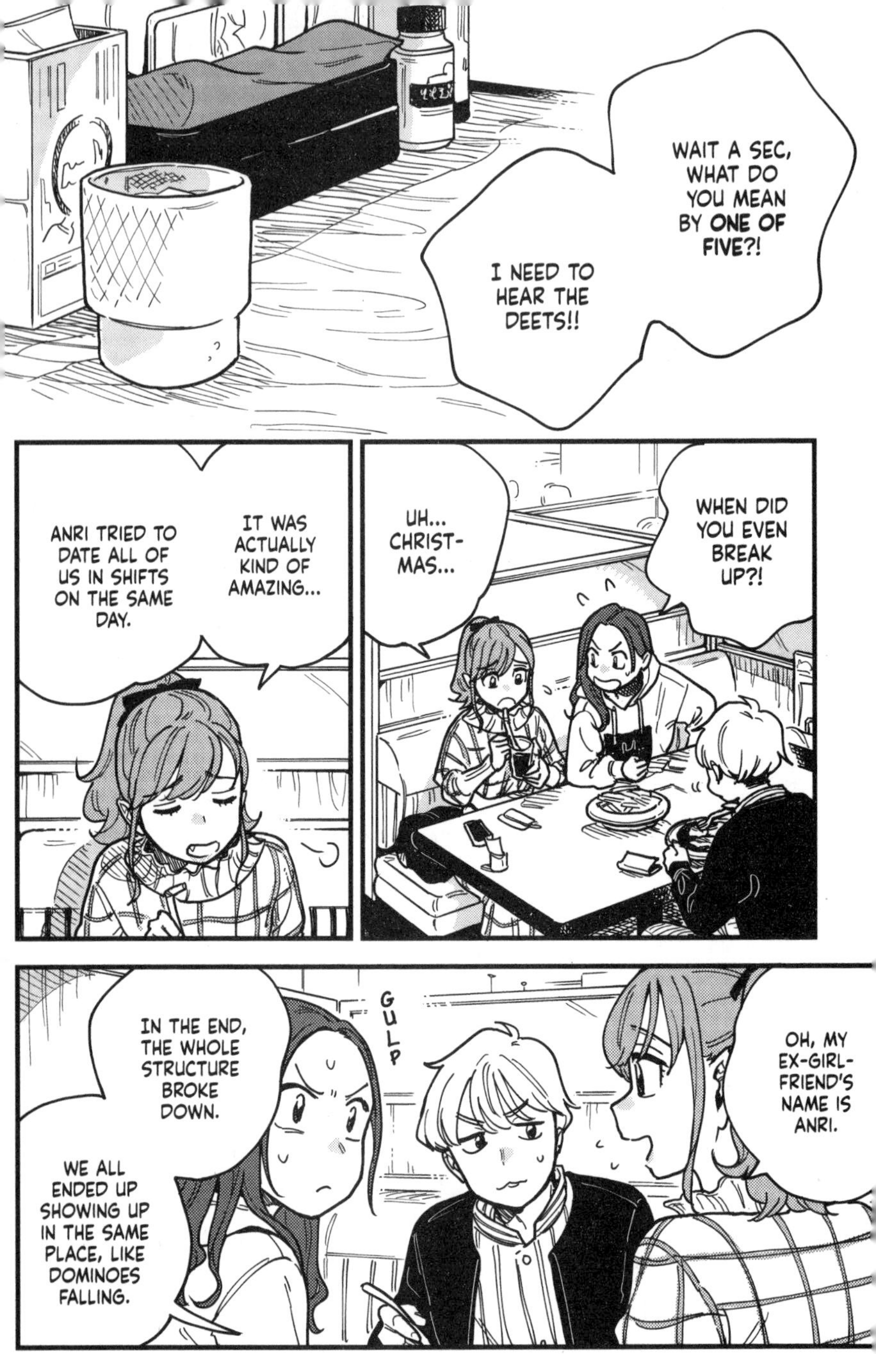
WAIT A SEC, WHAT DO YOU MEAN BY **ONE OF FIVE?!**
I NEED TO HEAR THE DEETS!!
WHEN DID YOU EVEN BREAK UP?!
UH... CHRIST-MAS...
IT WAS ACTUALLY KIND OF AMAZING...
ANRI TRIED TO DATE ALL OF US IN SHIFTS ON THE SAME DAY.
OH, MY EX-GIRL-FRIEND'S NAME IS ANRI.
GULP
IN THE END, THE WHOLE STRUCTURE BROKE DOWN.
WE ALL ENDED UP SHOWING UP IN THE SAME PLACE, LIKE DOMINOES FALLING.

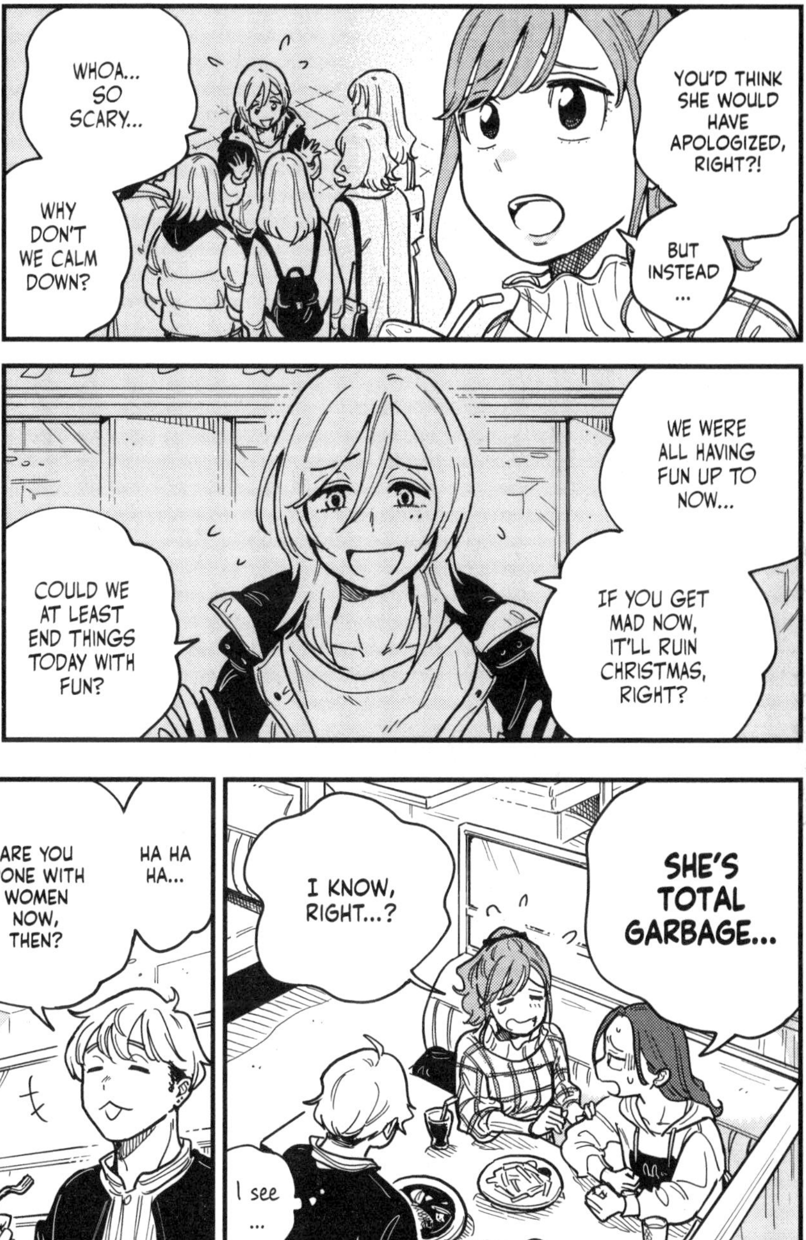
YOU'D THINK SHE WOULD HAVE APOLOGIZED, RIGHT?!
BUT INSTEAD ...
WHOA... SO SCARY...
WHY DON'T WE CALM DOWN?
WE WERE ALL HAVING FUN UP TO NOW...
IF YOU GET MAD NOW, IT'LL RUIN CHRISTMAS, RIGHT?
COULD WE AT LEAST END THINGS TODAY WITH FUN?
SHE'S TOTAL GARBAGE...
I KNOW, RIGHT...?
I see ...
HA HA HA...
ARE YOU DONE WITH WOMEN NOW, THEN?

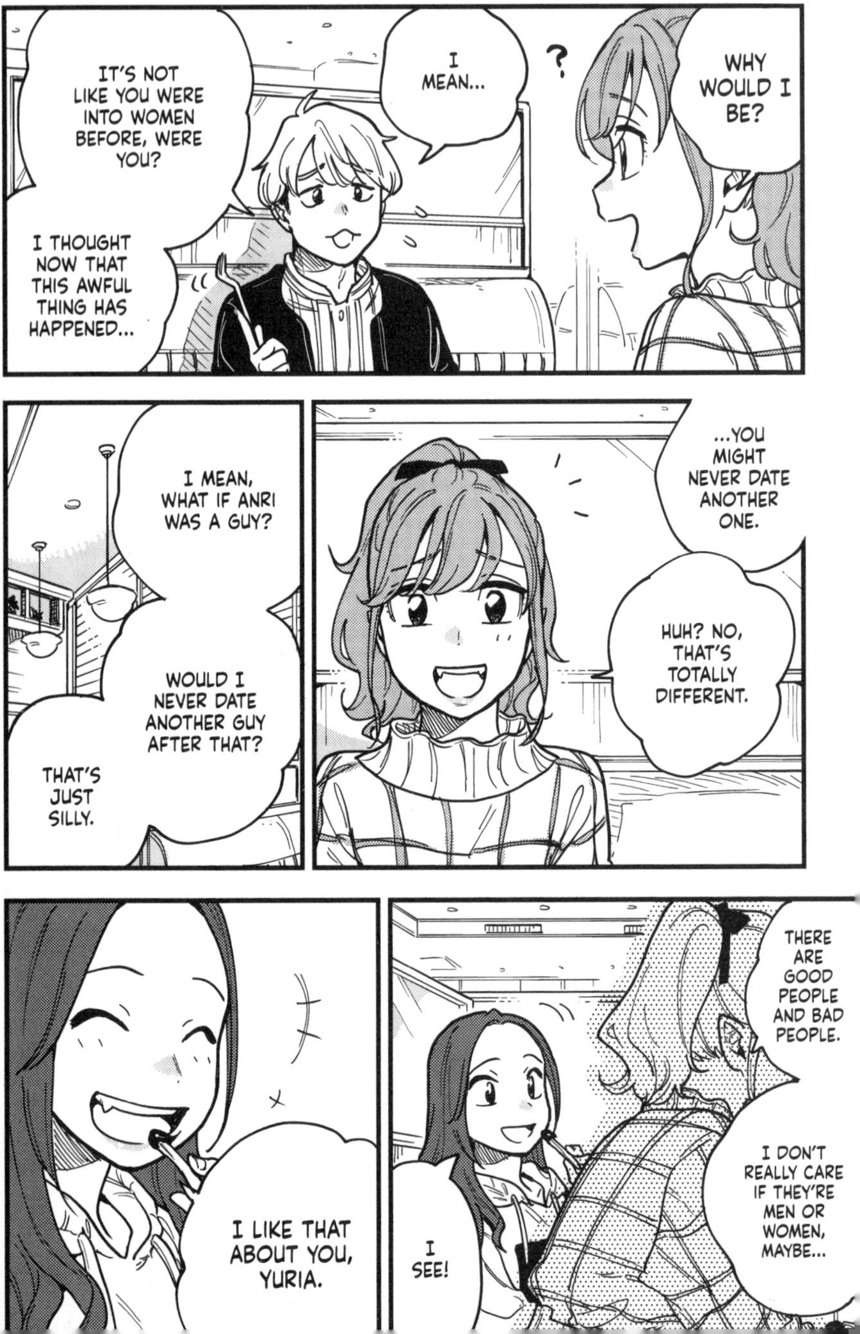
WHY WOULD I BE?
?
I MEAN...
IT'S NOT LIKE YOU WERE INTO WOMEN BEFORE, WERE YOU?
I THOUGHT NOW THAT THIS AWFUL THING HAS HAPPENED...
...YOU MIGHT NEVER DATE ANOTHER ONE.
HUH? NO, THAT'S TOTALLY DIFFERENT.
I MEAN, WHAT IF ANRI WAS A GUY?
WOULD I NEVER DATE ANOTHER GUY AFTER THAT?
THAT'S JUST SILLY.
THERE ARE GOOD PEOPLE AND BAD PEOPLE.
I DON'T REALLY CARE IF THEY'RE MEN OR WOMEN, MAYBE...
I SEE!
I LIKE THAT ABOUT YOU, YURIA.

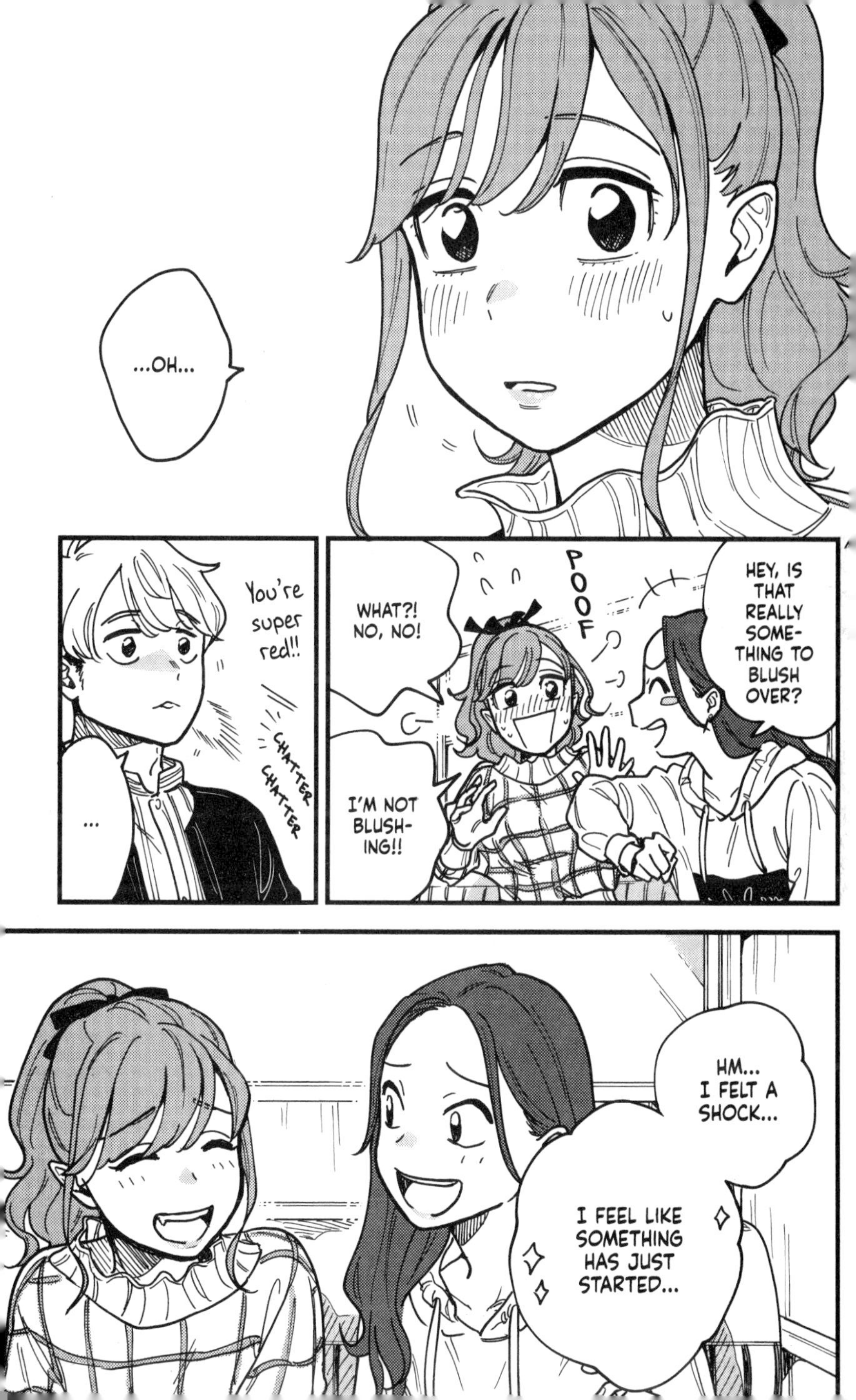
...OH...
HEY, IS THAT REALLY SOME-THING TO BLUSH OVER?
POOF
WHAT?! NO, NO!
I'M NOT BLUSH-ING!!
You're super red!!
CHATTER CHATTER
...
HM... I FELT A SHOCK...
I FEEL LIKE SOMETHING HAS JUST STARTED...

How Do We
Relationship?

Chapter 44: A Sweet Counterattack

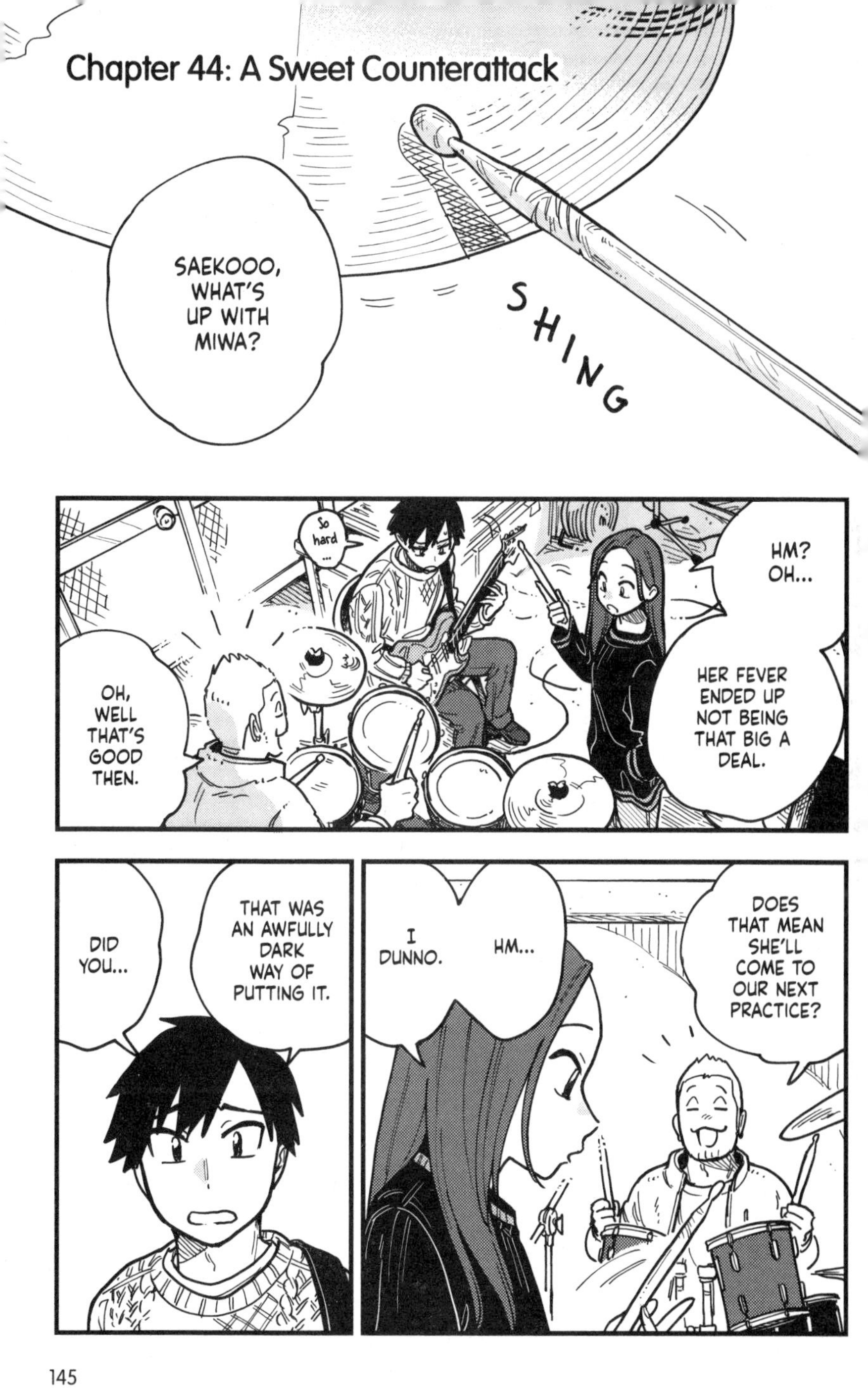
SHING
SAEKOOO, WHAT'S UP WITH MIWA?
HM? OH...
HER FEVER ENDED UP NOT BEING THAT BIG A DEAL.
So hard...
OH, WELL THAT'S GOOD THEN.
DOES THAT MEAN SHE'LL COME TO OUR NEXT PRACTICE?
HM...
I DUNNO.
THAT WAS AN AWFULLY DARK WAY OF PUTTING IT.
DID YOU...

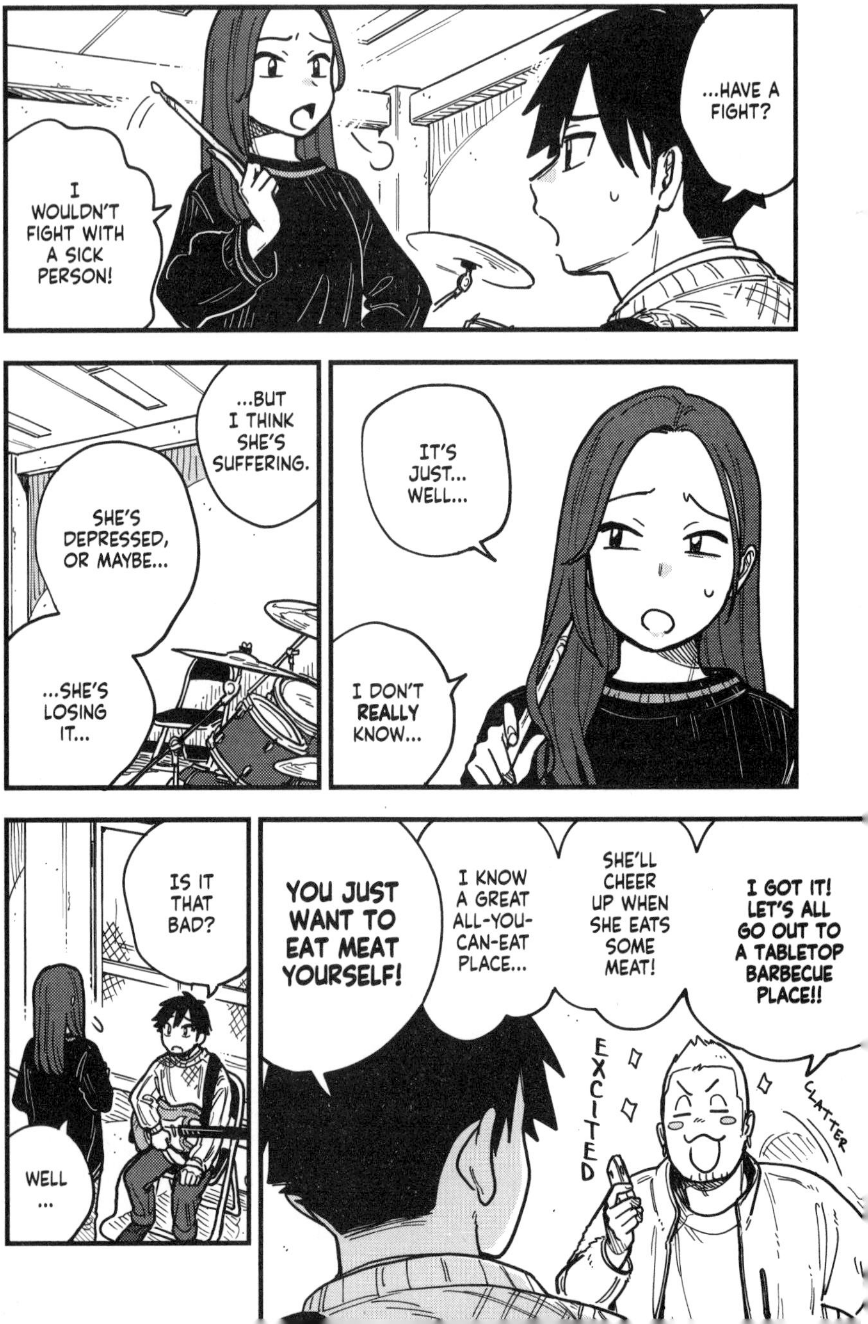
...HAVE A FIGHT?
I WOULDN'T FIGHT WITH A SICK PERSON!
IT'S JUST... WELL...
I DON'T REALLY KNOW...
...BUT I THINK SHE'S SUFFERING.
SHE'S DEPRESSED, OR MAYBE...
...SHE'S LOSING IT...
I GOT IT! LET'S ALL GO OUT TO A TABLETOP BARBECUE PLACE!!
CLATTER
SHE'LL CHEER UP WHEN SHE EATS SOME MEAT!
EXCITED
I KNOW A GREAT ALL-YOU-CAN-EAT PLACE...
YOU JUST WANT TO EAT MEAT YOURSELF!
IS IT THAT BAD?
WELL ...

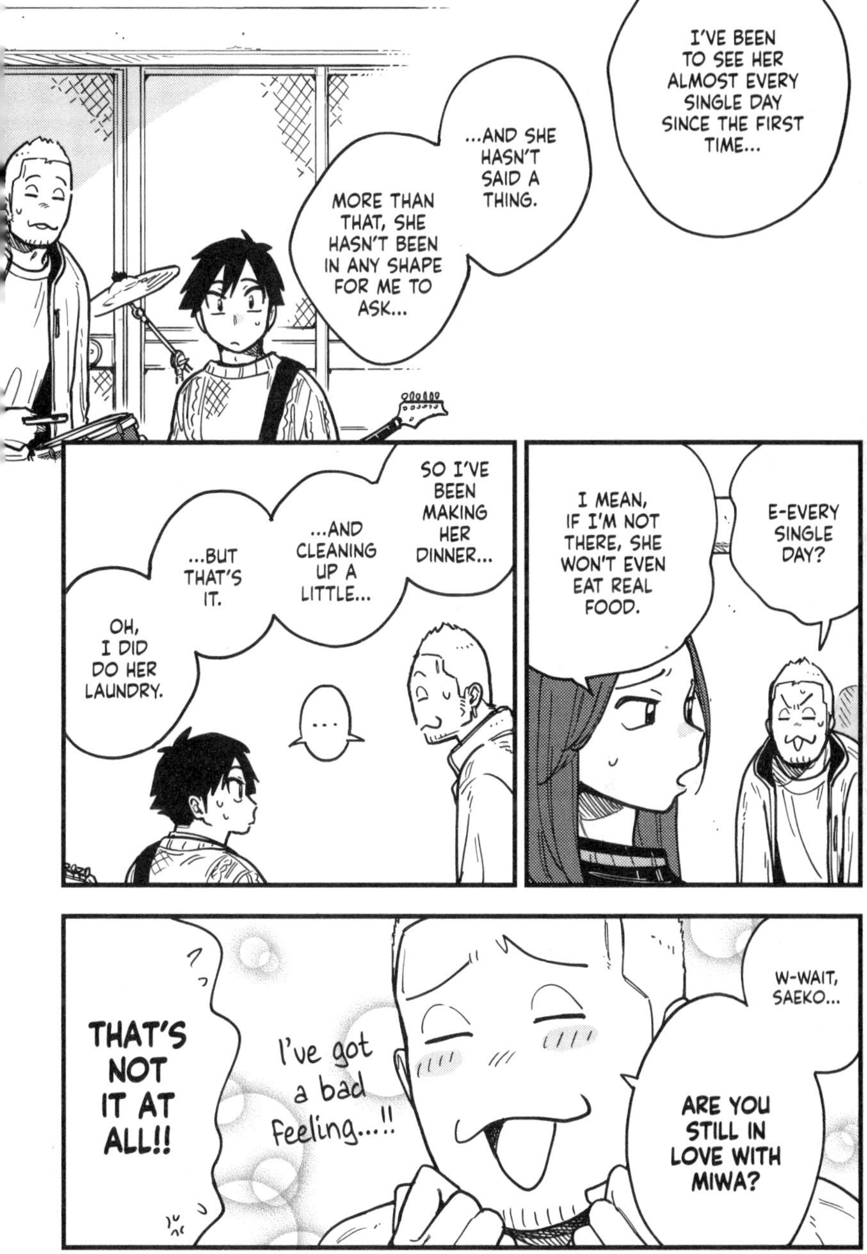
I'VE BEEN TO SEE HER ALMOST EVERY SINGLE DAY SINCE THE FIRST TIME...
...AND SHE HASN'T SAID A THING.
MORE THAN THAT, SHE HASN'T BEEN IN ANY SHAPE FOR ME TO ASK...
E-EVERY SINGLE DAY?
I MEAN, IF I'M NOT THERE, SHE WON'T EVEN EAT REAL FOOD.
SO I'VE BEEN MAKING HER DINNER...
...AND CLEANING UP A LITTLE...
...BUT THAT'S IT.
OH, I DID DO HER LAUNDRY.
...
W-WAIT, SAEKO...
ARE YOU STILL IN LOVE WITH MIWA?
I've got a bad feeling...!!
THAT'S NOT IT AT ALL!!

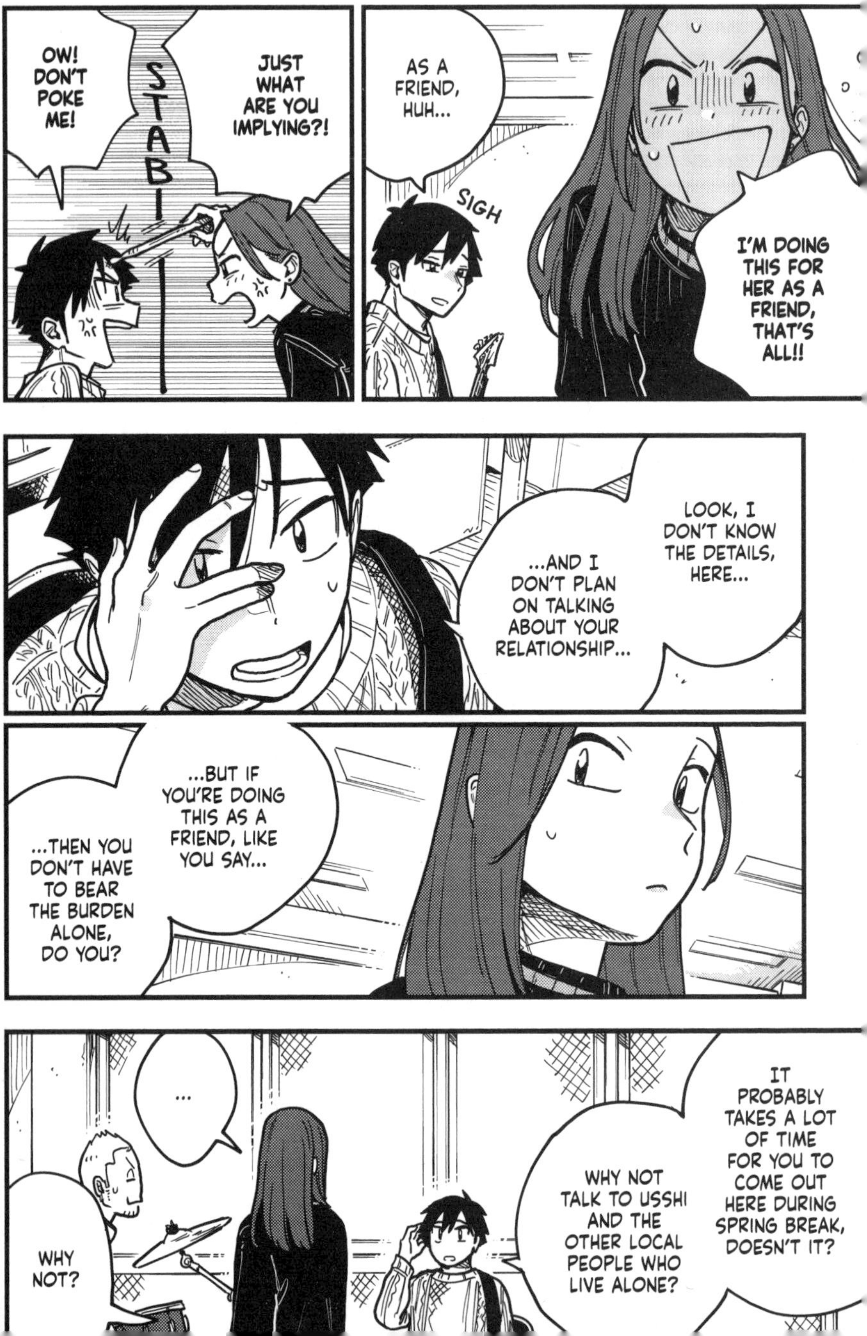
I'M DOING THIS FOR HER AS A FRIEND, THAT'S ALL!!
AS A FRIEND, HUH...
SIGH
JUST WHAT ARE YOU IMPLYING?!
STAB!
OW! DON'T POKE ME!
LOOK, I DON'T KNOW THE DETAILS, HERE...
...AND I DON'T PLAN ON TALKING ABOUT YOUR RELATIONSHIP...
...BUT IF YOU'RE DOING THIS AS A FRIEND, LIKE YOU SAY...
...THEN YOU DON'T HAVE TO BEAR THE BURDEN ALONE, DO YOU?
IT PROBABLY TAKES A LOT OF TIME FOR YOU TO COME OUT HERE DURING SPRING BREAK, DOESN'T IT?
WHY NOT TALK TO USSHI AND THE OTHER LOCAL PEOPLE WHO LIVE ALONE?
...
WHY NOT?

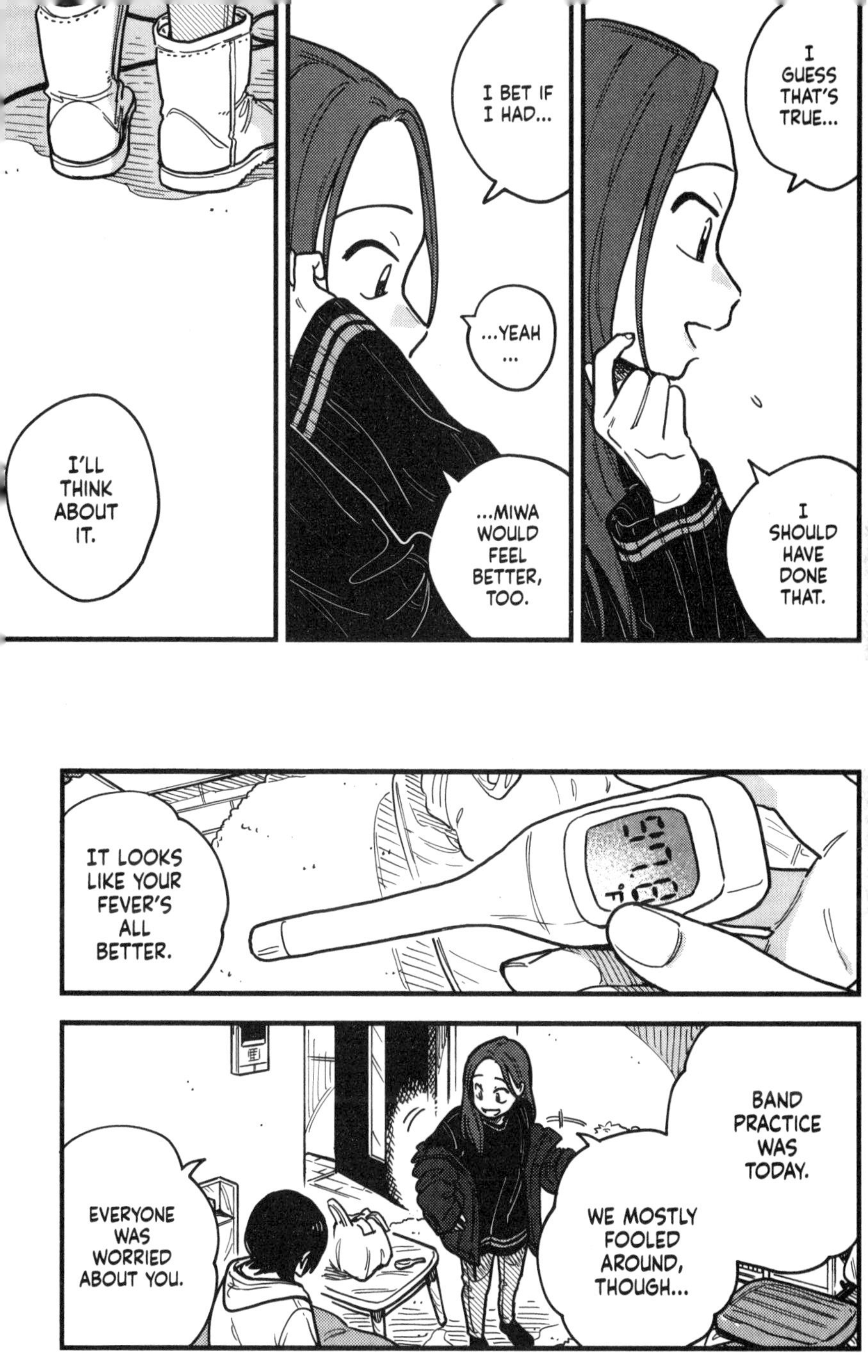
I GUESS THAT'S TRUE...
I SHOULD HAVE DONE THAT.
I BET IF I HAD...
...YEAH ...
...MIWA WOULD FEEL BETTER, TOO.
I'LL THINK ABOUT IT.
IT LOOKS LIKE YOUR FEVER'S ALL BETTER.
BAND PRACTICE WAS TODAY.
WE MOSTLY FOOLED AROUND, THOUGH...
EVERYONE WAS WORRIED ABOUT YOU.

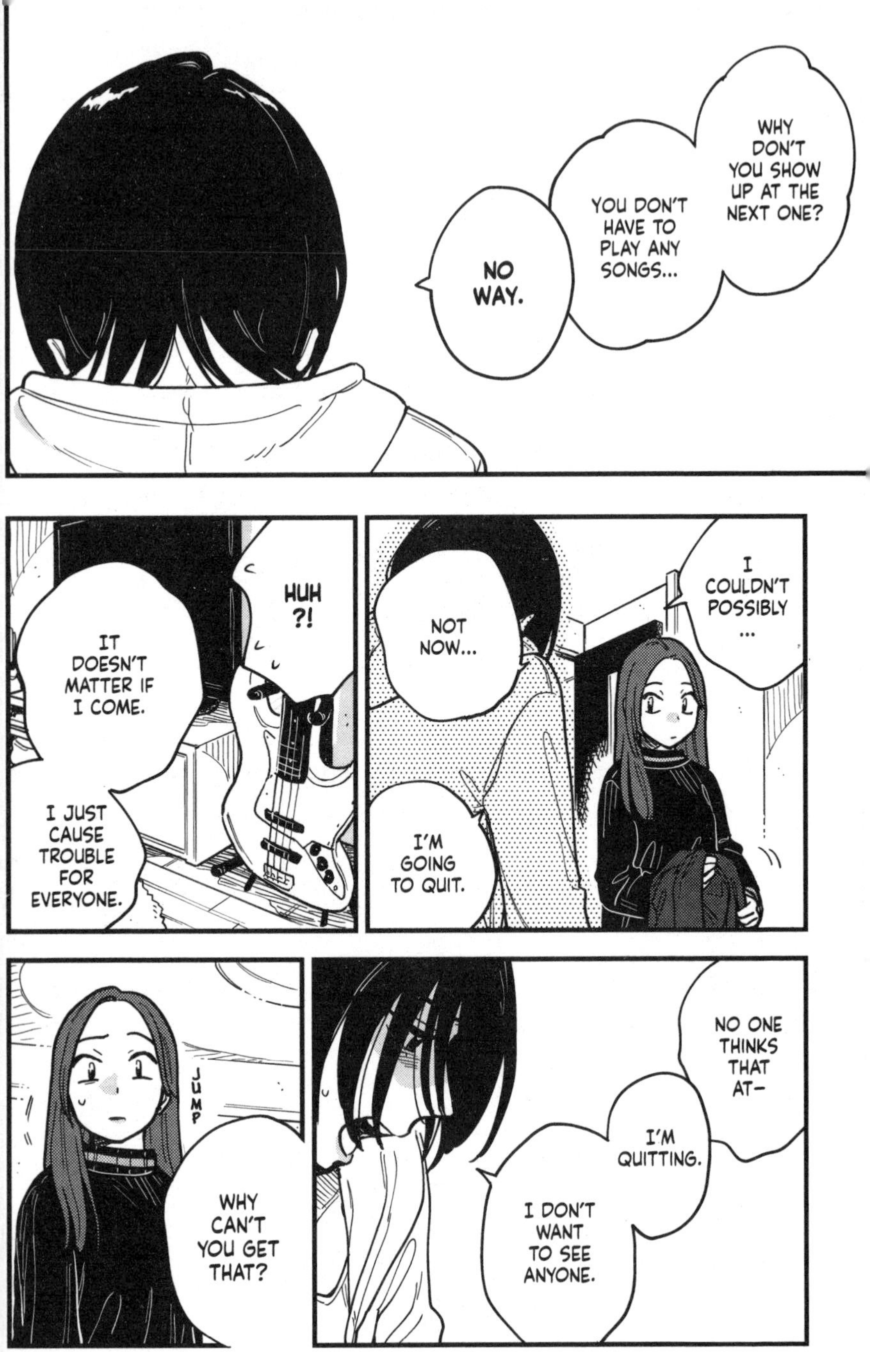
WHY DON'T YOU SHOW UP AT THE NEXT ONE?
YOU DON'T HAVE TO PLAY ANY SONGS...
NO WAY.
I COULDN'T POSSIBLY ...
NOT NOW...
I'M GOING TO QUIT.
HUH ?!
IT DOESN'T MATTER IF I COME.
I JUST CAUSE TROUBLE FOR EVERYONE.
NO ONE THINKS THAT AT–
I'M QUITTING.
I DON'T WANT TO SEE ANYONE.
JUMP
WHY CAN'T YOU GET THAT?

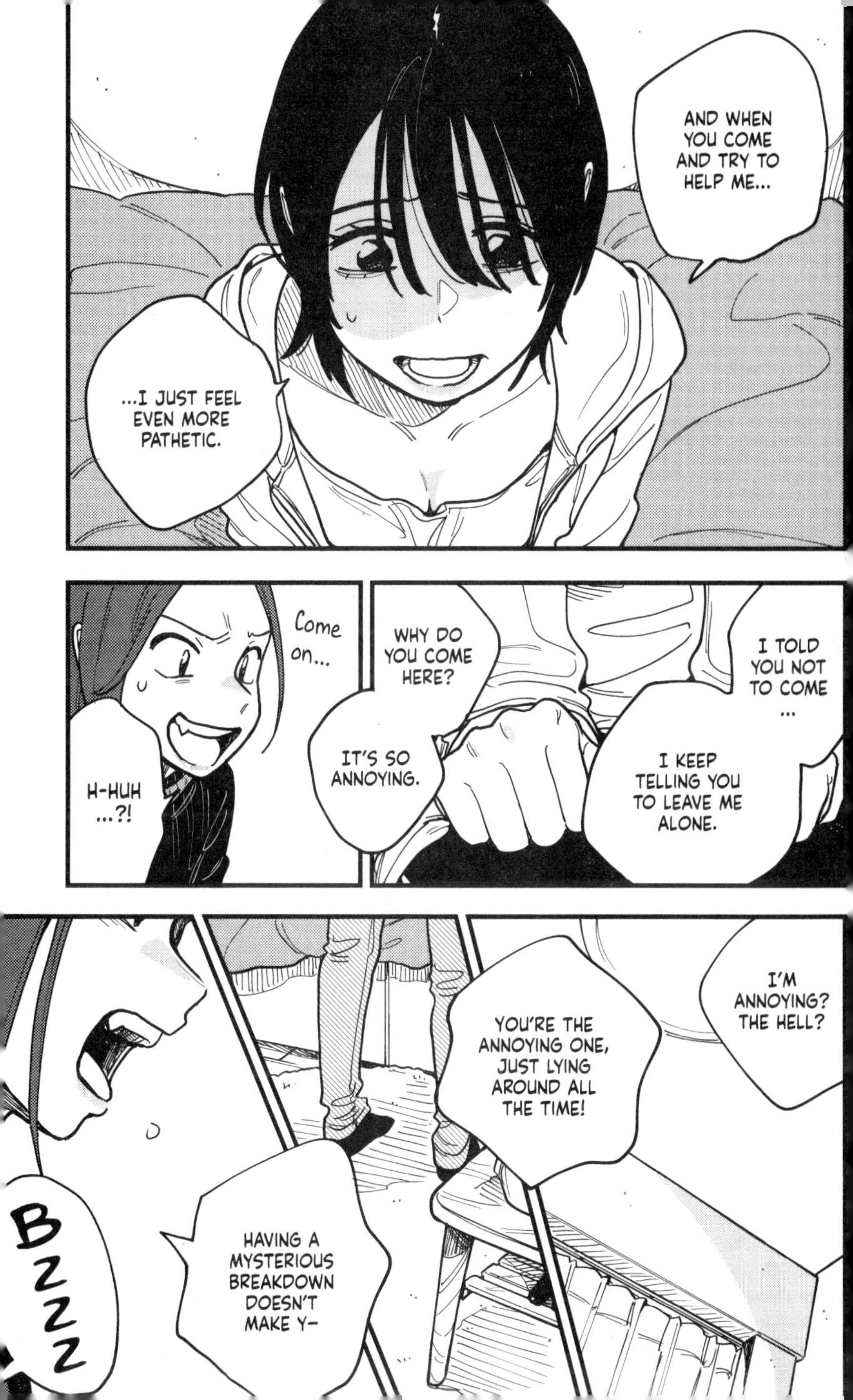
AND WHEN YOU COME AND TRY TO HELP ME...
...I JUST FEEL EVEN MORE PATHETIC.
I TOLD YOU NOT TO COME ...
I KEEP TELLING YOU TO LEAVE ME ALONE.
WHY DO YOU COME HERE?
IT'S SO ANNOYING.
Come on...
H-HUH ...?!
I'M ANNOYING? THE HELL?
YOU'RE THE ANNOYING ONE, JUST LYING AROUND ALL THE TIME!
HAVING A MYSTERIOUS BREAKDOWN DOESN'T MAKE Y-
BZZZ

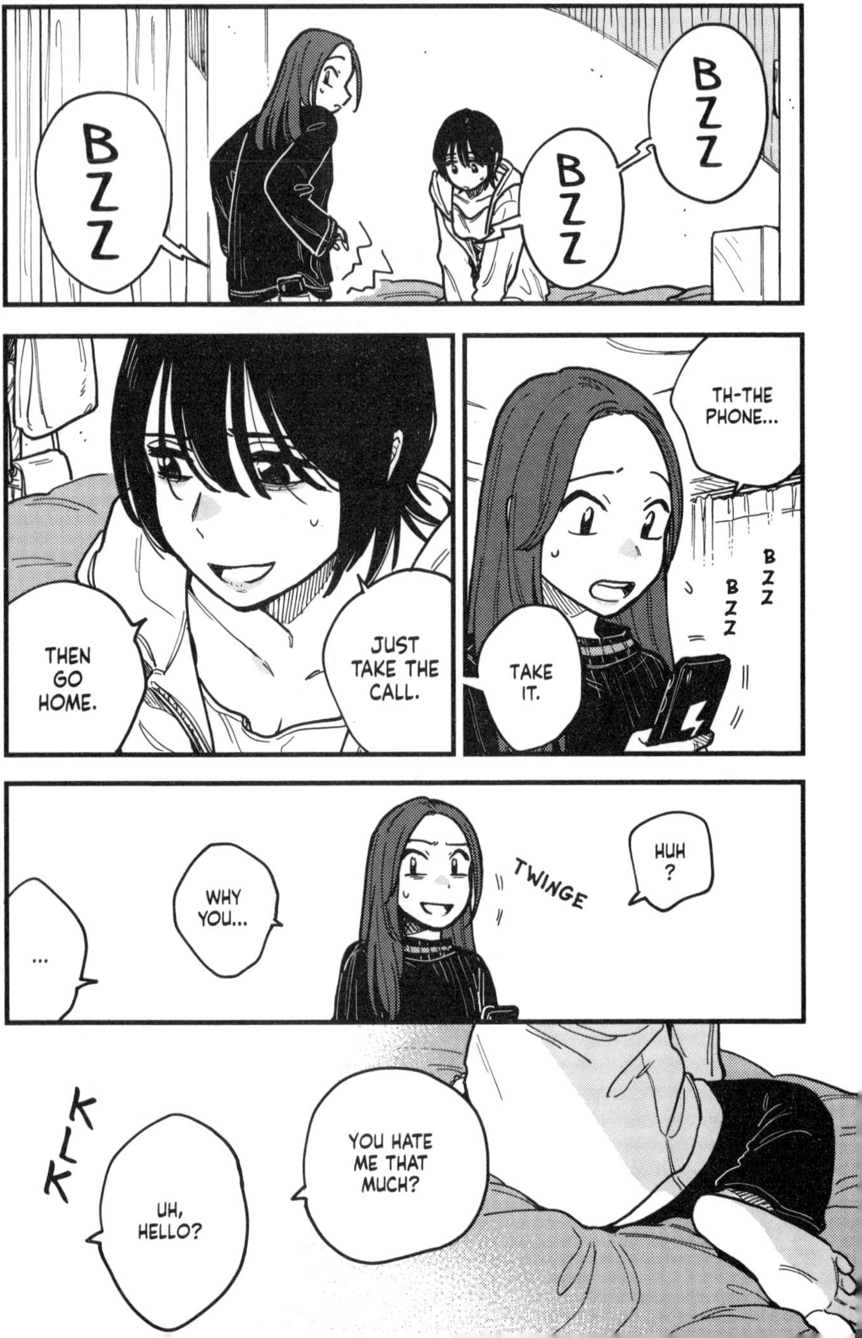
BZZ
BZZ
BZZ
TH-THE PHONE...
BZZ
BZZ
TAKE IT.
JUST TAKE THE CALL.
THEN GO HOME.
HUH?
TWINGE
WHY YOU...
...
YOU HATE ME THAT MUCH?
UH, HELLO?
KLIK

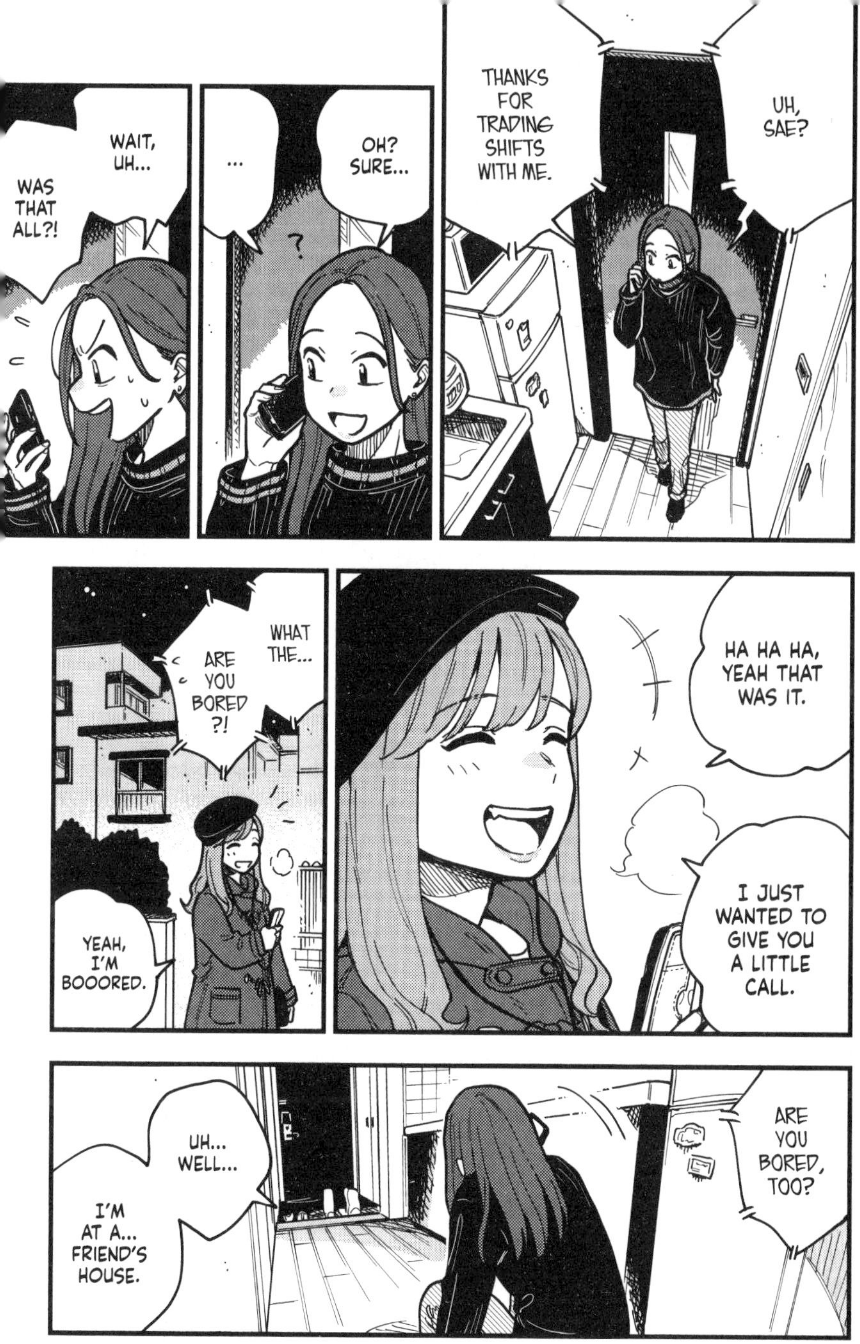
UH, SAE?
THANKS FOR TRADING SHIFTS WITH ME.
OH? SURE...
...
WAIT, UH...
WAS THAT ALL?!
HA HA HA, YEAH THAT WAS IT.
I JUST WANTED TO GIVE YOU A LITTLE CALL.
WHAT THE...
ARE YOU BORED?!
YEAH, I'M BOOORED.
ARE YOU BORED, TOO?
UH... WELL...
I'M AT A... FRIEND'S HOUSE.

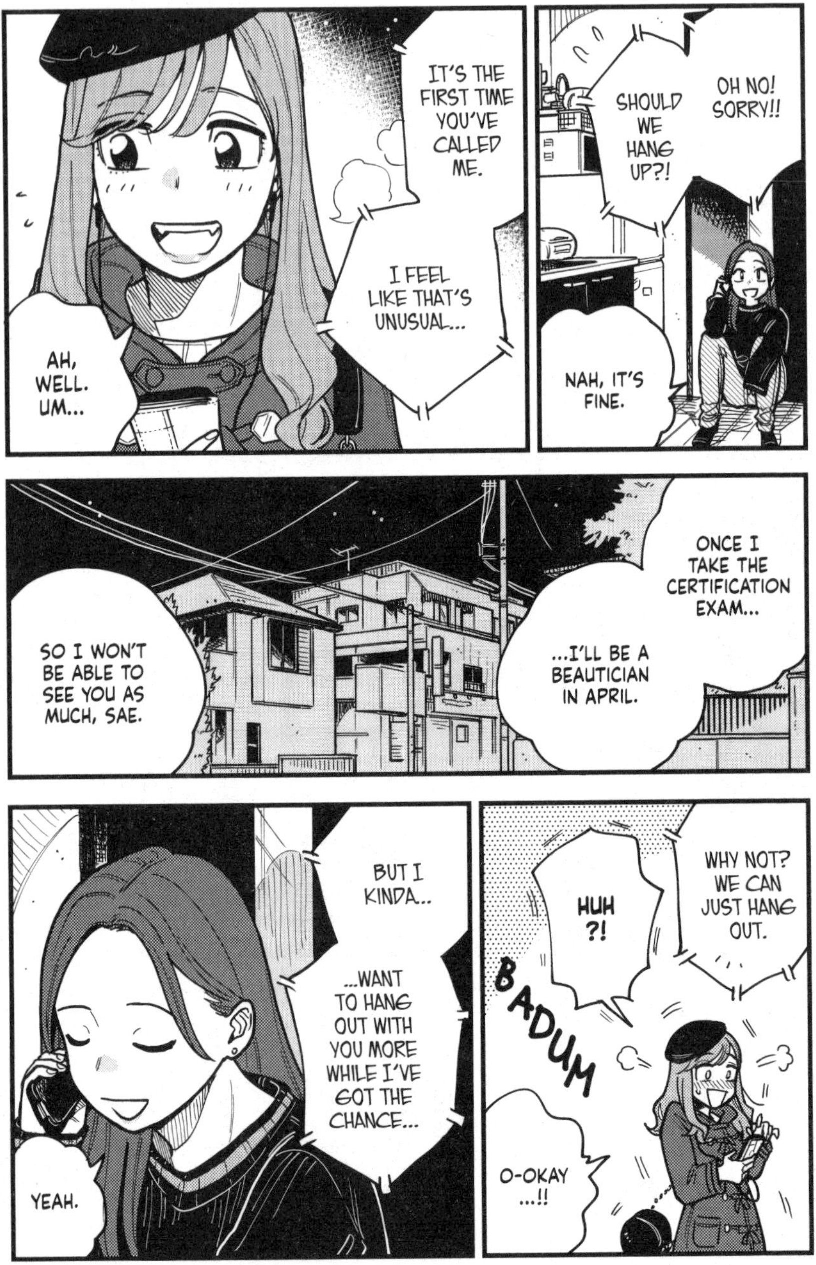
OH NO! SORRY!!
SHOULD WE HANG UP?!
NAH, IT'S FINE.
IT'S THE FIRST TIME YOU'VE CALLED ME.
I FEEL LIKE THAT'S UNUSUAL...
AH, WELL. UM...
ONCE I TAKE THE CERTIFICATION EXAM...
...I'LL BE A BEAUTICIAN IN APRIL.
SO I WON'T BE ABLE TO SEE YOU AS MUCH, SAE.
WHY NOT? WE CAN JUST HANG OUT.
HUH ?!
BADUM
O-OKAY ...!!
BUT I KINDA...
...WANT TO HANG OUT WITH YOU MORE WHILE I'VE GOT THE CHANCE...
YEAH.

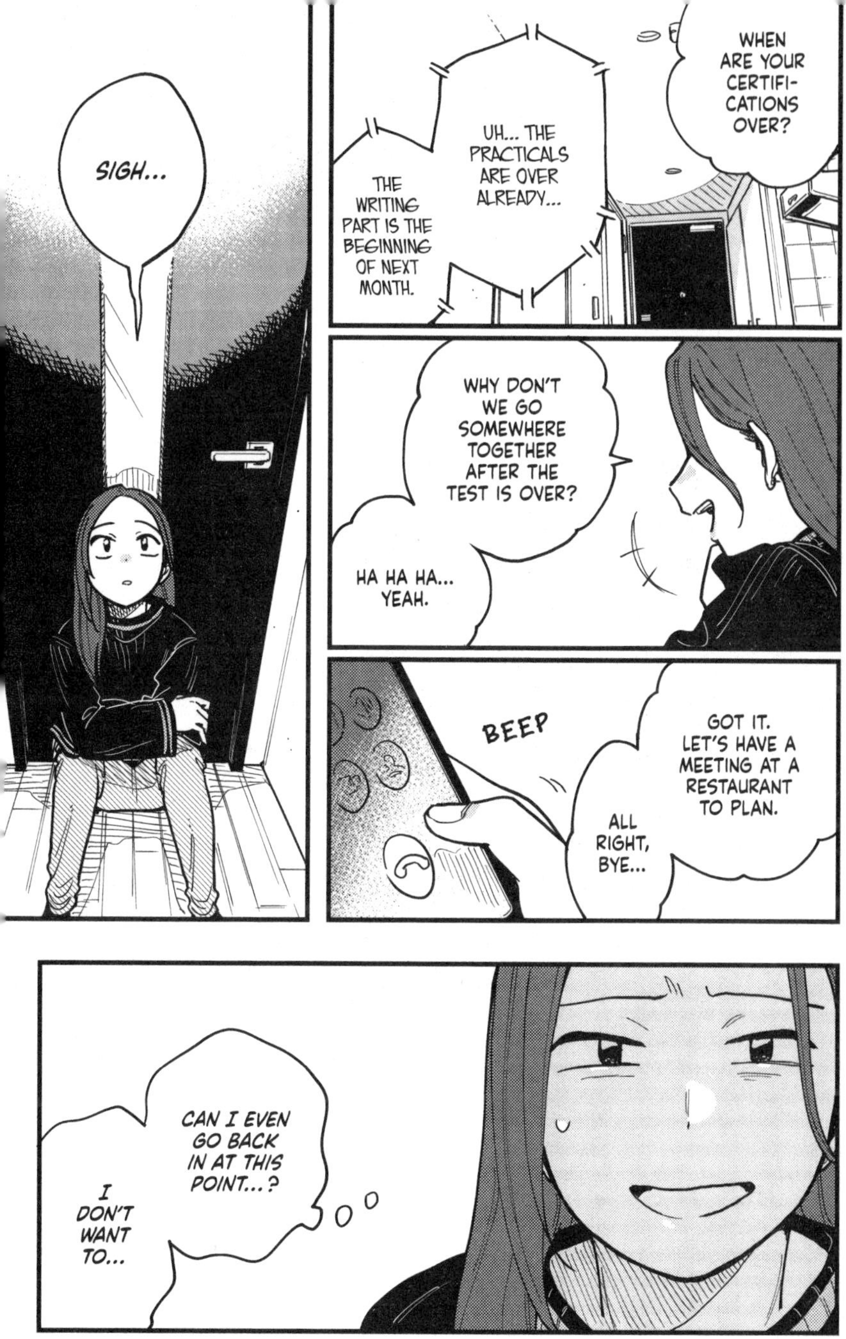
WHEN ARE YOUR CERTIFI-CATIONS OVER?
UH... THE PRACTICALS ARE OVER ALREADY...
THE WRITING PART IS THE BEGINNING OF NEXT MONTH.
WHY DON'T WE GO SOMEWHERE TOGETHER AFTER THE TEST IS OVER?
HA HA HA... YEAH.
GOT IT. LET'S HAVE A MEETING AT A RESTAURANT TO PLAN.
ALL RIGHT, BYE...
BEEP
SIGH...
CAN I EVEN GO BACK IN AT THIS POINT...?
I DON'T WANT TO...

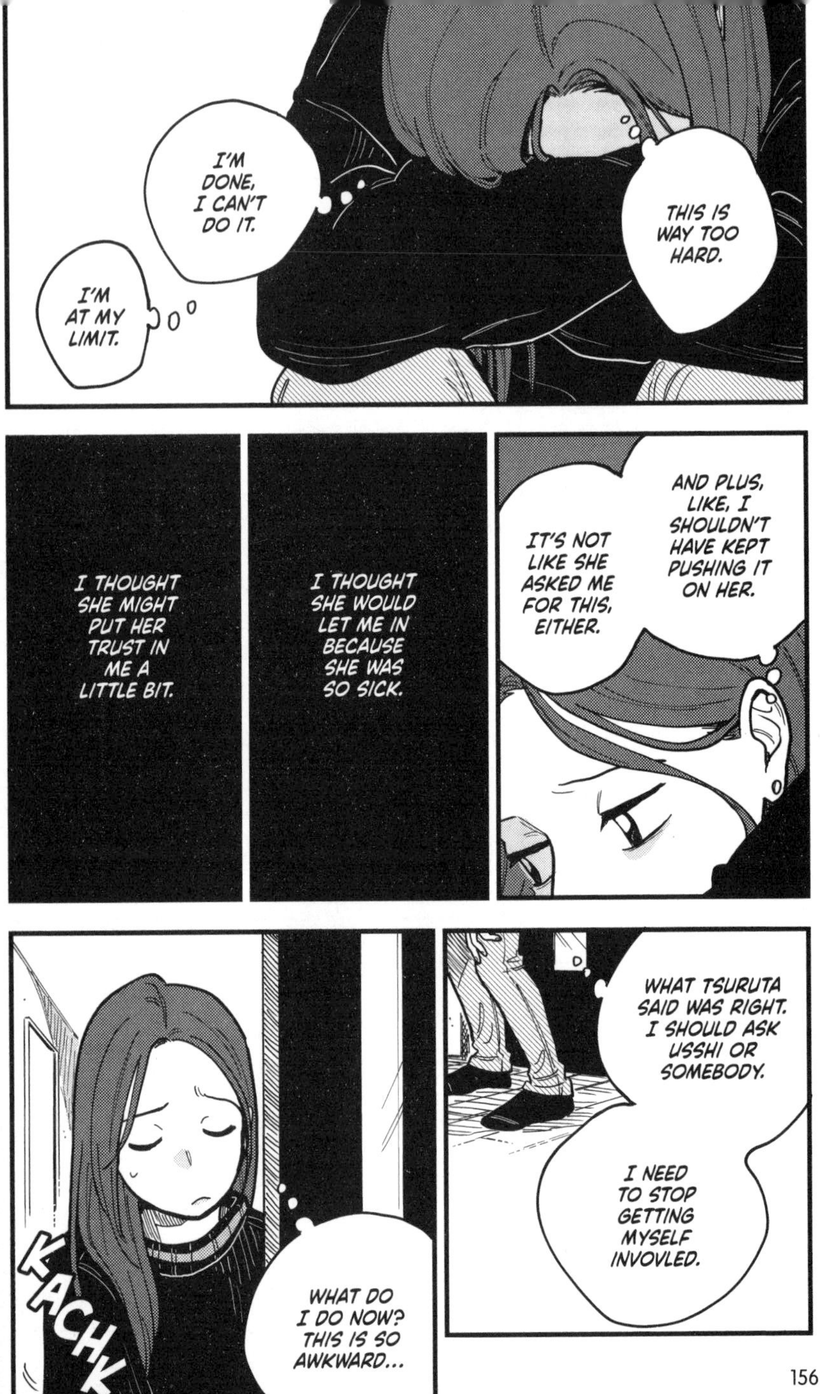
THIS IS WAY TOO HARD.
I'M DONE, I CAN'T DO IT.
I'M AT MY LIMIT.
AND PLUS, LIKE, I SHOULDN'T HAVE KEPT PUSHING IT ON HER.
IT'S NOT LIKE SHE ASKED ME FOR THIS, EITHER.
I THOUGHT SHE WOULD LET ME IN BECAUSE SHE WAS SO SICK.
I THOUGHT SHE MIGHT PUT HER TRUST IN ME A LITTLE BIT.
WHAT TSURUTA SAID WAS RIGHT. I SHOULD ASK USSHI OR SOMEBODY.
I NEED TO STOP GETTING MYSELF INVOVLED.
WHAT DO I DO NOW? THIS IS SO AWKWARD...
KACHK

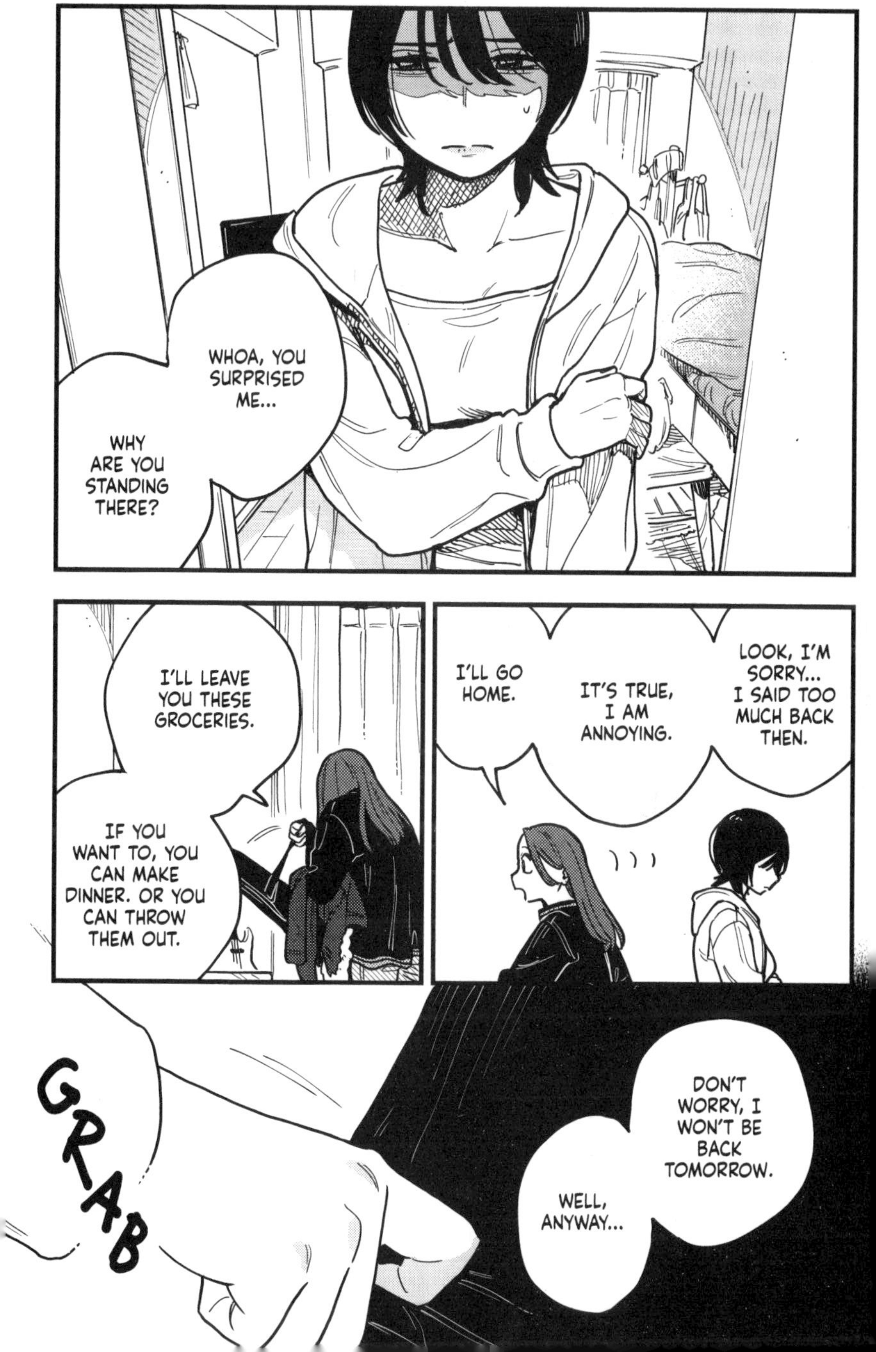
WHOA, YOU SURPRISED ME...
WHY ARE YOU STANDING THERE?
LOOK, I'M SORRY... I SAID TOO MUCH BACK THEN.
IT'S TRUE, I AM ANNOYING.
I'LL GO HOME.
I'LL LEAVE YOU THESE GROCERIES.
IF YOU WANT TO, YOU CAN MAKE DINNER. OR YOU CAN THROW THEM OUT.
DON'T WORRY, I WON'T BE BACK TOMORROW.
WELL, ANYWAY...
GRAB

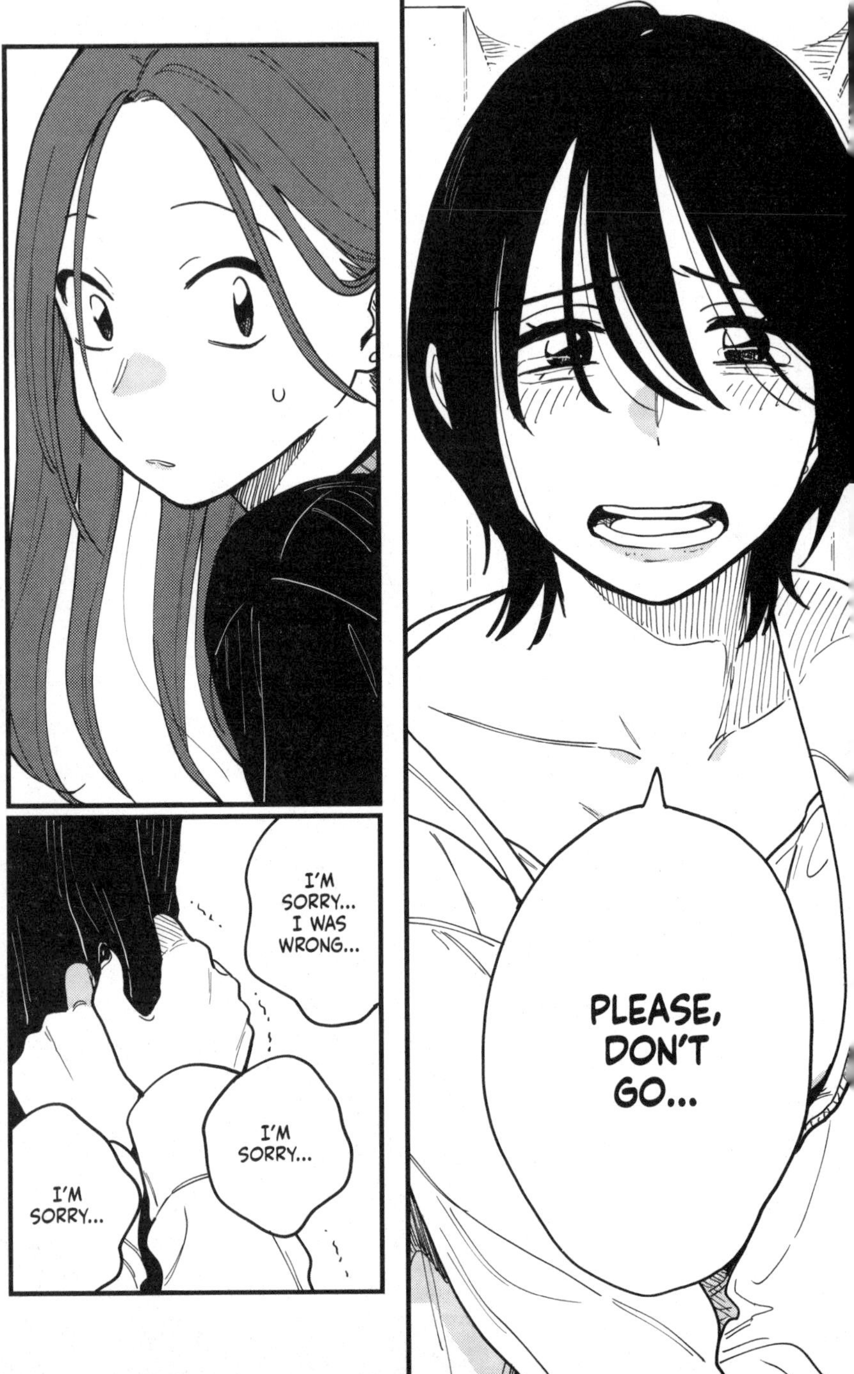
PLEASE, DON'T GO...
I'M SORRY... I WAS WRONG...
I'M SORRY...
I'M SORRY...

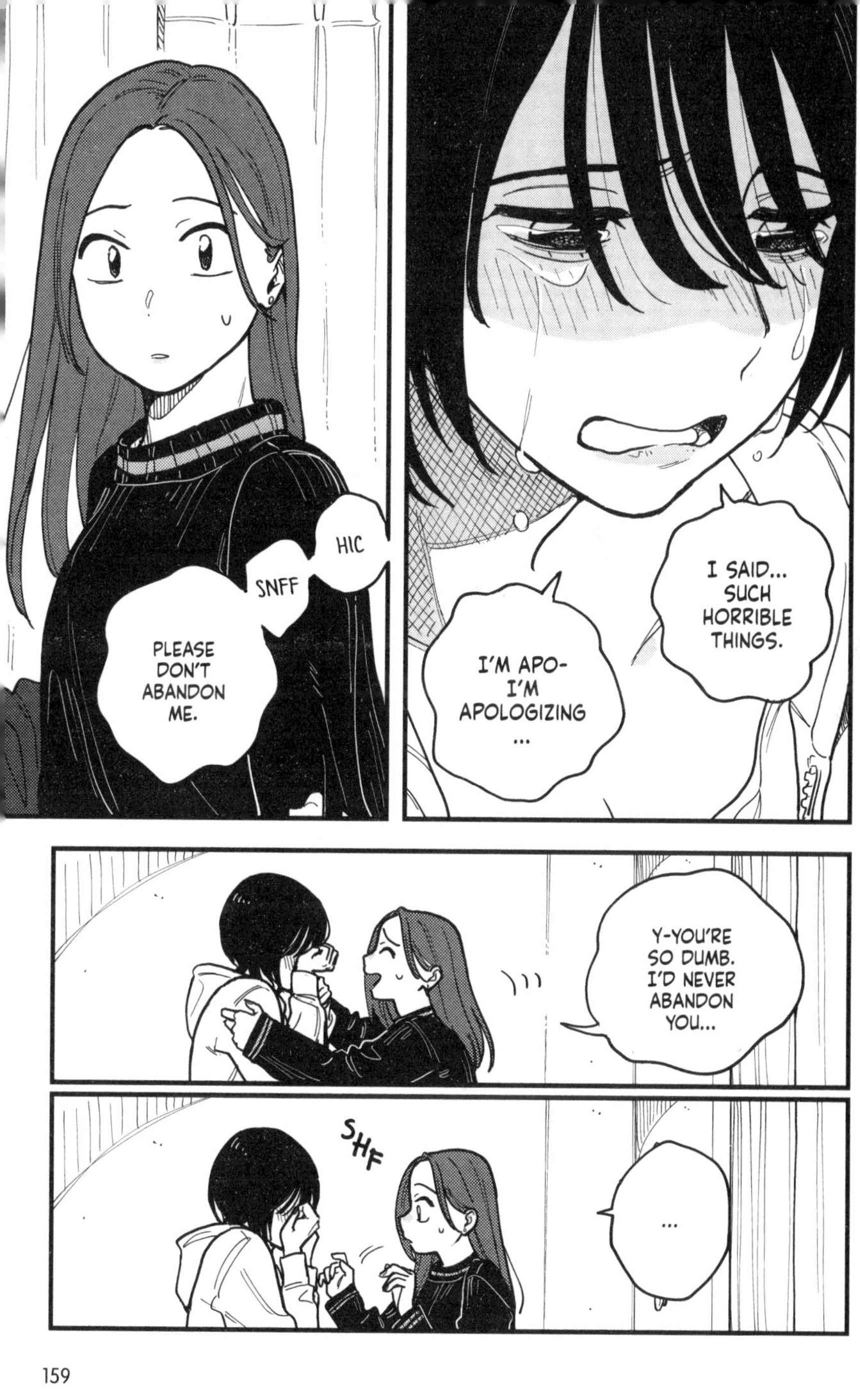
I SAID... SUCH HORRIBLE THINGS.
I'M APO- I'M APOLOGIZING ...
HIC
SNFF
PLEASE DON'T ABANDON ME.
Y-YOU'RE SO DUMB. I'D NEVER ABANDON YOU...
...
SHF

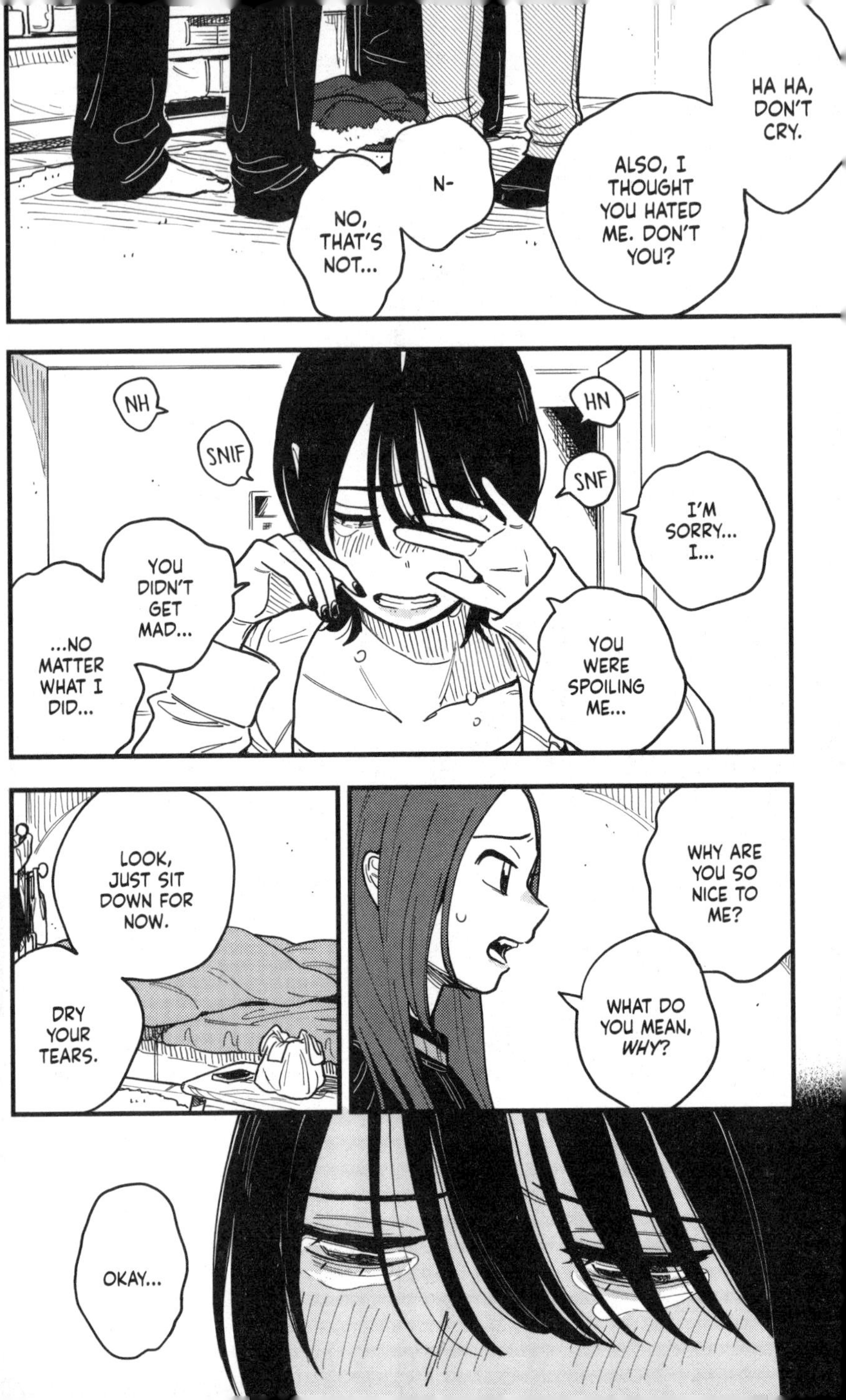
HA HA, DON'T CRY.
ALSO, I THOUGHT YOU HATED ME. DON'T YOU?
N-
NO, THAT'S NOT...
HN
SNF
I'M SORRY... I...
YOU WERE SPOILING ME...
NH
SNIF
YOU DIDN'T GET MAD...
...NO MATTER WHAT I DID...
WHY ARE YOU SO NICE TO ME?
WHAT DO YOU MEAN, *WHY*?
LOOK, JUST SIT DOWN FOR NOW.
DRY YOUR TEARS.
OKAY...

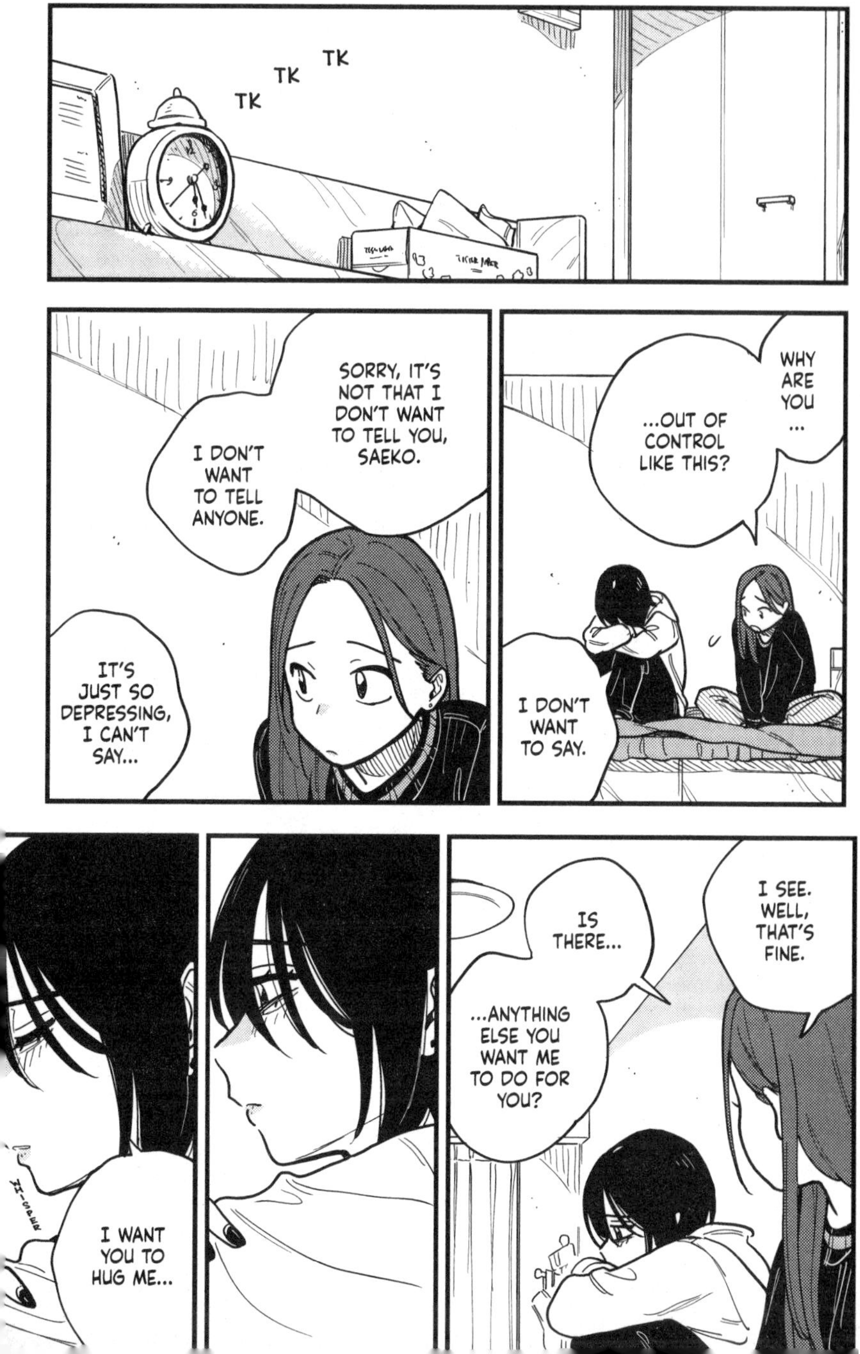
TK
TK
TK
WHY ARE YOU ...
...OUT OF CONTROL LIKE THIS?
I DON'T WANT TO SAY.
SORRY, IT'S NOT THAT I DON'T WANT TO TELL YOU, SAEKO.
I DON'T WANT TO TELL ANYONE.
IT'S JUST SO DEPRESSING, I CAN'T SAY...
I SEE. WELL, THAT'S FINE.
IS THERE...
...ANYTHING ELSE YOU WANT ME TO DO FOR YOU?
WHI-SPER
I WANT YOU TO HUG ME...

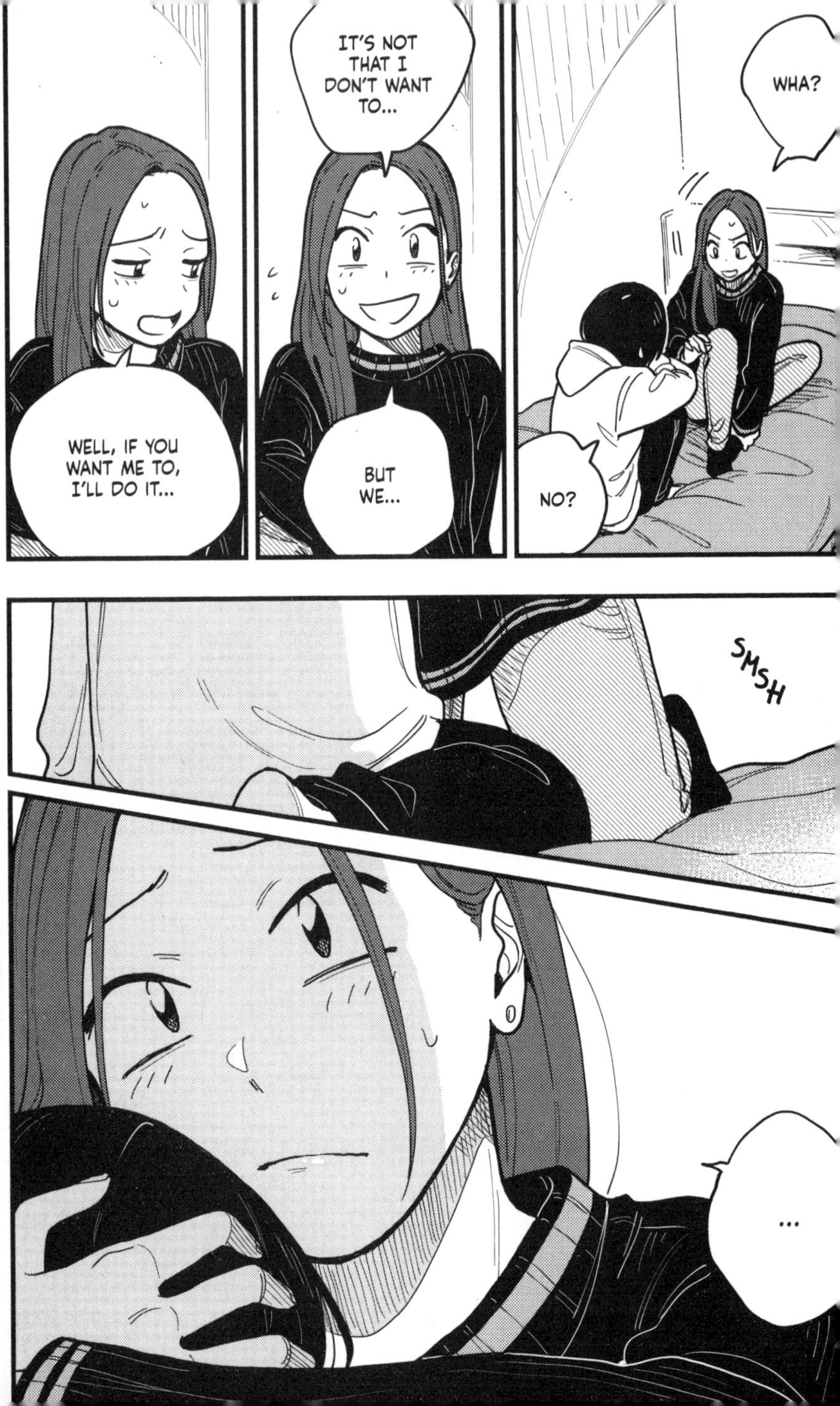
WHA?
NO?
IT'S NOT THAT I DON'T WANT TO...
BUT WE...
WELL, IF YOU WANT ME TO, I'LL DO IT...
SMSH
...

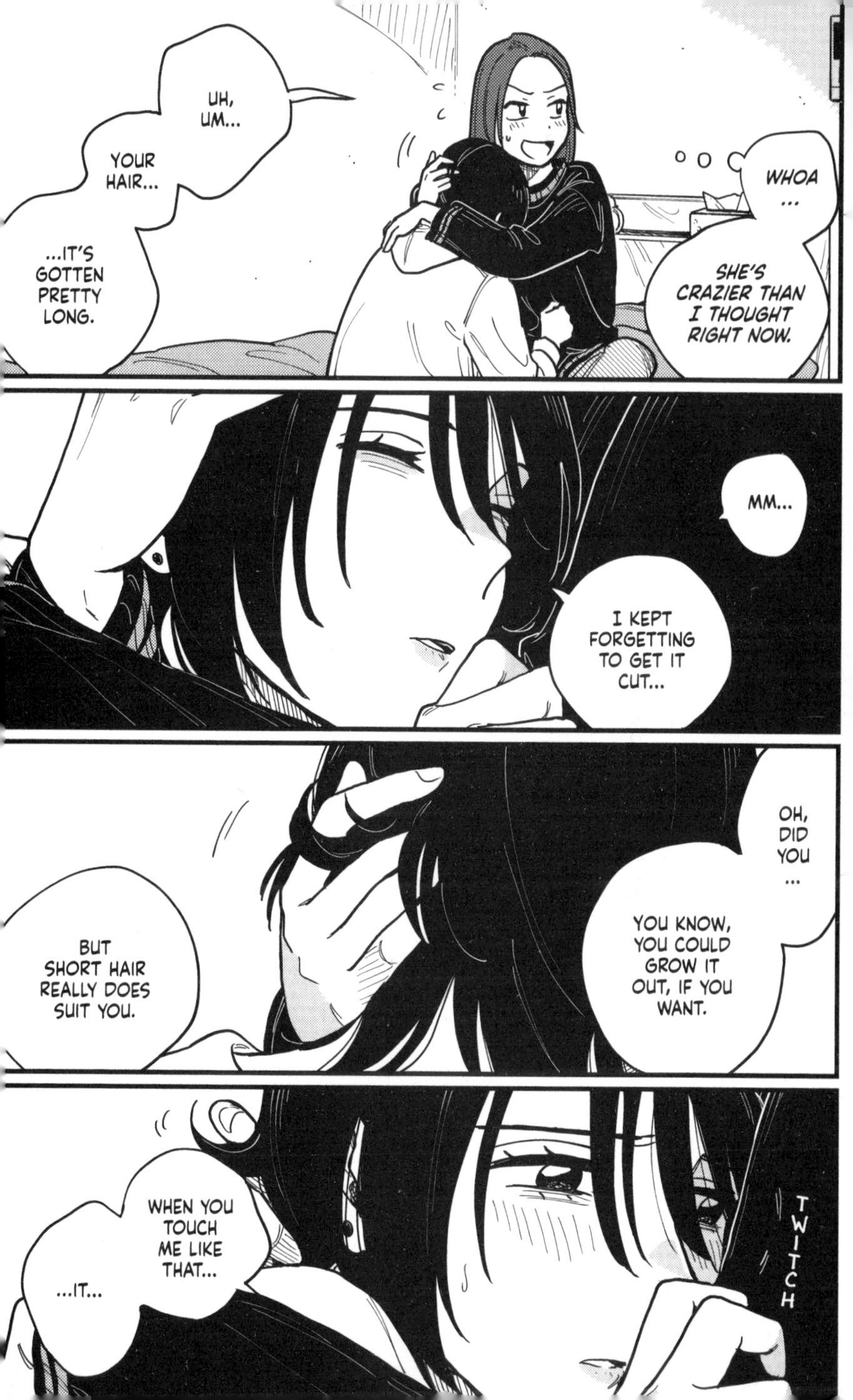
WHOA...
SHE'S CRAZIER THAN I THOUGHT RIGHT NOW.
UH, UM...
YOUR HAIR...
...IT'S GOTTEN PRETTY LONG.
MM...
I KEPT FORGETTING TO GET IT CUT...
OH, DID YOU...
YOU KNOW, YOU COULD GROW IT OUT, IF YOU WANT.
BUT SHORT HAIR REALLY DOES SUIT YOU.
TWITCH
WHEN YOU TOUCH ME LIKE THAT...
...IT...

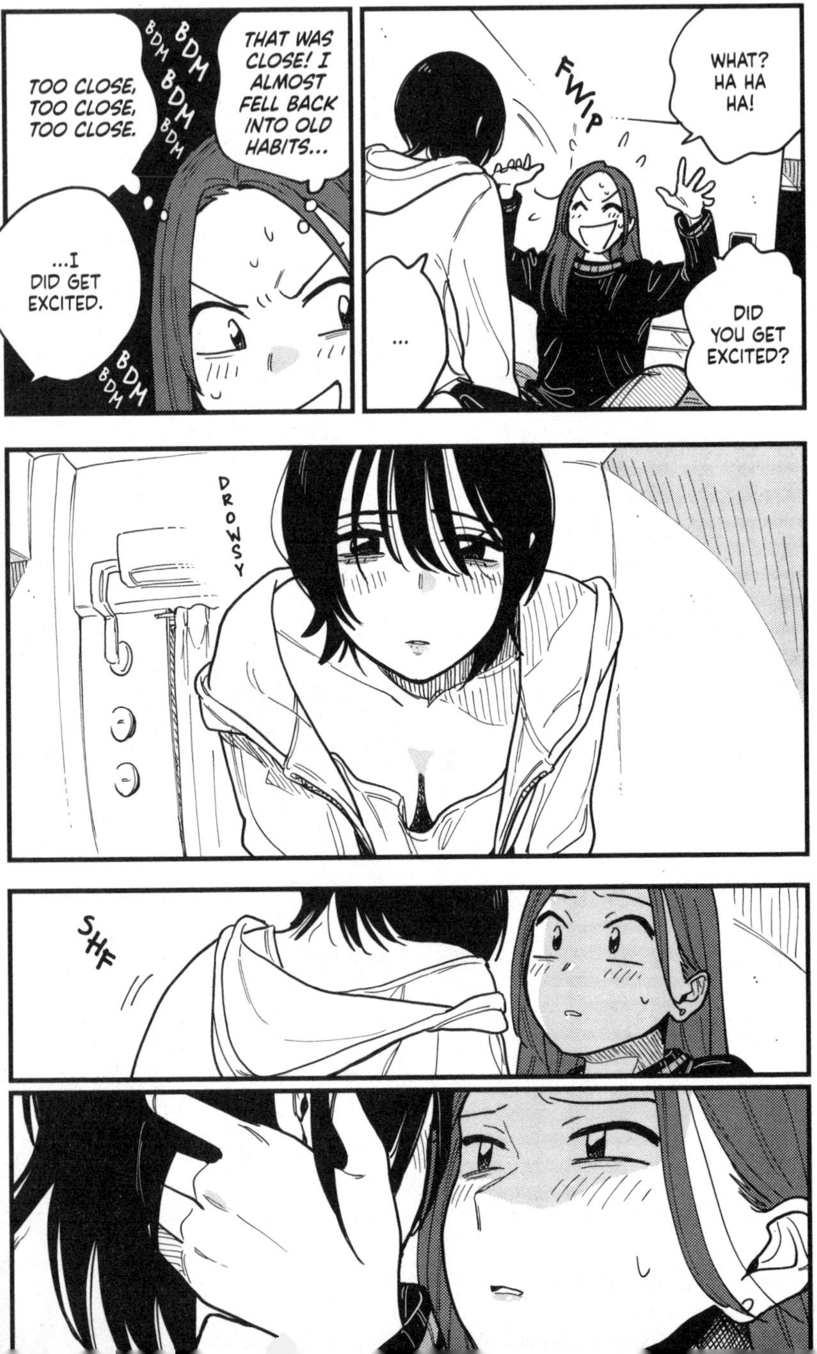
WHAT? HA HA HA!
FWIP
DID YOU GET EXCITED?
...
THAT WAS CLOSE! I ALMOST FELL BACK INTO OLD HABITS...
BDM BDM BDM BDM
TOO CLOSE, TOO CLOSE, TOO CLOSE.
...I DID GET EXCITED.
BDM BDM
DROWSY
SHF

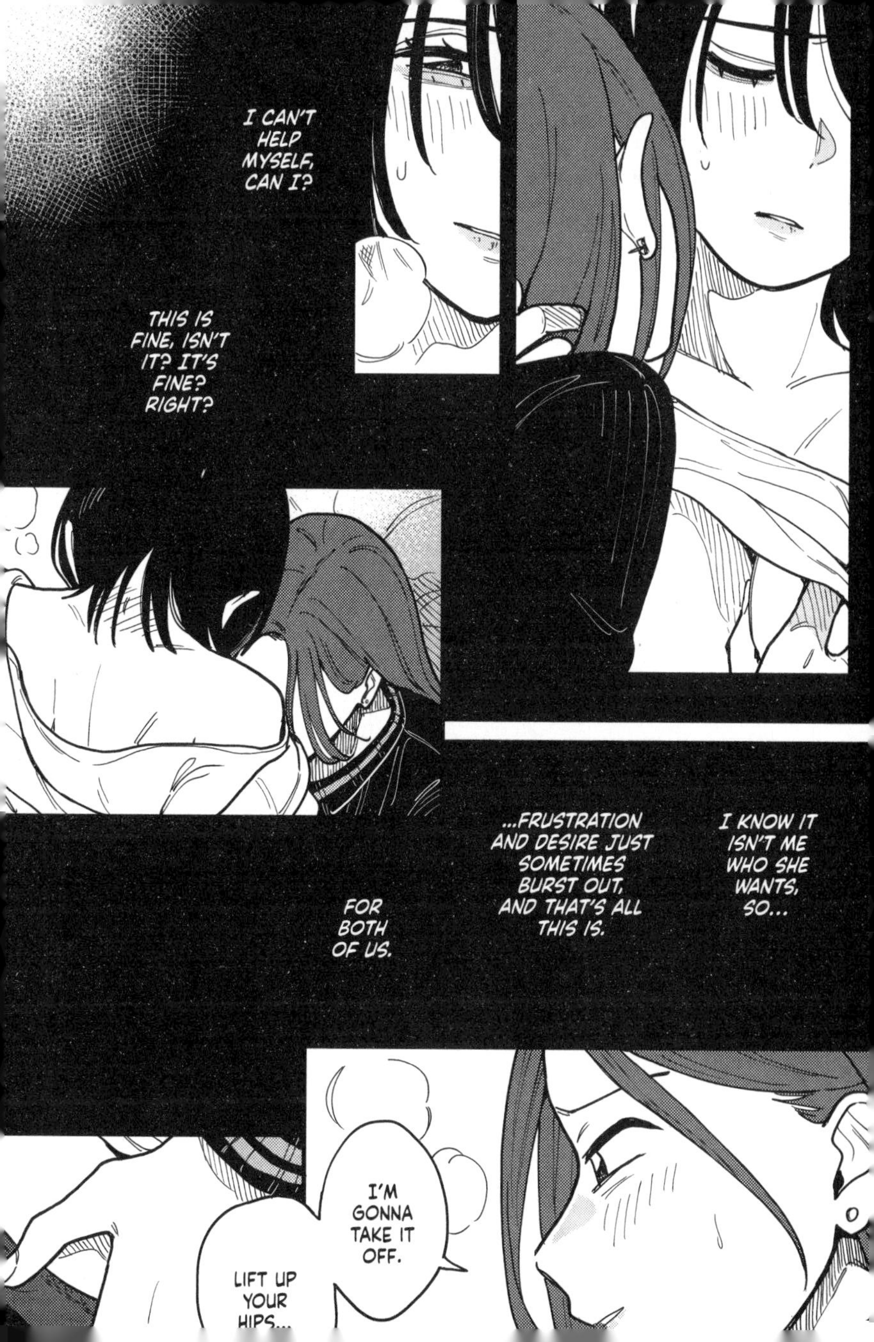
I CAN'T HELP MYSELF, CAN I?
THIS IS FINE, ISN'T IT? IT'S FINE? RIGHT?
I KNOW IT ISN'T ME WHO SHE WANTS, SO...
...FRUSTRATION AND DESIRE JUST SOMETIMES BURST OUT, AND THAT'S ALL THIS IS.
FOR BOTH OF US.
I'M GONNA TAKE IT OFF.
LIFT UP YOUR HIPS...

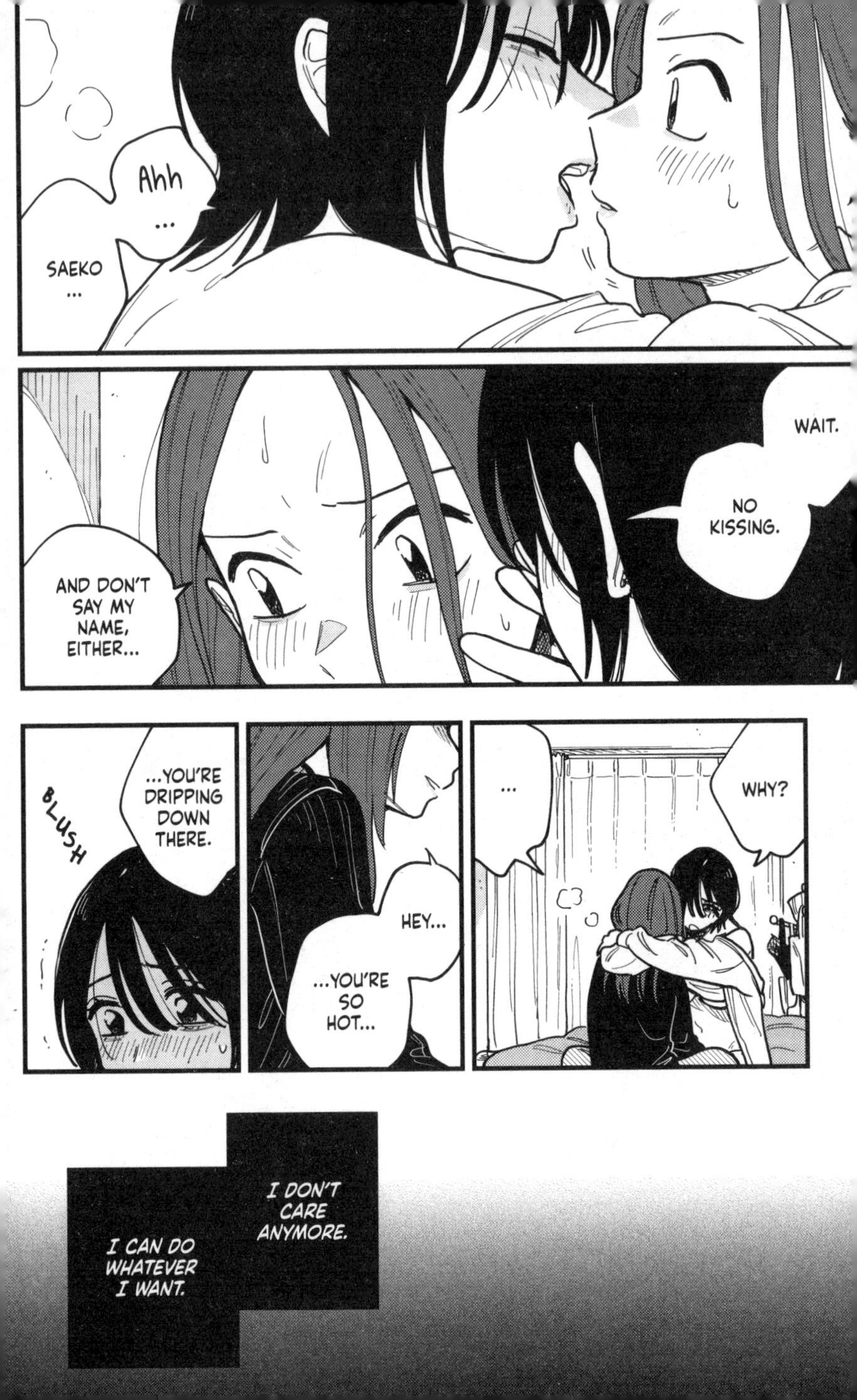

Ahh
...
SAEKO
...
WAIT.
NO KISSING.
AND DON'T SAY MY NAME, EITHER...
WHY?
...
HEY...
...YOU'RE SO HOT...
...YOU'RE DRIPPING DOWN THERE.
BLUSH
I DON'T CARE ANYMORE.
I CAN DO WHATEVER I WANT.

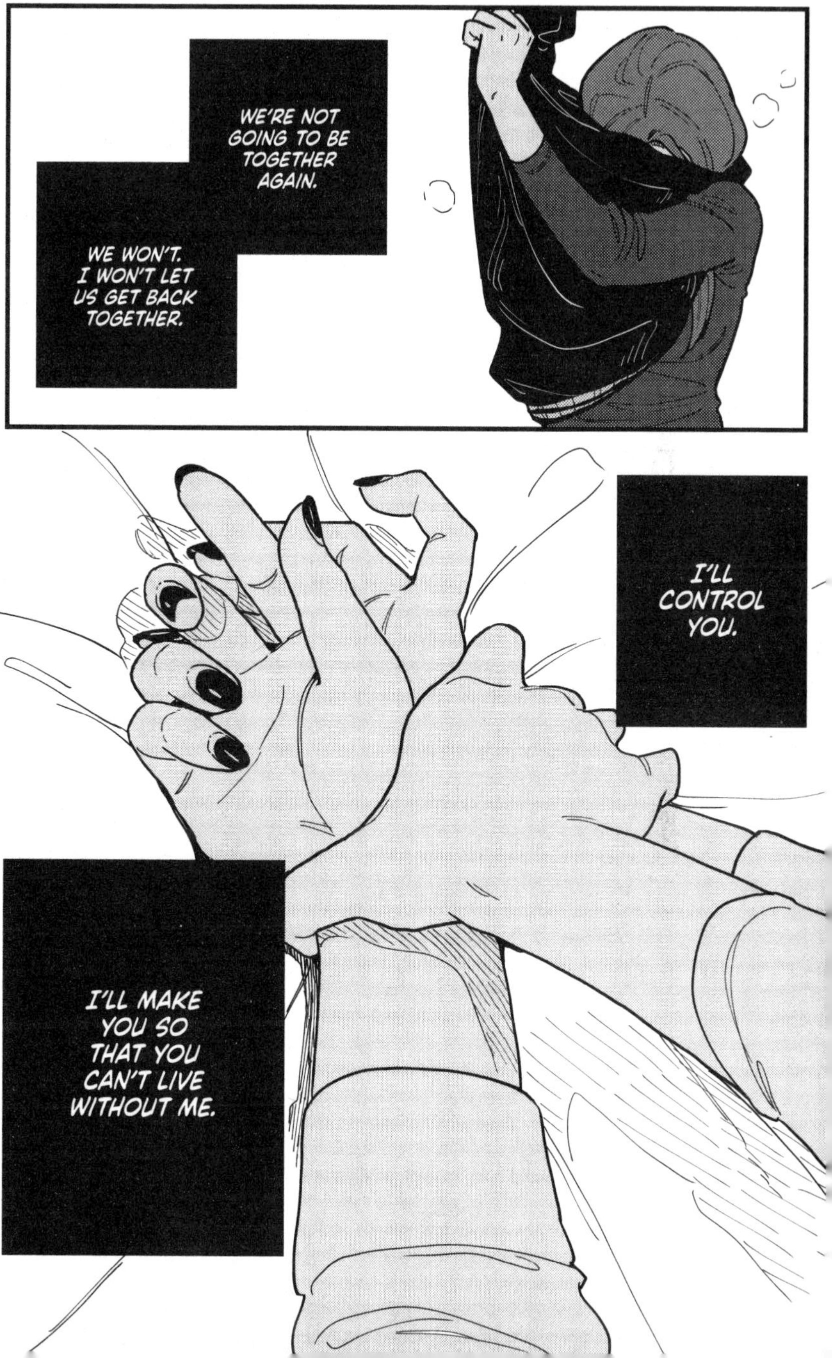
WE'RE NOT GOING TO BE TOGETHER AGAIN.
WE WON'T. I WON'T LET US GET BACK TOGETHER.
I'LL CONTROL YOU.
I'LL MAKE YOU SO THAT YOU CAN'T LIVE WITHOUT ME.

How Do We Relationship?

Chapter 45: If You Make a Mistake…

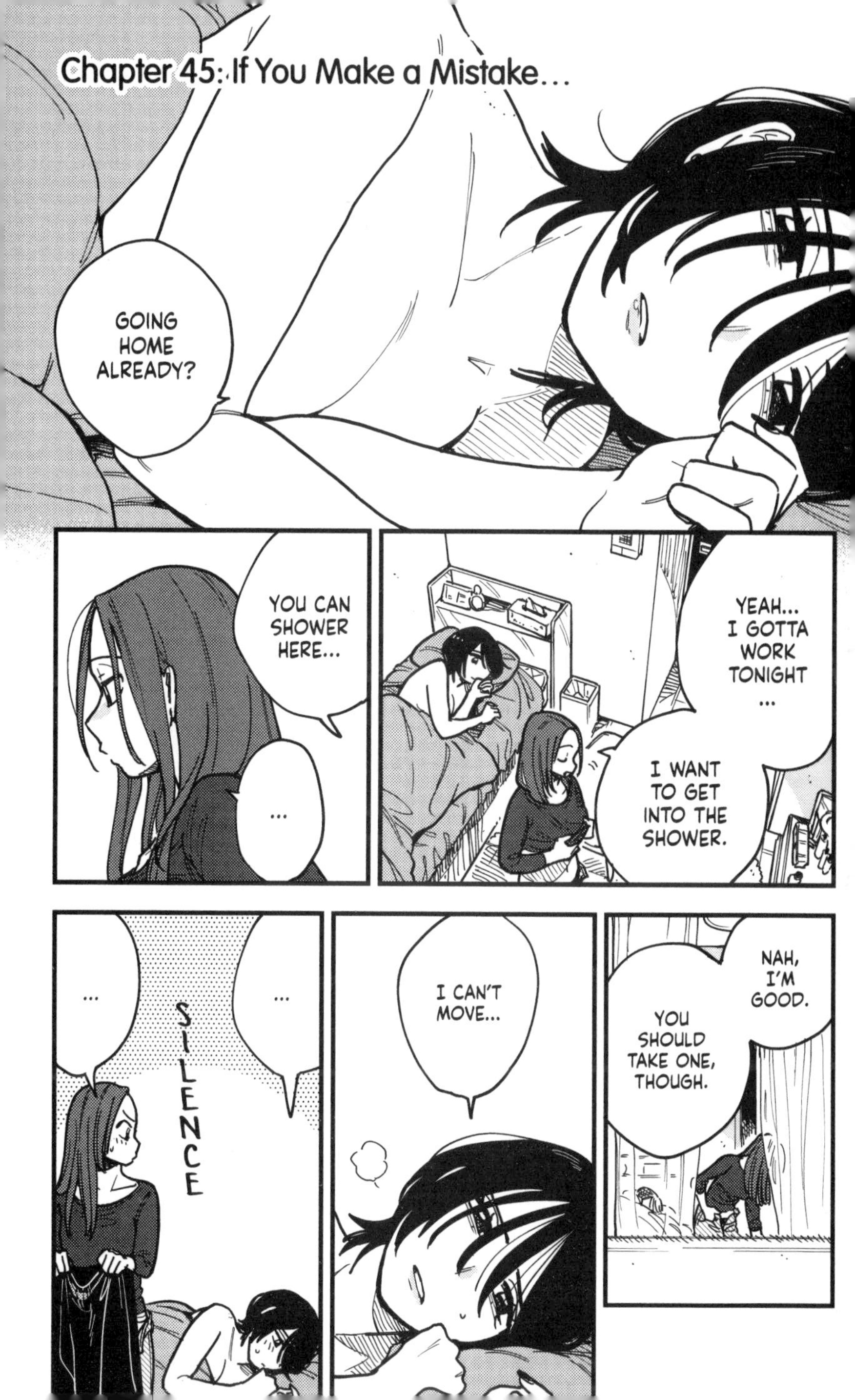
GOING HOME ALREADY?
YEAH... I GOTTA WORK TONIGHT...
I WANT TO GET INTO THE SHOWER.
YOU CAN SHOWER HERE...
...
NAH, I'M GOOD.
YOU SHOULD TAKE ONE, THOUGH.
I CAN'T MOVE...
...
...
SILENCE

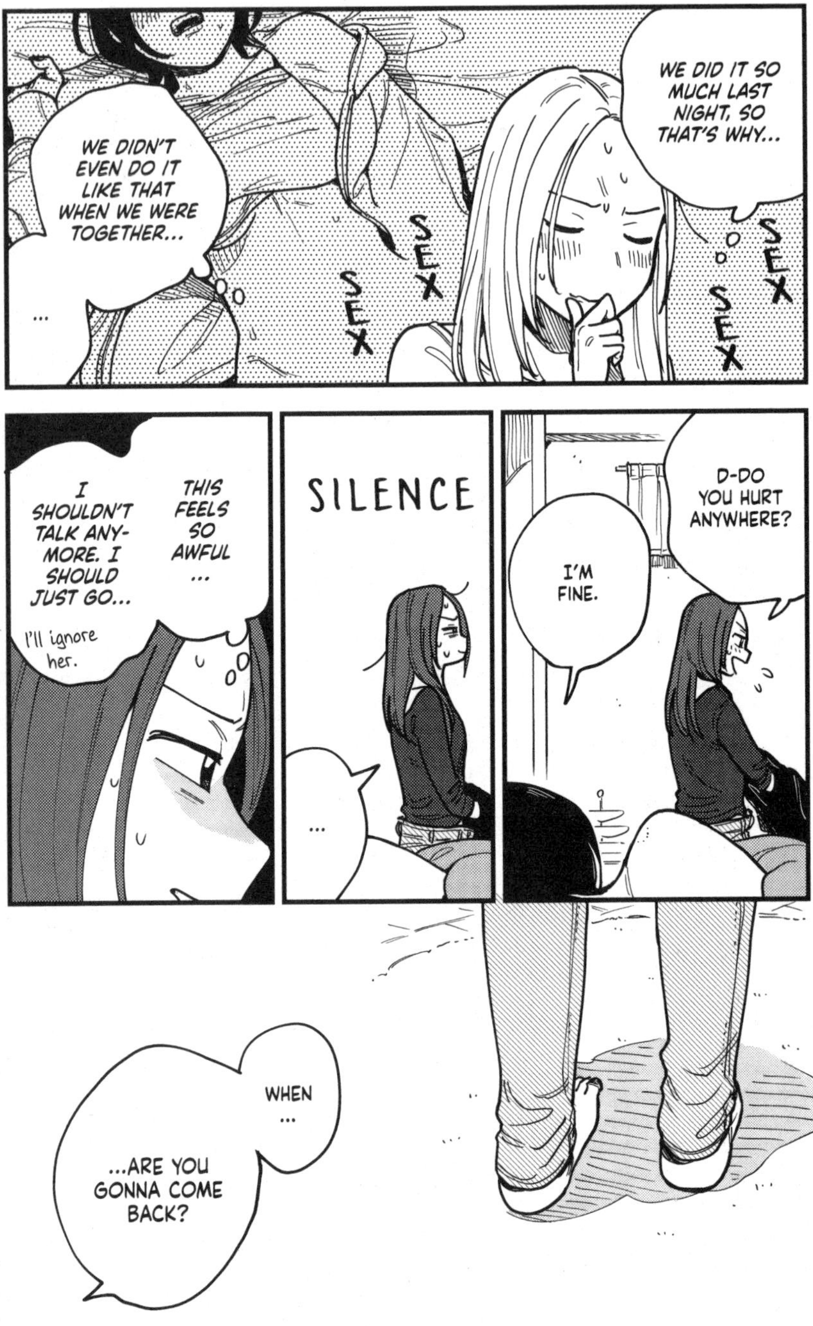
WE DID IT SO MUCH LAST NIGHT, SO THAT'S WHY...
SEX SEX
WE DIDN'T EVEN DO IT LIKE THAT WHEN WE WERE TOGETHER...
SEX SEX
...
D-DO YOU HURT ANYWHERE?
I'M FINE.
SILENCE
...
THIS FEELS SO AWFUL...
I SHOULDN'T TALK ANY-MORE. I SHOULD JUST GO...
I'll ignore her.
WHEN...
...ARE YOU GONNA COME BACK?

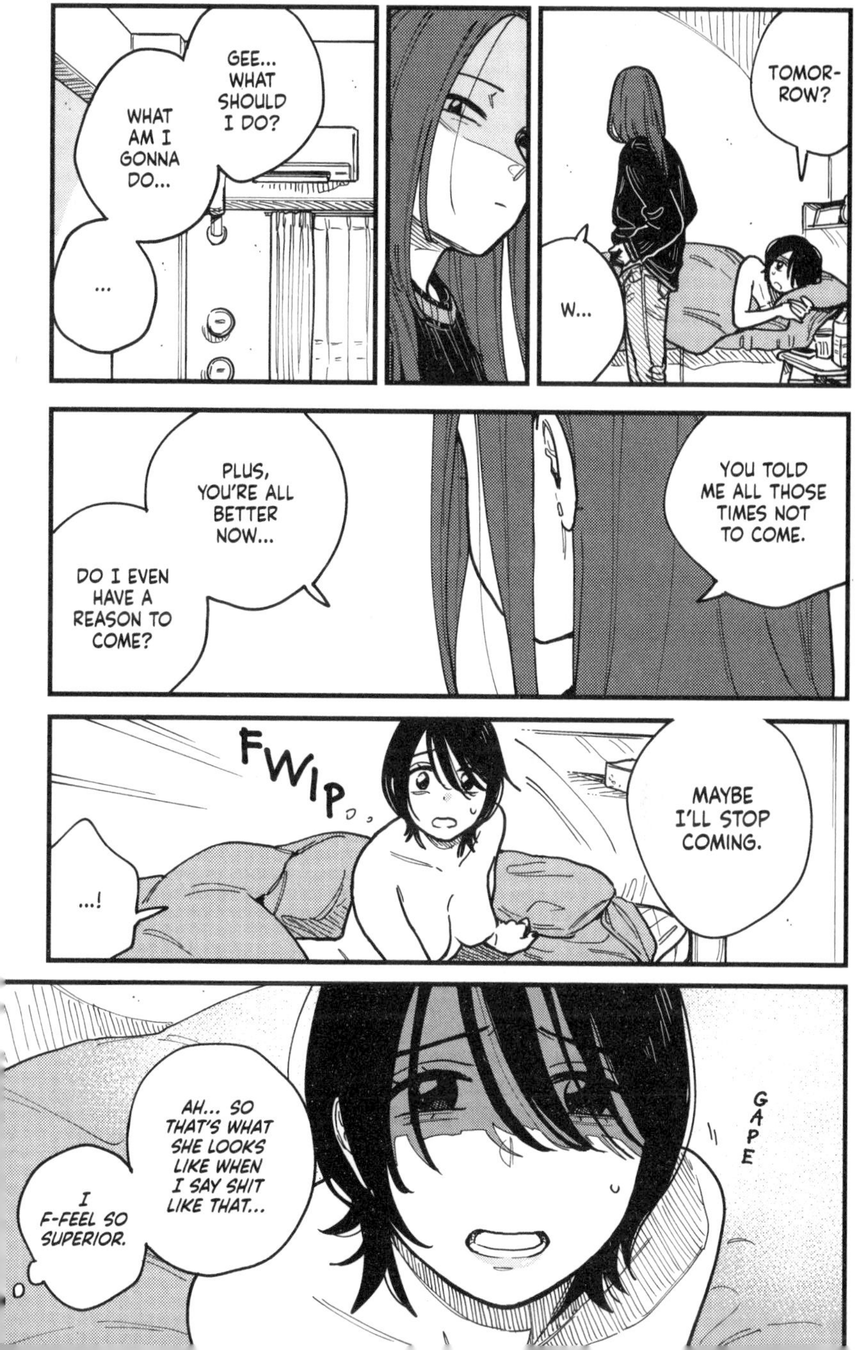
TOMOR-ROW?
W...
GEE... WHAT SHOULD I DO?
WHAT AM I GONNA DO...
...
YOU TOLD ME ALL THOSE TIMES NOT TO COME.
PLUS, YOU'RE ALL BETTER NOW...
DO I EVEN HAVE A REASON TO COME?
MAYBE I'LL STOP COMING.
FWIP
...!
GAPE
AH... SO THAT'S WHAT SHE LOOKS LIKE WHEN I SAY SHIT LIKE THAT...
I F-FEEL SO SUPERIOR.

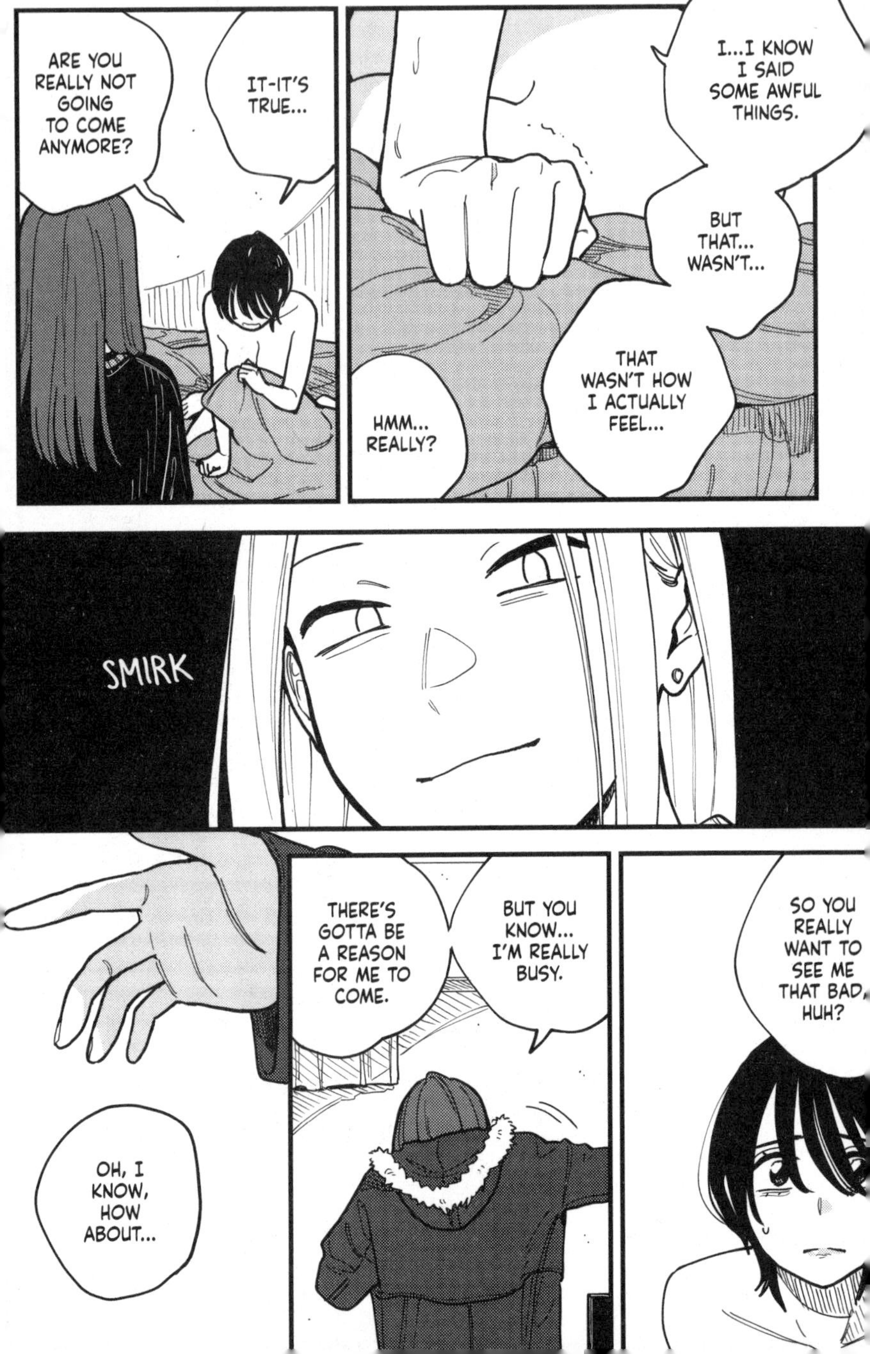
I...I KNOW I SAID SOME AWFUL THINGS.
BUT THAT... WASN'T...
THAT WASN'T HOW I ACTUALLY FEEL...
HMM... REALLY?
IT-IT'S TRUE...
ARE YOU REALLY NOT GOING TO COME ANYMORE?
SMIRK
SO YOU REALLY WANT TO SEE ME THAT BAD, HUH?
BUT YOU KNOW... I'M REALLY BUSY.
THERE'S GOTTA BE A REASON FOR ME TO COME.
OH, I KNOW, HOW ABOUT...

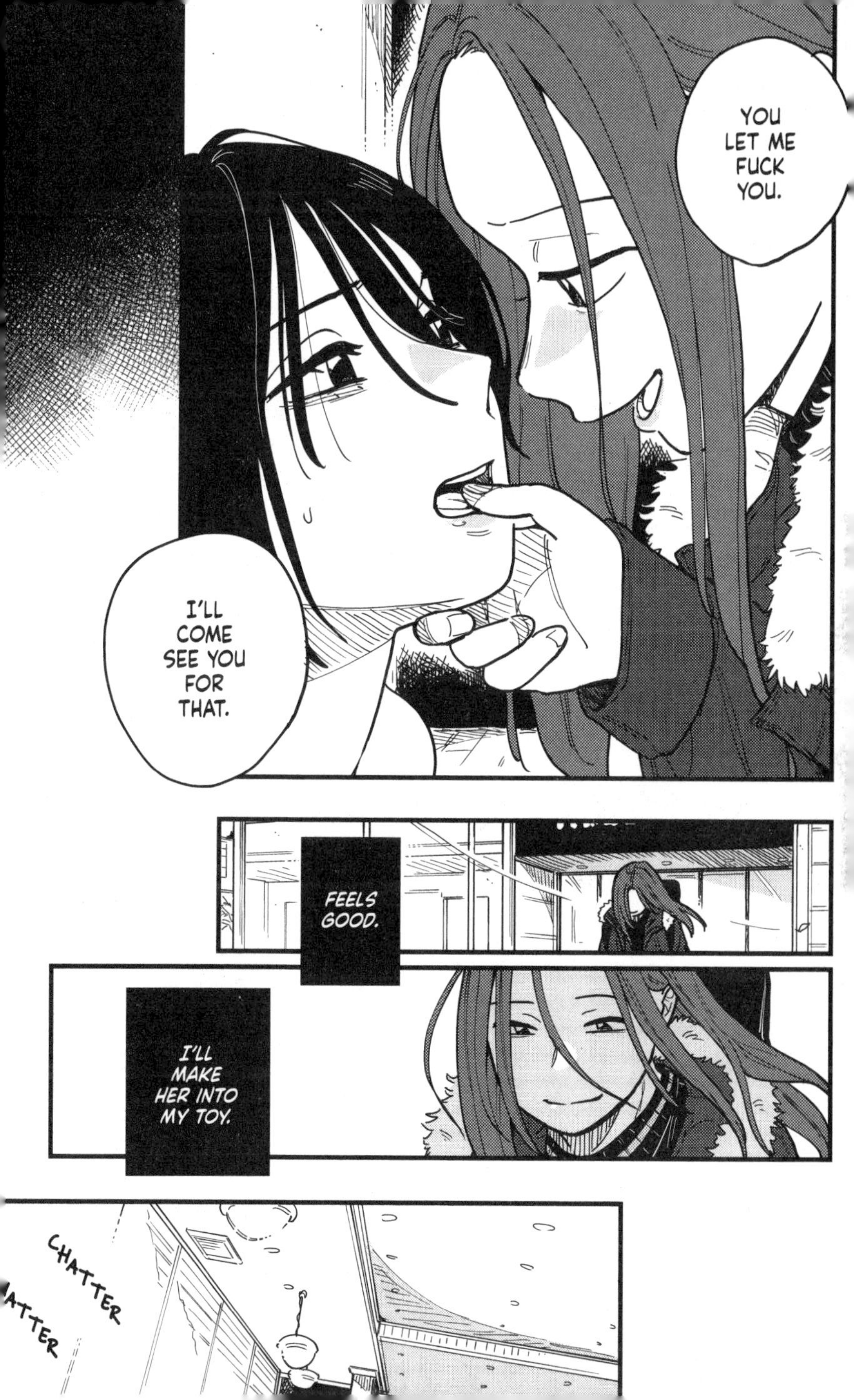
YOU LET ME FUCK YOU.
I'LL COME SEE YOU FOR THAT.
FEELS GOOD.
I'LL MAKE HER INTO MY TOY.
CHATTER
CHATTER

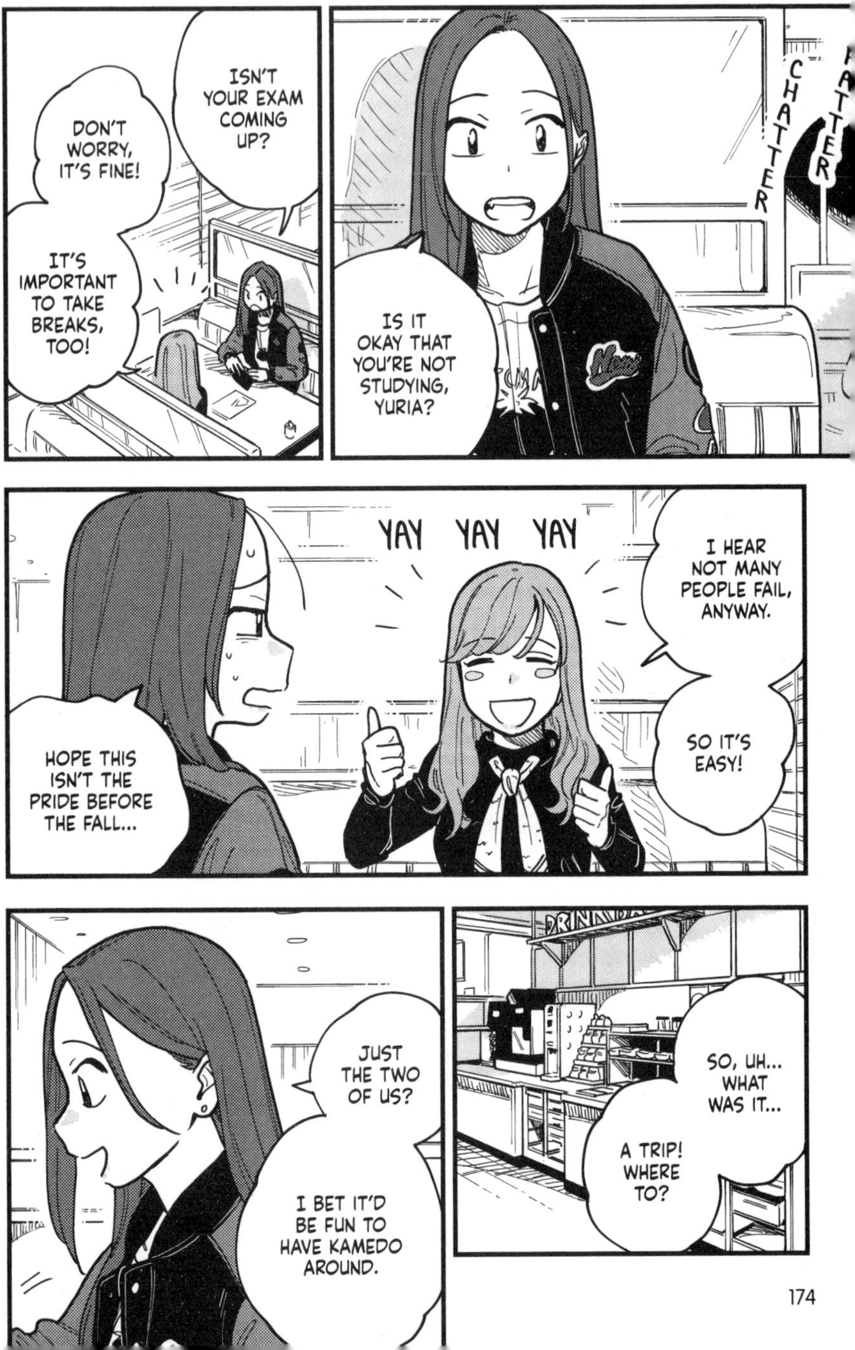
CHATTER
CHATTER
IS IT OKAY THAT YOU'RE NOT STUDYING, YURIA?
ISN'T YOUR EXAM COMING UP?
DON'T WORRY, IT'S FINE!
IT'S IMPORTANT TO TAKE BREAKS, TOO!
I HEAR NOT MANY PEOPLE FAIL, ANYWAY.
SO IT'S EASY!
YAY YAY YAY
HOPE THIS ISN'T THE PRIDE BEFORE THE FALL...
SO, UH... WHAT WAS IT...
A TRIP! WHERE TO?
JUST THE TWO OF US?
I BET IT'D BE FUN TO HAVE KAMEDO AROUND.

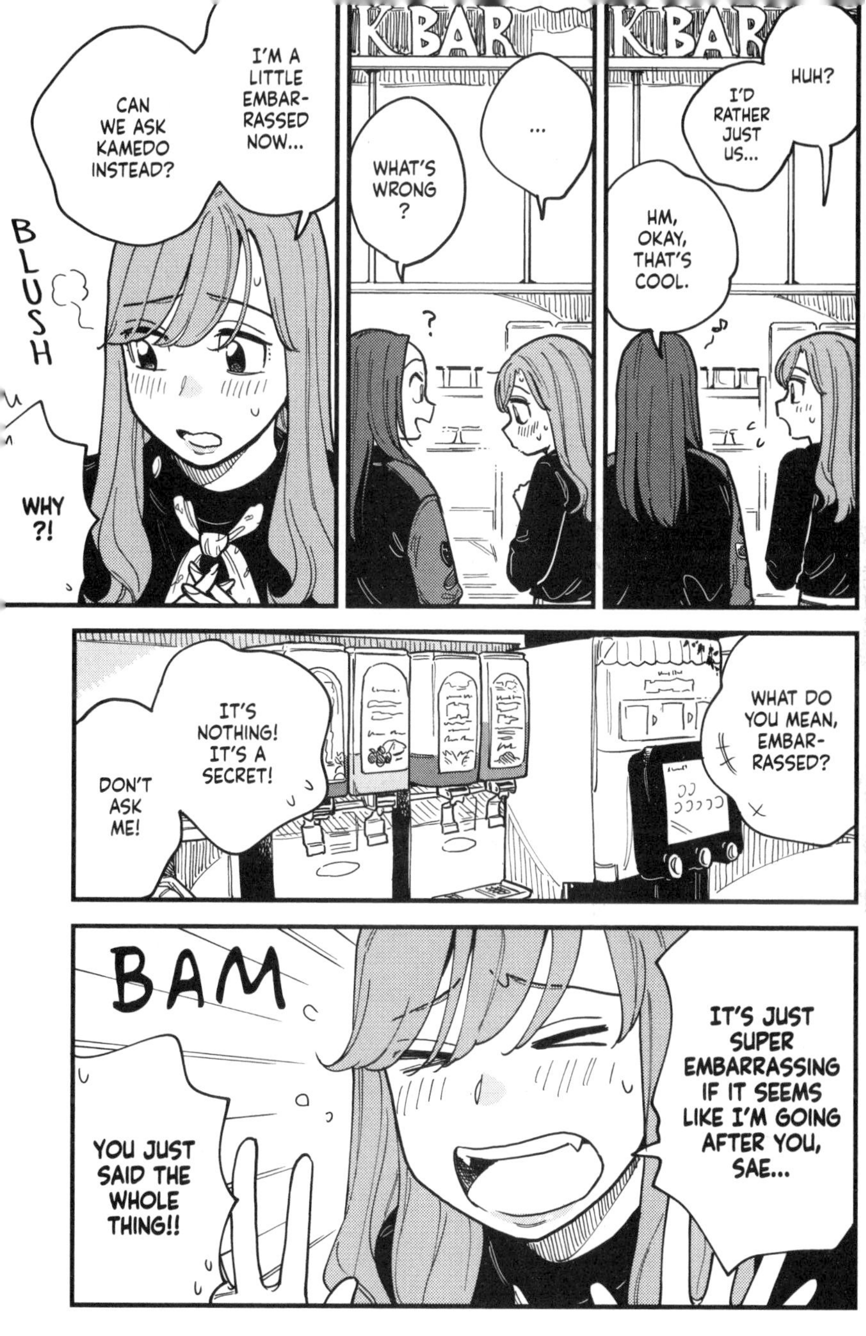
HUH?
I'D RATHER JUST US...
HM, OKAY, THAT'S COOL.
...
WHAT'S WRONG?
I'M A LITTLE EMBARRASSED NOW...
CAN WE ASK KAMEDO INSTEAD?
BLUSH
WHY?!
WHAT DO YOU MEAN, EMBARRASSED?
IT'S NOTHING! IT'S A SECRET!
DON'T ASK ME!
IT'S JUST SUPER EMBARRASSING IF IT SEEMS LIKE I'M GOING AFTER YOU, SAE...
BAM
YOU JUST SAID THE WHOLE THING!!

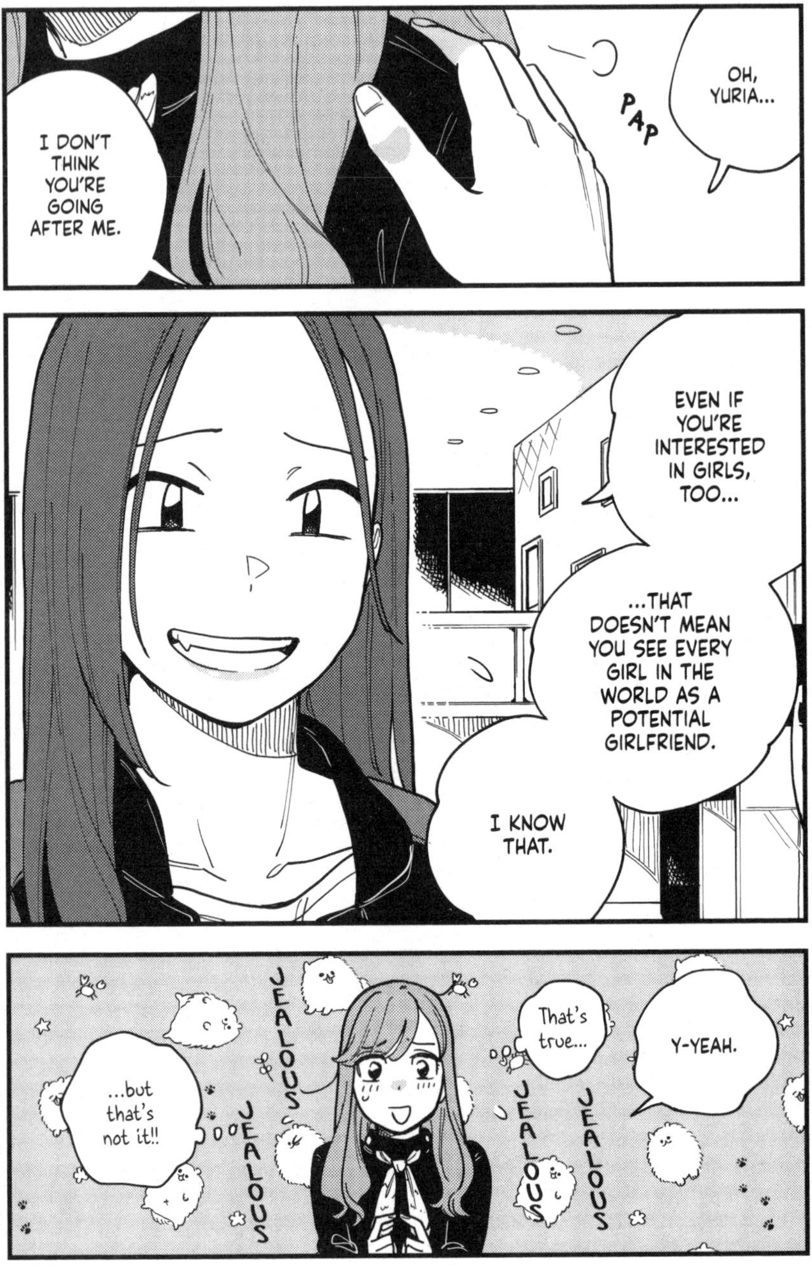
OH, YURIA...
PAP
I DON'T THINK YOU'RE GOING AFTER ME.
EVEN IF YOU'RE INTERESTED IN GIRLS, TOO...
...THAT DOESN'T MEAN YOU SEE EVERY GIRL IN THE WORLD AS A POTENTIAL GIRLFRIEND.
I KNOW THAT.
Y-YEAH.
JEALOUS
That's true...
JEALOUS
JEALOUS
JEALOUS
...but that's not it!!

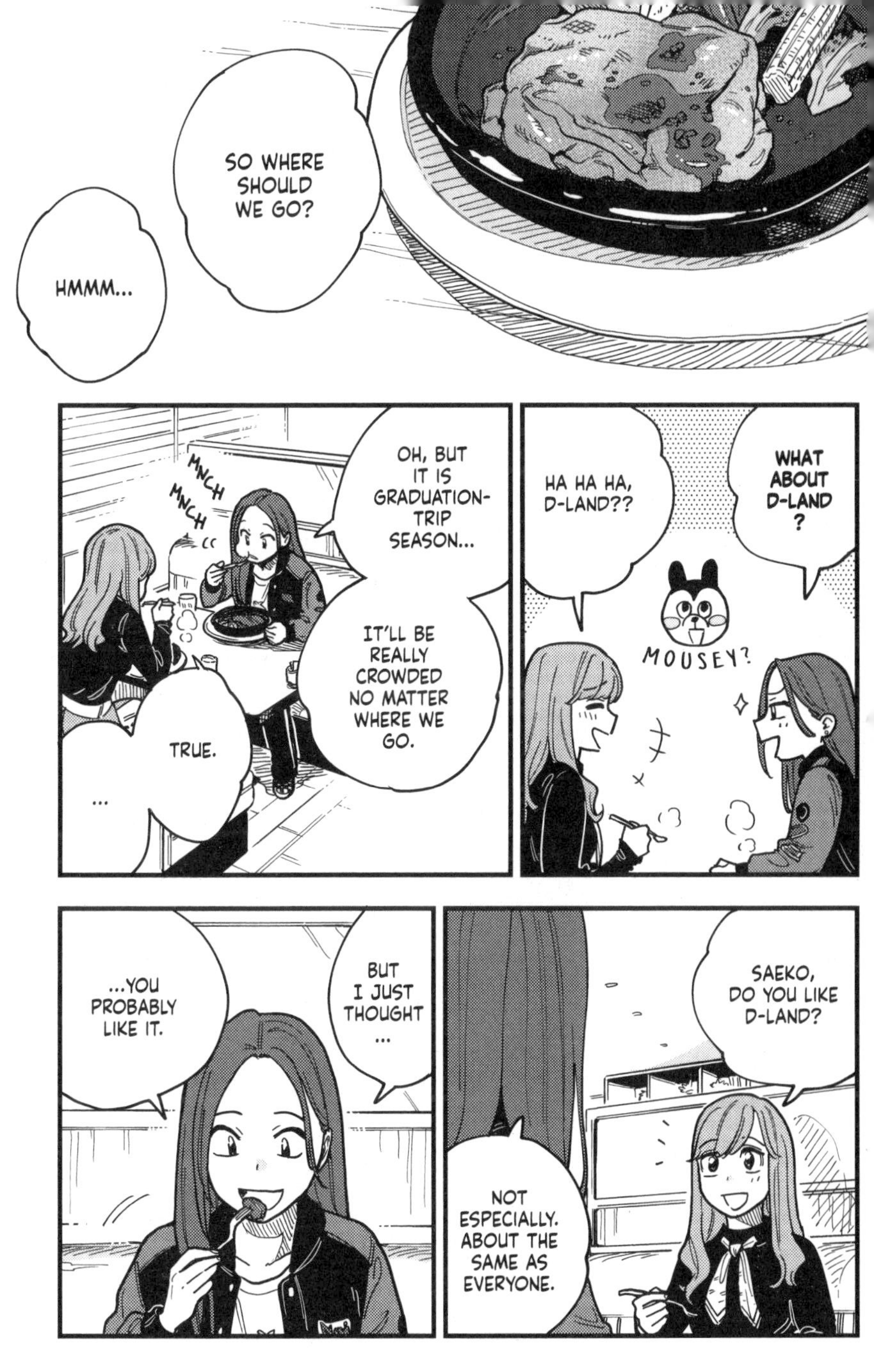
SO WHERE SHOULD WE GO?
HMMM...
WHAT ABOUT D-LAND?
MOUSEY?
HA HA HA, D-LAND??
OH, BUT IT IS GRADUATION-TRIP SEASON...
MNCH MNCH
IT'LL BE REALLY CROWDED NO MATTER WHERE WE GO.
TRUE.
...
SAEKO, DO YOU LIKE D-LAND?
NOT ESPECIALLY. ABOUT THE SAME AS EVERYONE.
BUT I JUST THOUGHT...
...YOU PROBABLY LIKE IT.

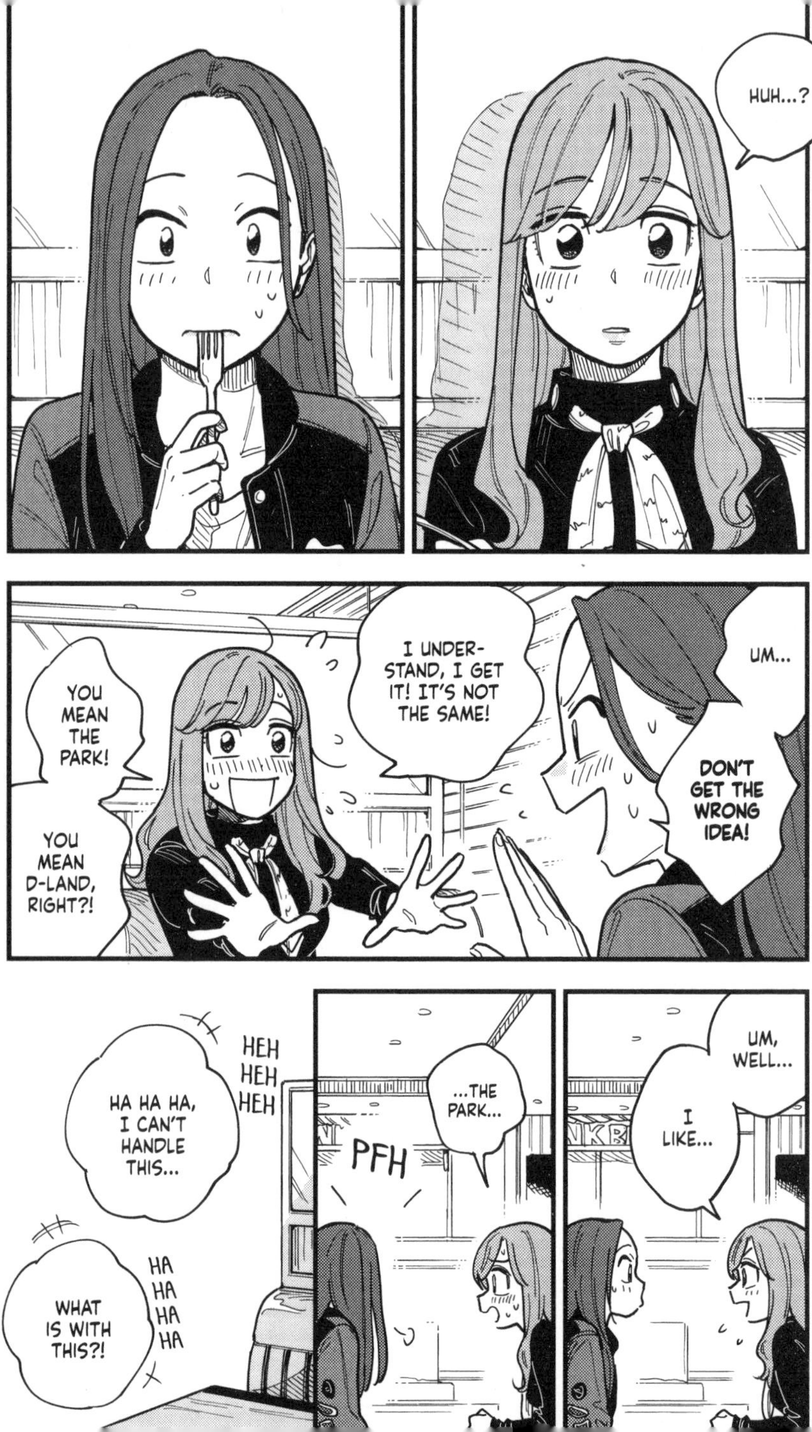
HUH...?
UM...
DON'T GET THE WRONG IDEA!
I UNDER-STAND, I GET IT! IT'S NOT THE SAME!
YOU MEAN THE PARK!
YOU MEAN D-LAND, RIGHT?!
UM, WELL...
I LIKE...
...THE PARK...
PFH
HEH HEH HEH
HA HA HA, I CAN'T HANDLE THIS...
HA HA HA HA
WHAT IS WITH THIS?!

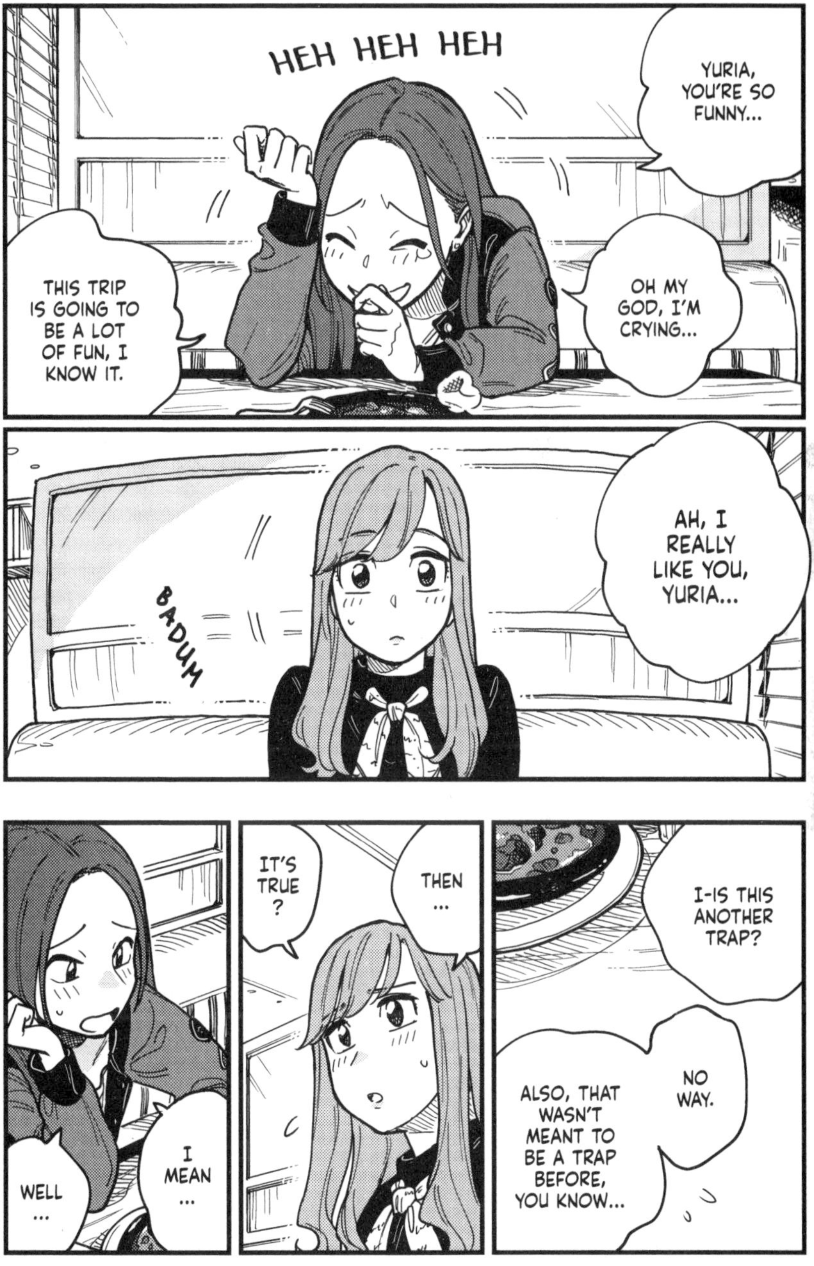
YURIA, YOU'RE SO FUNNY...
HEH HEH HEH
OH MY GOD, I'M CRYING...
THIS TRIP IS GOING TO BE A LOT OF FUN, I KNOW IT.
AH, I REALLY LIKE YOU, YURIA...
BADUM
I-IS THIS ANOTHER TRAP?
NO WAY.
ALSO, THAT WASN'T MEANT TO BE A TRAP BEFORE, YOU KNOW...
THEN ...
IT'S TRUE ?
I MEAN ...
WELL ...

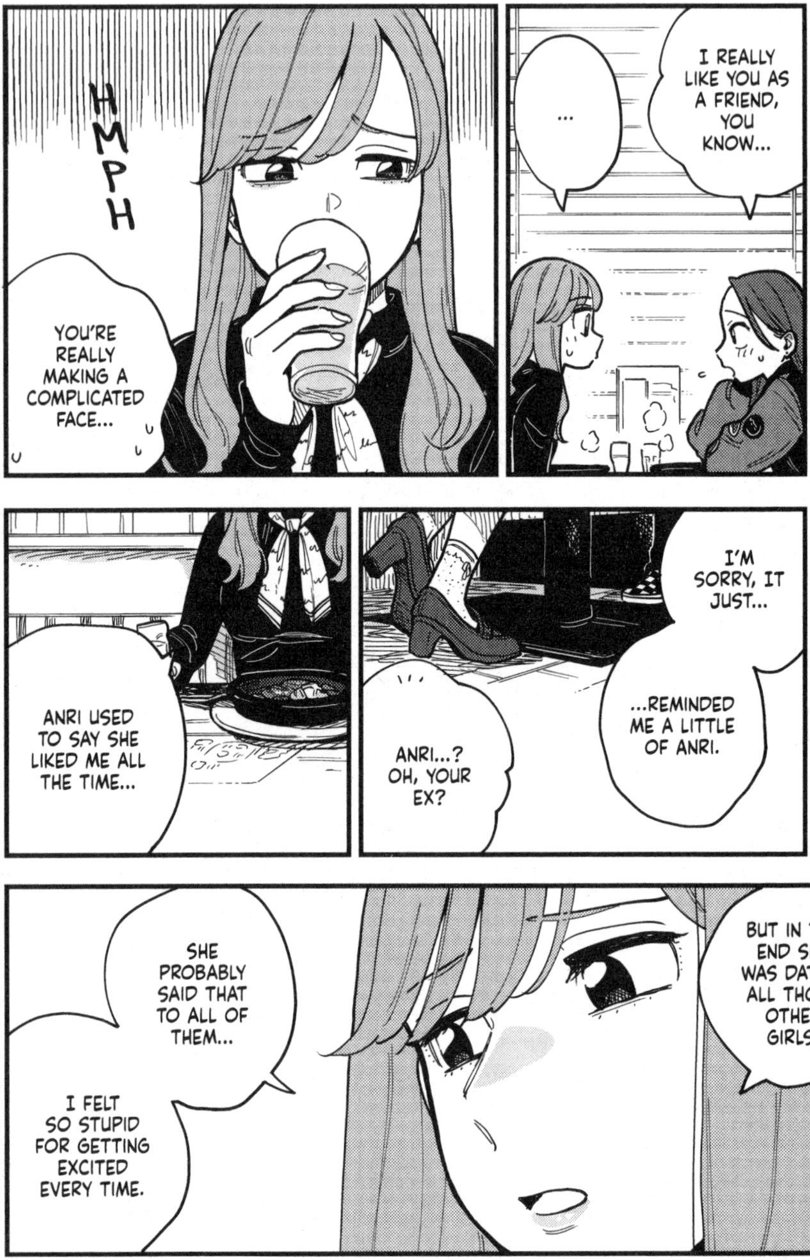
I REALLY LIKE YOU AS A FRIEND, YOU KNOW...
...
HMPH
YOU'RE REALLY MAKING A COMPLICATED FACE...
I'M SORRY, IT JUST...
...REMINDED ME A LITTLE OF ANRI.
ANRI...? OH, YOUR EX?
ANRI USED TO SAY SHE LIKED ME ALL THE TIME...
BUT IN THE END SHE WAS DATING ALL THOSE OTHER GIRLS.
SHE PROBABLY SAID THAT TO ALL OF THEM...
I FELT SO STUPID FOR GETTING EXCITED EVERY TIME.

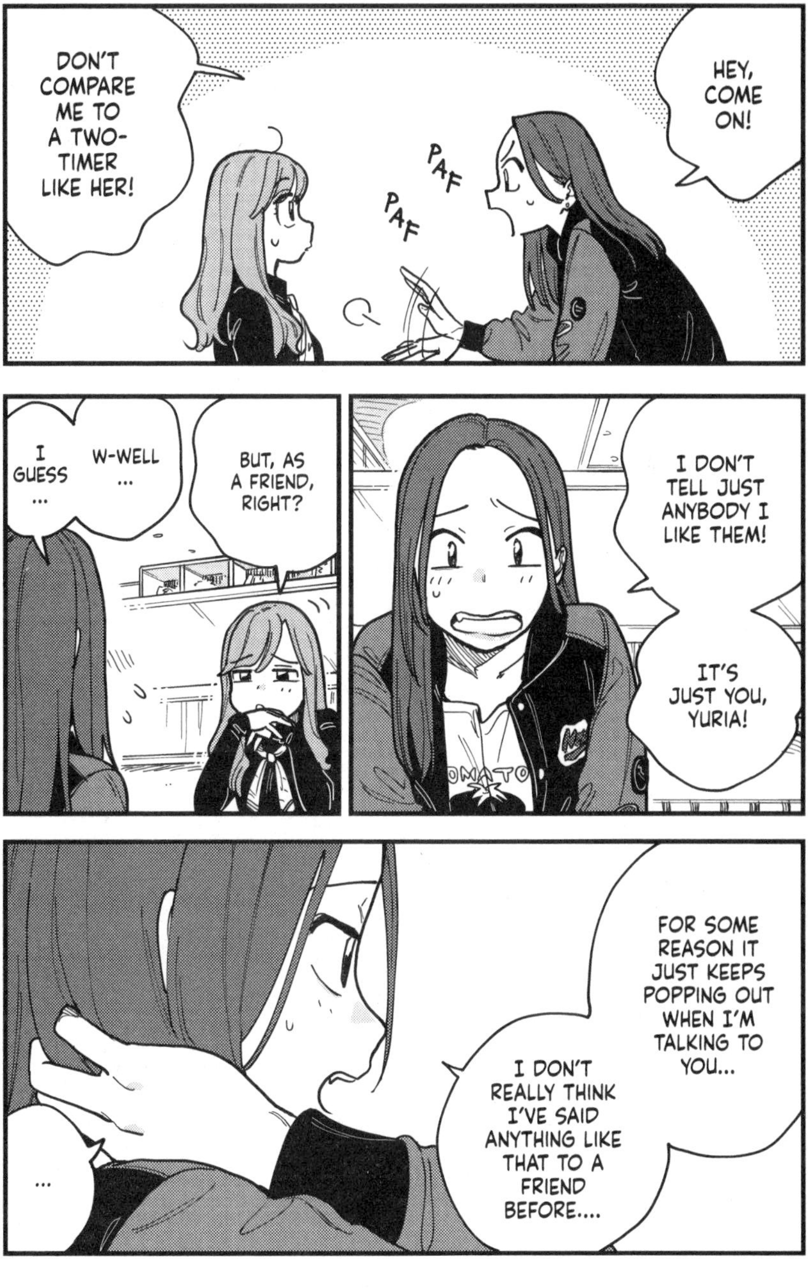
HEY, COME ON!
DON'T COMPARE ME TO A TWO-TIMER LIKE HER!
PAF
PAF
I DON'T TELL JUST ANYBODY I LIKE THEM!
IT'S JUST YOU, YURIA!
BUT, AS A FRIEND, RIGHT?
W-WELL ...
I GUESS ...
FOR SOME REASON IT JUST KEEPS POPPING OUT WHEN I'M TALKING TO YOU...
I DON'T REALLY THINK I'VE SAID ANYTHING LIKE THAT TO A FRIEND BEFORE....
...

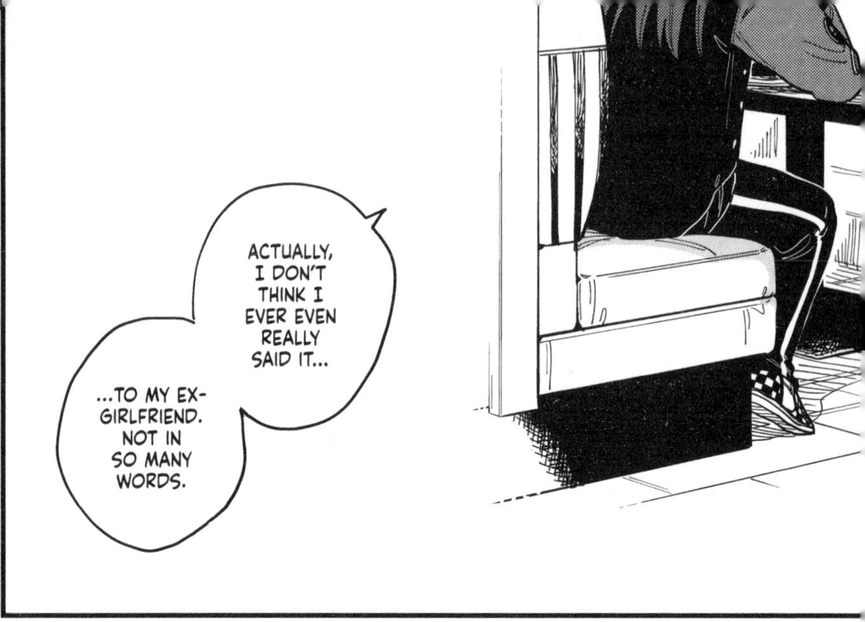
ACTUALLY, I DON'T THINK I EVER EVEN REALLY SAID IT...
...TO MY EX-GIRLFRIEND. NOT IN SO MANY WORDS.

AHH... THAT'S RIGHT...

I NEVER GOT ANYTHING ACROSS TO HER, DID I?

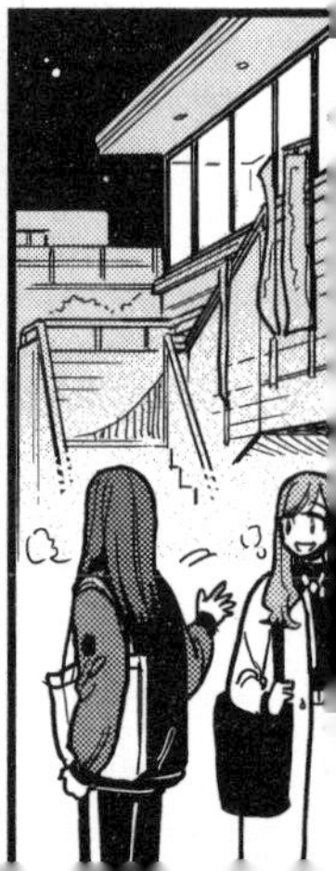

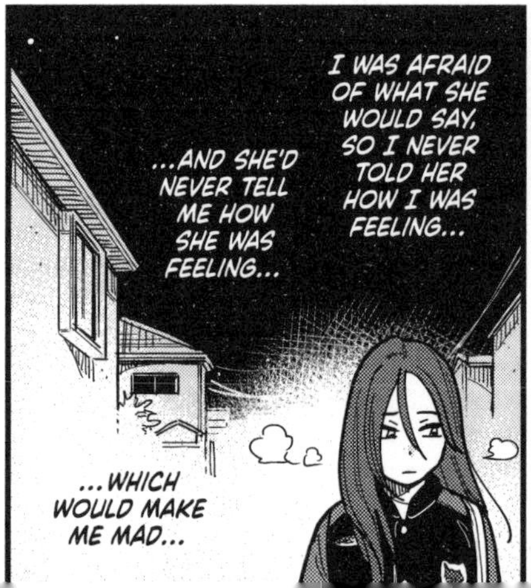
I WAS AFRAID OF WHAT SHE WOULD SAY, SO I NEVER TOLD HER HOW I WAS FEELING...
...AND SHE'D NEVER TELL ME HOW SHE WAS FEELING...
...WHICH WOULD MAKE ME MAD...

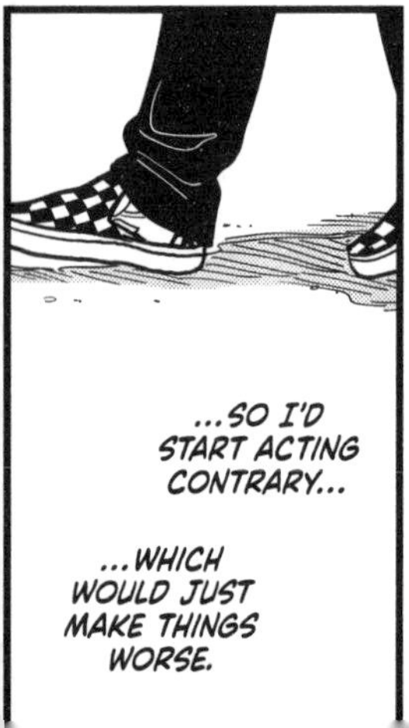
...SO I'D START ACTING CONTRARY...
...WHICH WOULD JUST MAKE THINGS WORSE.

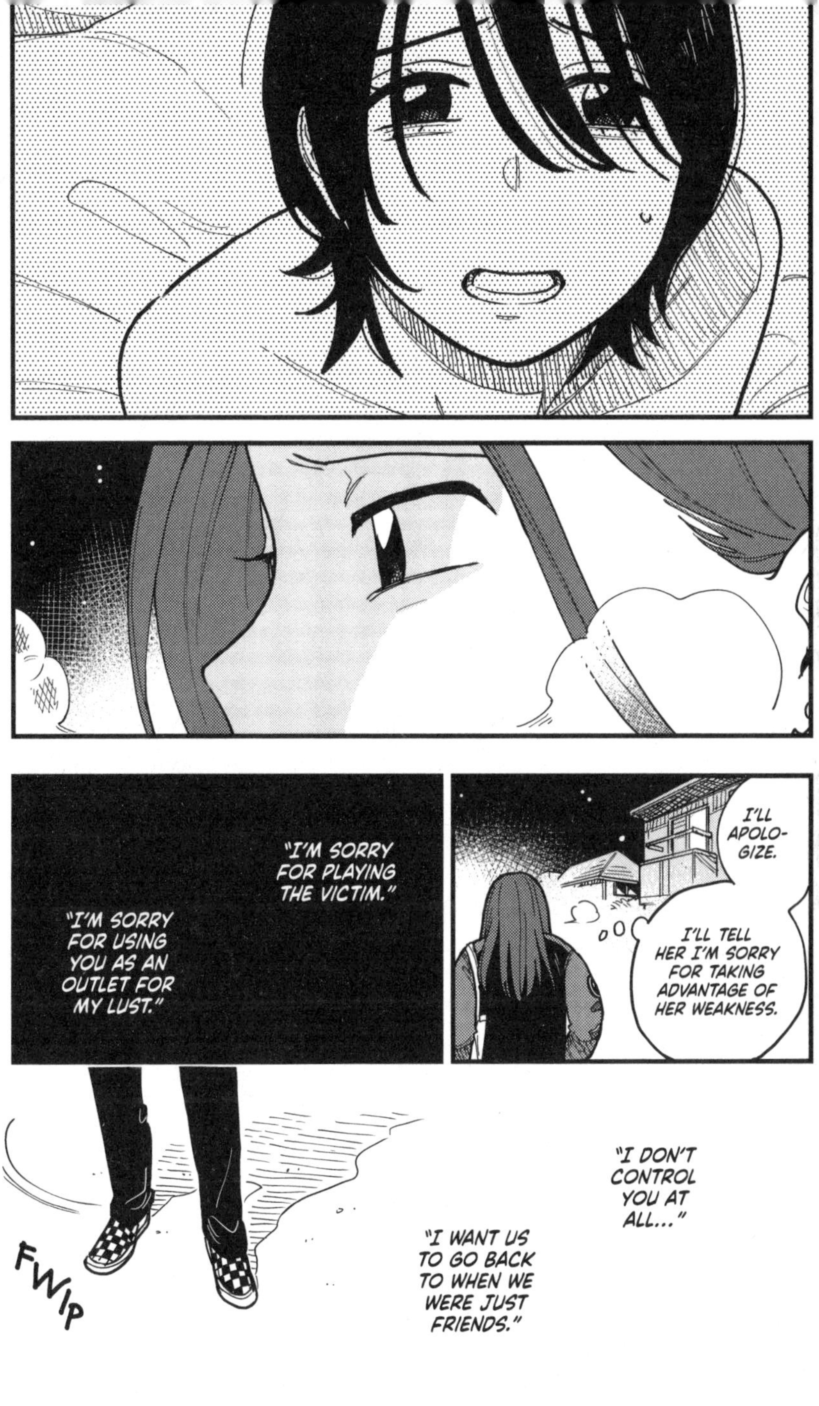
I'LL APOLOGIZE.
I'LL TELL HER I'M SORRY FOR TAKING ADVANTAGE OF HER WEAKNESS.
"I'M SORRY FOR PLAYING THE VICTIM."
"I'M SORRY FOR USING YOU AS AN OUTLET FOR MY LUST."
"I DON'T CONTROL YOU AT ALL..."
"I WANT US TO GO BACK TO WHEN WE WERE JUST FRIENDS."
FWIP

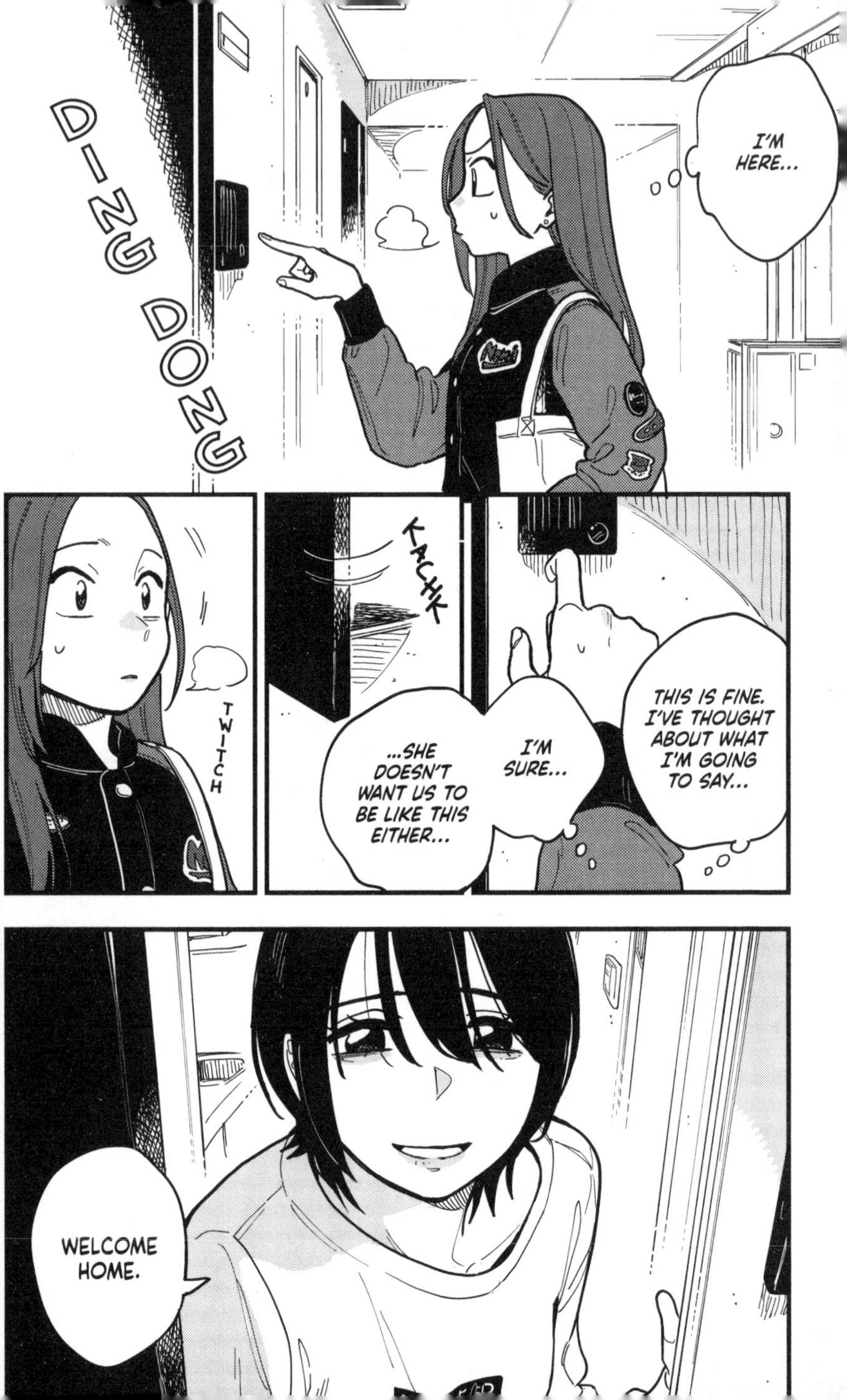
I'M HERE...
DING DONG
THIS IS FINE. I'VE THOUGHT ABOUT WHAT I'M GOING TO SAY...
I'M SURE...
...SHE DOESN'T WANT US TO BE LIKE THIS EITHER...
KACHK
TWITCH
WELCOME HOME.

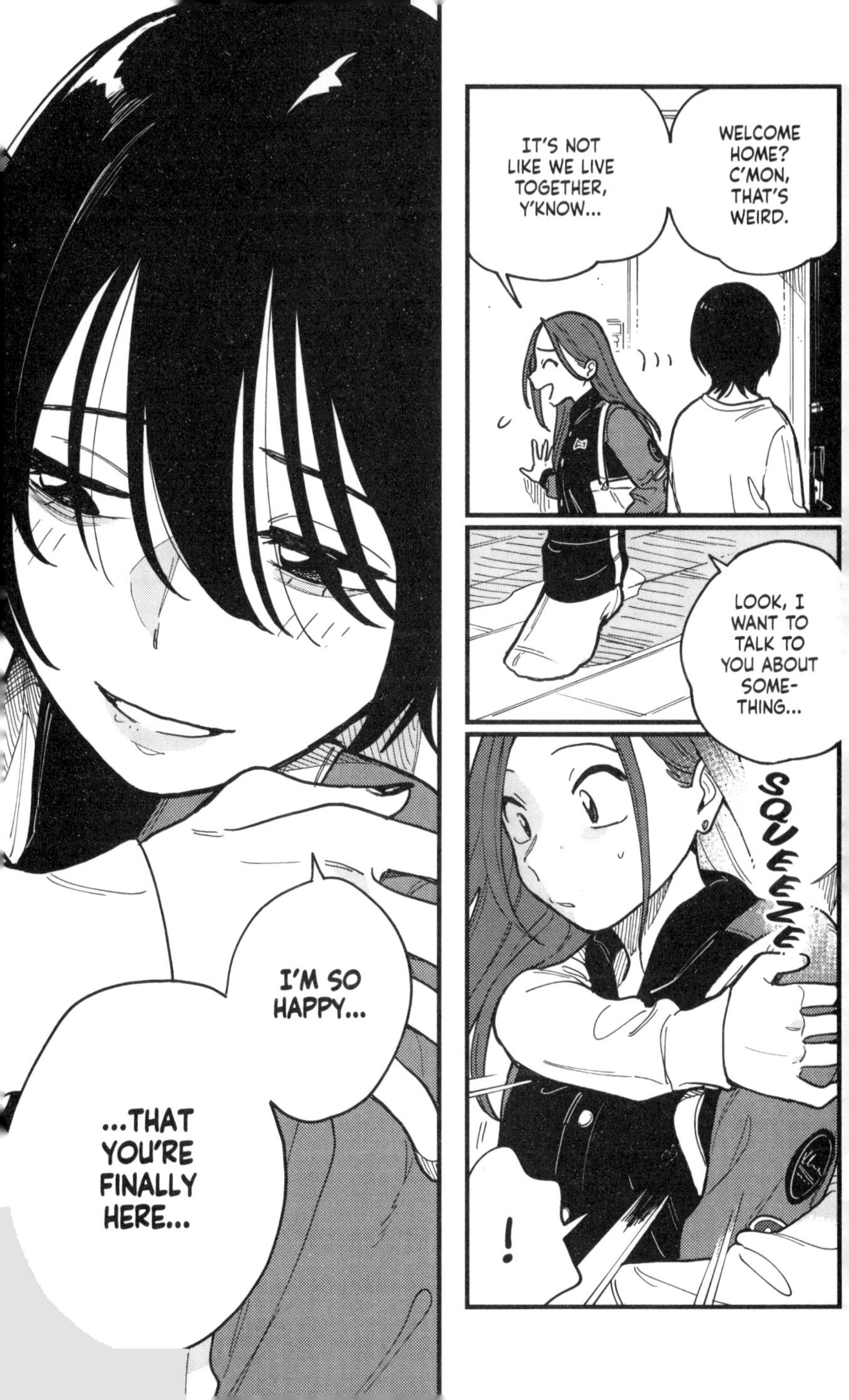
WELCOME HOME? C'MON, THAT'S WEIRD.
IT'S NOT LIKE WE LIVE TOGETHER, Y'KNOW...
LOOK, I WANT TO TALK TO YOU ABOUT SOME-THING...
SQUEEZE
!
I'M SO HAPPY...
...THAT YOU'RE FINALLY HERE...

HOW DO WE RELATIONSHIP?

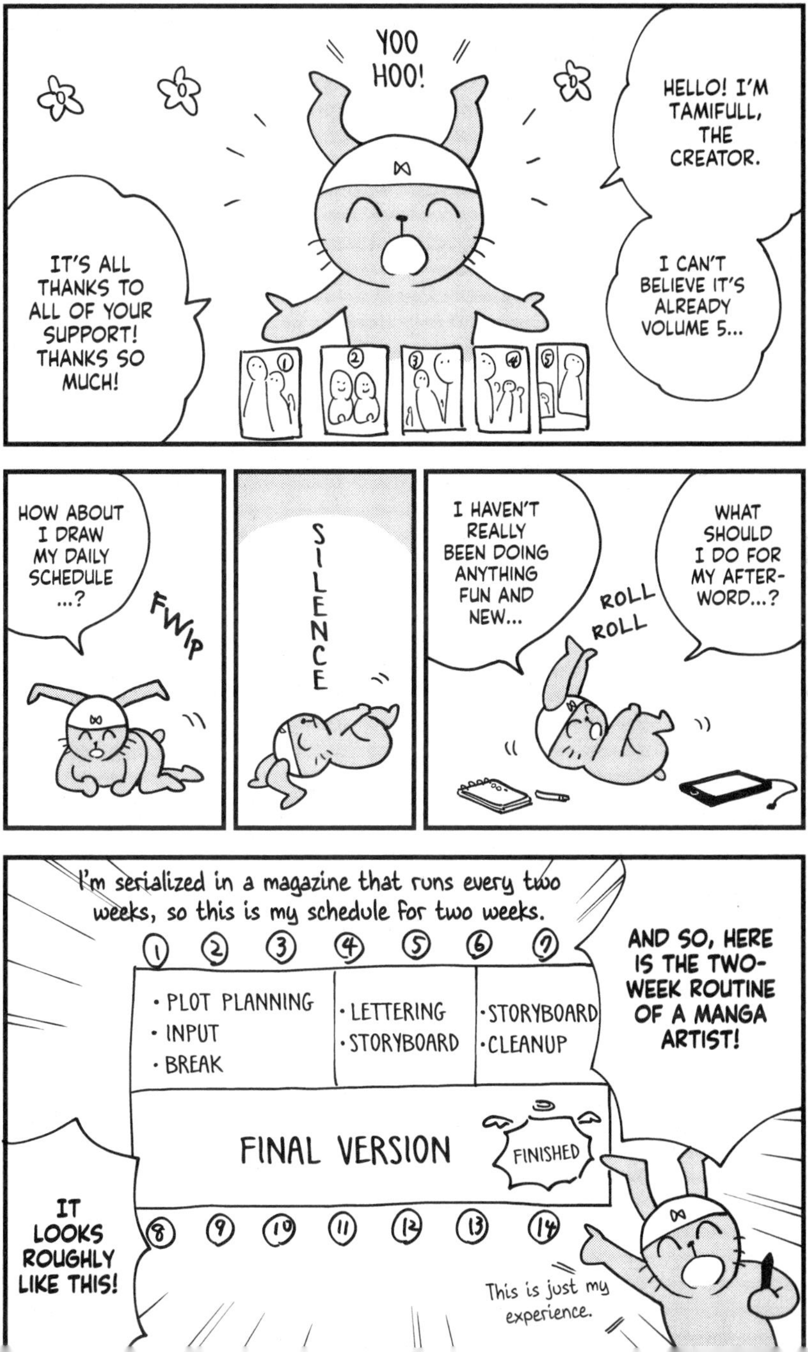
HELLO! I'M TAMIFULL, THE CREATOR.
YOO HOO!
I CAN'T BELIEVE IT'S ALREADY VOLUME 5...
IT'S ALL THANKS TO ALL OF YOUR SUPPORT! THANKS SO MUCH!
WHAT SHOULD I DO FOR MY AFTER-WORD...?
ROLL ROLL
I HAVEN'T REALLY BEEN DOING ANYTHING FUN AND NEW...
SILENCE
HOW ABOUT I DRAW MY DAILY SCHEDULE ...?
FWIP
AND SO, HERE IS THE TWO-WEEK ROUTINE OF A MANGA ARTIST!
I'm serialized in a magazine that runs every two weeks, so this is my schedule for two weeks.
1 2 3 4 5 6 7
· PLOT PLANNING · INPUT · BREAK
· LETTERING · STORYBOARD
· STORYBOARD · CLEANUP
FINAL VERSION
FINISHED
8 9 10 11 12 13 14
This is just my experience.
IT LOOKS ROUGHLY LIKE THIS!

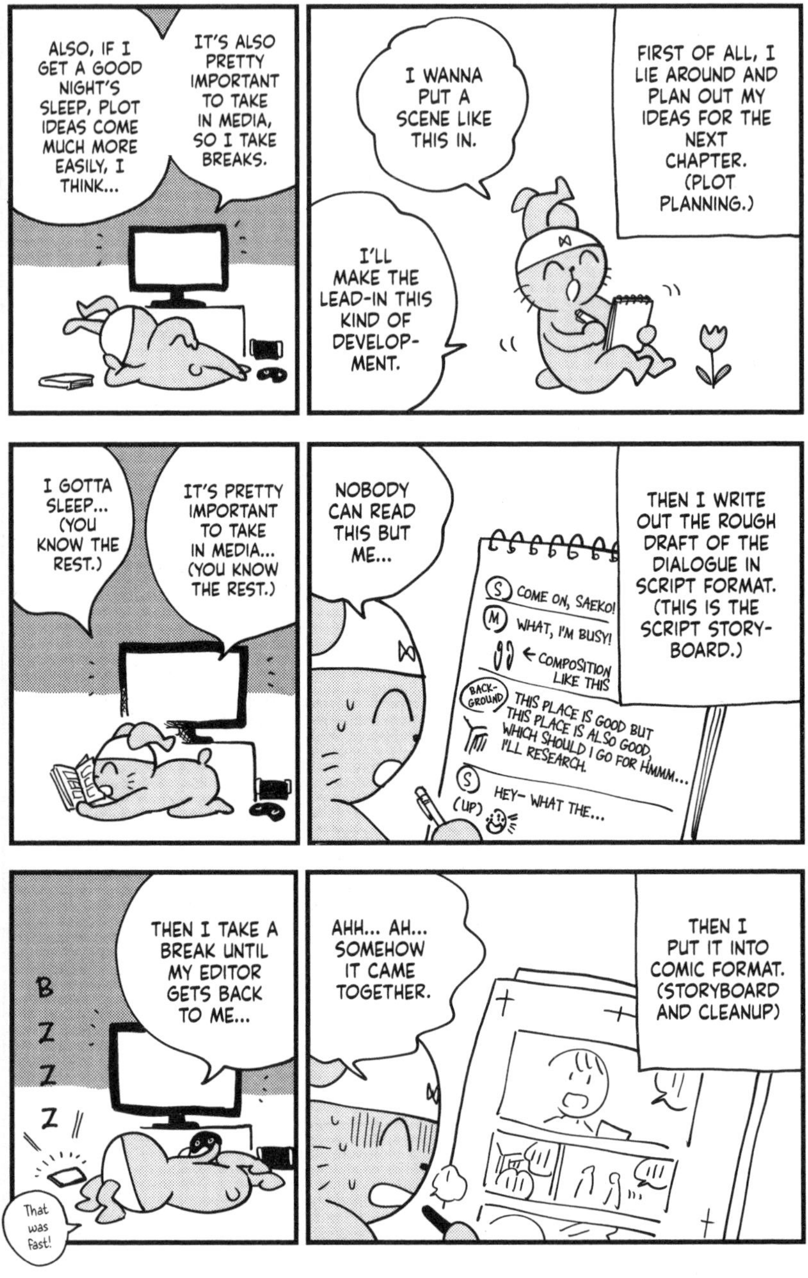
FIRST OF ALL, I LIE AROUND AND PLAN OUT MY IDEAS FOR THE NEXT CHAPTER. (PLOT PLANNING.)
I WANNA PUT A SCENE LIKE THIS IN.
I'LL MAKE THE LEAD-IN THIS KIND OF DEVELOP-MENT.
IT'S ALSO PRETTY IMPORTANT TO TAKE IN MEDIA, SO I TAKE BREAKS.
ALSO, IF I GET A GOOD NIGHT'S SLEEP, PLOT IDEAS COME MUCH MORE EASILY, I THINK...
THEN I WRITE OUT THE ROUGH DRAFT OF THE DIALOGUE IN SCRIPT FORMAT. (THIS IS THE SCRIPT STORY-BOARD.)
NOBODY CAN READ THIS BUT ME...
S COME ON, SAEKO!
M WHAT, I'M BUSY!
← COMPOSITION LIKE THIS
BACK-GROUND THIS PLACE IS GOOD BUT THIS PLACE IS ALSO GOOD, WHICH SHOULD I GO FOR HMMM... I'LL RESEARCH.
S HEY- WHAT THE...
(UP)
IT'S PRETTY IMPORTANT TO TAKE IN MEDIA... (YOU KNOW THE REST.)
I GOTTA SLEEP... (YOU KNOW THE REST.)
THEN I PUT IT INTO COMIC FORMAT. (STORYBOARD AND CLEANUP)
AHH... AH... SOMEHOW IT CAME TOGETHER.
THEN I TAKE A BREAK UNTIL MY EDITOR GETS BACK TO ME...
BZZZ
That was fast!

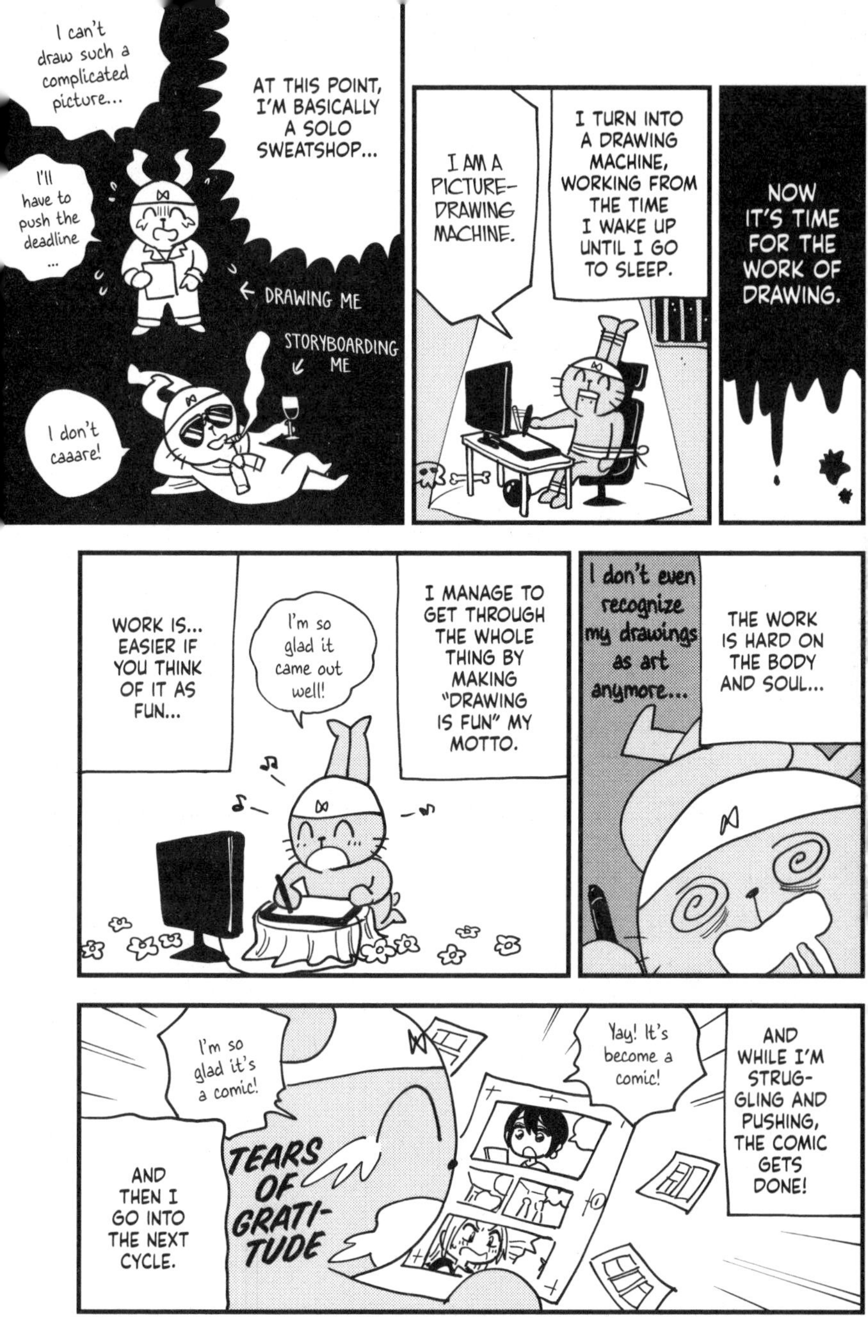
NOW IT'S TIME FOR THE WORK OF DRAWING.
I TURN INTO A DRAWING MACHINE, WORKING FROM THE TIME I WAKE UP UNTIL I GO TO SLEEP.
I AM A PICTURE-DRAWING MACHINE.
AT THIS POINT, I'M BASICALLY A SOLO SWEATSHOP...
I can't draw such a complicated picture...
I'll have to push the deadline...
DRAWING ME
STORYBOARDING ME
I don't caaare!
THE WORK IS HARD ON THE BODY AND SOUL...
I don't even recognize my drawings as art anymore...
I MANAGE TO GET THROUGH THE WHOLE THING BY MAKING "DRAWING IS FUN" MY MOTTO.
I'm so glad it came out well!
WORK IS... EASIER IF YOU THINK OF IT AS FUN...
AND WHILE I'M STRUG-GLING AND PUSHING, THE COMIC GETS DONE!
Yay! It's become a comic!
I'm so glad it's a comic!
TEARS OF GRATI-TUDE
AND THEN I GO INTO THE NEXT CYCLE.

HOW DO WE RELATIONSHIP VOLUME 5 COMMENTARY TRACK COMIC

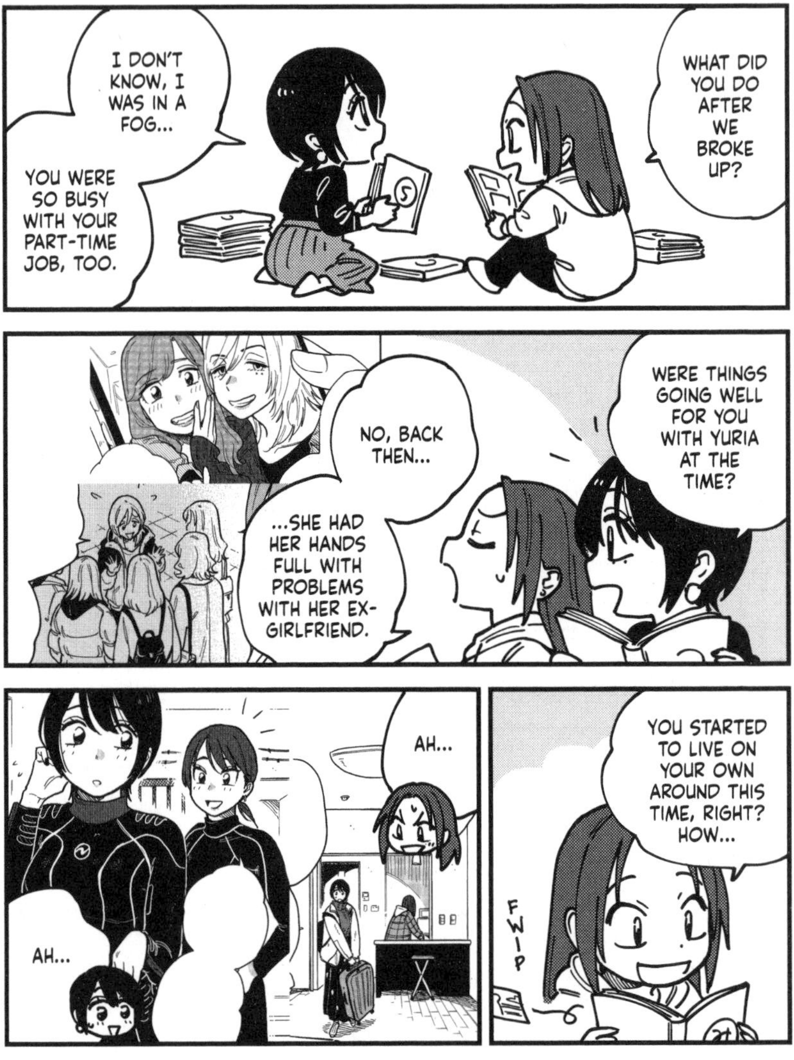
WHAT DID YOU DO AFTER WE BROKE UP?
I DON'T KNOW, I WAS IN A FOG...
YOU WERE SO BUSY WITH YOUR PART-TIME JOB, TOO.
WERE THINGS GOING WELL FOR YOU WITH YURIA AT THE TIME?
NO, BACK THEN...
...SHE HAD HER HANDS FULL WITH PROBLEMS WITH HER EX-GIRLFRIEND.
YOU STARTED TO LIVE ON YOUR OWN AROUND THIS TIME, RIGHT? HOW...
FWIP
AH...
AH...

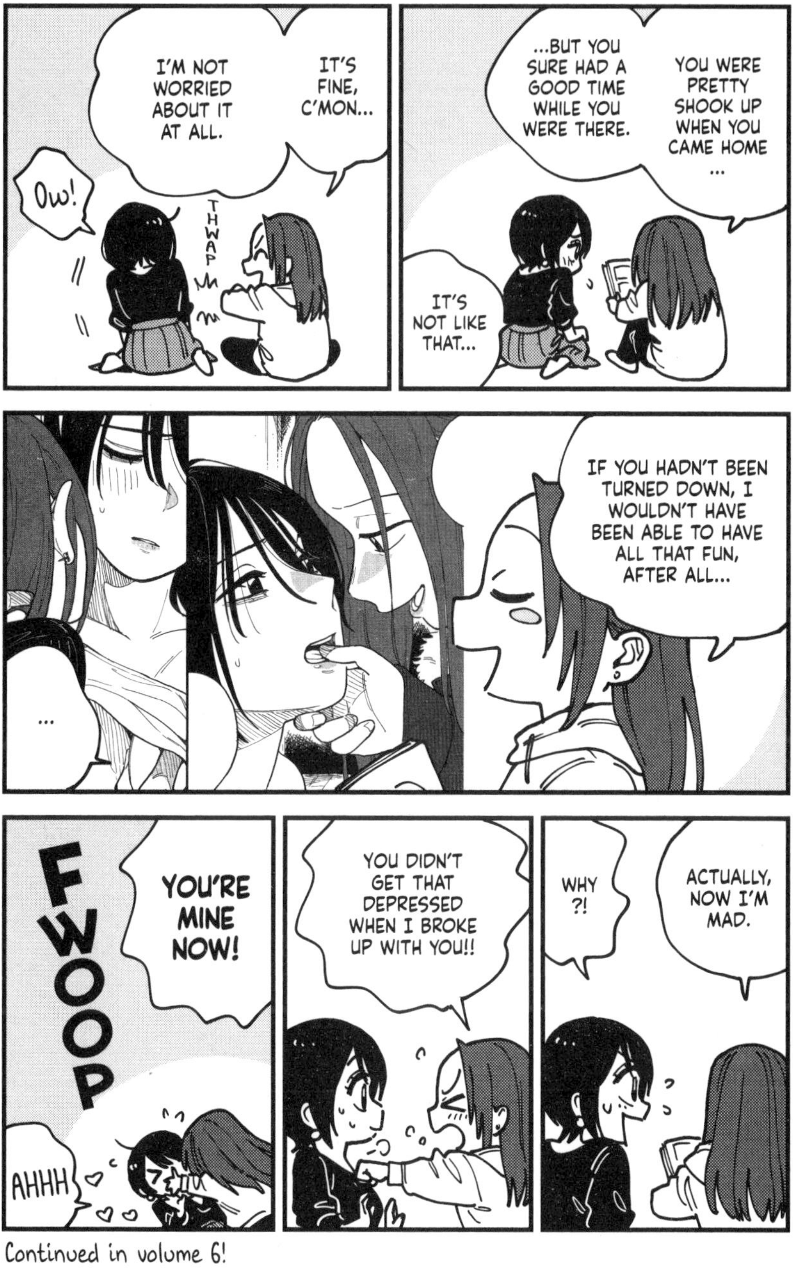
YOU WERE PRETTY SHOOK UP WHEN YOU CAME HOME ...
...BUT YOU SURE HAD A GOOD TIME WHILE YOU WERE THERE.
IT'S NOT LIKE THAT...
IT'S FINE, C'MON...
I'M NOT WORRIED ABOUT IT AT ALL.
THWAP
Ow!
IF YOU HADN'T BEEN TURNED DOWN, I WOULDN'T HAVE BEEN ABLE TO HAVE ALL THAT FUN, AFTER ALL...
...
ACTUALLY, NOW I'M MAD.
WHY ?!
YOU DIDN'T GET THAT DEPRESSED WHEN I BROKE UP WITH YOU!!
YOU'RE MINE NOW!
FWOOP
AHHH

Continued in volume 6!

Tamifull

Since we're entering a new arc in the story,

I decided to refresh the cover design too.

It's always exciting to begin new things.

How Do We Relationship?

VOLUME 5

VIZ MEDIA EDITION

STORY AND ART BY
Tamifull

ENGLISH TRANSLATION & ADAPTATION
Abby Lehrke

TOUCH-UP ART & LETTERING
Joanna Estep

DESIGN
Alice Lewis

EDITOR
Pancha Diaz

TSUKIATTE AGETEMO IIKANA Vol. 5
by TAMIFULL
© 2019 TAMIFULL
All rights reserved.
Original Japanese edition published by SHOGAKUKAN.
English translation rights in the United States of America, Canada, the United
Kingdom, Ireland, Australia and New Zealand arranged with SHOGAKUKAN.

Printed in the U.S.A.

Published by VIZ Media, LLC.
P.O. Box 77010
San Francisco, CA 94107

10 9 8 7 6 5 4 3 2 1
First printing, February 2022

VIZ MEDIA

viz.com

Revolutionary Girl
UTENA

AFTER-the-REVOLUTION

Story and Art by **Chiho Saito**   Original Concept by **Be-Papas**

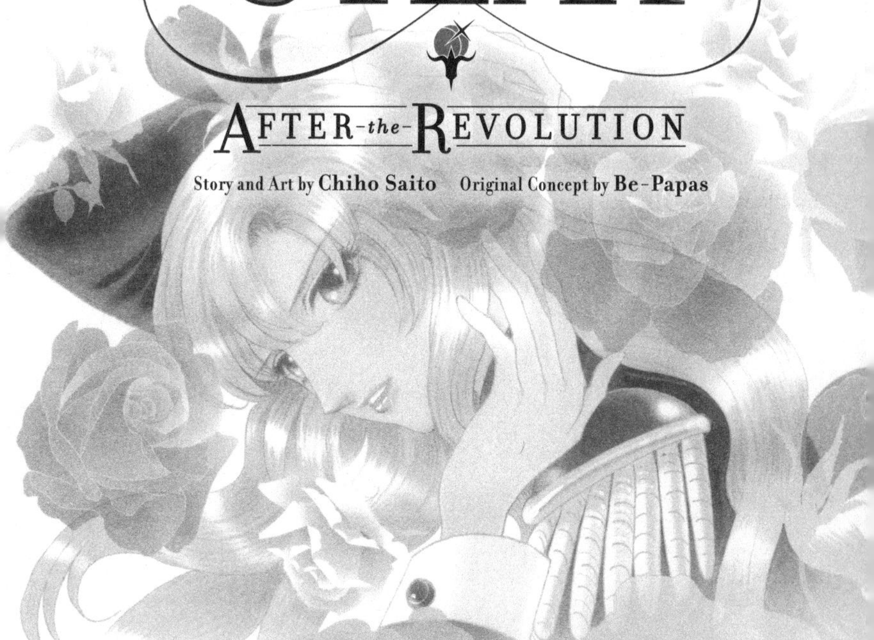

Three short stories set after Utena's revolution!

Utena has saved Anthy by defeating Akio in the final duel, but in doing so she has vanished from the world. Now the student council members at Ohtori Academy find themselves in their own revolutions.

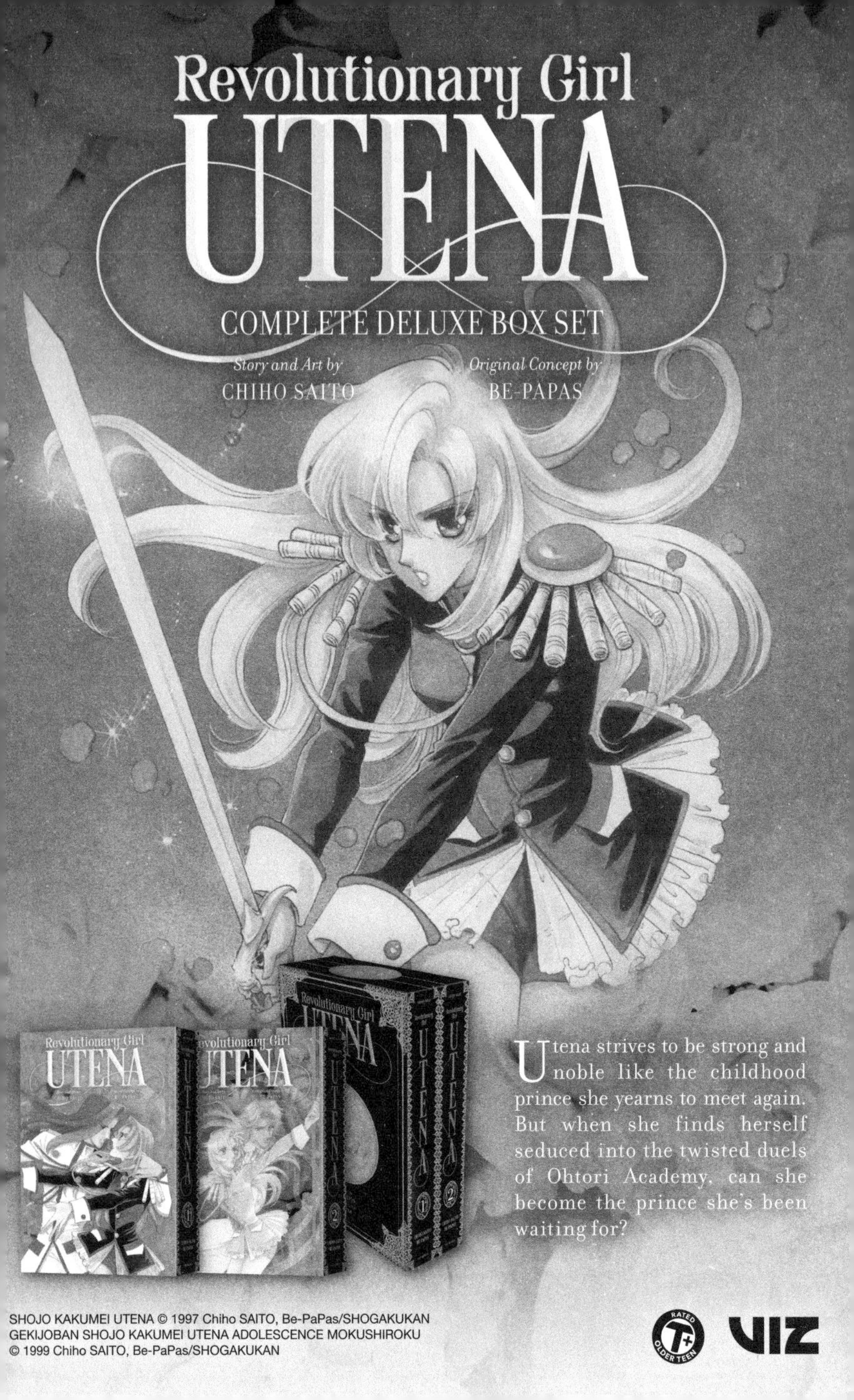

Revolutionary Girl
UTENA

COMPLETE DELUXE BOX SET

Story and Art by
CHIHO SAITO

Original Concept by
BE-PAPAS

Utena strives to be strong and noble like the childhood prince she yearns to meet again. But when she finds herself seduced into the twisted duels of Ohtori Academy, can she become the prince she's been waiting for?

VIZ

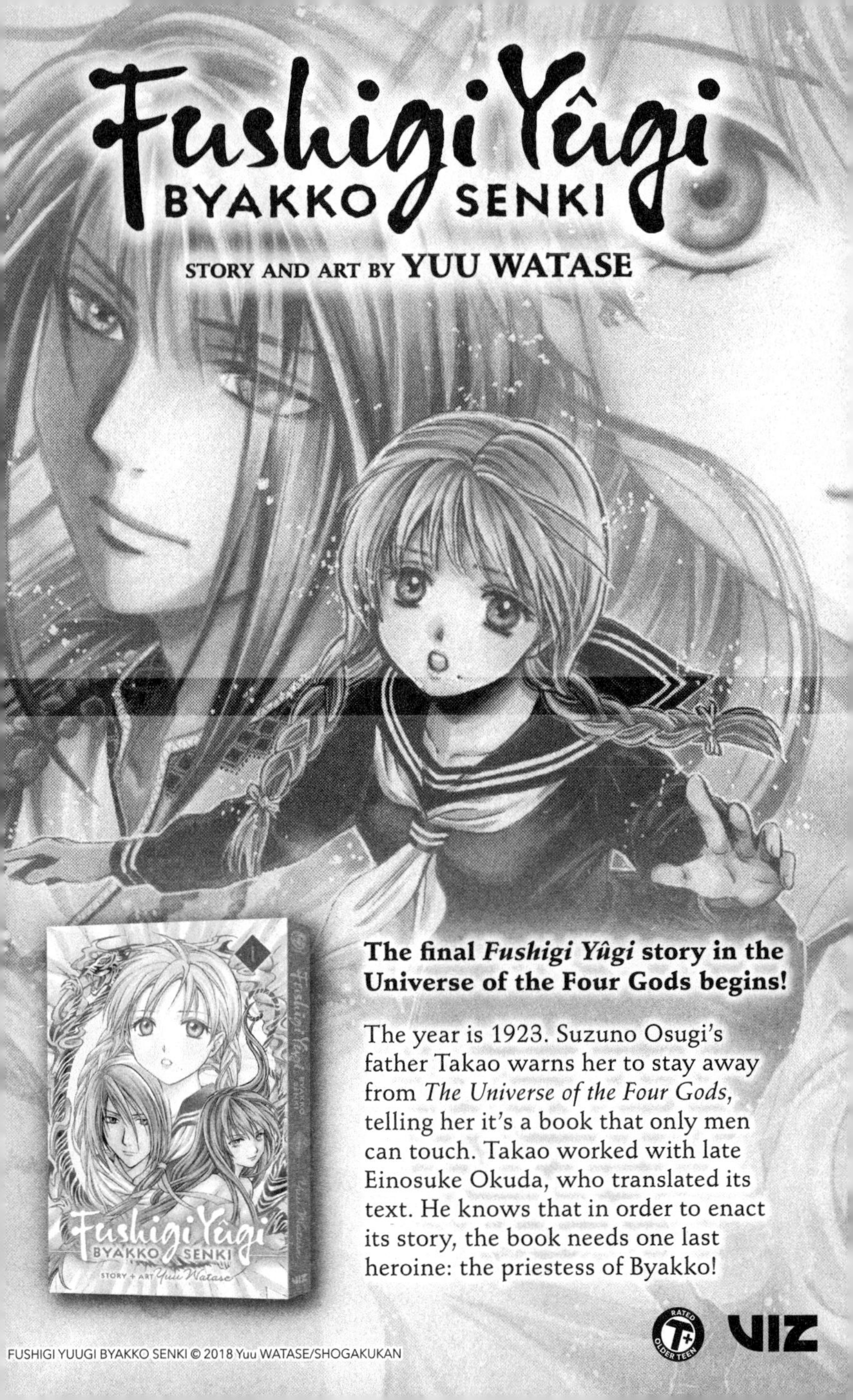
Fushigi Yûgi
BYAKKO SENKI
STORY AND ART BY YUU WATASE
The final Fushigi Yûgi story in the Universe of the Four Gods begins!
The year is 1923. Suzuno Osugi's father Takao warns her to stay away from The Universe of the Four Gods, telling her it's a book that only men can touch. Takao worked with late Einosuke Okuda, who translated its text. He knows that in order to enact its story, the book needs one last heroine: the priestess of Byakko!
Fushigi Yûgi
BYAKKO SENKI
STORY + ART Yuu Watase
RATED T+ OLDER TEEN
VIZ